# DOORWAY TO HELL

COLLECTED COMIC STRIPS
from the pages of

**BBC**
# DOCTOR WHO
MAGAZINE™

panini comics

# Contents

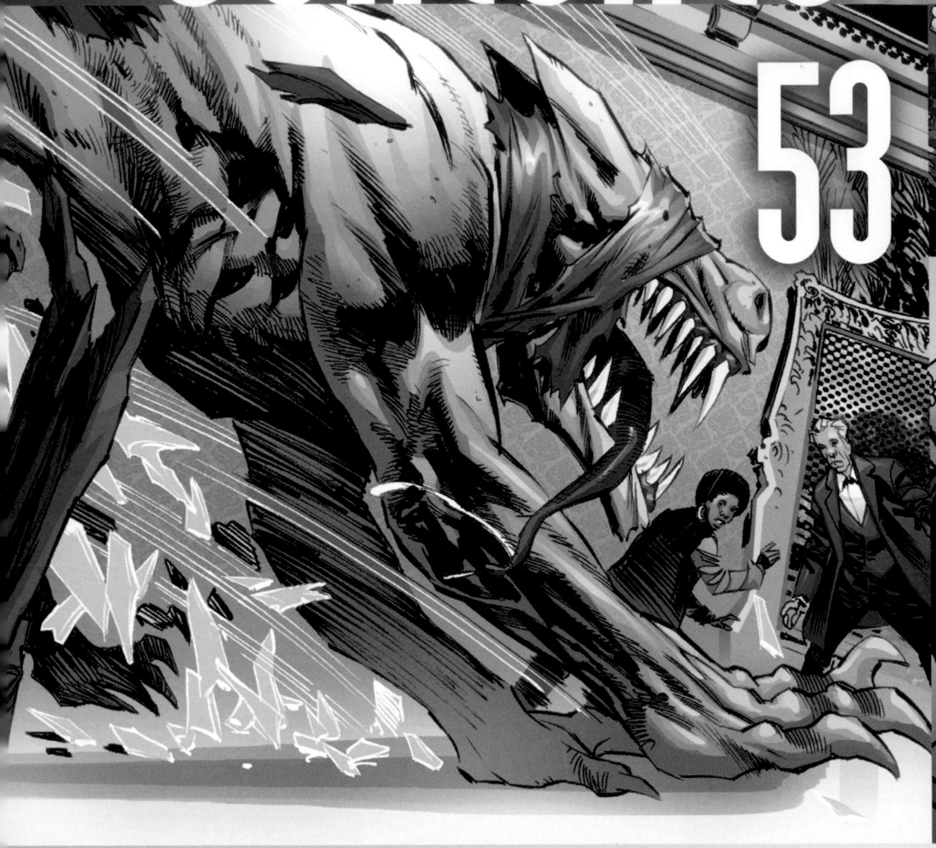

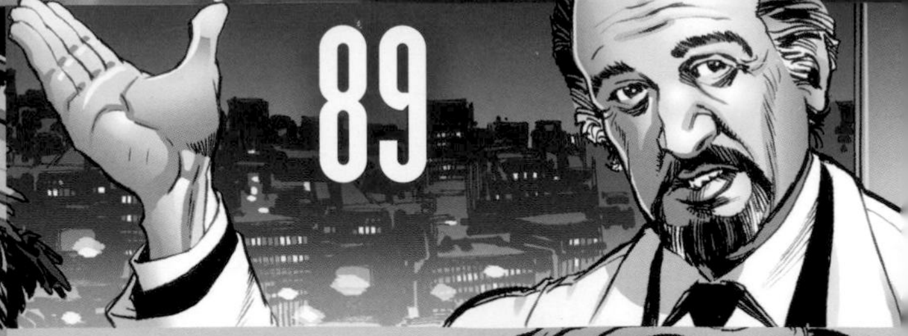

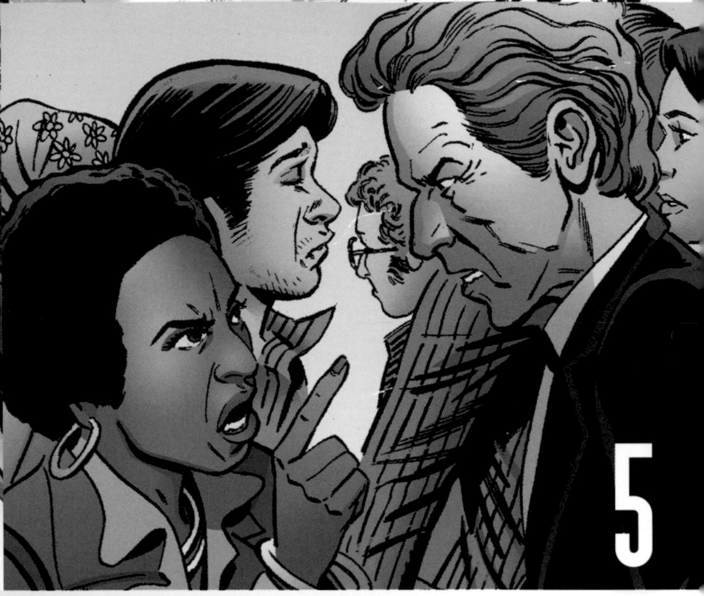




Project Editors **TOM SPILSBURY & SCOTT GRAY** Designer **PERI GODBOLD**
Cover pencils and inks by **DAVID A ROACH** Cover colours by **JAMES OFFREDI**

Head of Production **MARK IRVINE** Managing Editor **ALAN O'KEEFE** Managing Director **MIKE RIDDELL**

Special thanks to **PETER CAPALDI, STEVEN MOFFAT, BRIAN MINCHIN, EDWARD RUSSELL, RICHARD ATKINSON, PETER WARE, EMILY COOK and all the writers and artists whose work is presented herein.**

MIX Paper from responsible sources FSC www.fsc.org FSC® C010353

*Doctor Who* Graphic Novel #25: *Doorway to Hell*. Published by Panini UK. Office of publication: Brockbourne House, 77 Mount Ephraim, Tunbridge Wells, Kent TN4 8BS.



Printed in the UK. ISBN 978-1-84653-834-6

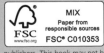

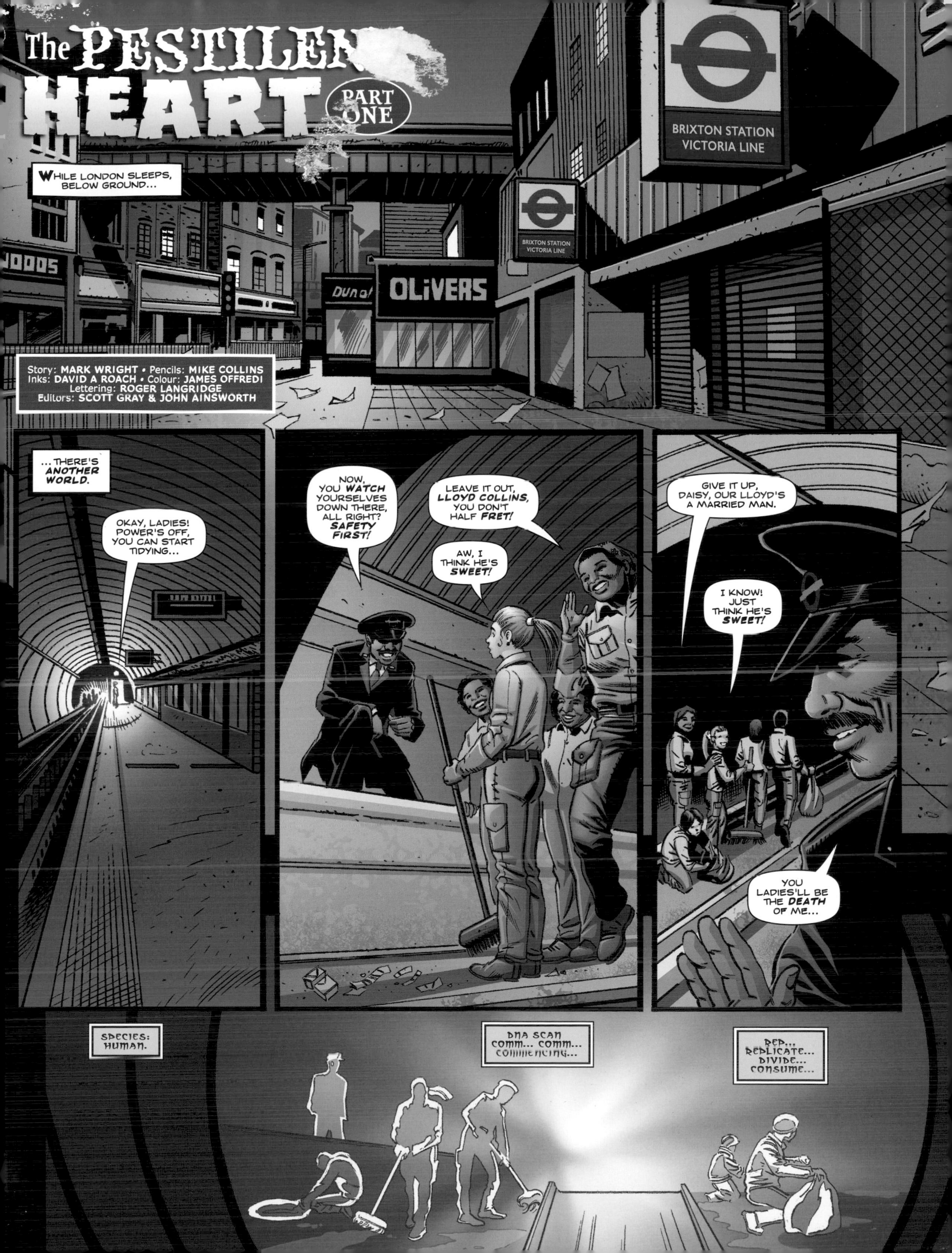
The PESTILEN
HEART
PART ONE
BRIXTON STATION VICTORIA LINE
WHILE LONDON SLEEPS, BELOW GROUND...
OLIVERS
BRIXTON STATION VICTORIA LINE
Story: MARK WRIGHT • Pencils: MIKE COLLINS
Inks: DAVID A ROACH • Colour: JAMES OFFREDI
Lettering: ROGER LANGRIDGE
Editors: SCOTT GRAY & JOHN AINSWORTH
...THERE'S ANOTHER WORLD.
OKAY, LADIES! POWER'S OFF, YOU CAN START TIDYING...
NOW, YOU WATCH YOURSELVES DOWN THERE, ALL RIGHT? SAFETY FIRST!
LEAVE IT OUT, LLOYD COLLINS, YOU DON'T HALF FRET!
AW, I THINK HE'S SWEET!
GIVE IT UP, DAISY, OUR LLOYD'S A MARRIED MAN.
I KNOW! JUST THINK HE'S SWEET!
YOU LADIES'LL BE THE DEATH OF ME...
SPECIES: HUMAN.
DNA SCAN COMM... COMM... COMMENCING...
REP... REPLICATE... DIVIDE... CONSUME...

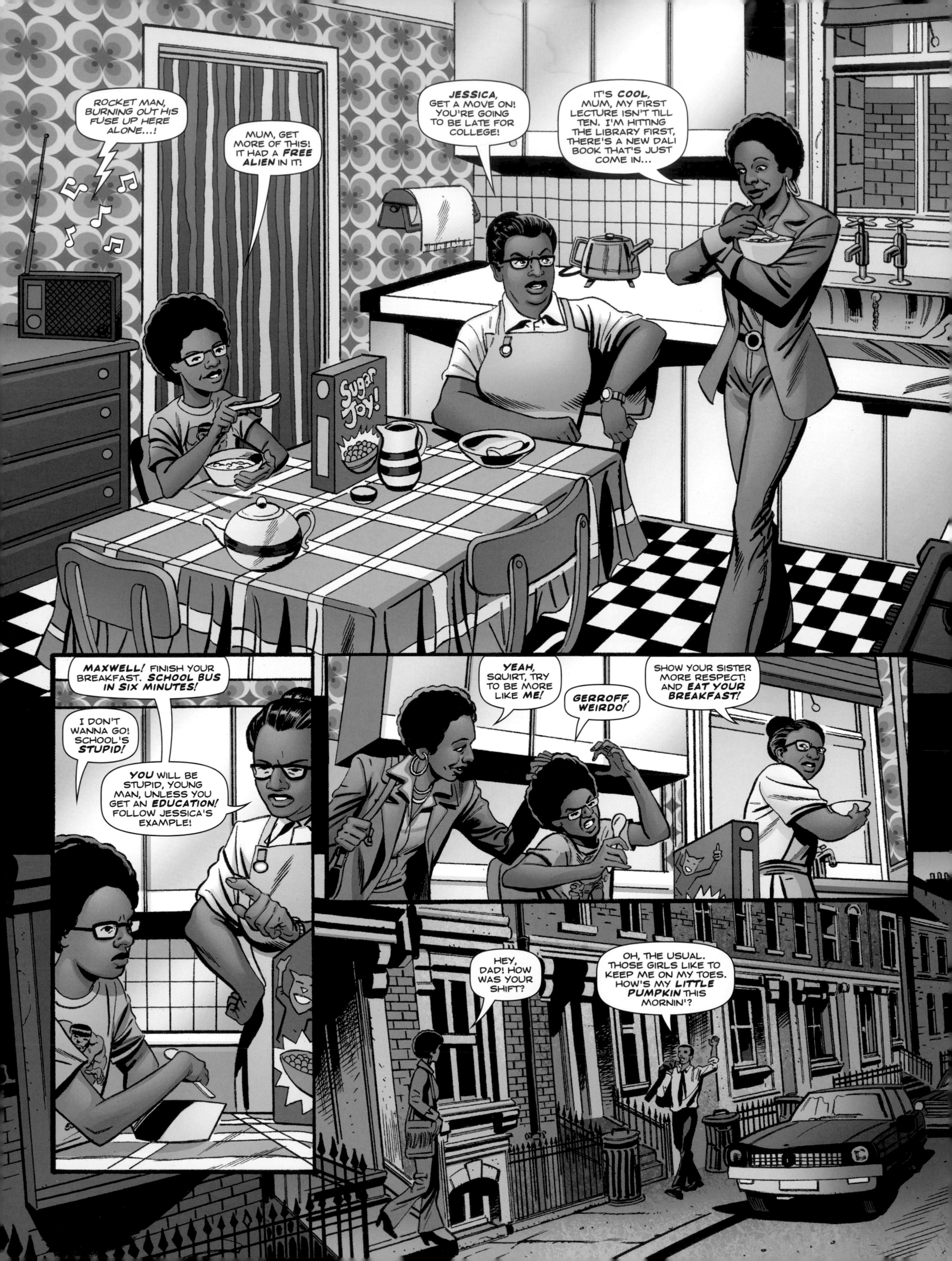
ROCKET MAN, BURNING OUT HIS FUSE UP HERE ALONE...!
MUM, GET MORE OF THIS! IT HAD A FREE ALIEN IN IT!
JESSICA, GET A MOVE ON! YOU'RE GOING TO BE LATE FOR COLLEGE!
IT'S COOL, MUM, MY FIRST LECTURE ISN'T TILL TEN. I'M HITTING THE LIBRARY FIRST, THERE'S A NEW DALI BOOK THAT'S JUST COME IN...
Sugar Joy!
MAXWELL! FINISH YOUR BREAKFAST. SCHOOL BUS IN SIX MINUTES!
I DON'T WANNA GO! SCHOOL'S STUPID!
YOU WILL BE STUPID, YOUNG MAN, UNLESS YOU GET AN EDUCATION! FOLLOW JESSICA'S EXAMPLE!
YEAH, SQUIRT, TRY TO BE MORE LIKE ME!
GERROFF, WEIRDO!
SHOW YOUR SISTER MORE RESPECT! AND EAT YOUR BREAKFAST!
HEY, DAD! HOW WAS YOUR SHIFT?
OH, THE USUAL. THOSE GIRLS LIKE TO KEEP ME ON MY TOES. HOW'S MY LITTLE PUMPKIN THIS MORNIN'?

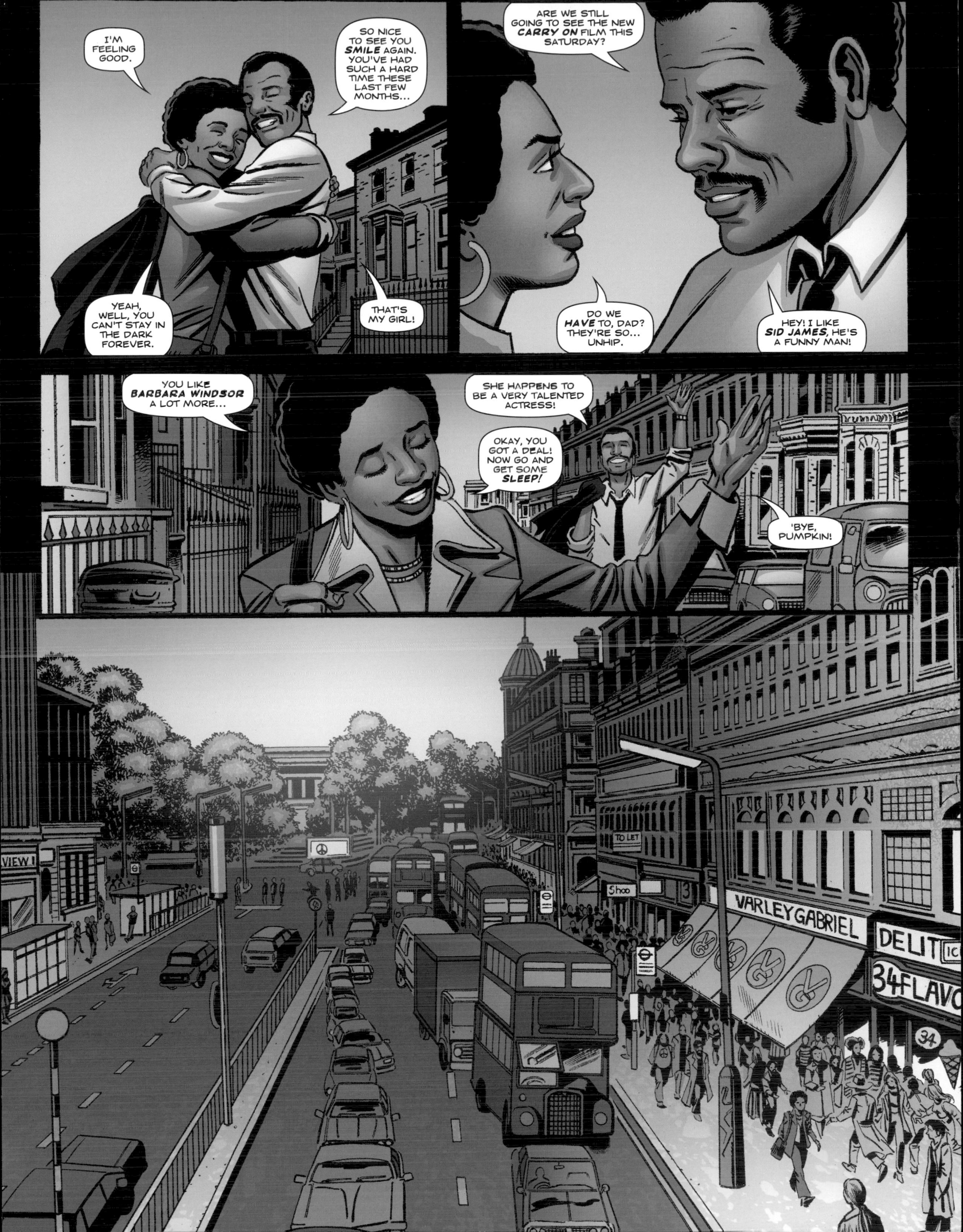
I'M FEELING GOOD.
SO NICE TO SEE YOU SMILE AGAIN. YOU'VE HAD SUCH A HARD TIME THESE LAST FEW MONTHS...
YEAH, WELL, YOU CAN'T STAY IN THE DARK FOREVER.
THAT'S MY GIRL!
ARE WE STILL GOING TO SEE THE NEW CARRY ON FILM THIS SATURDAY?
DO WE HAVE TO, DAD? THEY'RE SO... UNHIP.
HEY! I LIKE SID JAMES, HE'S A FUNNY MAN!
YOU LIKE BARBARA WINDSOR A LOT MORE...
SHE HAPPENS TO BE A VERY TALENTED ACTRESS!
OKAY, YOU GOT A DEAL! NOW GO AND GET SOME SLEEP!
'BYE, PUMPKIN!
VIEW
TO LET
Shoo
VARLEYGABRIEL
DELIT
34FLAVO
34

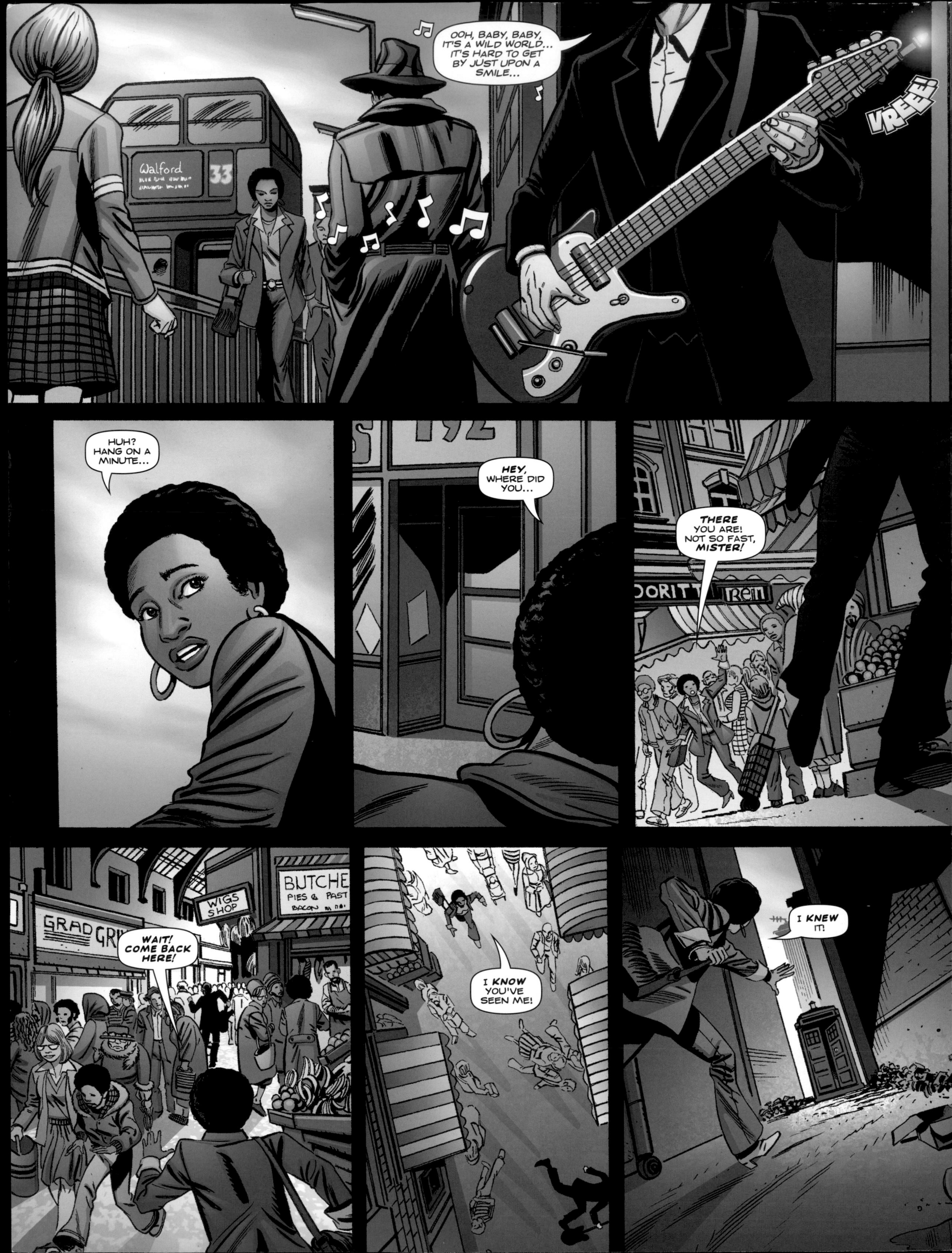

OOH, BABY, BABY, IT'S A WILD WORLD... IT'S HARD TO GET BY JUST UPON A SMILE...
VREEE!
Walford
33
HUH? HANG ON A MINUTE...
HEY, WHERE DID YOU...
THERE YOU ARE! NOT SO FAST, MISTER!
WAIT! COME BACK HERE!
WIGS SHOP
I KNOW YOU'VE SEEN ME!
I KNEW IT!

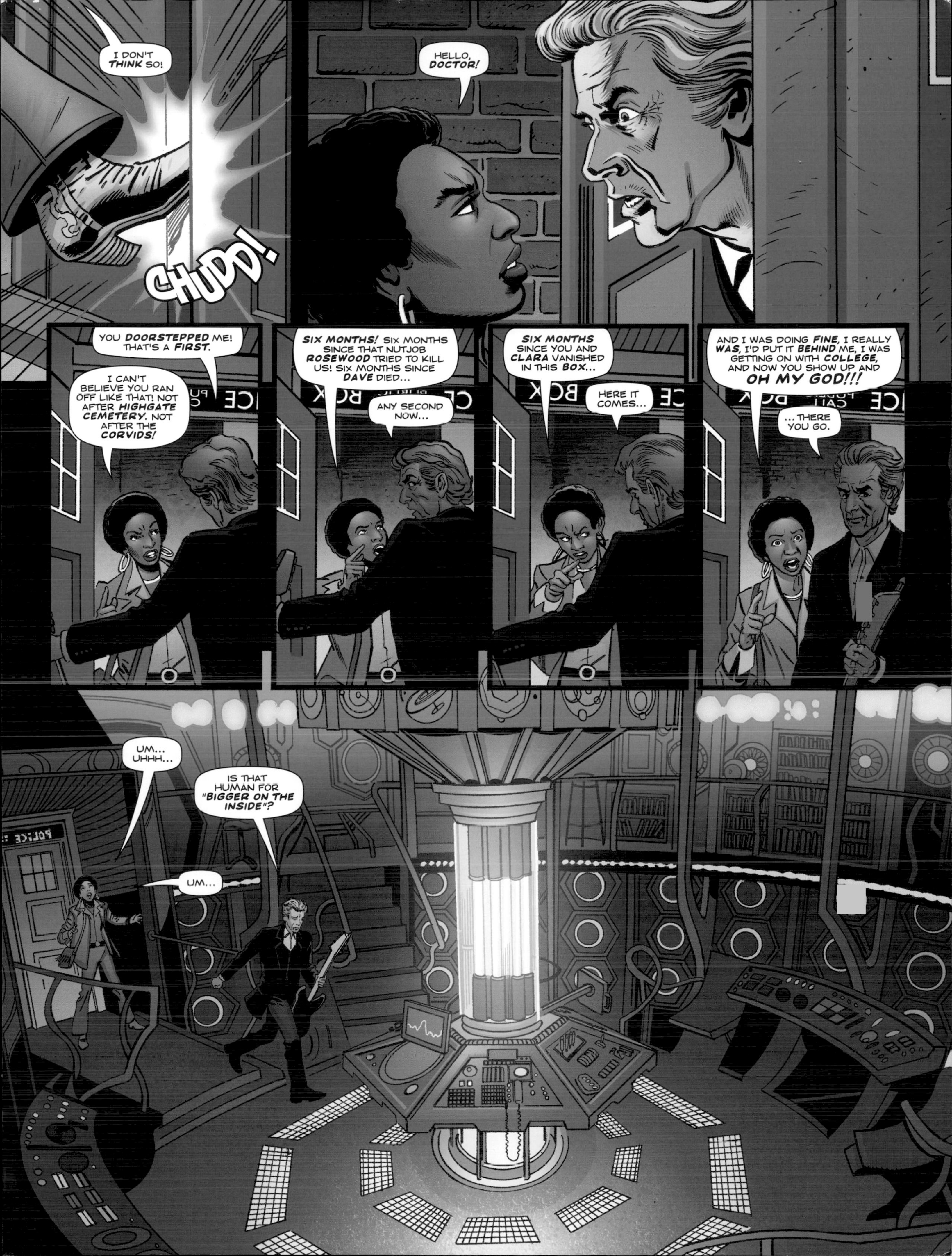
I DON'T THINK SO!
CHUDD!
HELLO, DOCTOR!
YOU DOORSTEPPED ME! THAT'S A FIRST.
I CAN'T BELIEVE YOU RAN OFF LIKE THAT! NOT AFTER HIGHGATE CEMETERY. NOT AFTER THE CORVIDS!
SIX MONTHS! SIX MONTHS SINCE THAT NUTJOB ROSEWOOD TRIED TO KILL US! SIX MONTHS SINCE DAVE DIED...
ANY SECOND NOW...
SIX MONTHS SINCE YOU AND CLARA VANISHED IN THIS BOX...
HERE IT COMES...
AND I WAS DOING FINE, I REALLY WAS, I'D PUT IT BEHIND ME, I WAS GETTING ON WITH COLLEGE, AND NOW YOU SHOW UP AND OH MY GOD!!!
...THERE YOU GO.
UM... UHHH...
IS THAT HUMAN FOR "BIGGER ON THE INSIDE"?
UM...

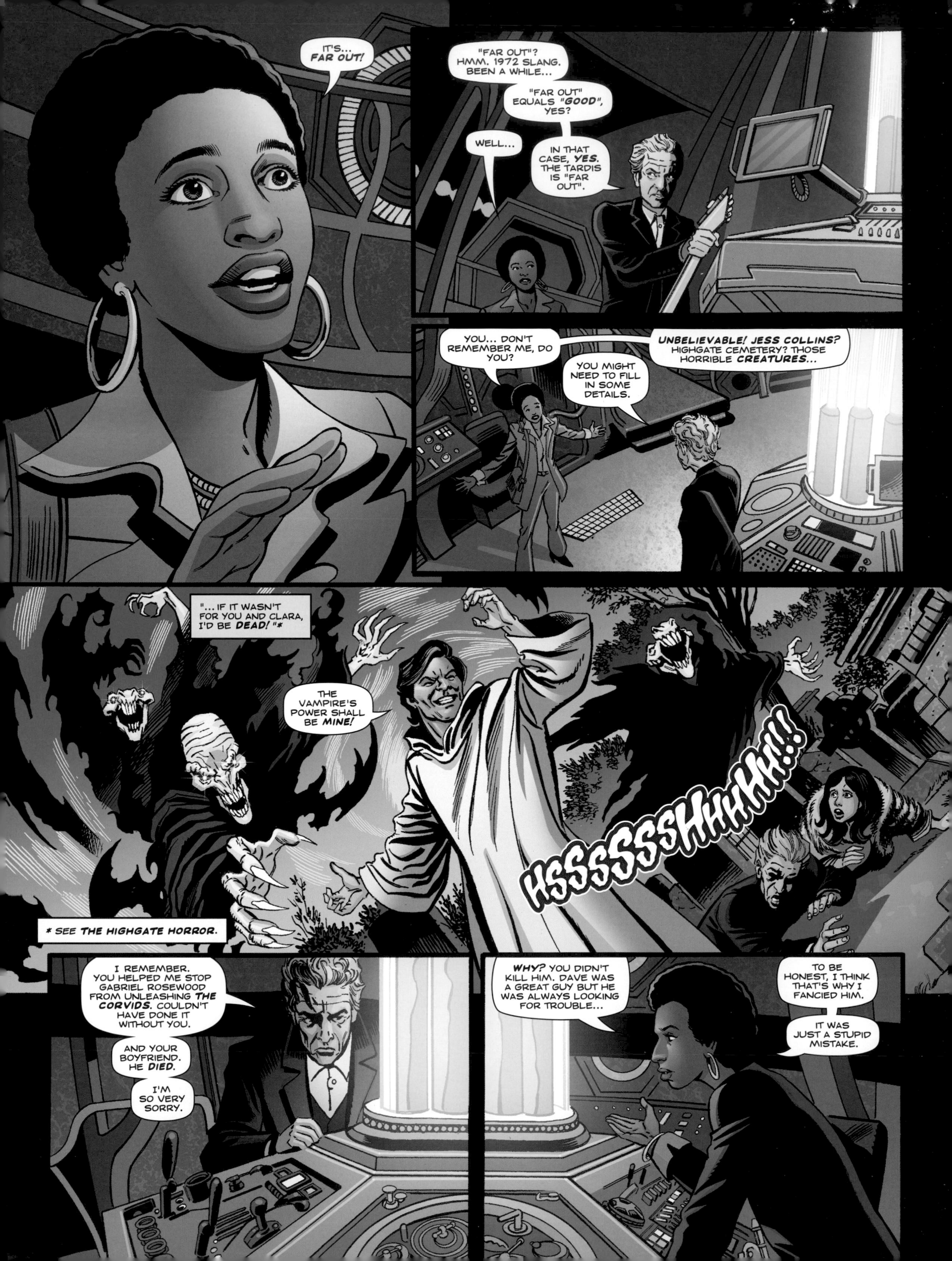
IT'S... FAR OUT!
"FAR OUT"? HMM. 1972 SLANG. BEEN A WHILE...
"FAR OUT" EQUALS "GOOD", YES?
WELL...
IN THAT CASE, YES. THE TARDIS IS "FAR OUT".
YOU... DON'T REMEMBER ME, DO YOU?
UNBELIEVABLE! JESS COLLINS? HIGHGATE CEMETERY? THOSE HORRIBLE CREATURES...
YOU MIGHT NEED TO FILL IN SOME DETAILS.
"...IF IT WASN'T FOR YOU AND CLARA, I'D BE DEAD!"*
THE VAMPIRE'S POWER SHALL BE MINE!
HSSSSSSSHHHHH!!!
* SEE THE HIGHGATE HORROR.
I REMEMBER. YOU HELPED ME STOP GABRIEL ROSEWOOD FROM UNLEASHING THE CORVIDS. COULDN'T HAVE DONE IT WITHOUT YOU.
AND YOUR BOYFRIEND. HE DIED.
I'M SO VERY SORRY.
WHY? YOU DIDN'T KILL HIM. DAVE WAS A GREAT GUY BUT HE WAS ALWAYS LOOKING FOR TROUBLE...
TO BE HONEST, I THINK THAT'S WHY I FANCIED HIM.
IT WAS JUST A STUPID MISTAKE.

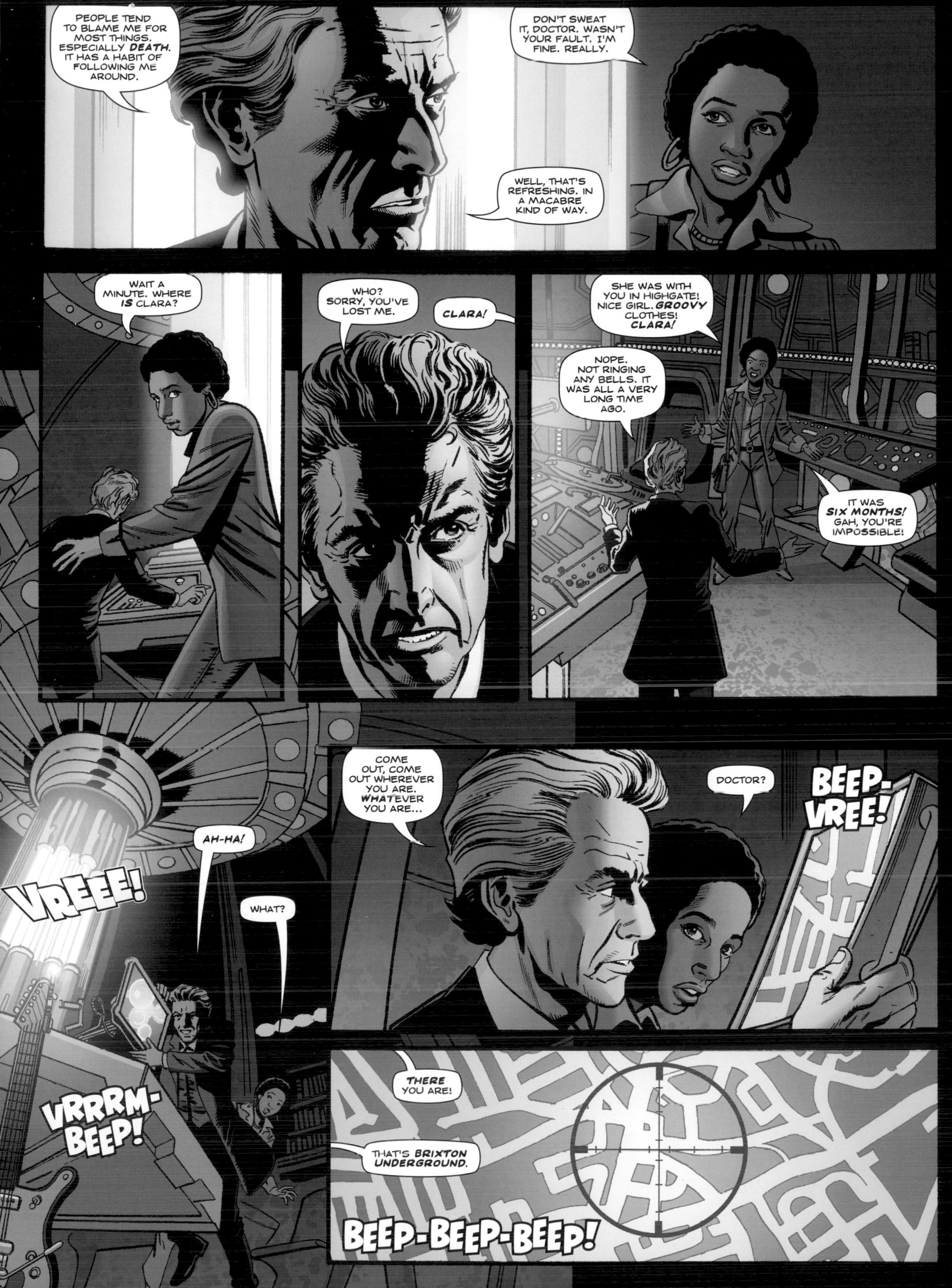
PEOPLE TEND TO BLAME ME FOR MOST THINGS. ESPECIALLY DEATH. IT HAS A HABIT OF FOLLOWING ME AROUND.
DON'T SWEAT IT, DOCTOR. WASN'T YOUR FAULT. I'M FINE. REALLY.
WELL, THAT'S REFRESHING. IN A MACABRE KIND OF WAY.
WAIT A MINUTE. WHERE IS CLARA?
WHO? SORRY, YOU'VE LOST ME.
CLARA!
SHE WAS WITH YOU IN HIGHGATE! NICE GIRL. GROOVY CLOTHES! CLARA!
NOPE. NOT RINGING ANY BELLS. IT WAS ALL A VERY LONG TIME AGO.
IT WAS SIX MONTHS! GAH, YOU'RE IMPOSSIBLE!
VREEE!
AH-HA!
WHAT?
VRRRM-BEEP!
COME OUT, COME OUT WHEREVER YOU ARE. WHATEVER YOU ARE...
DOCTOR?
BEEP-VREE!
THERE YOU ARE!
THAT'S BRIXTON UNDERGROUND.
BEEP-BEEP-BEEP!

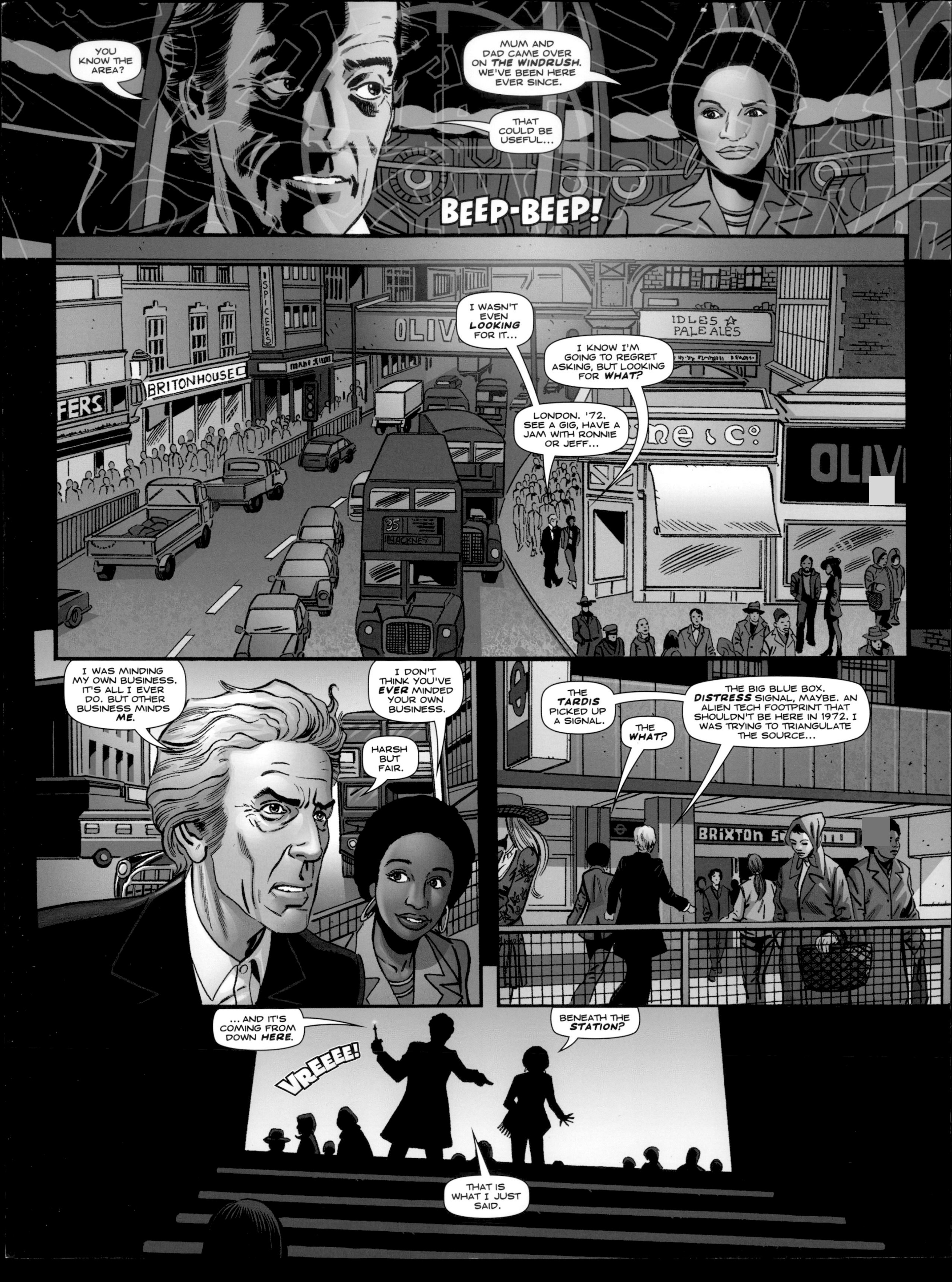
YOU KNOW THE AREA?
MUM AND DAD CAME OVER ON THE WINDRUSH. WE'VE BEEN HERE EVER SINCE.
THAT COULD BE USEFUL...
BEEP-BEEP!
I WASN'T EVEN LOOKING FOR IT...
I KNOW I'M GOING TO REGRET ASKING, BUT LOOKING FOR WHAT?
LONDON. '72. SEE A GIG, HAVE A JAM WITH RONNIE OR JEFF...
I WAS MINDING MY OWN BUSINESS. IT'S ALL I EVER DO. BUT OTHER BUSINESS MINDS ME.
I DON'T THINK YOU'VE EVER MINDED YOUR OWN BUSINESS.
HARSH BUT FAIR.
THE TARDIS PICKED UP A SIGNAL.
THE WHAT?
THE BIG BLUE BOX. DISTRESS SIGNAL, MAYBE. AN ALIEN TECH FOOTPRINT THAT SHOULDN'T BE HERE IN 1972. I WAS TRYING TO TRIANGULATE THE SOURCE...
... AND IT'S COMING FROM DOWN HERE.
VREEEE!
BENEATH THE STATION?
THAT IS WHAT I JUST SAID.

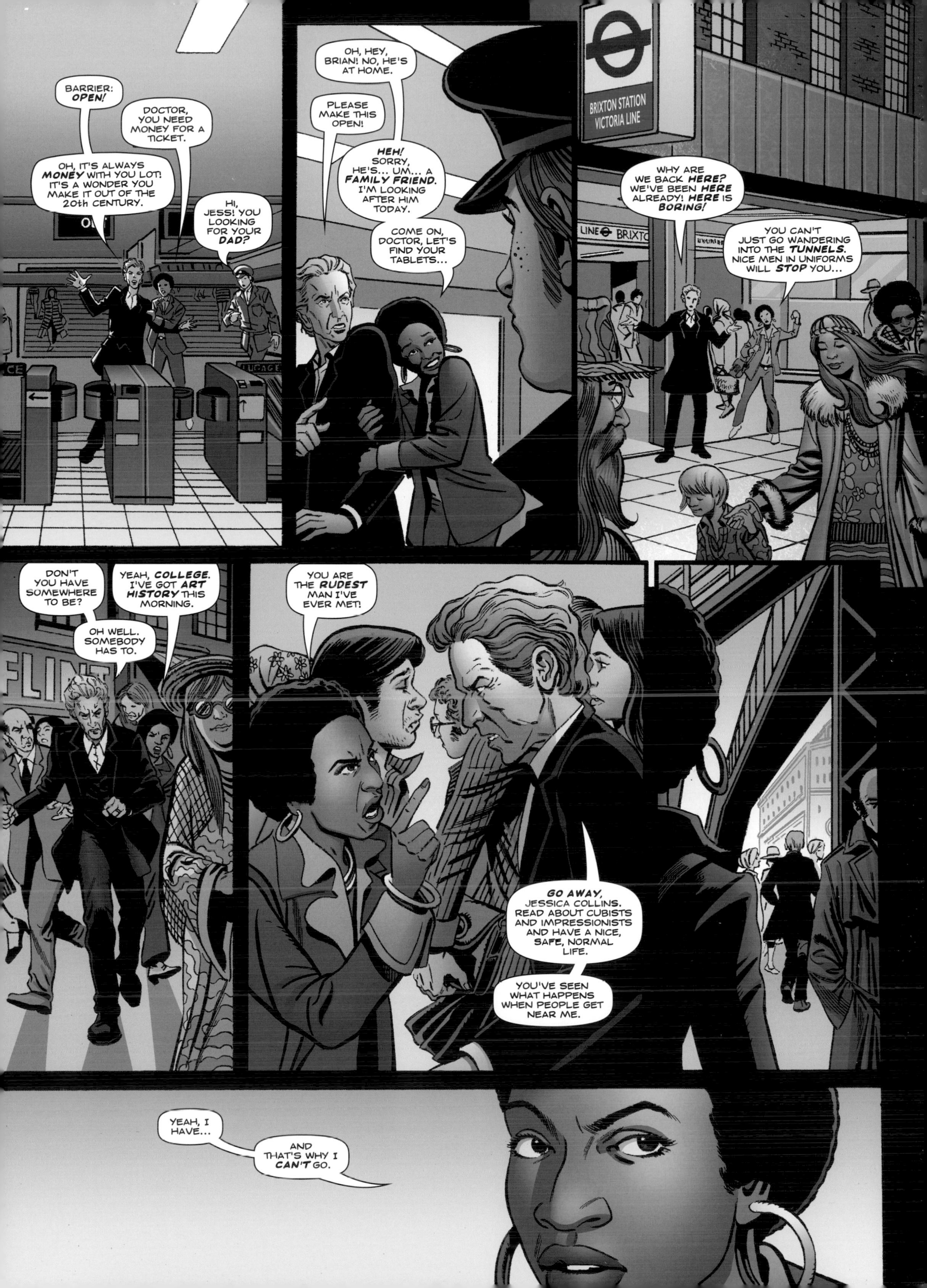
BARRIER: OPEN!
DOCTOR, YOU NEED MONEY FOR A TICKET.
OH, IT'S ALWAYS MONEY WITH YOU LOT! IT'S A WONDER YOU MAKE IT OUT OF THE 20th CENTURY.
HI, JESS! YOU LOOKING FOR YOUR DAD?
OH, HEY, BRIAN! NO, HE'S AT HOME.
PLEASE MAKE THIS OPEN!
HEH! SORRY, HE'S... UM... A FAMILY FRIEND. I'M LOOKING AFTER HIM TODAY.
COME ON, DOCTOR, LET'S FIND YOUR TABLETS...
BRIXTON STATION
VICTORIA LINE
WHY ARE WE BACK HERE? WE'VE BEEN HERE ALREADY! HERE IS BORING!
YOU CAN'T JUST GO WANDERING INTO THE TUNNELS. NICE MEN IN UNIFORMS WILL STOP YOU...
DON'T YOU HAVE SOMEWHERE TO BE?
YEAH, COLLEGE. I'VE GOT ART HISTORY THIS MORNING.
OH WELL. SOMEBODY HAS TO.
YOU ARE THE RUDEST MAN I'VE EVER MET!
GO AWAY, JESSICA COLLINS. READ ABOUT CUBISTS AND IMPRESSIONISTS AND HAVE A NICE, SAFE, NORMAL LIFE.
YOU'VE SEEN WHAT HAPPENS WHEN PEOPLE GET NEAR ME.
YEAH, I HAVE...
AND THAT'S WHY I CAN'T GO.

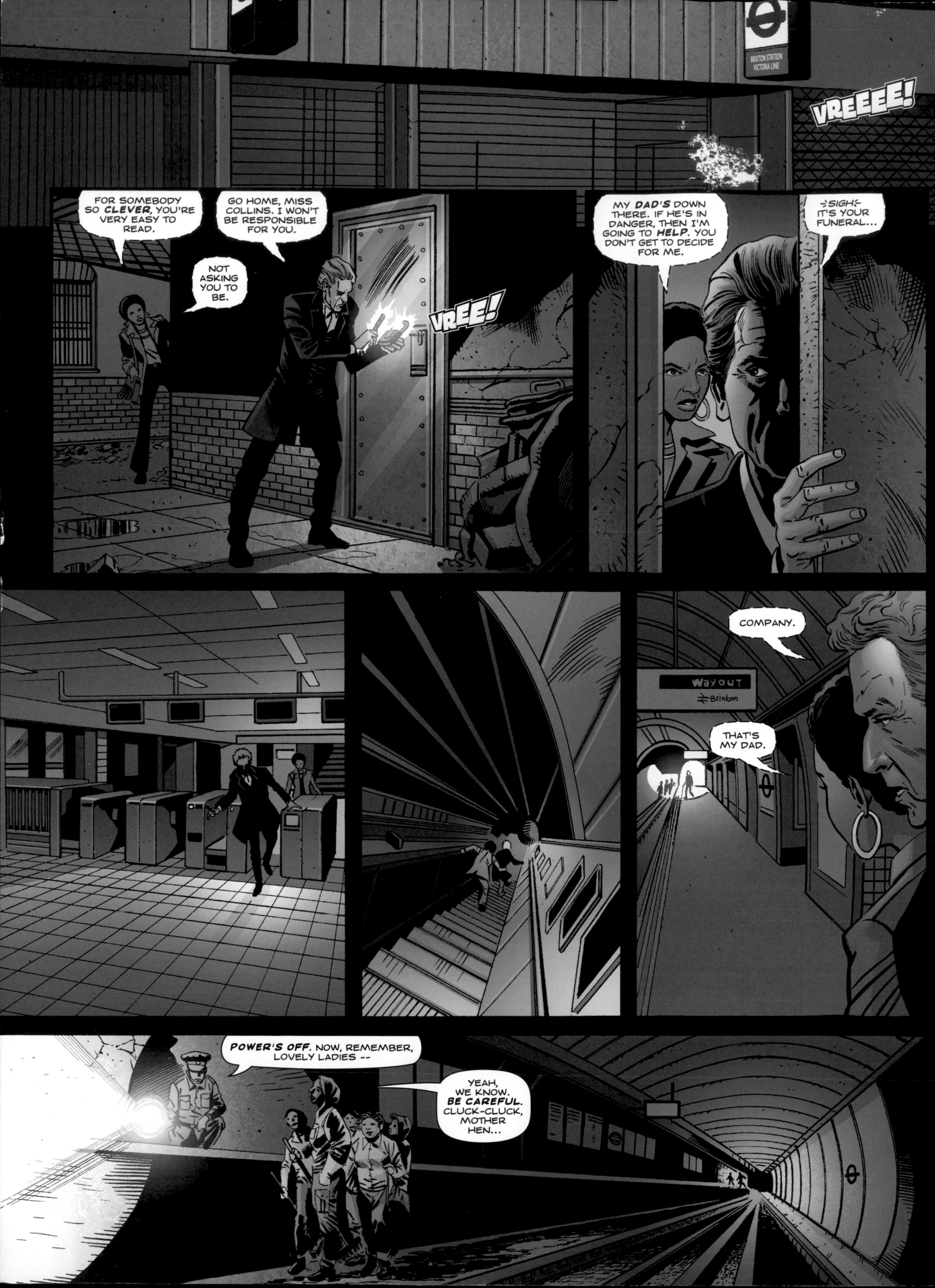
BRIXTON STATION VICTORIA LINE
VREEEE!
FOR SOMEBODY SO CLEVER, YOU'RE VERY EASY TO READ.
GO HOME, MISS COLLINS. I WON'T BE RESPONSIBLE FOR YOU.
NOT ASKING YOU TO BE.
VREE!
MY DAD'S DOWN THERE. IF HE'S IN DANGER, THEN I'M GOING TO HELP. YOU DON'T GET TO DECIDE FOR ME.
-SIGH- IT'S YOUR FUNERAL...
COMPANY.
Way out
Brixton
THAT'S MY DAD.
POWER'S OFF. NOW, REMEMBER, LOVELY LADIES --
YEAH, WE KNOW. BE CAREFUL. CLUCK-CLUCK, MOTHER HEN...

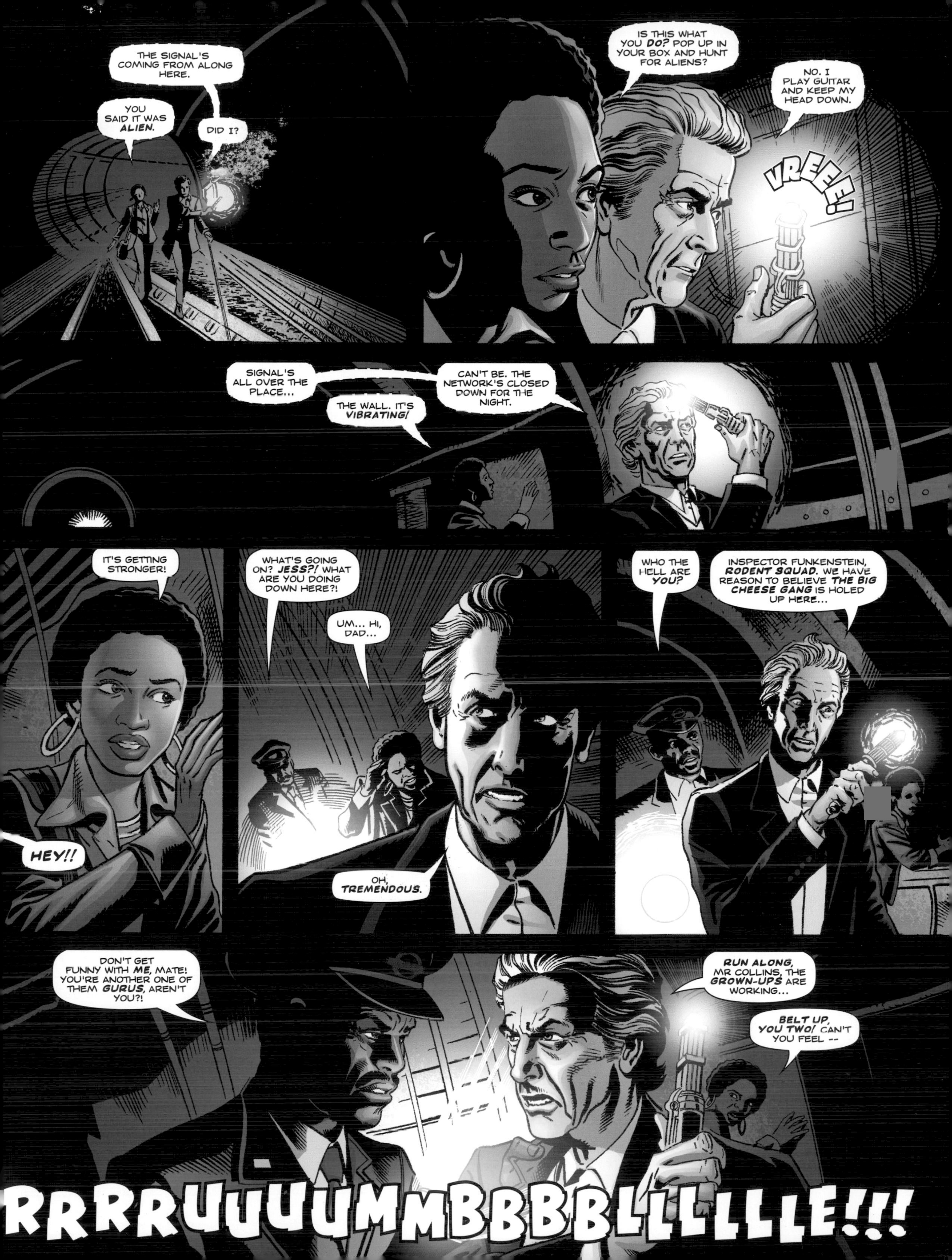
THE SIGNAL'S COMING FROM ALONG HERE.
YOU SAID IT WAS ALIEN.
DID I?
IS THIS WHAT YOU DO? POP UP IN YOUR BOX AND HUNT FOR ALIENS?
NO. I PLAY GUITAR AND KEEP MY HEAD DOWN.
VREEE!
SIGNAL'S ALL OVER THE PLACE...
CAN'T BE. THE NETWORK'S CLOSED DOWN FOR THE NIGHT.
THE WALL. IT'S VIBRATING!
IT'S GETTING STRONGER!
HEY!!
WHAT'S GOING ON? JESS?! WHAT ARE YOU DOING DOWN HERE?!
UM... HI, DAD...
OH, TREMENDOUS.
WHO THE HELL ARE YOU?
INSPECTOR FUNKENSTEIN, RODENT SQUAD. WE HAVE REASON TO BELIEVE THE BIG CHEESE GANG IS HOLED UP HERE...
DON'T GET FUNNY WITH ME, MATE! YOU'RE ANOTHER ONE OF THEM GURUS, AREN'T YOU?!
RUN ALONG, MR COLLINS, THE GROWN-UPS ARE WORKING...
BELT UP, YOU TWO! CAN'T YOU FEEL --
RRRRUUUUMMBBBBLLLLLLE!!!

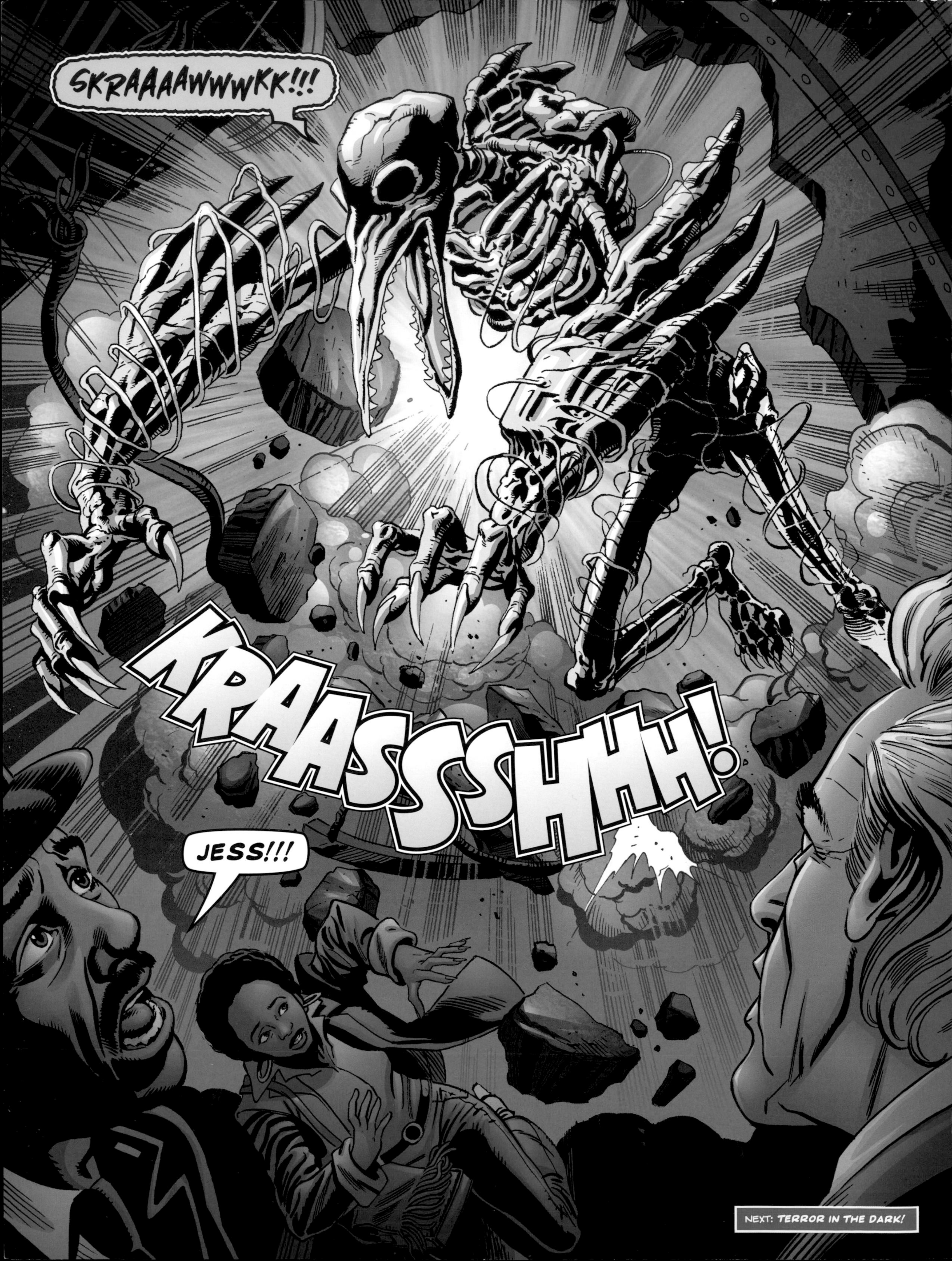
SKRAAAAWWWKK!!!
KRAASSSHHH!
JESS!!!
NEXT: TERROR IN THE DARK!

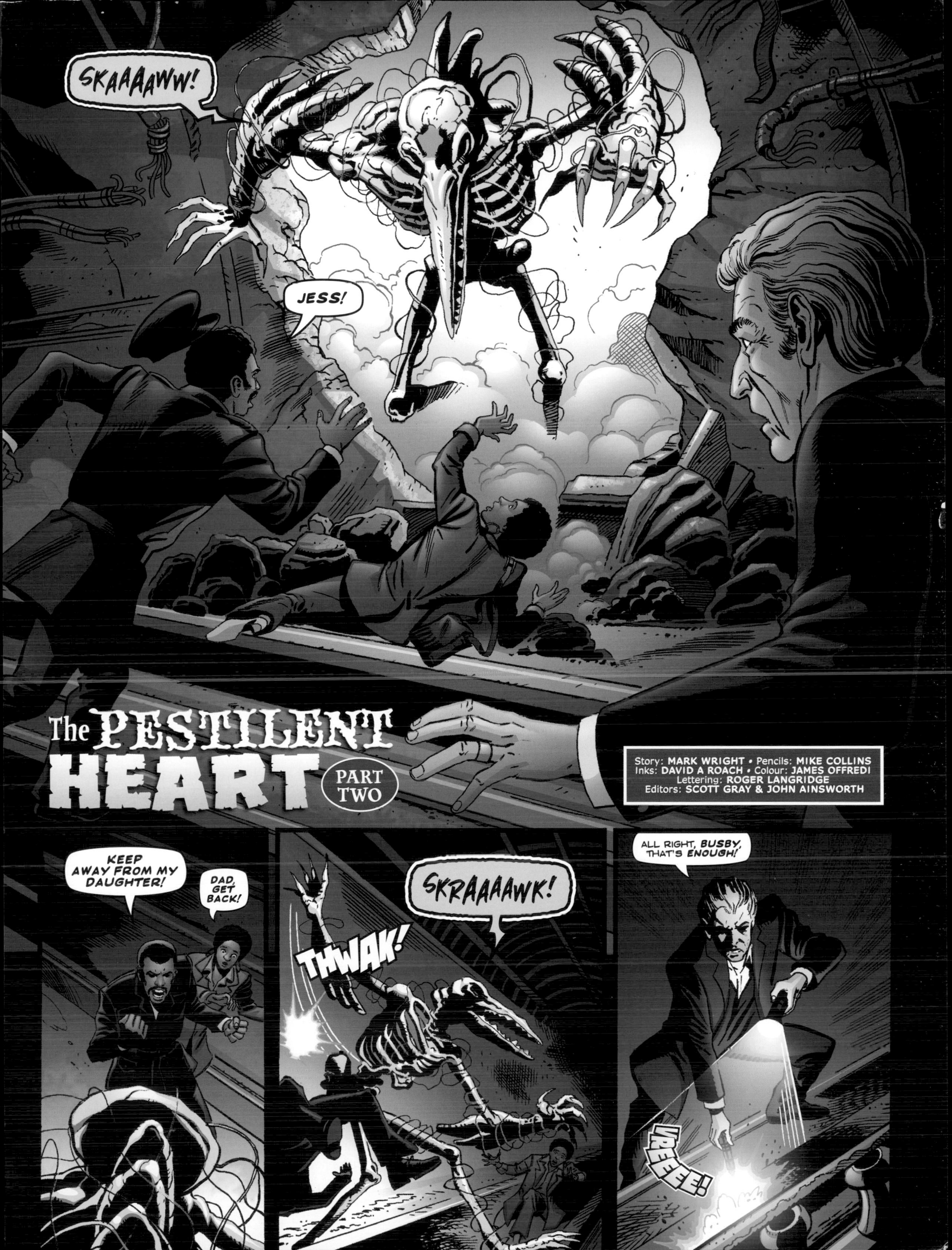
SKAAAAWW!
JESS!
The PESTILENT HEART PART TWO
Story: MARK WRIGHT • Pencils: MIKE COLLINS
Inks: DAVID A ROACH • Colour: JAMES OFFREDI
Lettering: ROGER LANGRIDGE
Editors: SCOTT GRAY & JOHN AINSWORTH
KEEP AWAY FROM MY DAUGHTER!
DAD, GET BACK!
SKRAAAAWK!
THWAK!
ALL RIGHT, BUSBY, THAT'S ENOUGH!
VREEEE!

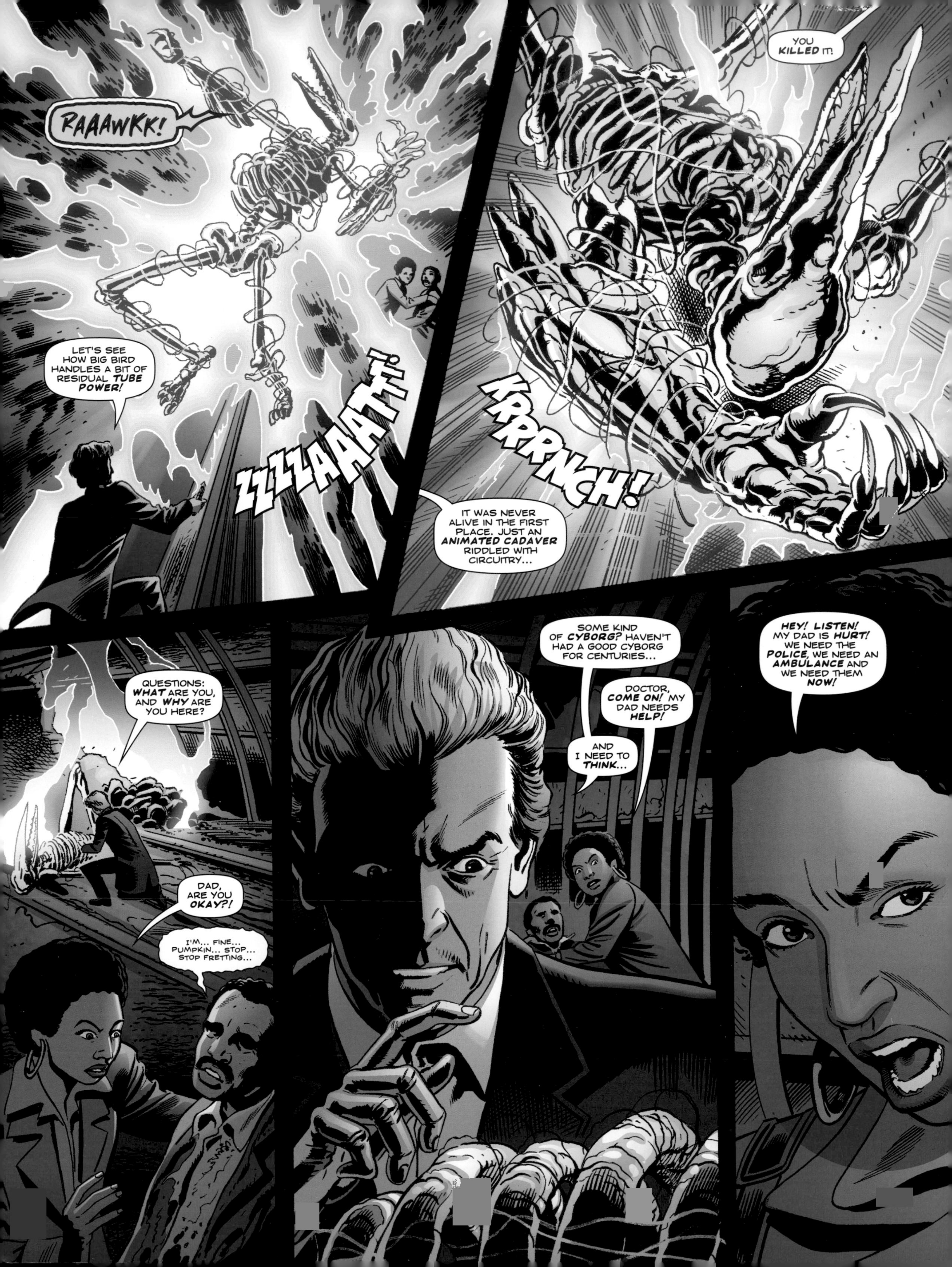
RAAAWKK!
LET'S SEE HOW BIG BIRD HANDLES A BIT OF RESIDUAL TUBE POWER!
ZZZZAAAT!
YOU KILLED IT!
KRRRNCH!
IT WAS NEVER ALIVE IN THE FIRST PLACE. JUST AN ANIMATED CADAVER RIDDLED WITH CIRCUITRY...
QUESTIONS: WHAT ARE YOU, AND WHY ARE YOU HERE?
DAD, ARE YOU OKAY?!
I'M... FINE... PUMPKIN... STOP... STOP FRETTING...
SOME KIND OF CYBORG? HAVEN'T HAD A GOOD CYBORG FOR CENTURIES...
DOCTOR, COME ON! MY DAD NEEDS HELP!
AND I NEED TO THINK...
HEY! LISTEN! MY DAD IS HURT! WE NEED THE POLICE, WE NEED AN AMBULANCE AND WE NEED THEM NOW!

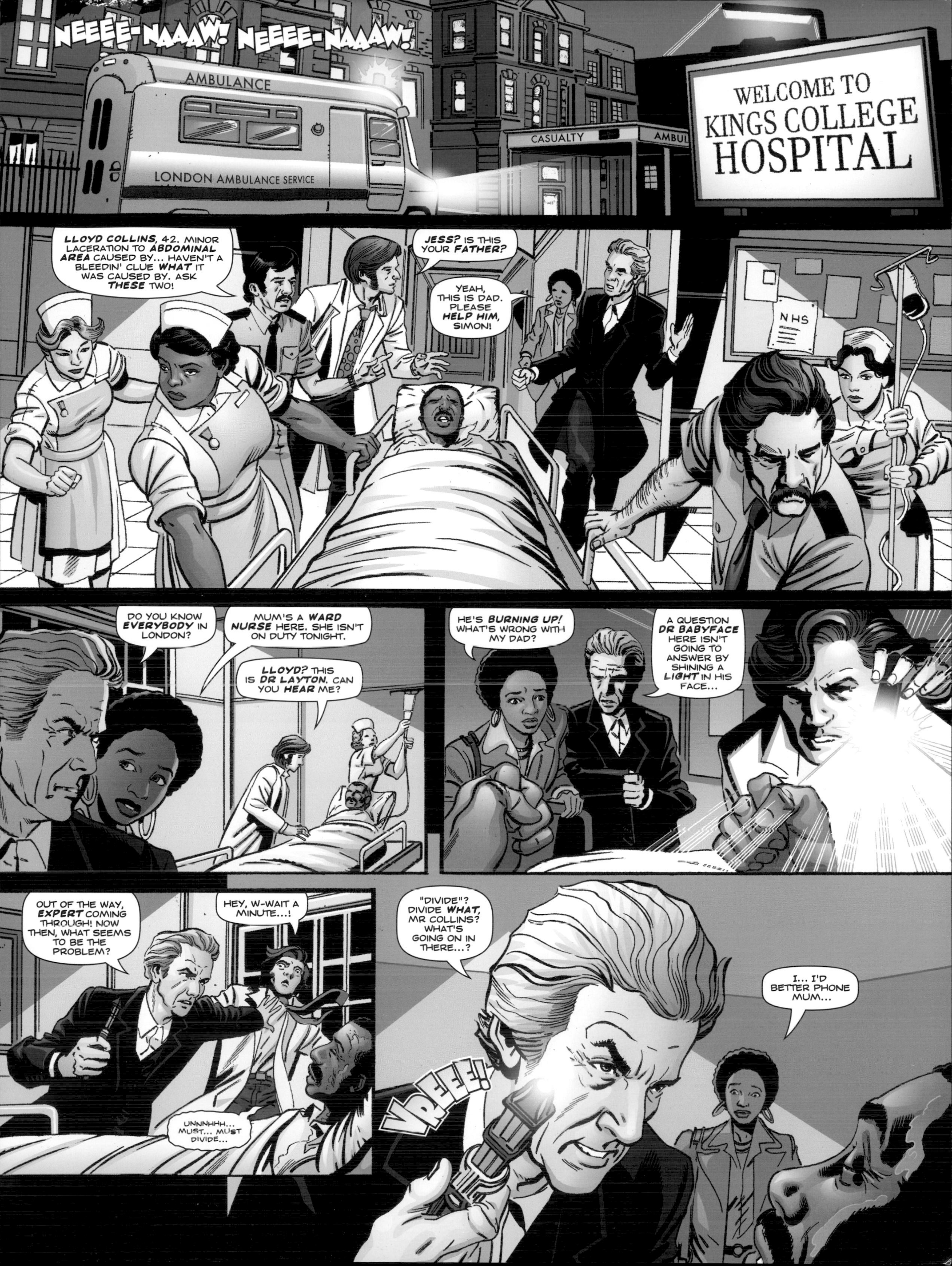
NEEEE-NAAAW! NEEEE-NAAAW!
AMBULANCE
LONDON AMBULANCE SERVICE
CASUALTY
AMBUL
WELCOME TO KINGS COLLEGE HOSPITAL
LLOYD COLLINS, 42. MINOR LACERATION TO ABDOMINAL AREA CAUSED BY... HAVEN'T A BLEEDIN' CLUE WHAT IT WAS CAUSED BY. ASK THESE TWO!
JESS? IS THIS YOUR FATHER?
YEAH, THIS IS DAD. PLEASE HELP HIM, SIMON!
NHS
DO YOU KNOW EVERYBODY IN LONDON?
MUM'S A WARD NURSE HERE. SHE ISN'T ON DUTY TONIGHT.
LLOYD? THIS IS DR LAYTON. CAN YOU HEAR ME?
HE'S BURNING UP! WHAT'S WRONG WITH MY DAD?
A QUESTION DR BABYFACE HERE ISN'T GOING TO ANSWER BY SHINING A LIGHT IN HIS FACE...
OUT OF THE WAY, EXPERT COMING THROUGH! NOW THEN, WHAT SEEMS TO BE THE PROBLEM?
HEY, W-WAIT A MINUTE...!
UNNNHHH... MUST... MUST DIVIDE...
"DIVIDE"? DIVIDE WHAT, MR COLLINS? WHAT'S GOING ON IN THERE...?
VREEE!
I... I'D BETTER PHONE MUM...

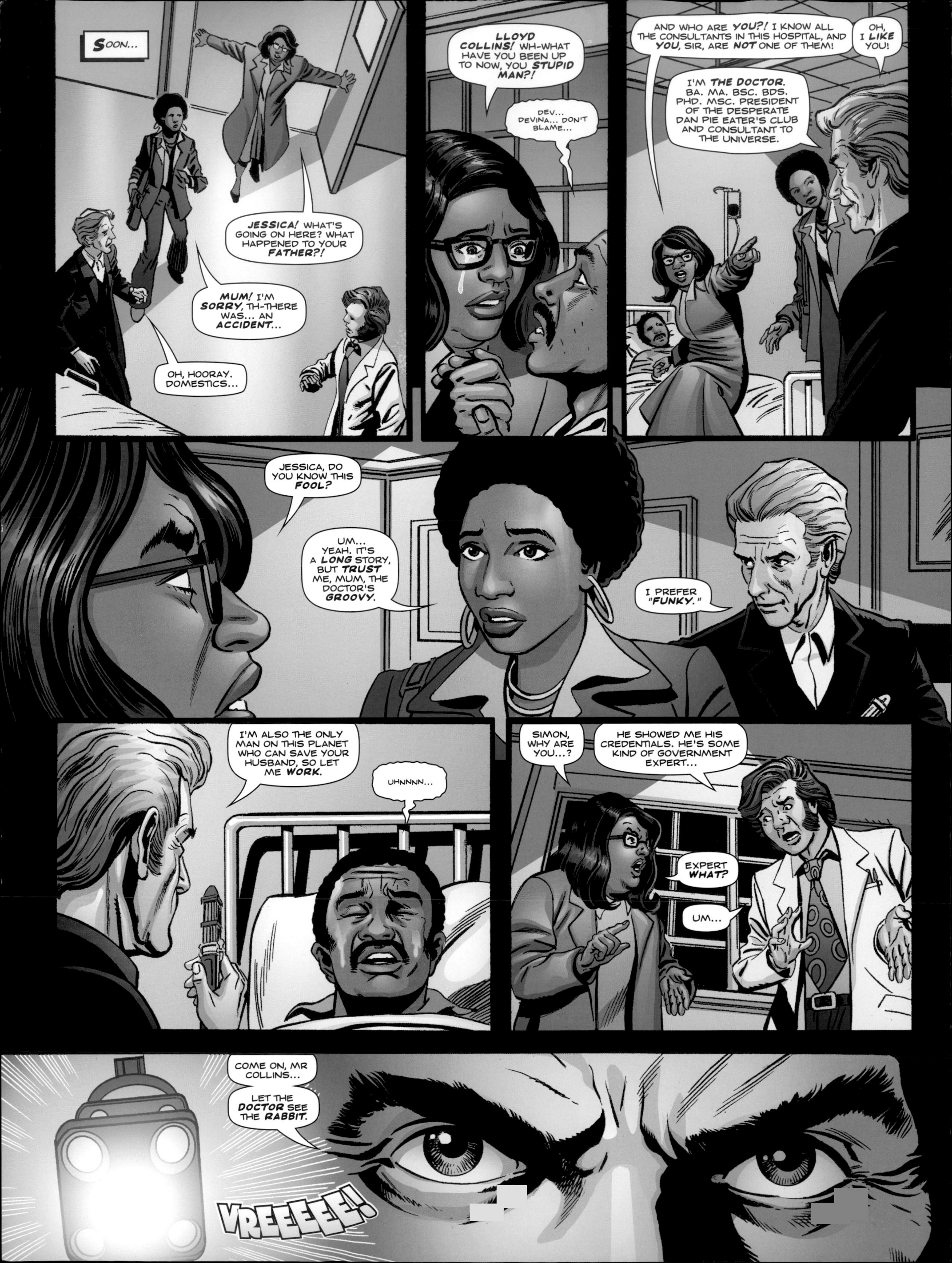

SOON...
JESSICA! WHAT'S GOING ON HERE? WHAT HAPPENED TO YOUR FATHER?!
MUM! I'M SORRY, TH-THERE WAS... AN ACCIDENT...
OH, HOORAY. DOMESTICS...
LLOYD COLLINS! WH-WHAT HAVE YOU BEEN UP TO NOW, YOU STUPID MAN?!
DEV... DEVINA... DON'T BLAME...
AND WHO ARE YOU?! I KNOW ALL THE CONSULTANTS IN THIS HOSPITAL, AND YOU, SIR, ARE NOT ONE OF THEM!
OH, I LIKE YOU!
I'M THE DOCTOR. BA. MA. BSC. BDS. PHD. MSC. PRESIDENT OF THE DESPERATE DAN PIE EATER'S CLUB AND CONSULTANT TO THE UNIVERSE.
JESSICA, DO YOU KNOW THIS FOOL?
UM... YEAH. IT'S A LONG STORY, BUT TRUST ME, MUM, THE DOCTOR'S GROOVY.
I PREFER "FUNKY."
I'M ALSO THE ONLY MAN ON THIS PLANET WHO CAN SAVE YOUR HUSBAND, SO LET ME WORK.
UHNNNN...
SIMON, WHY ARE YOU...?
HE SHOWED ME HIS CREDENTIALS. HE'S SOME KIND OF GOVERNMENT EXPERT...
EXPERT WHAT?
UM...
COME ON, MR COLLINS...
LET THE DOCTOR SEE THE RABBIT.
VREEEEE!

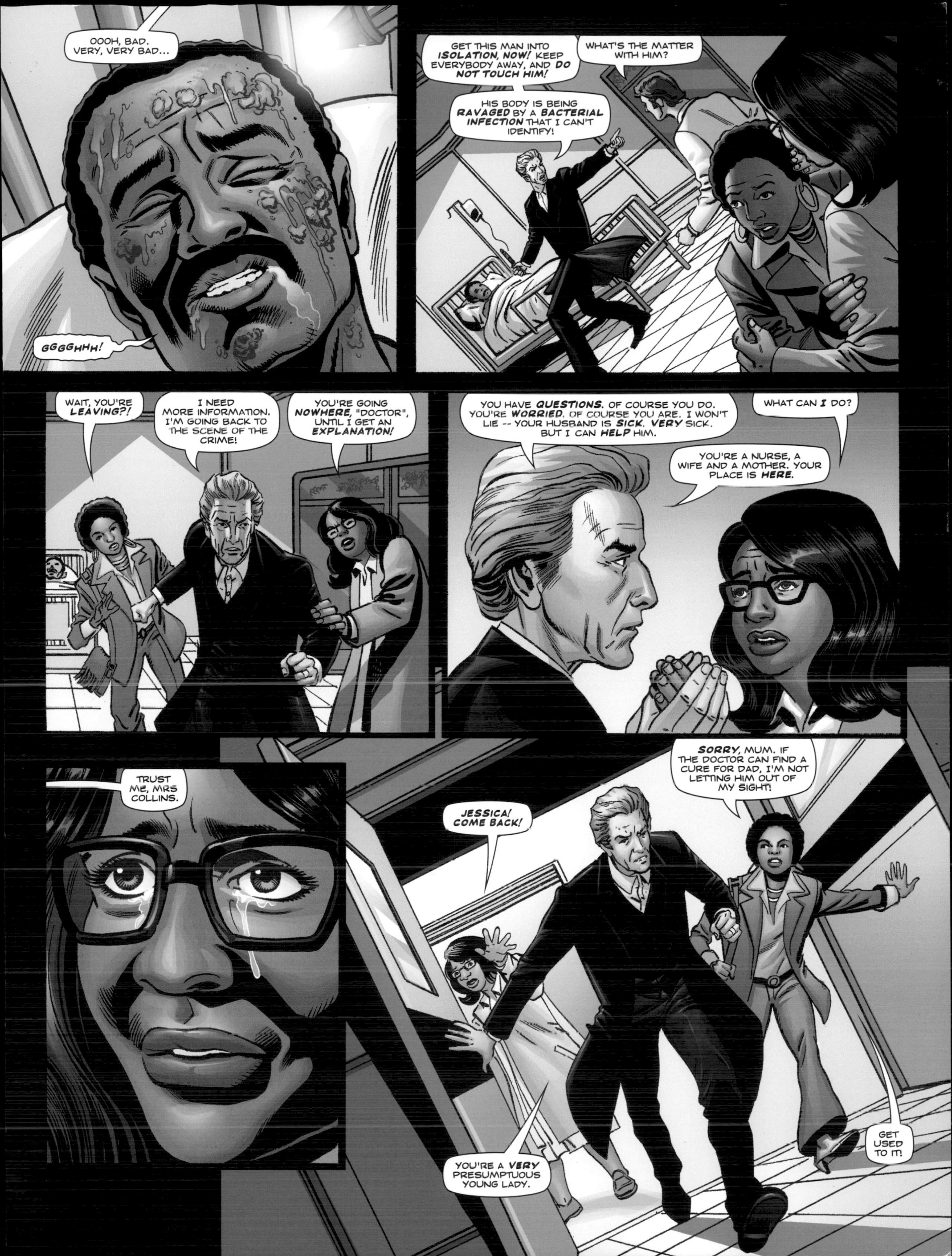

OOOH, BAD. VERY, VERY BAD...
GGGGHHH!
GET THIS MAN INTO ISOLATION, NOW! KEEP EVERYBODY AWAY, AND DO NOT TOUCH HIM!
WHAT'S THE MATTER WITH HIM?
HIS BODY IS BEING RAVAGED BY A BACTERIAL INFECTION THAT I CAN'T IDENTIFY!
WAIT, YOU'RE LEAVING?!
I NEED MORE INFORMATION. I'M GOING BACK TO THE SCENE OF THE CRIME!
YOU'RE GOING NOWHERE, "DOCTOR", UNTIL I GET AN EXPLANATION!
YOU HAVE QUESTIONS. OF COURSE YOU DO. YOU'RE WORRIED. OF COURSE YOU ARE. I WON'T LIE -- YOUR HUSBAND IS SICK. VERY SICK. BUT I CAN HELP HIM.
WHAT CAN I DO?
YOU'RE A NURSE, A WIFE AND A MOTHER. YOUR PLACE IS HERE.
TRUST ME, MRS COLLINS.
SORRY, MUM. IF THE DOCTOR CAN FIND A CURE FOR DAD, I'M NOT LETTING HIM OUT OF MY SIGHT!
JESSICA! COME BACK!
YOU'RE A VERY PRESUMPTUOUS YOUNG LADY.
GET USED TO IT!

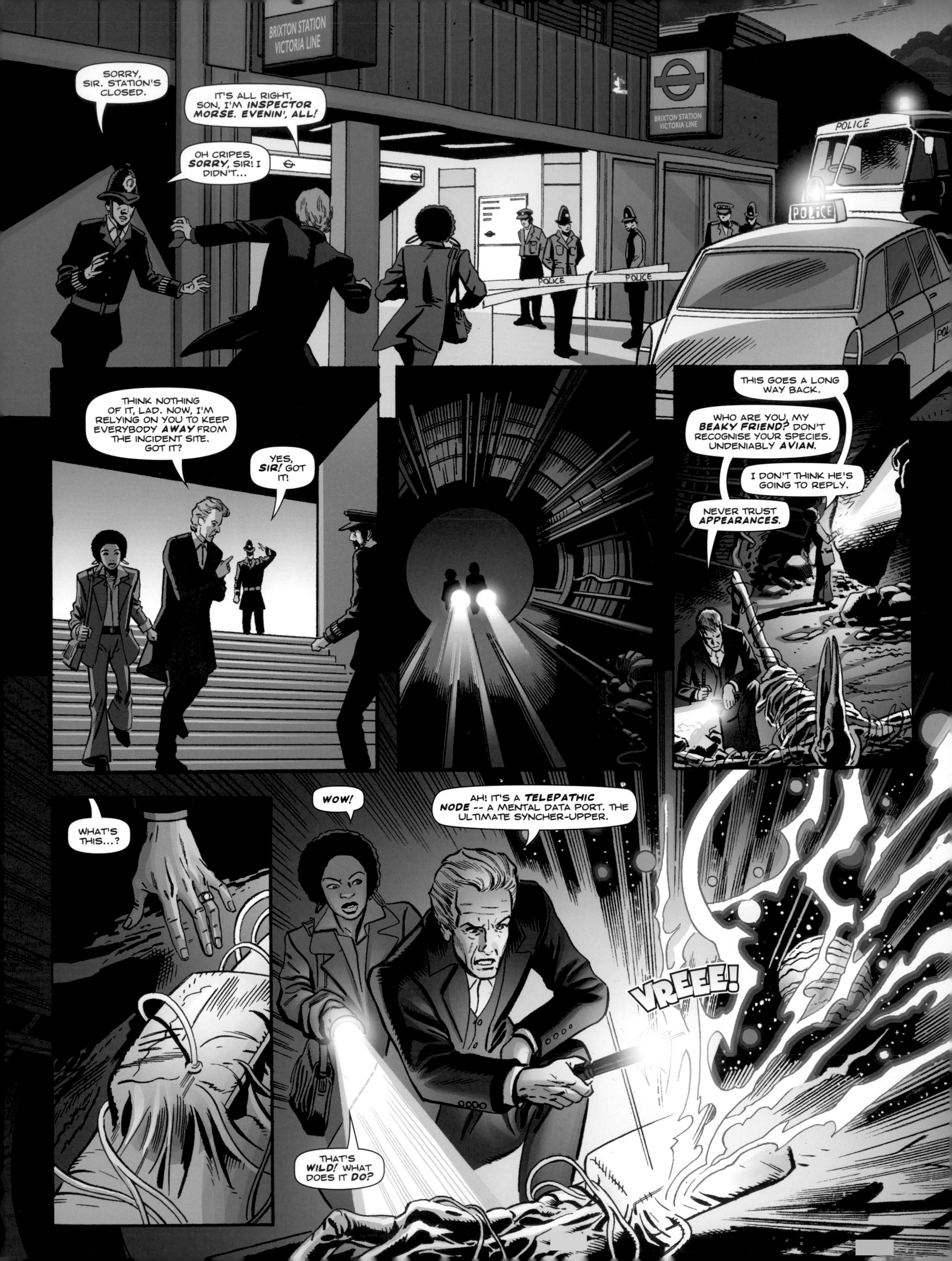
BRIXTON STATION VICTORIA LINE
SORRY, SIR. STATION'S CLOSED.
IT'S ALL RIGHT, SON, I'M INSPECTOR MORSE. EVENIN', ALL!
OH CRIPES, SORRY, SIR! I DIDN'T...
BRIXTON STATION VICTORIA LINE
POLICE
POLICE
POLICE
POLICE
THINK NOTHING OF IT, LAD. NOW, I'M RELYING ON YOU TO KEEP EVERYBODY AWAY FROM THE INCIDENT SITE. GOT IT?
YES, SIR! GOT IT!
THIS GOES A LONG WAY BACK.
WHO ARE YOU, MY BEAKY FRIEND? DON'T RECOGNISE YOUR SPECIES. UNDENIABLY AVIAN.
I DON'T THINK HE'S GOING TO REPLY.
NEVER TRUST APPEARANCES.
WHAT'S THIS...?
WOW!
AH! IT'S A TELEPATHIC NODE -- A MENTAL DATA PORT. THE ULTIMATE SYNCHER-UPPER.
VREEE!
THAT'S WILD! WHAT DOES IT DO?

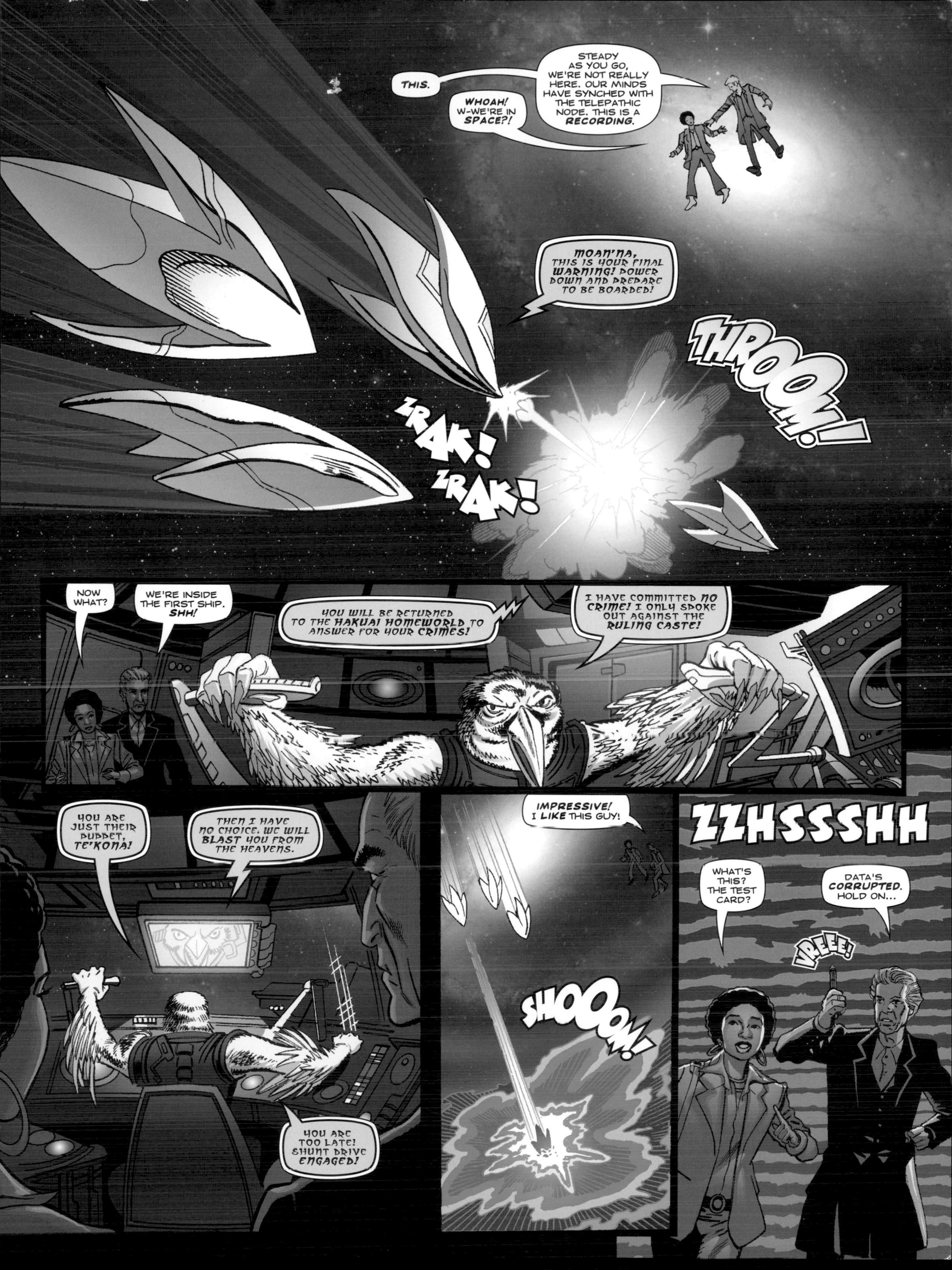

THIS.
STEADY AS YOU GO, WE'RE NOT REALLY HERE. OUR MINDS HAVE SYNCHED WITH THE TELEPATHIC NODE. THIS IS A RECORDING.
WHOAH! W-WE'RE IN SPACE?!
MOAN'NA, THIS IS YOUR FINAL WARNING! POWER DOWN AND PREPARE TO BE BOARDED!
THROOM!
ZRAK! ZRAK!
NOW WHAT?
WE'RE INSIDE THE FIRST SHIP. SHH!
YOU WILL BE RETURNED TO THE HAKUAI HOMEWORLD TO ANSWER FOR YOUR CRIMES!
I HAVE COMMITTED NO CRIME! I ONLY SPOKE OUT AGAINST THE RULING CASTE!
YOU ARE JUST THEIR PUPPET, TE'KONA!
THEN I HAVE NO CHOICE. WE WILL BLAST YOU FROM THE HEAVENS.
YOU ARE TOO LATE! SHUNT DRIVE ENGAGED!
IMPRESSIVE! I LIKE THIS GUY!
SHOOOM!
ZZHSSSHH
WHAT'S THIS? THE TEST CARD?
DATA'S CORRUPTED. HOLD ON...
VREEE!

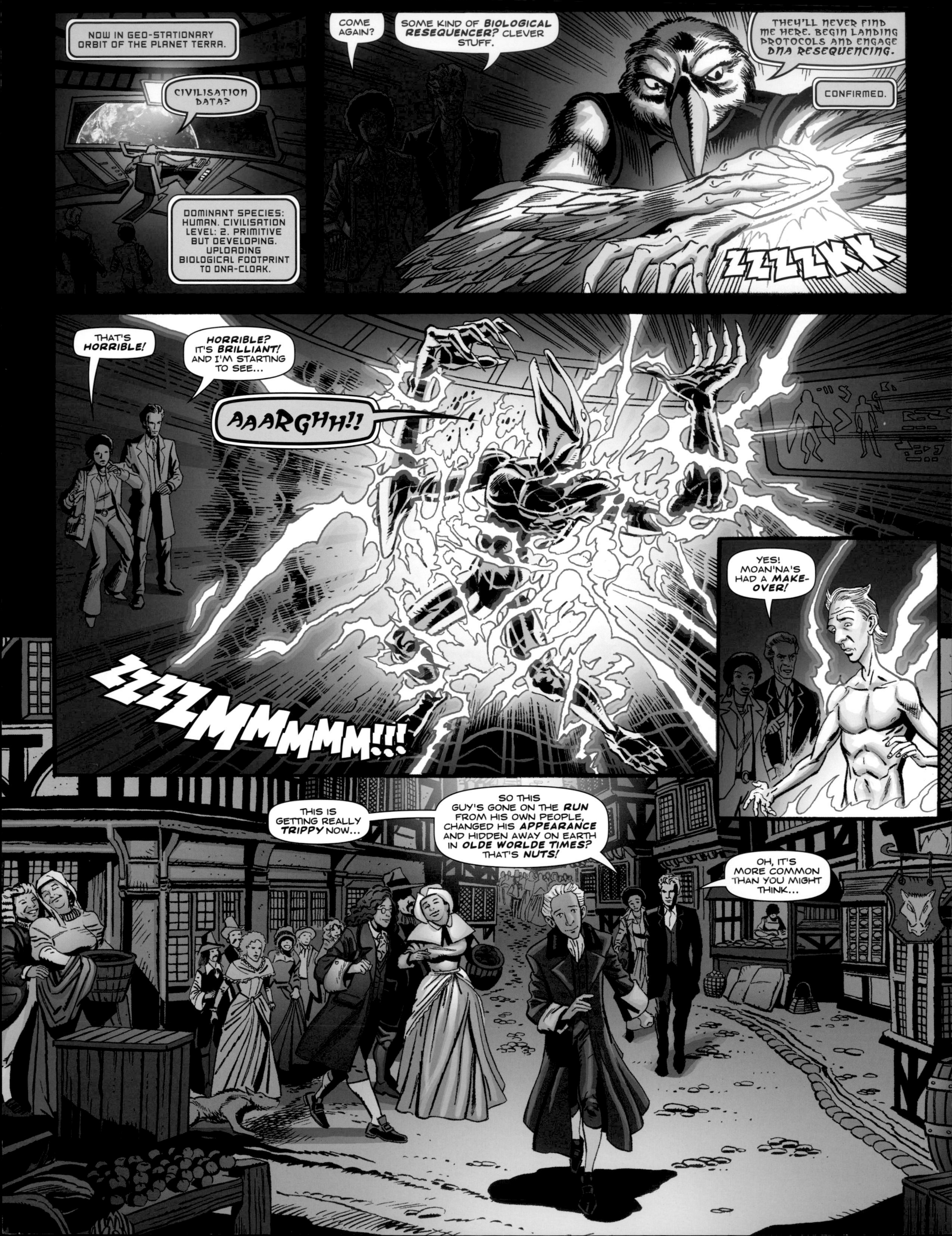
NOW IN GEO-STATIONARY ORBIT OF THE PLANET TERRA.
CIVILISATION DATA?
DOMINANT SPECIES: HUMAN. CIVILISATION LEVEL: 2. PRIMITIVE BUT DEVELOPING. UPLOADING BIOLOGICAL FOOTPRINT TO DNA-CLOAK.
COME AGAIN?
SOME KIND OF BIOLOGICAL RESEQUENCER? CLEVER STUFF.
THEY'LL NEVER FIND ME HERE. BEGIN LANDING PROTOCOLS AND ENGAGE DNA RESEQUENCING.
CONFIRMED.
ZZZZKK
THAT'S HORRIBLE!
HORRIBLE? IT'S BRILLIANT! AND I'M STARTING TO SEE...
AAARGHH!!
ZZZZMMMMMM!!!
YES! MOAN'NA'S HAD A MAKE-OVER!
THIS IS GETTING REALLY TRIPPY NOW...
SO THIS GUY'S GONE ON THE RUN FROM HIS OWN PEOPLE, CHANGED HIS APPEARANCE AND HIDDEN AWAY ON EARTH IN OLDE WORLDE TIMES? THAT'S NUTS!
OH, IT'S MORE COMMON THAN YOU MIGHT THINK...

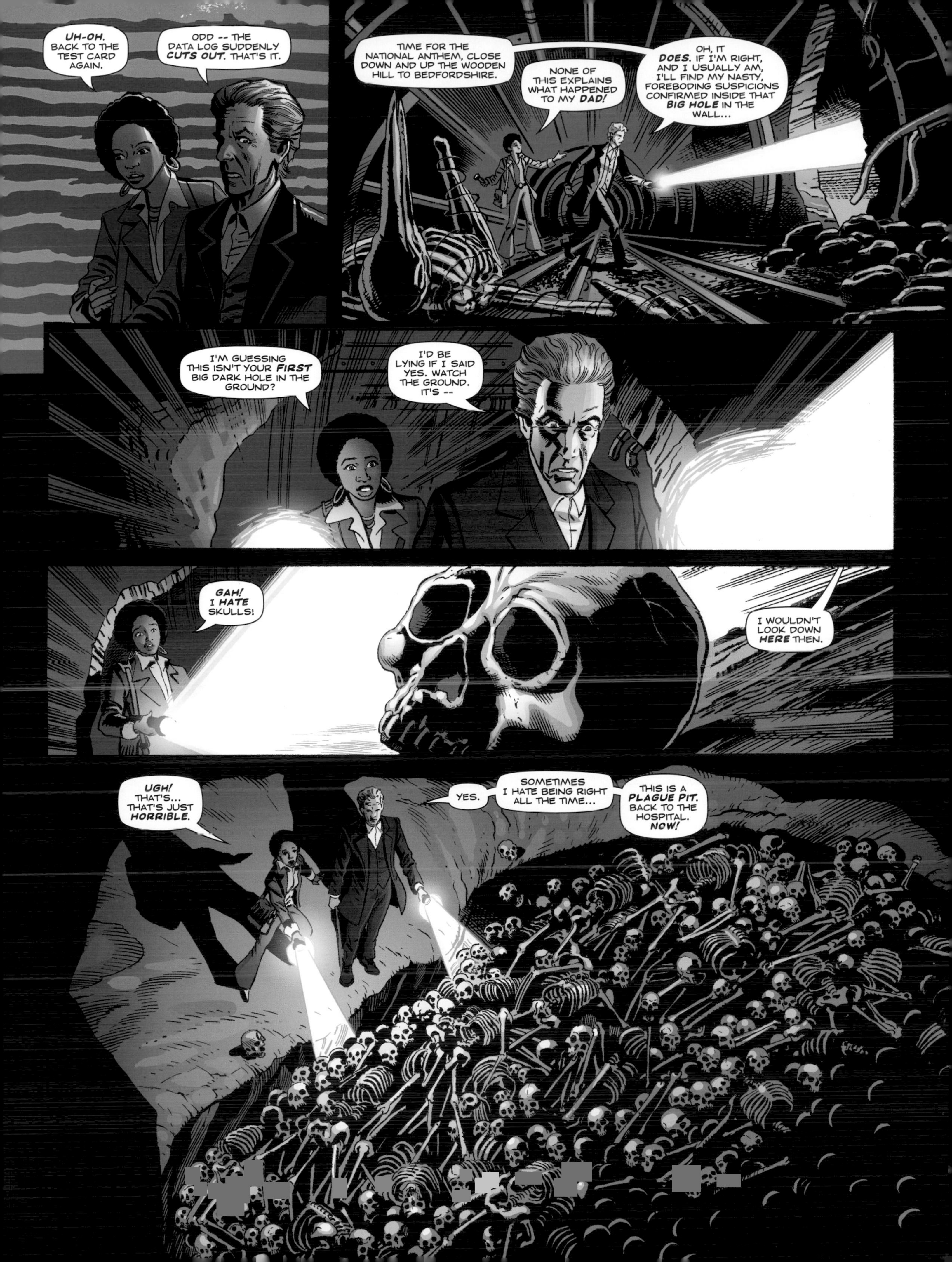
UH-OH. BACK TO THE TEST CARD AGAIN.
ODD -- THE DATA LOG SUDDENLY CUTS OUT. THAT'S IT.
TIME FOR THE NATIONAL ANTHEM, CLOSE DOWN AND UP THE WOODEN HILL TO BEDFORDSHIRE.
NONE OF THIS EXPLAINS WHAT HAPPENED TO MY DAD!
OH, IT DOES. IF I'M RIGHT, AND I USUALLY AM, I'LL FIND MY NASTY, FOREBODING SUSPICIONS CONFIRMED INSIDE THAT BIG HOLE IN THE WALL...
I'M GUESSING THIS ISN'T YOUR FIRST BIG DARK HOLE IN THE GROUND?
I'D BE LYING IF I SAID YES. WATCH THE GROUND. IT'S --
GAH! I HATE SKULLS!
I WOULDN'T LOOK DOWN HERE THEN.
UGH! THAT'S... THAT'S JUST HORRIBLE.
YES.
SOMETIMES I HATE BEING RIGHT ALL THE TIME...
THIS IS A PLAGUE PIT. BACK TO THE HOSPITAL. NOW!

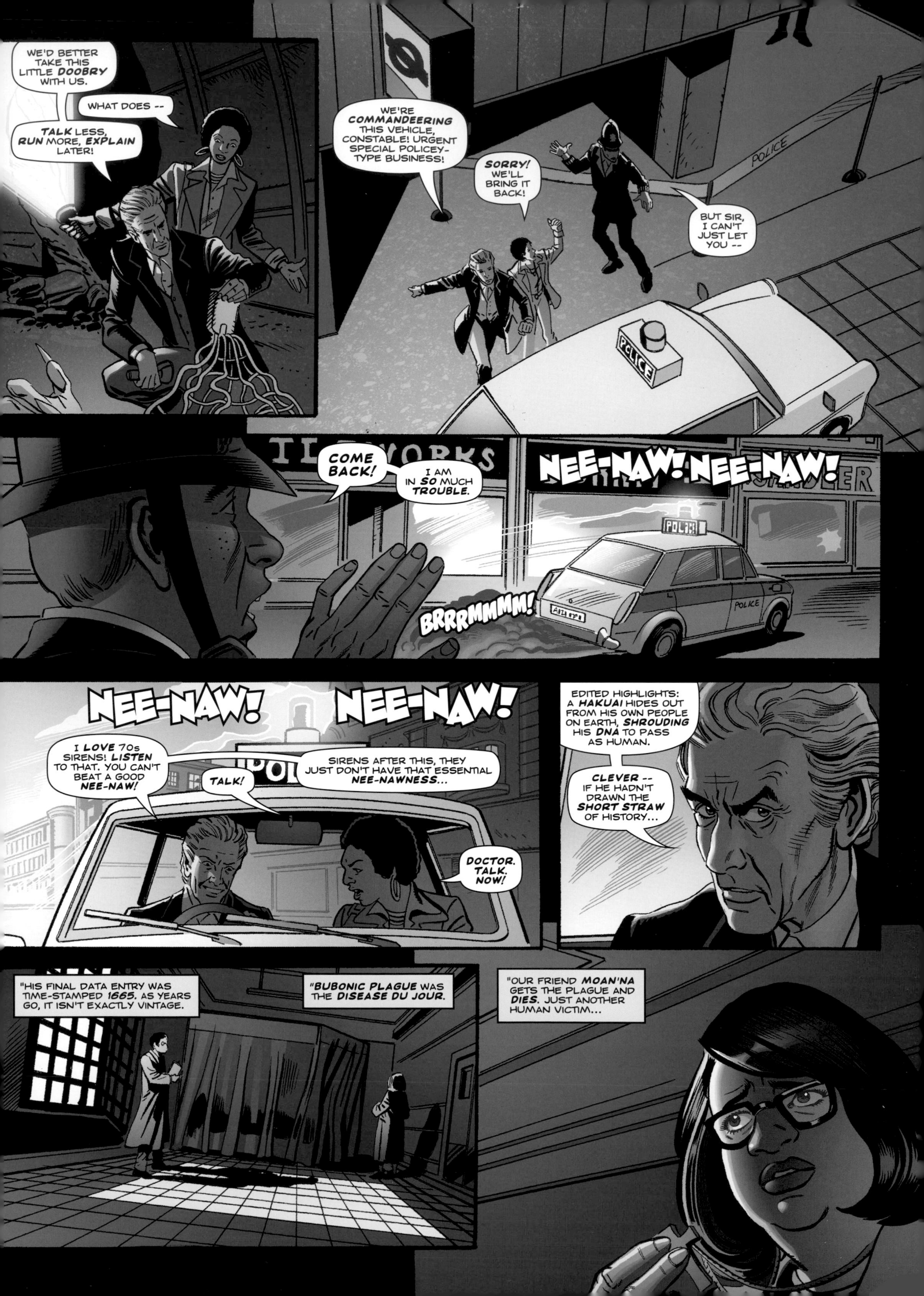
WE'D BETTER TAKE THIS LITTLE DOOBRY WITH US.
WHAT DOES --
TALK LESS, RUN MORE, EXPLAIN LATER!
WE'RE COMMANDEERING THIS VEHICLE, CONSTABLE! URGENT SPECIAL POLICEY-TYPE BUSINESS!
SORRY! WE'LL BRING IT BACK!
BUT SIR, I CAN'T JUST LET YOU --
POLICE
COME BACK!
I AM IN SO MUCH TROUBLE.
NEE-NAW! NEE-NAW!
BRRRMMMM!
POLICE
NEE-NAW! NEE-NAW!
I LOVE 70s SIRENS! LISTEN TO THAT. YOU CAN'T BEAT A GOOD NEE-NAW!
TALK!
SIRENS AFTER THIS, THEY JUST DON'T HAVE THAT ESSENTIAL NEE-NAWNESS...
DOCTOR. TALK. NOW!
EDITED HIGHLIGHTS: A HAKUAI HIDES OUT FROM HIS OWN PEOPLE ON EARTH, SHROUDING HIS DNA TO PASS AS HUMAN.
CLEVER -- IF HE HADN'T DRAWN THE SHORT STRAW OF HISTORY...
"HIS FINAL DATA ENTRY WAS TIME-STAMPED 1665. AS YEARS GO, IT ISN'T EXACTLY VINTAGE.
"BUBONIC PLAGUE WAS THE DISEASE DU JOUR.
"OUR FRIEND MOAN'NA GETS THE PLAGUE AND DIES. JUST ANOTHER HUMAN VICTIM...

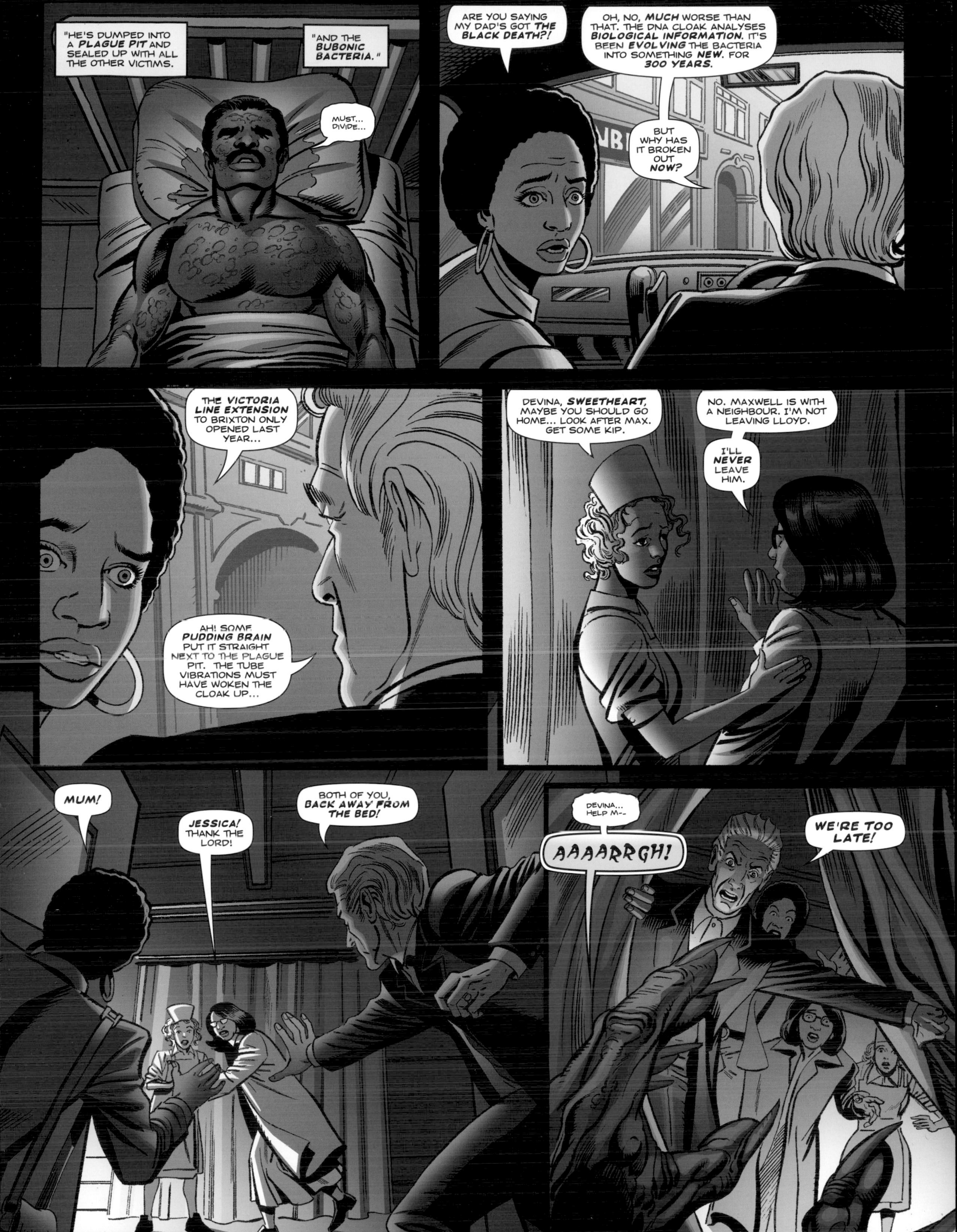
"HE'S DUMPED INTO A PLAGUE PIT AND SEALED UP WITH ALL THE OTHER VICTIMS.
"AND THE BUBONIC BACTERIA."
MUST... DIVIDE...
ARE YOU SAYING MY DAD'S GOT THE BLACK DEATH?!
OH, NO, MUCH WORSE THAN THAT. THE DNA CLOAK ANALYSES BIOLOGICAL INFORMATION. IT'S BEEN EVOLVING THE BACTERIA INTO SOMETHING NEW. FOR 300 YEARS.
BUT WHY HAS IT BROKEN OUT NOW?
THE VICTORIA LINE EXTENSION TO BRIXTON ONLY OPENED LAST YEAR...
AH! SOME PUDDING BRAIN PUT IT STRAIGHT NEXT TO THE PLAGUE PIT. THE TUBE VIBRATIONS MUST HAVE WOKEN THE CLOAK UP...
DEVINA, SWEETHEART, MAYBE YOU SHOULD GO HOME... LOOK AFTER MAX. GET SOME KIP.
NO. MAXWELL IS WITH A NEIGHBOUR. I'M NOT LEAVING LLOYD.
I'LL NEVER LEAVE HIM.
MUM!
JESSICA! THANK THE LORD!
BOTH OF YOU, BACK AWAY FROM THE BED!
DEVINA... HELP M--
AAAARRGH!
WE'RE TOO LATE!

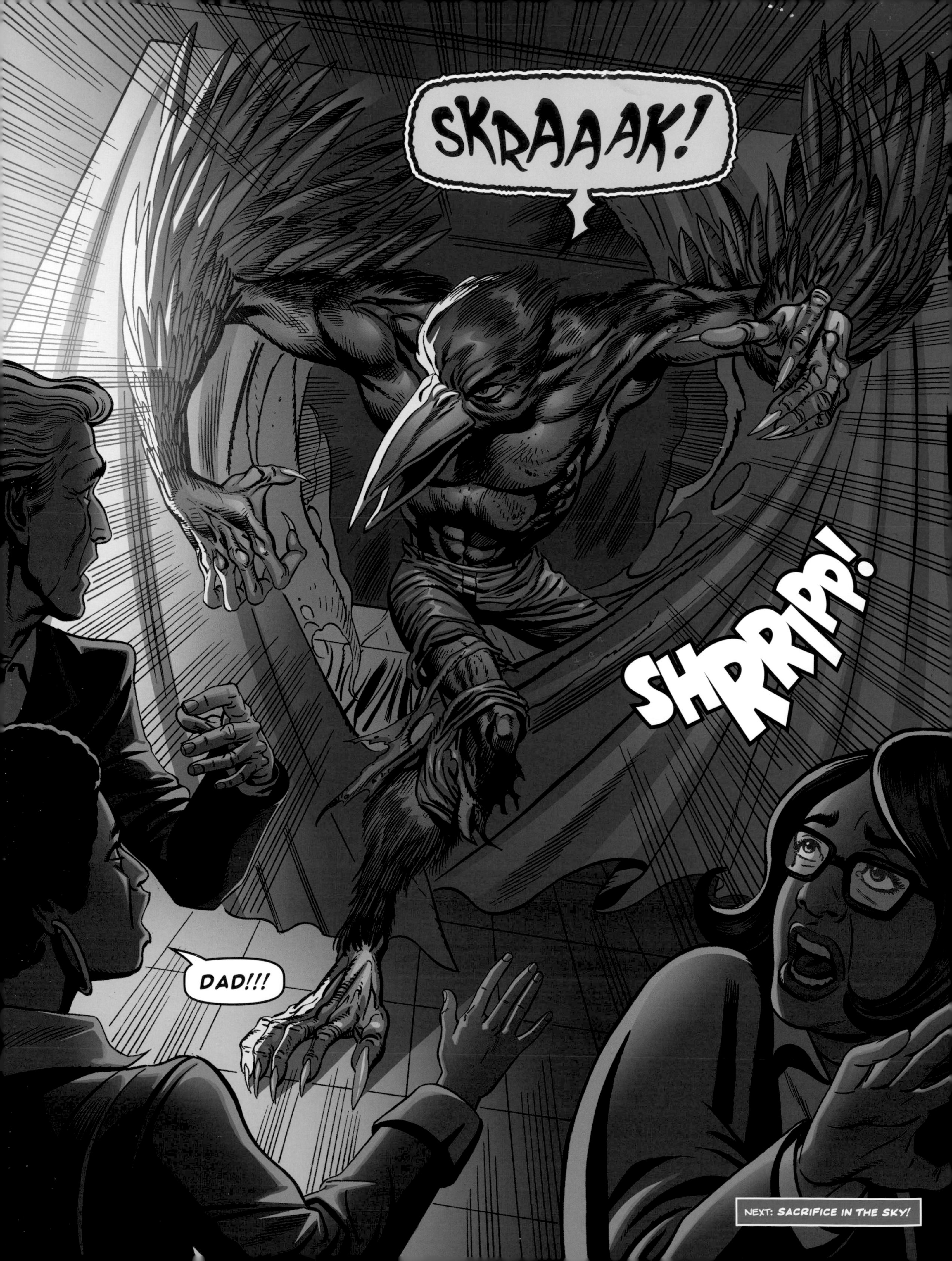
SKRAAAK!
SHRRIPP!
DAD!!!
NEXT: SACRIFICE IN THE SKY!

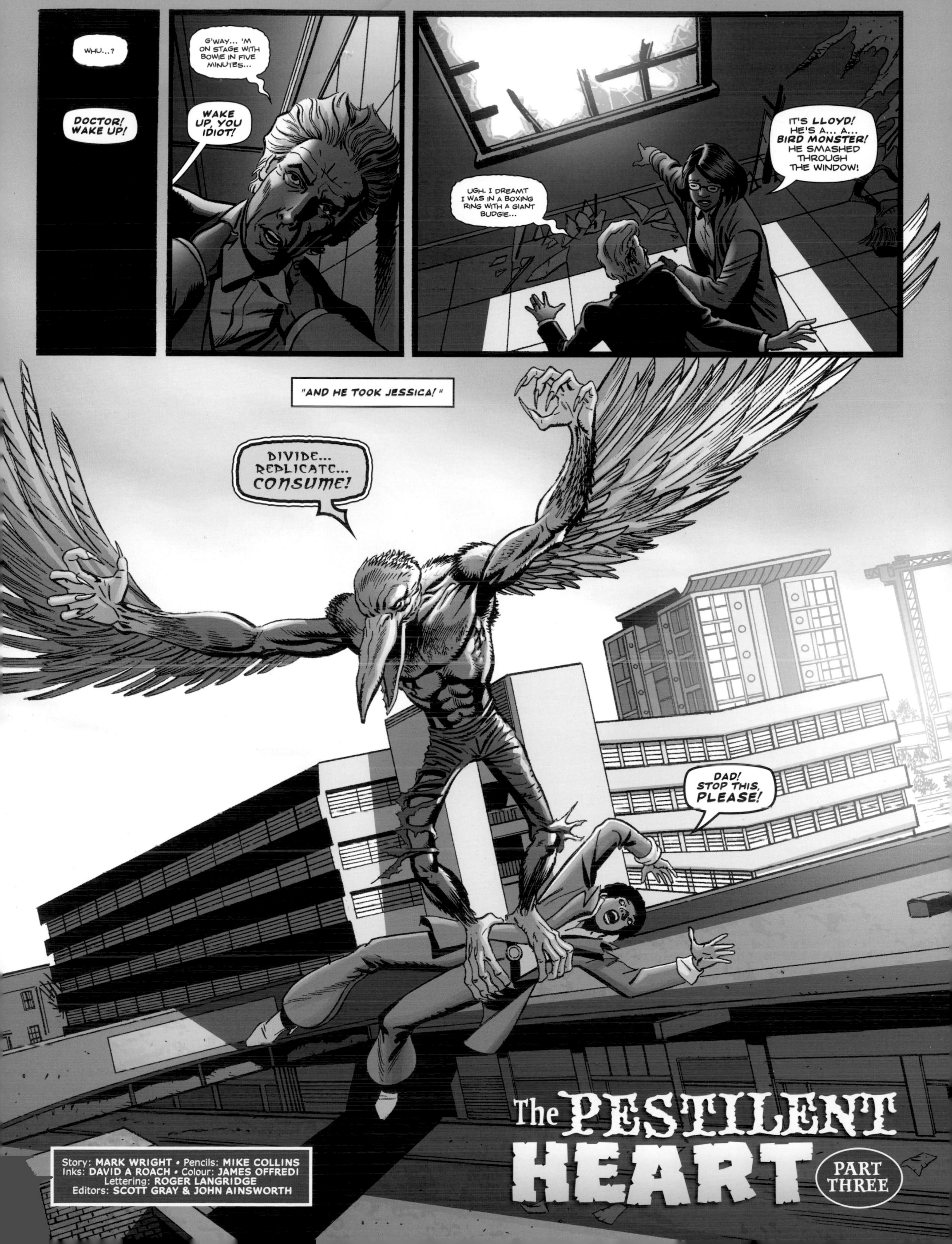
WHU...?
DOCTOR! WAKE UP!
G'WAY... 'M ON STAGE WITH BOWIE IN FIVE MINUTES...
WAKE UP, YOU IDIOT!
IT'S LLOYD! HE'S A... A... BIRD MONSTER! HE SMASHED THROUGH THE WINDOW!
UGH. I DREAMT I WAS IN A BOXING RING WITH A GIANT BUDGIE...
"AND HE TOOK JESSICA!"
DIVIDE... REPLICATE... CONSUME!
DAD! STOP THIS, PLEASE!
The PESTILENT HEART PART THREE
Story: MARK WRIGHT • Pencils: MIKE COLLINS
Inks: DAVID A ROACH • Colour: JAMES OFFREDI
Lettering: ROGER LANGRIDGE
Editors: SCOTT GRAY & JOHN AINSWORTH

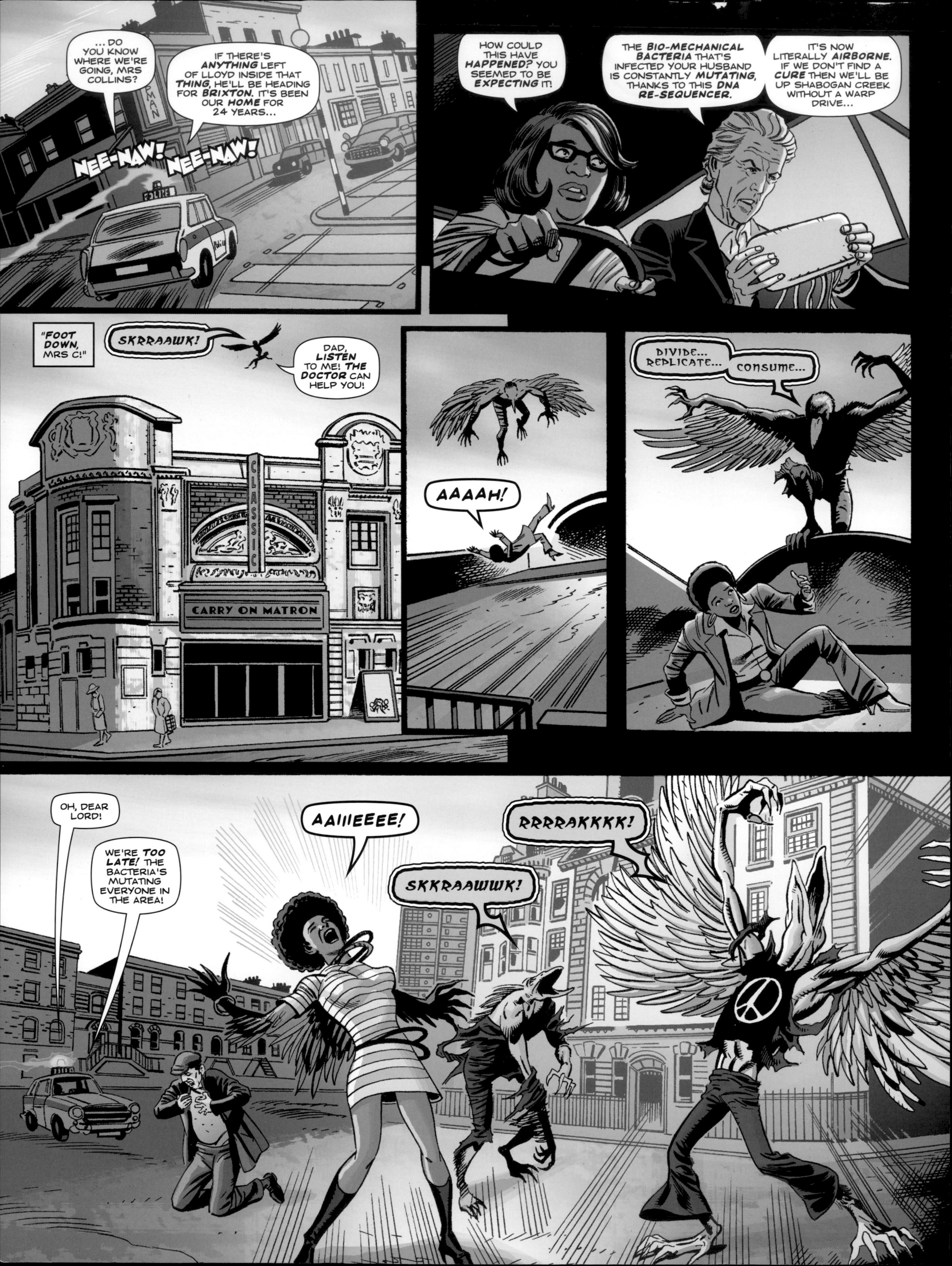
... DO YOU KNOW WHERE WE'RE GOING, MRS COLLINS?
IF THERE'S ANYTHING LEFT OF LLOYD INSIDE THAT THING, HE'LL BE HEADING FOR BRIXTON. IT'S BEEN OUR HOME FOR 24 YEARS...
NEE-NAW! NEE-NAW!
HOW COULD THIS HAVE HAPPENED? YOU SEEMED TO BE EXPECTING IT!
THE BIO-MECHANICAL BACTERIA THAT'S INFECTED YOUR HUSBAND IS CONSTANTLY MUTATING, THANKS TO THIS DNA RE-SEQUENCER.
IT'S NOW LITERALLY AIRBORNE. IF WE DON'T FIND A CURE THEN WE'LL BE UP SHABOGAN CREEK WITHOUT A WARP DRIVE...
"FOOT DOWN, MRS C!"
SKRRAAWK!
DAD, LISTEN TO ME! THE DOCTOR CAN HELP YOU!
CLASSIC
CARRY ON MATRON
AAAAH!
DIVIDE... REPLICATE...
CONSUME...
OH, DEAR LORD!
WE'RE TOO LATE! THE BACTERIA'S MUTATING EVERYONE IN THE AREA!
AAIIEEEE!
SKKRAAWWK!
RRRRAKKKK!

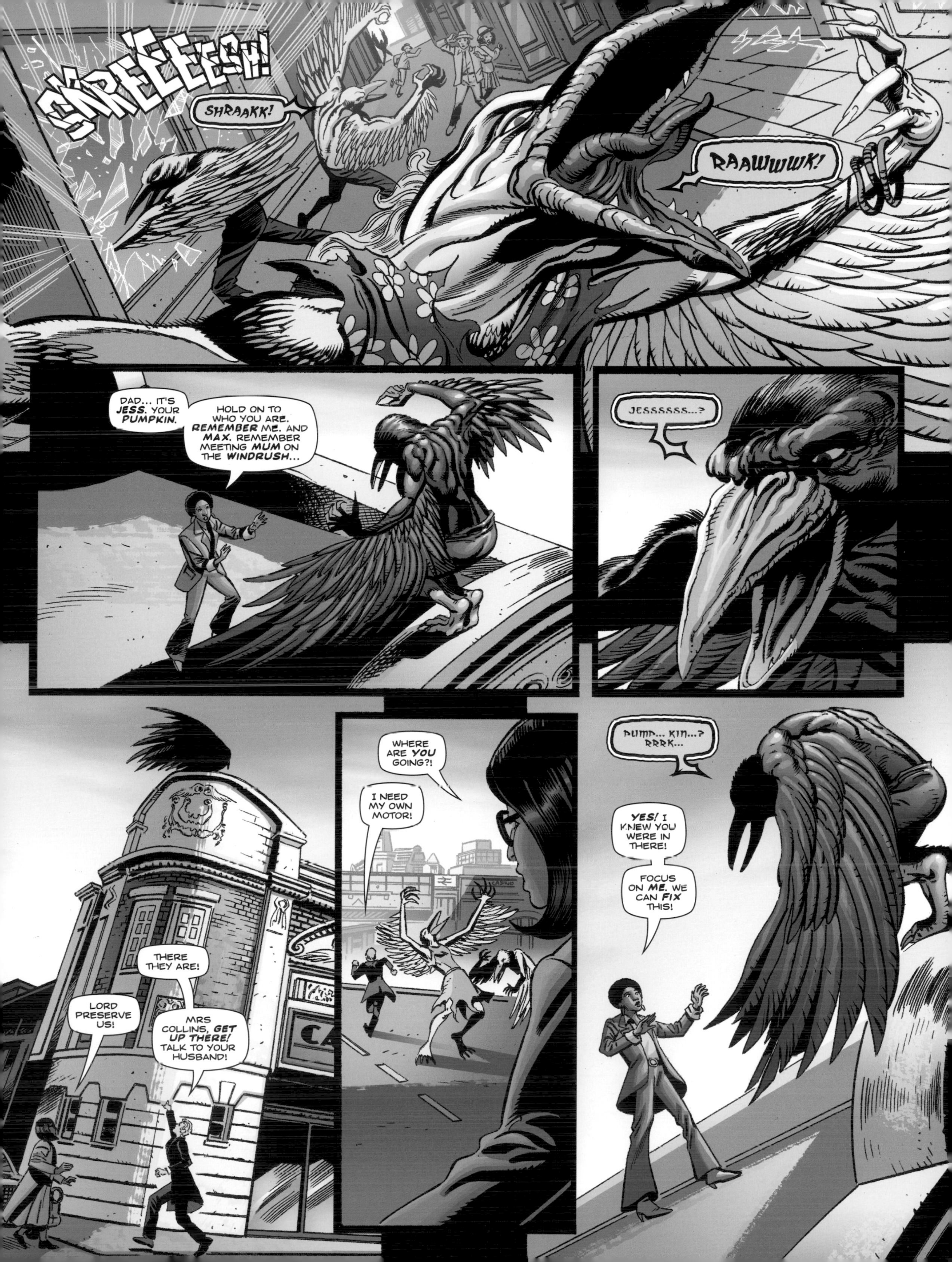
SKREEEESH!
SHRAAKK!
RAAWWWK!
DAD... IT'S JESS. YOUR PUMPKIN.
HOLD ON TO WHO YOU ARE. REMEMBER ME. AND MAX. REMEMBER MEETING MUM ON THE WINDRUSH...
JESSSSSS...?
THERE THEY ARE!
LORD PRESERVE US!
MRS COLLINS, GET UP THERE! TALK TO YOUR HUSBAND!
WHERE ARE YOU GOING?!
I NEED MY OWN MOTOR!
PUMP... KIN...? RRRK...
YES! I KNEW YOU WERE IN THERE!
FOCUS ON ME. WE CAN FIX THIS!

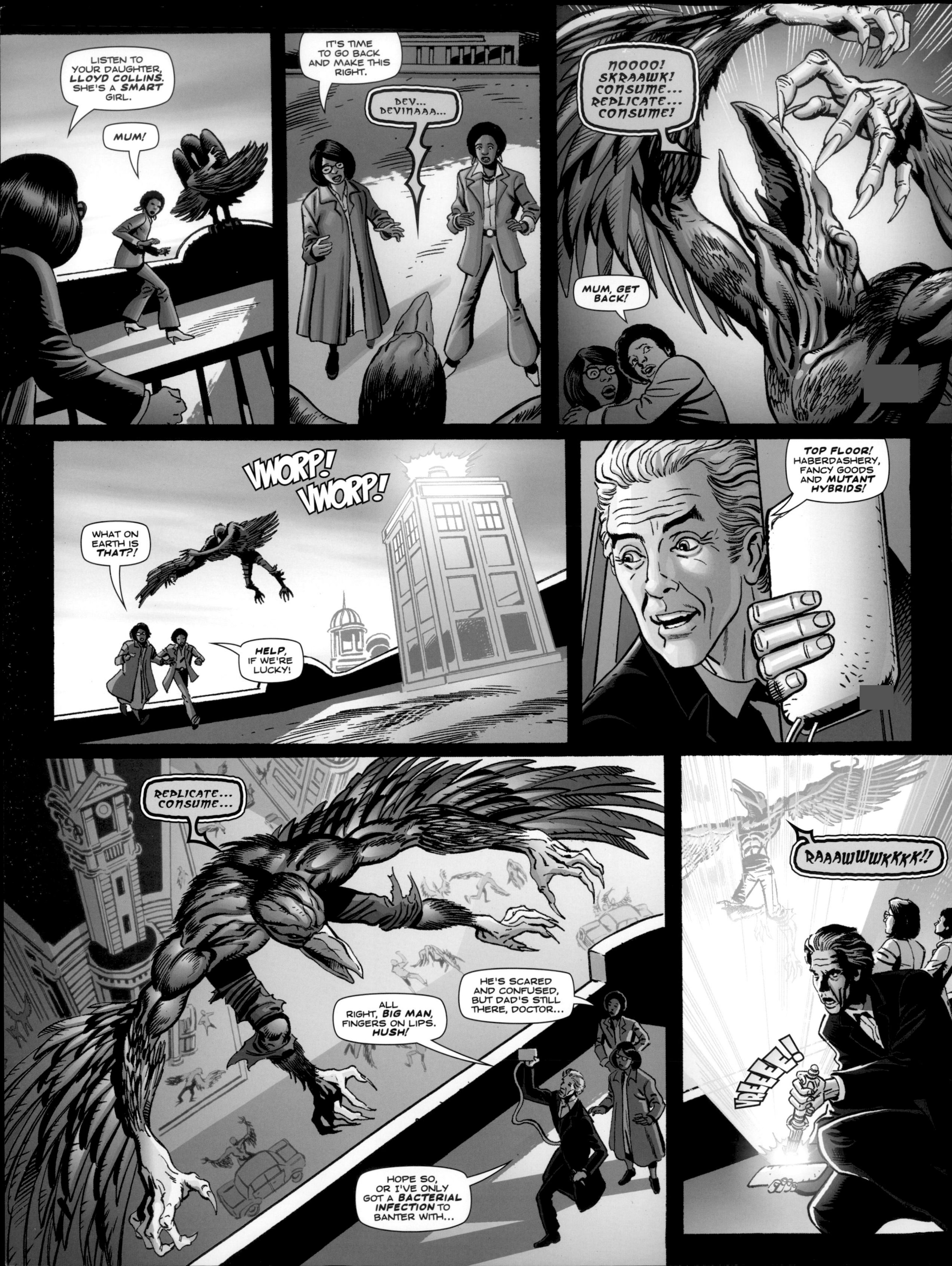

LISTEN TO YOUR DAUGHTER, LLOYD COLLINS. SHE'S A SMART GIRL.
MUM!
IT'S TIME TO GO BACK AND MAKE THIS RIGHT.
DEV... DEVINAAA...
NOOOO! SKRAAWK! CONSUME... REPLICATE... CONSUME!
MUM, GET BACK!
VWORP! VWORP!
WHAT ON EARTH IS THAT?!
HELP, IF WE'RE LUCKY!
TOP FLOOR! HABERDASHERY, FANCY GOODS AND MUTANT HYBRIDS!
REPLICATE... CONSUME...
HE'S SCARED AND CONFUSED, BUT DAD'S STILL THERE, DOCTOR...
ALL RIGHT, BIG MAN, FINGERS ON LIPS. HUSH!
HOPE SO, OR I'VE ONLY GOT A BACTERIAL INFECTION TO BANTER WITH...
RAAAWWWKKKK!!
VREEEE!!

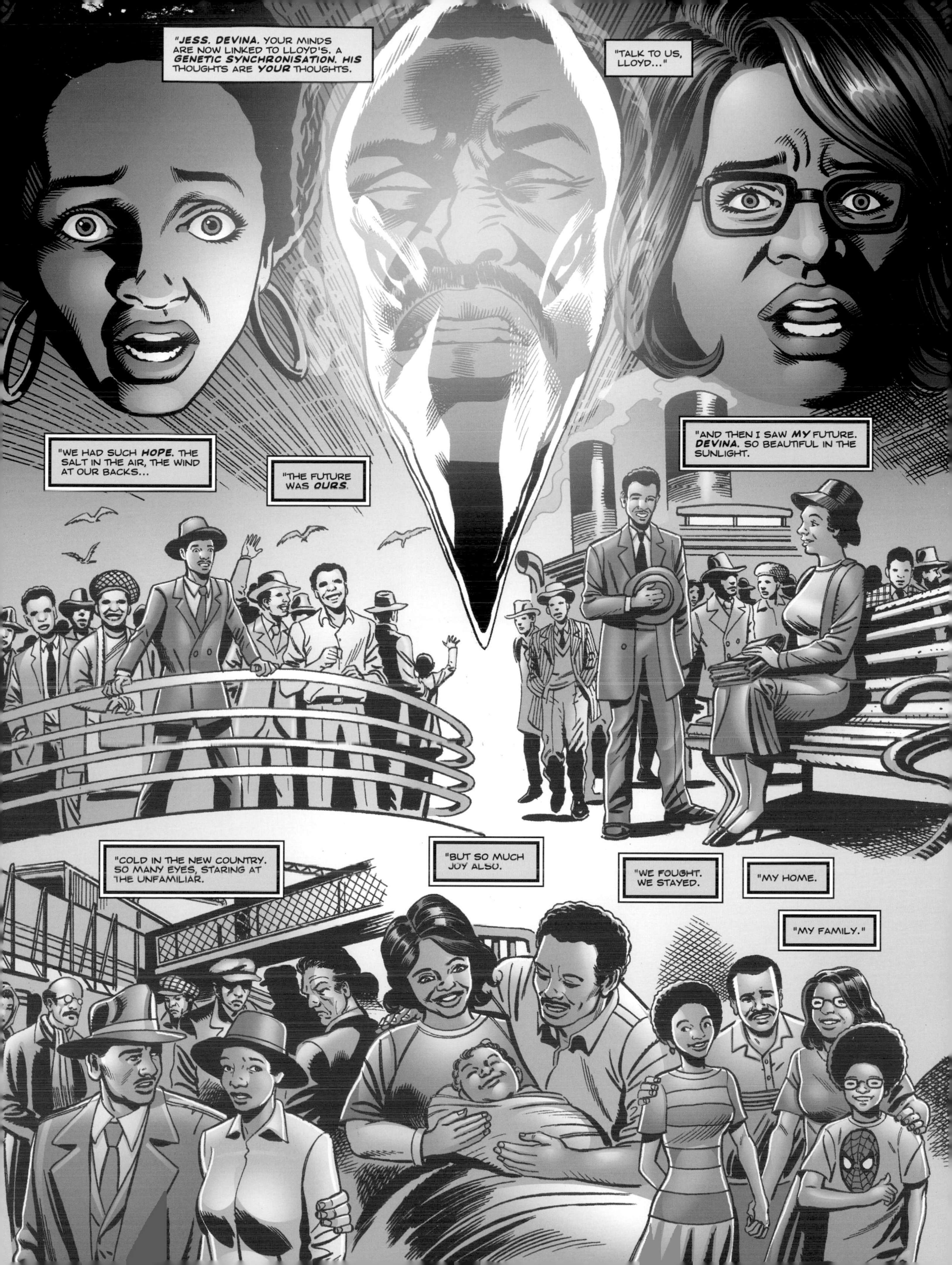
"JESS. DEVINA. YOUR MINDS ARE NOW LINKED TO LLOYD'S. A GENETIC SYNCHRONISATION. HIS THOUGHTS ARE YOUR THOUGHTS.
"TALK TO US, LLOYD..."
"WE HAD SUCH HOPE. THE SALT IN THE AIR, THE WIND AT OUR BACKS...
"THE FUTURE WAS OURS.
"AND THEN I SAW MY FUTURE. DEVINA. SO BEAUTIFUL IN THE SUNLIGHT.
"COLD IN THE NEW COUNTRY. SO MANY EYES, STARING AT THE UNFAMILIAR.
"BUT SO MUCH JOY ALSO.
"WE FOUGHT. WE STAYED.
"MY HOME.
"MY FAMILY."

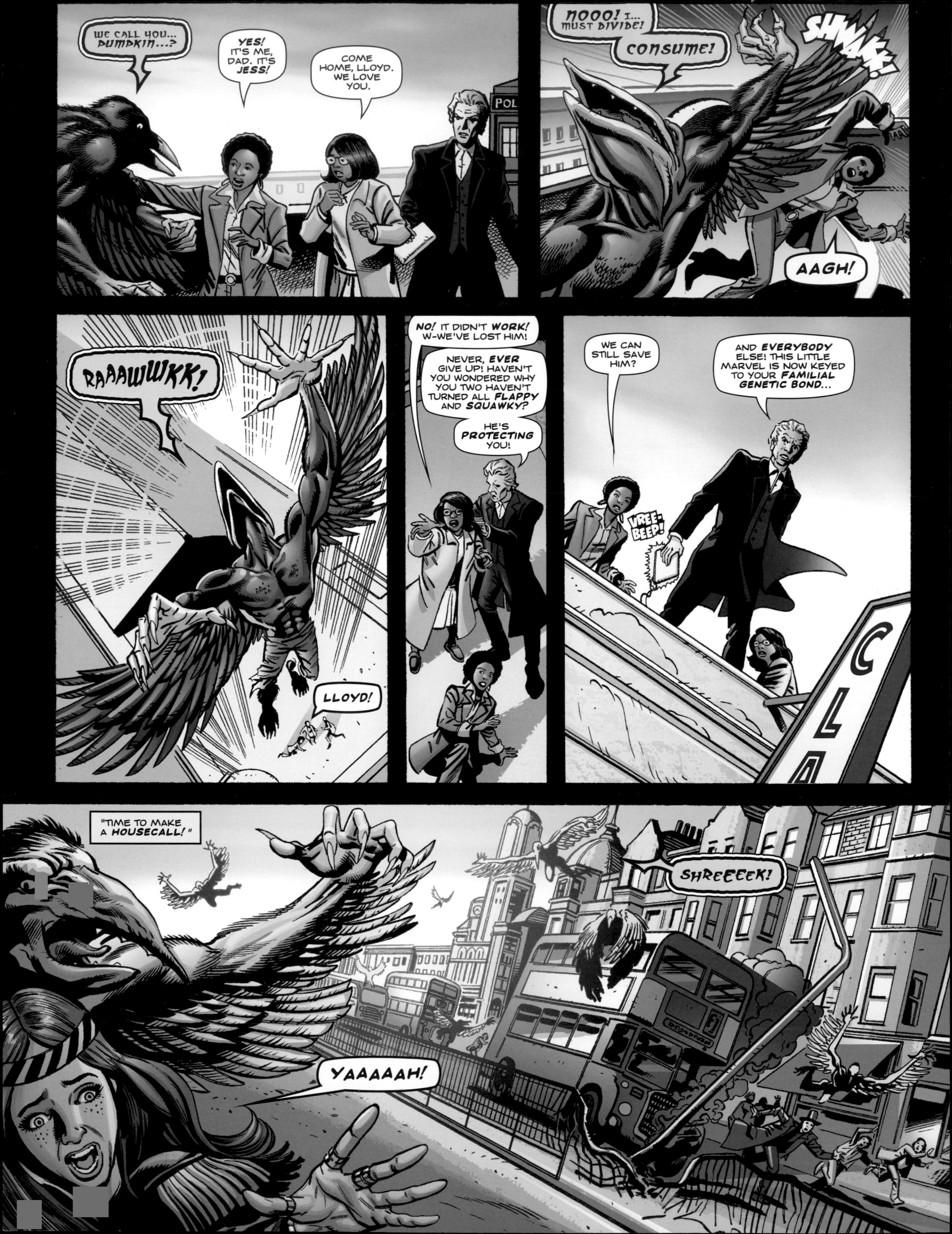

WE CALL YOU... PUMPKIN...?
YES! IT'S ME, DAD. IT'S JESS!
COME HOME, LLOYD. WE LOVE YOU.
NOOO! I... MUST DIVIDE!
CONSUME!
SHWAK!
AAGH!
RAAAWWKK!
LLOYD!
NO! IT DIDN'T WORK! W-WE'VE LOST HIM!
NEVER, EVER GIVE UP! HAVEN'T YOU WONDERED WHY YOU TWO HAVEN'T TURNED ALL FLAPPY AND SQUAWKY?
HE'S PROTECTING YOU!
WE CAN STILL SAVE HIM?
AND EVERYBODY ELSE! THIS LITTLE MARVEL IS NOW KEYED TO YOUR FAMILIAL GENETIC BOND...
VREE-BEEP!
"TIME TO MAKE A HOUSECALL!"
SHREEEEK!
YAAAAAH!

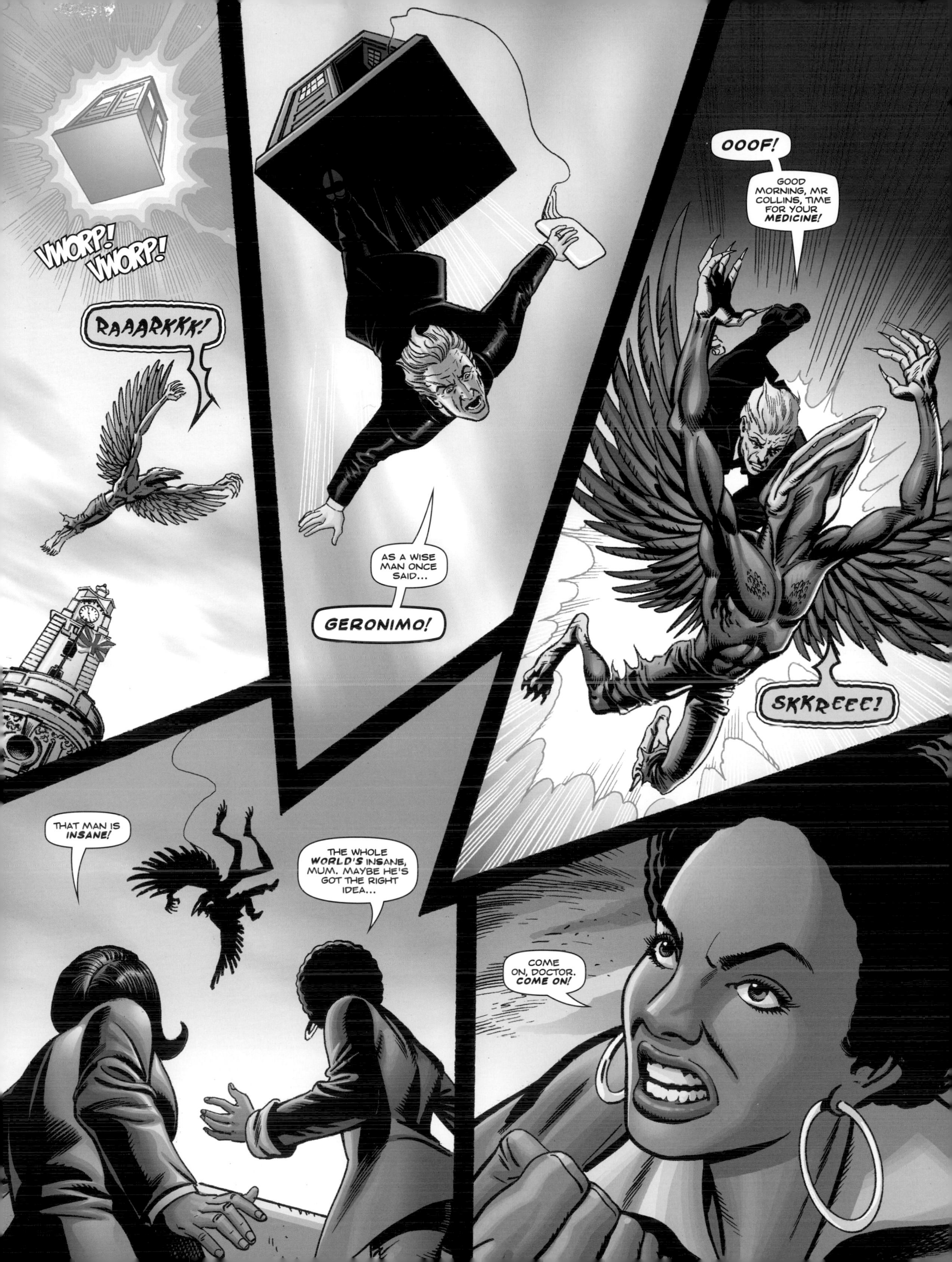
VWORP! VWORP!
RAAARKKK!
AS A WISE MAN ONCE SAID...
GERONIMO!
OOOF!
GOOD MORNING, MR COLLINS, TIME FOR YOUR MEDICINE!
SKKREEE!
THAT MAN IS INSANE!
THE WHOLE WORLD'S INSANE, MUM. MAYBE HE'S GOT THE RIGHT IDEA...
COME ON, DOCTOR. COME ON!

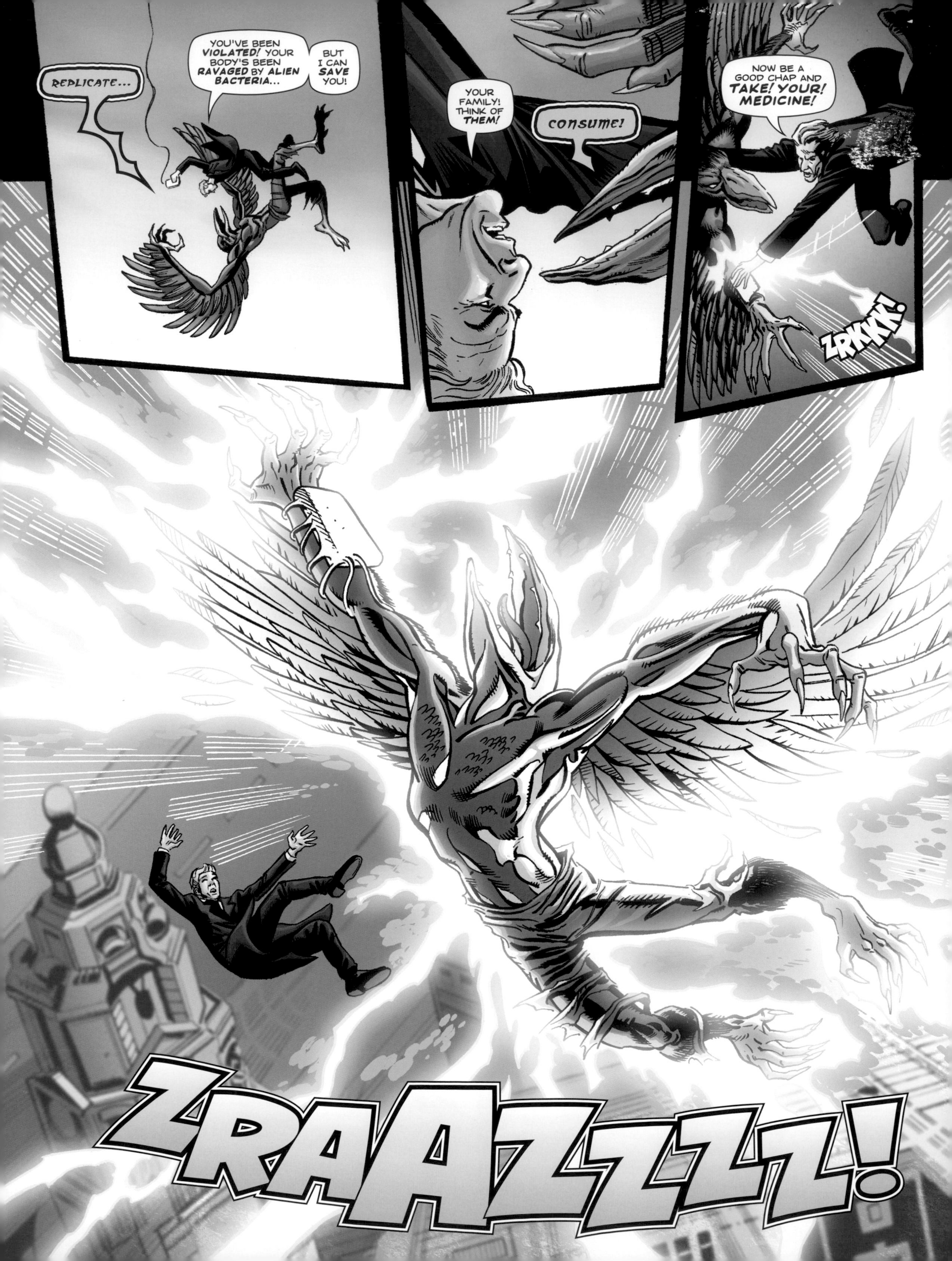
REPLICATE...
YOU'VE BEEN VIOLATED! YOUR BODY'S BEEN RAVAGED BY ALIEN BACTERIA...
BUT I CAN SAVE YOU!
YOUR FAMILY! THINK OF THEM!
CONSUME!
NOW BE A GOOD CHAP AND TAKE! YOUR! MEDICINE!
ZRKKK!
ZRAAZZZZ!

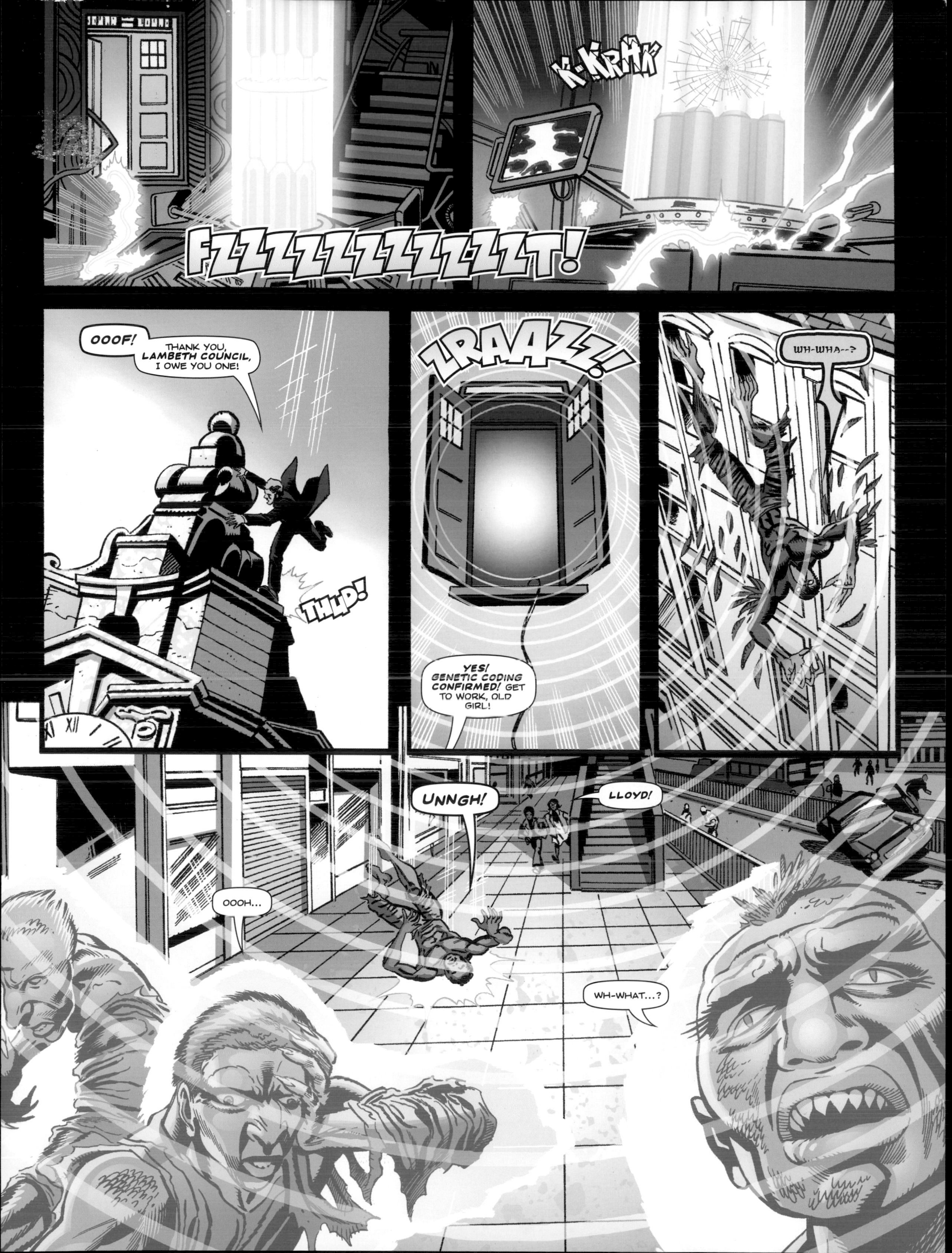
K-KRAK!
FZZZZZZZZZZZZZT!
OOOF!
THANK YOU, LAMBETH COUNCIL, I OWE YOU ONE!
THUD!
ZRAAZZ!
YES! GENETIC CODING CONFIRMED! GET TO WORK, OLD GIRL!
WH-WHA--?
UNNGH!
LLOYD!
OOOH...
WH-WHAT...?

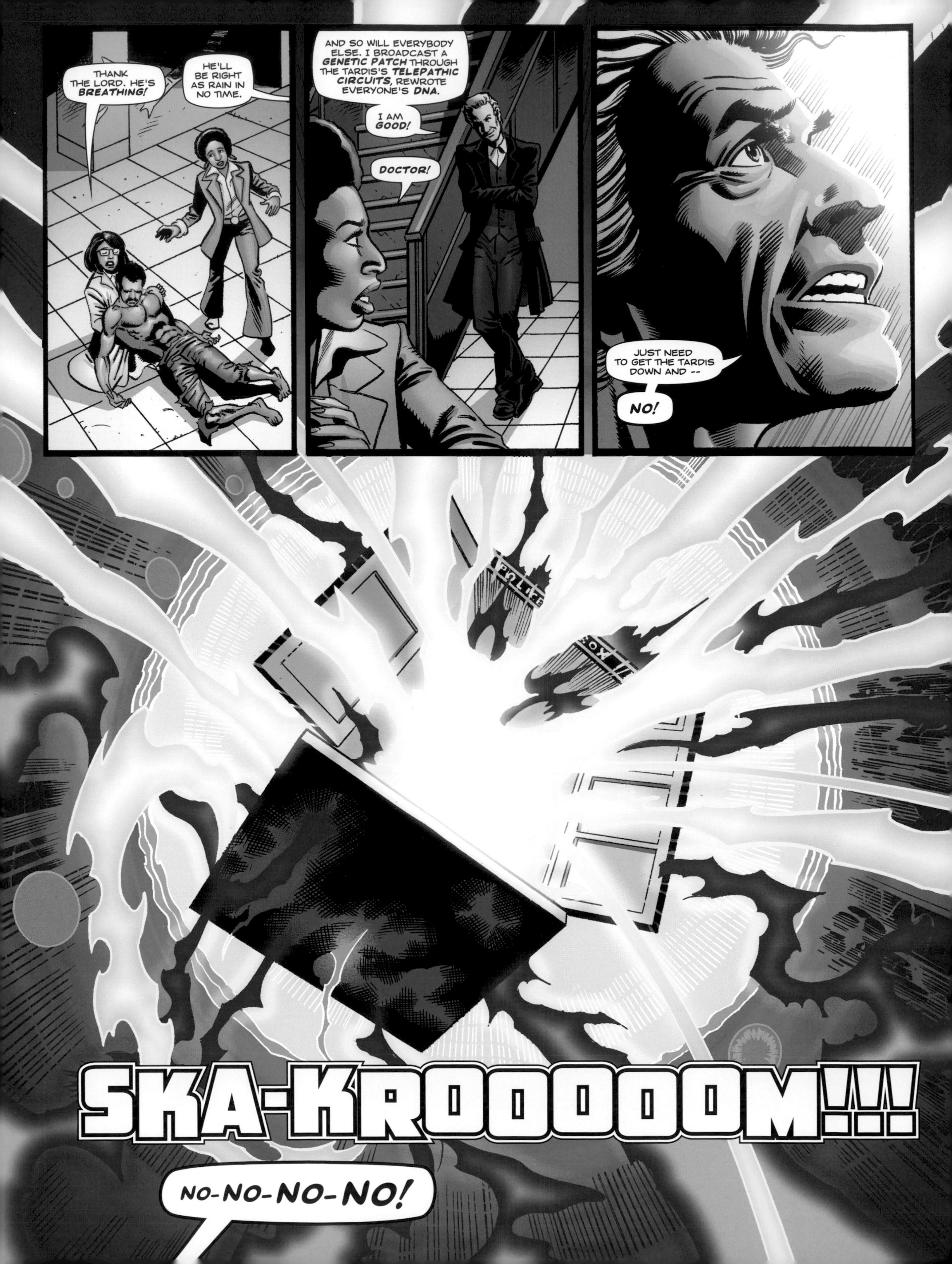

THANK THE LORD. HE'S BREATHING!
HE'LL BE RIGHT AS RAIN IN NO TIME.
AND SO WILL EVERYBODY ELSE. I BROADCAST A GENETIC PATCH THROUGH THE TARDIS'S TELEPATHIC CIRCUITS, REWROTE EVERYONE'S DNA.
I AM GOOD!
DOCTOR!
JUST NEED TO GET THE TARDIS DOWN AND --
NO!
POLICE
BOX
SKA-KROOOOOOM!!!!
NO-NO-NO-NO!

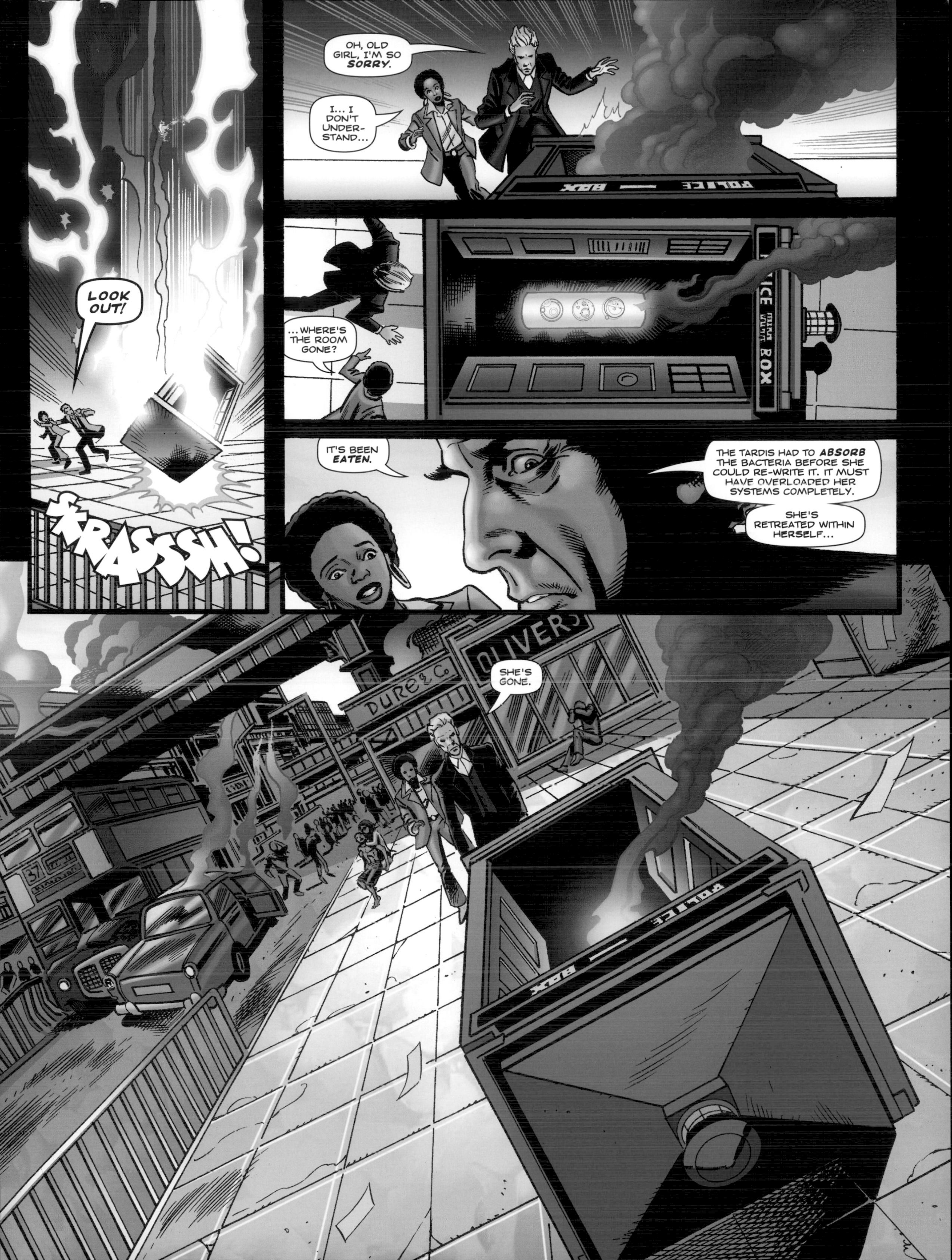
LOOK OUT!
SKRASSSH!
OH, OLD GIRL, I'M SO SORRY.
I... I DON'T UNDER-STAND...
POLICE BOX
...WHERE'S THE ROOM GONE?
IT'S BEEN EATEN.
THE TARDIS HAD TO ABSORB THE BACTERIA BEFORE SHE COULD RE-WRITE IT. IT MUST HAVE OVERLOADED HER SYSTEMS COMPLETELY.
SHE'S RETREATED WITHIN HERSELF...
OLIVERS
DURE & CO.
SHE'S GONE.

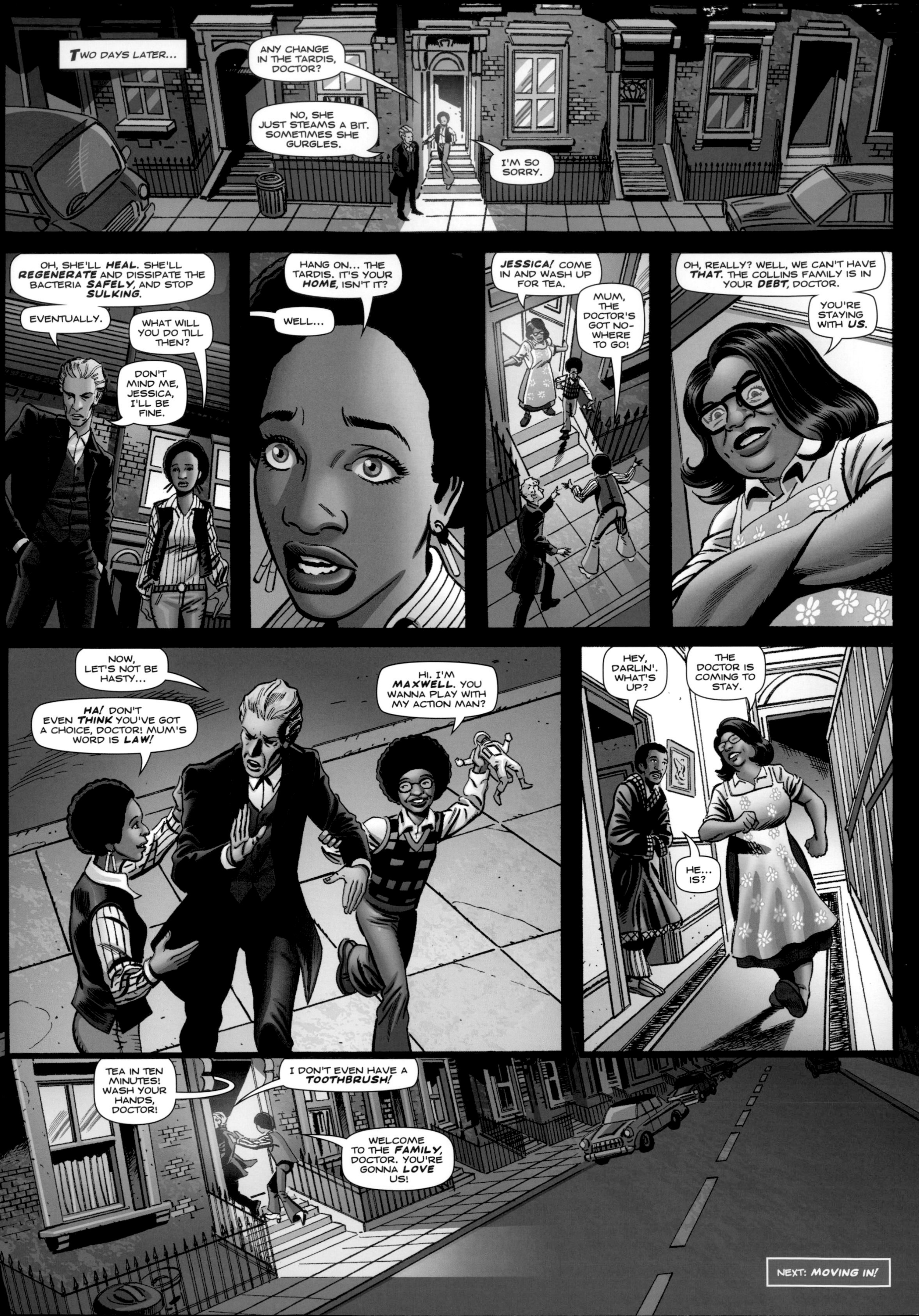
TWO DAYS LATER...
ANY CHANGE IN THE TARDIS, DOCTOR?
NO, SHE JUST STEAMS A BIT. SOMETIMES SHE GURGLES.
I'M SO SORRY.
OH, SHE'LL HEAL. SHE'LL REGENERATE AND DISSIPATE THE BACTERIA SAFELY, AND STOP SULKING.
EVENTUALLY.
WHAT WILL YOU DO TILL THEN?
DON'T MIND ME, JESSICA, I'LL BE FINE.
HANG ON... THE TARDIS. IT'S YOUR HOME, ISN'T IT?
WELL...
JESSICA! COME IN AND WASH UP FOR TEA.
MUM, THE DOCTOR'S GOT NO-WHERE TO GO!
OH, REALLY? WELL, WE CAN'T HAVE THAT. THE COLLINS FAMILY IS IN YOUR DEBT, DOCTOR.
YOU'RE STAYING WITH US.
NOW, LET'S NOT BE HASTY...
HA! DON'T EVEN THINK YOU'VE GOT A CHOICE, DOCTOR! MUM'S WORD IS LAW!
HI. I'M MAXWELL. YOU WANNA PLAY WITH MY ACTION MAN?
HEY, DARLIN'. WHAT'S UP?
THE DOCTOR IS COMING TO STAY.
HE... IS?
TEA IN TEN MINUTES! WASH YOUR HANDS, DOCTOR!
I DON'T EVEN HAVE A TOOTHBRUSH!
WELCOME TO THE FAMILY, DOCTOR. YOU'RE GONNA LOVE US!
NEXT: MOVING IN!

# MOVING IN

## Lloyd and the Doctor

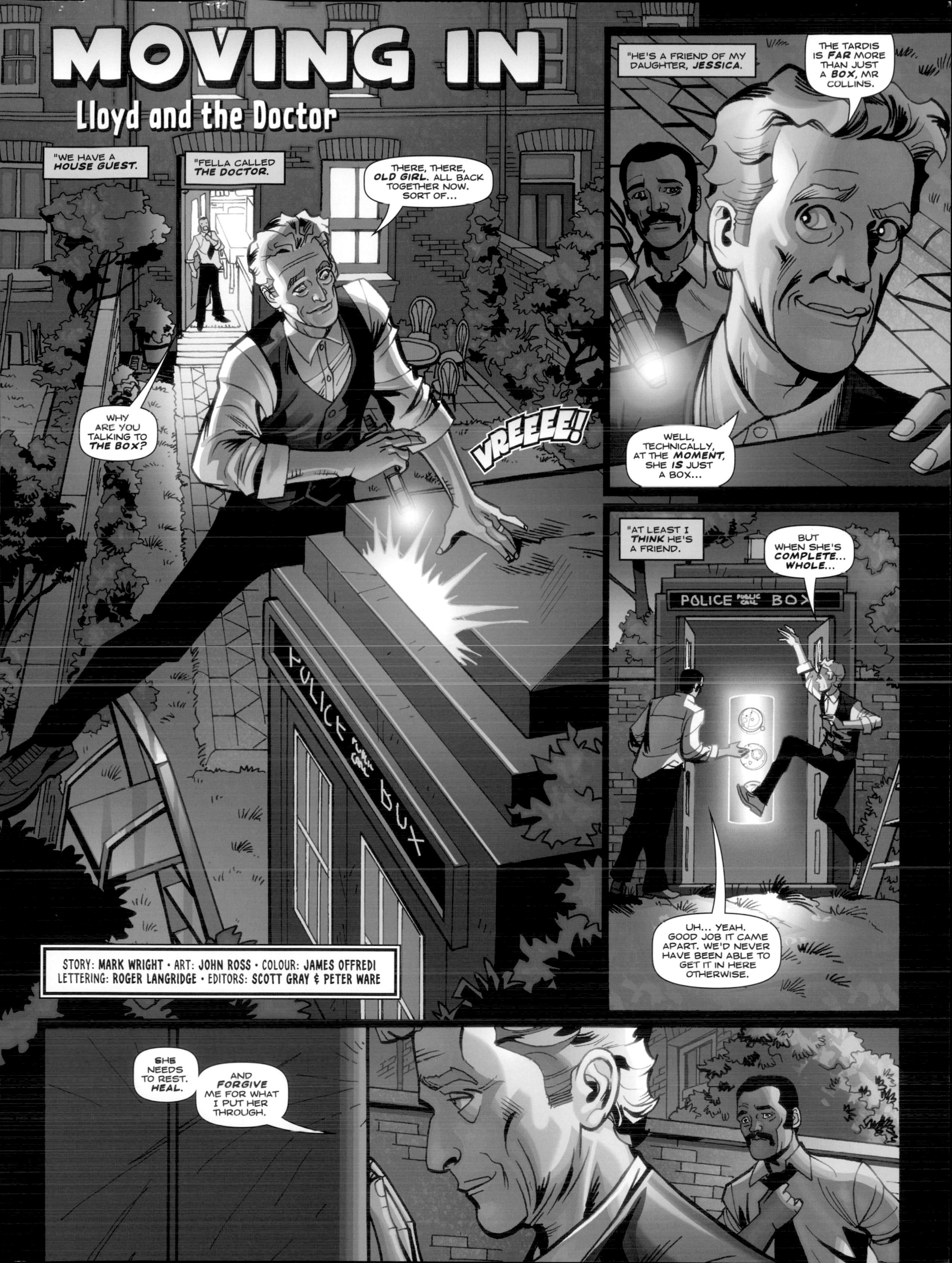

"WE HAVE A HOUSE GUEST.
"FELLA CALLED THE DOCTOR.
THERE, THERE, OLD GIRL. ALL BACK TOGETHER NOW. SORT OF...
WHY ARE YOU TALKING TO THE BOX?
VREEEEE!
POLICE PUBLIC CALL BOX
"HE'S A FRIEND OF MY DAUGHTER, JESSICA.
THE TARDIS IS FAR MORE THAN JUST A BOX, MR COLLINS.
WELL, TECHNICALLY, AT THE MOMENT, SHE IS JUST A BOX...
"AT LEAST I THINK HE'S A FRIEND.
BUT WHEN SHE'S COMPLETE... WHOLE...
POLICE PUBLIC CALL BOX
UH... YEAH. GOOD JOB IT CAME APART. WE'D NEVER HAVE BEEN ABLE TO GET IT IN HERE OTHERWISE.
SHE NEEDS TO REST. HEAL.
AND FORGIVE ME FOR WHAT I PUT HER THROUGH.


STORY: MARK WRIGHT • ART: JOHN ROSS • COLOUR: JAMES OFFREDI
LETTERING: ROGER LANGRIDGE • EDITORS: SCOTT GRAY & PETER WARE

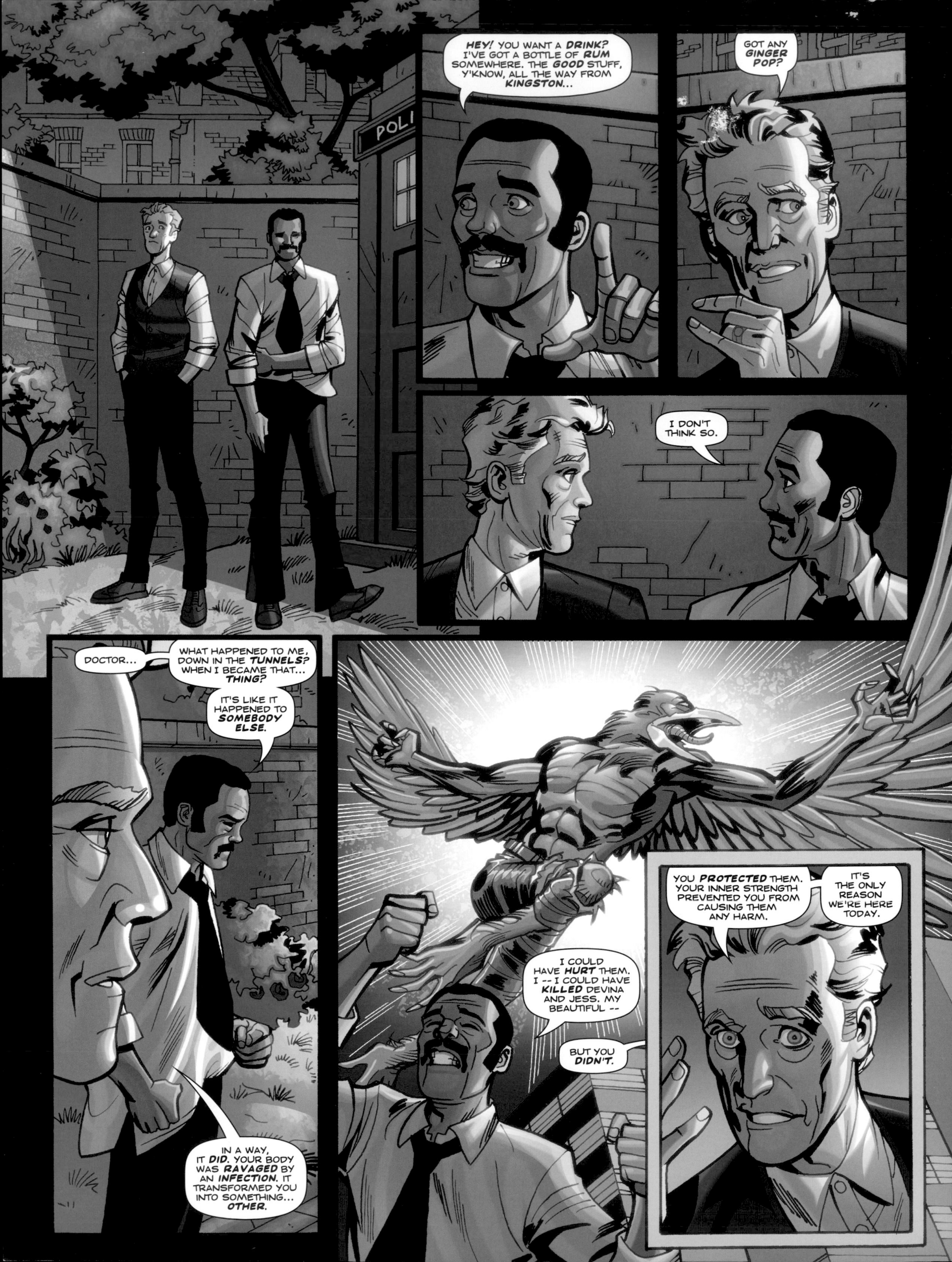
POLI
HEY! YOU WANT A DRINK? I'VE GOT A BOTTLE OF RUM SOMEWHERE. THE GOOD STUFF, Y'KNOW, ALL THE WAY FROM KINGSTON...
GOT ANY GINGER POP?
I DON'T THINK SO.
DOCTOR...
WHAT HAPPENED TO ME, DOWN IN THE TUNNELS? WHEN I BECAME THAT... THING?
IT'S LIKE IT HAPPENED TO SOMEBODY ELSE.
IN A WAY, IT DID. YOUR BODY WAS RAVAGED BY AN INFECTION. IT TRANSFORMED YOU INTO SOMETHING... OTHER.
I COULD HAVE HURT THEM. I -- I COULD HAVE KILLED DEVINA AND JESS. MY BEAUTIFUL --
BUT YOU DIDN'T.
YOU PROTECTED THEM. YOUR INNER STRENGTH PREVENTED YOU FROM CAUSING THEM ANY HARM.
IT'S THE ONLY REASON WE'RE HERE TODAY.

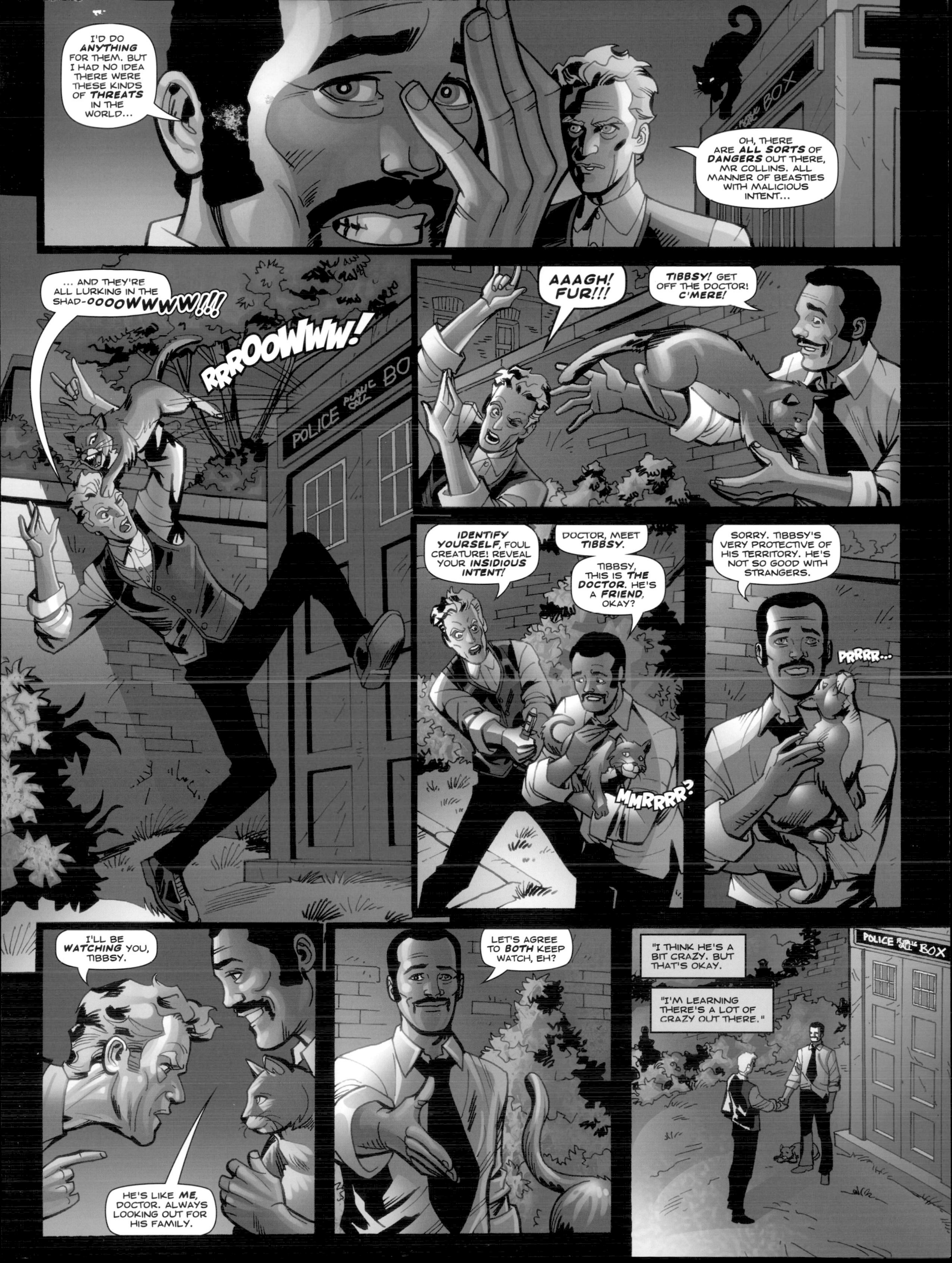
I'D DO ANYTHING FOR THEM. BUT I HAD NO IDEA THERE WERE THESE KINDS OF THREATS IN THE WORLD...
OH, THERE ARE ALL SORTS OF DANGERS OUT THERE, MR COLLINS. ALL MANNER OF BEASTIES WITH MALICIOUS INTENT...
... AND THEY'RE ALL LURKING IN THE SHAD-OOOOWWWW!!!
RRROOWWW!
POLICE PUBLIC CALL BOX
AAAGH! FUR!!!
TIBBSY! GET OFF THE DOCTOR! C'MERE!
IDENTIFY YOURSELF, FOUL CREATURE! REVEAL YOUR INSIDIOUS INTENT!
DOCTOR, MEET TIBBSY.
TIBBSY, THIS IS THE DOCTOR. HE'S A FRIEND, OKAY?
MMRRRR?
SORRY. TIBBSY'S VERY PROTECTIVE OF HIS TERRITORY. HE'S NOT SO GOOD WITH STRANGERS.
PRRRR...
I'LL BE WATCHING YOU, TIBBSY.
HE'S LIKE ME, DOCTOR. ALWAYS LOOKING OUT FOR HIS FAMILY.
LET'S AGREE TO BOTH KEEP WATCH, EH?
"I THINK HE'S A BIT CRAZY. BUT THAT'S OKAY.
"I'M LEARNING THERE'S A LOT OF CRAZY OUT THERE."
POLICE PUBLIC CALL BOX

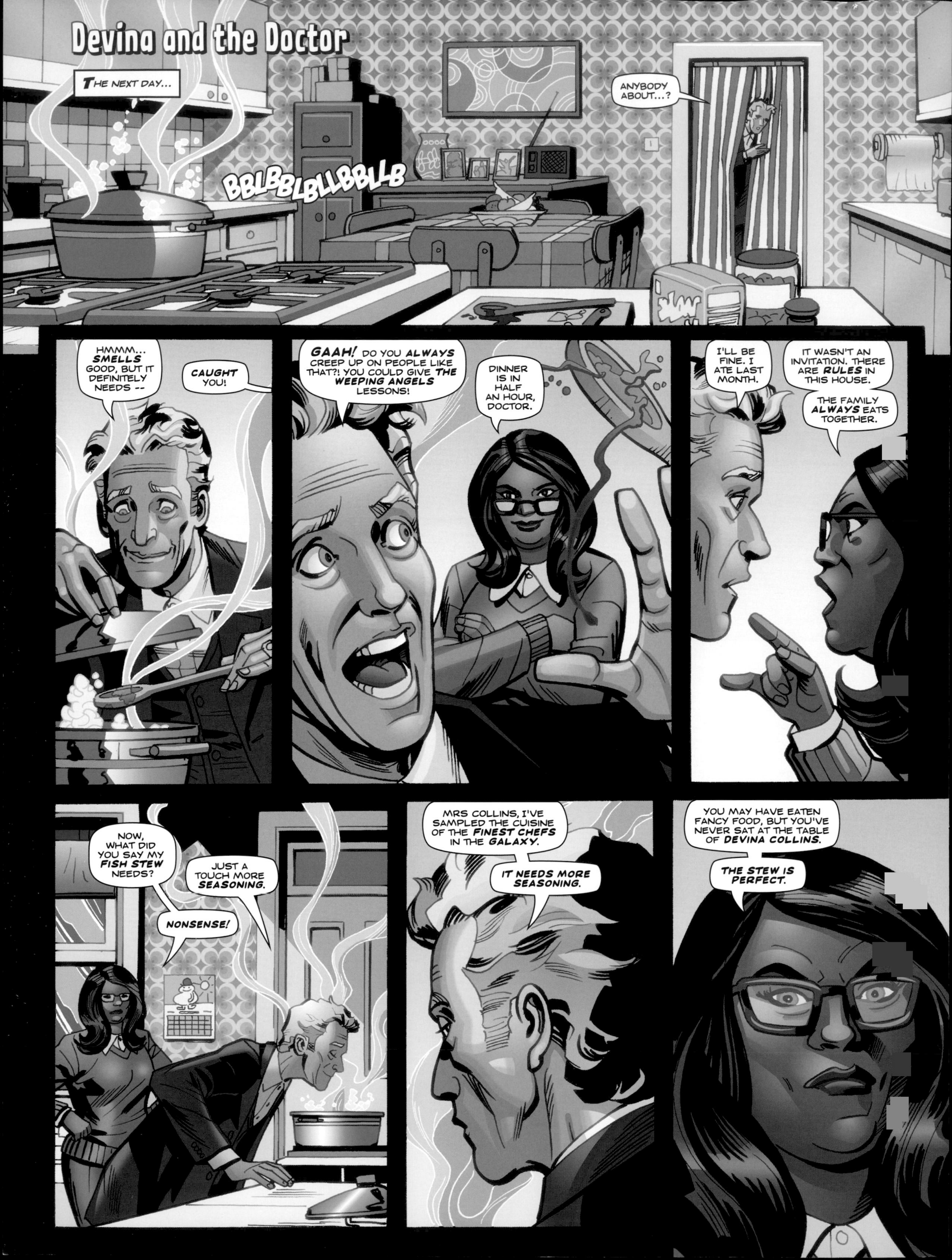
Devina and the Doctor
THE NEXT DAY...
BBLBBLBLLBBLLB
ANYBODY ABOUT...?
HMMM... SMELLS GOOD, BUT IT DEFINITELY NEEDS --
CAUGHT YOU!
GAAH! DO YOU ALWAYS CREEP UP ON PEOPLE LIKE THAT?! YOU COULD GIVE THE WEEPING ANGELS LESSONS!
DINNER IS IN HALF AN HOUR, DOCTOR.
I'LL BE FINE. I ATE LAST MONTH.
IT WASN'T AN INVITATION. THERE ARE RULES IN THIS HOUSE.
THE FAMILY ALWAYS EATS TOGETHER.
NOW, WHAT DID YOU SAY MY FISH STEW NEEDS?
JUST A TOUCH MORE SEASONING.
NONSENSE!
MRS COLLINS, I'VE SAMPLED THE CUISINE OF THE FINEST CHEFS IN THE GALAXY.
IT NEEDS MORE SEASONING.
YOU MAY HAVE EATEN FANCY FOOD, BUT YOU'VE NEVER SAT AT THE TABLE OF DEVINA COLLINS.
THE STEW IS PERFECT.

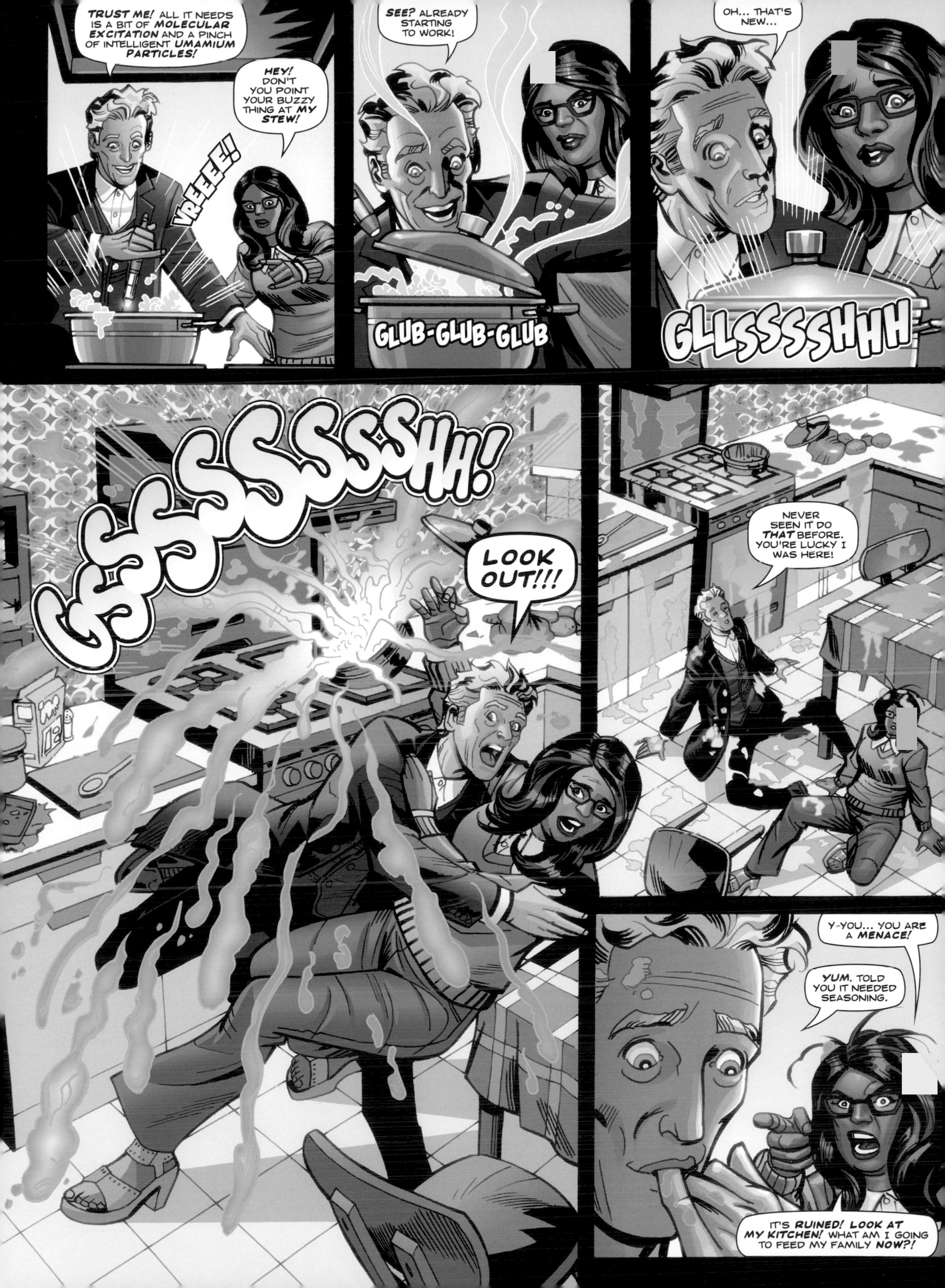
TRUST ME! ALL IT NEEDS IS A BIT OF MOLECULAR EXCITATION AND A PINCH OF INTELLIGENT UMAMIUM PARTICLES!
HEY! DON'T YOU POINT YOUR BUZZY THING AT MY STEW!
VREEEE!
SEE? ALREADY STARTING TO WORK!
GLUB-GLUB-GLUB
OH... THAT'S NEW...
GLLSSSSHHH
CSSSSSSSSHH!
LOOK OUT!!!
NEVER SEEN IT DO THAT BEFORE. YOU'RE LUCKY I WAS HERE!
Y-YOU... YOU ARE A MENACE!
YUM. TOLD YOU IT NEEDED SEASONING.
IT'S RUINED! LOOK AT MY KITCHEN! WHAT AM I GOING TO FEED MY FAMILY NOW?!

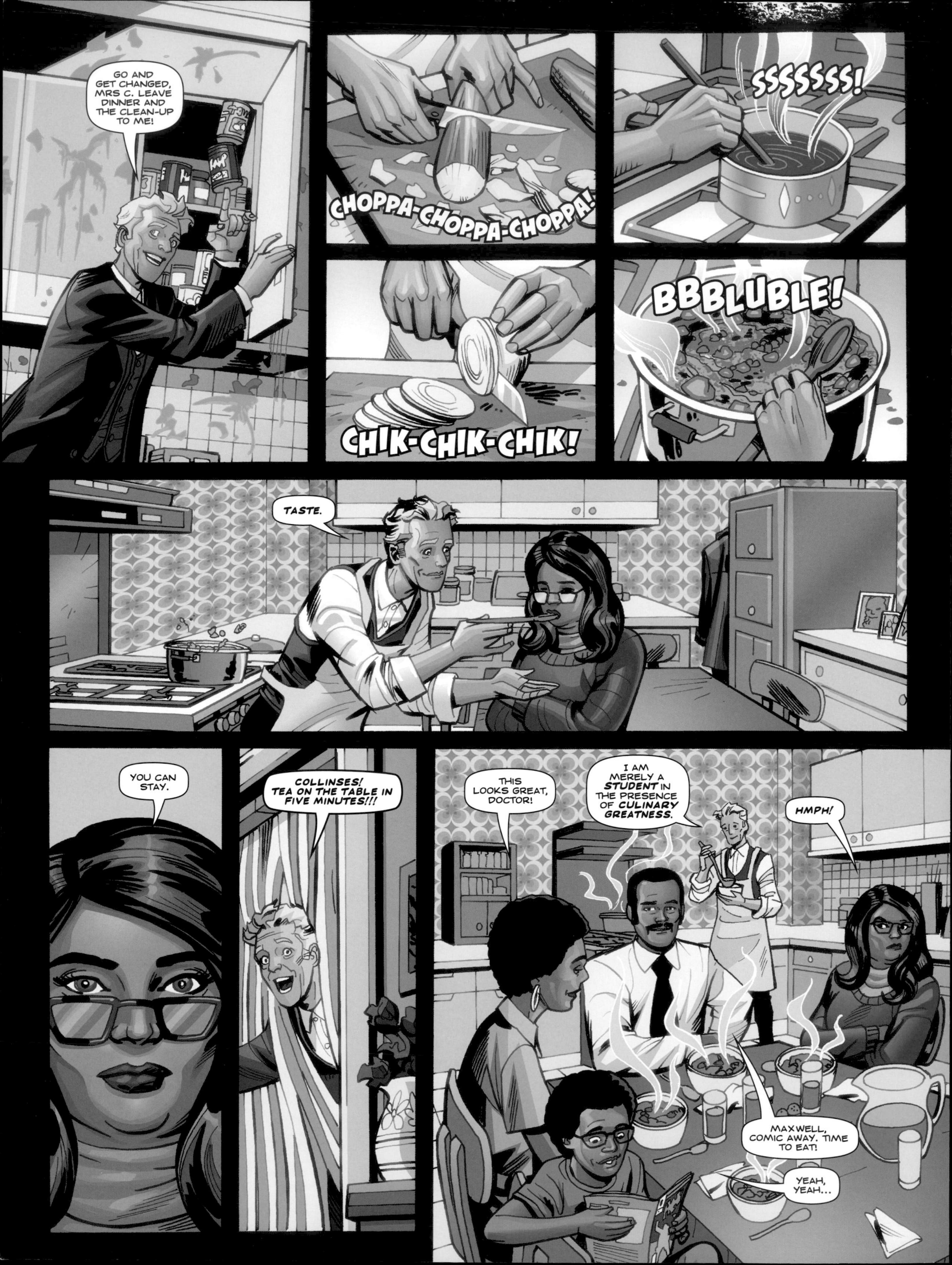
GO AND GET CHANGED, MRS C. LEAVE DINNER AND THE CLEAN-UP TO ME!
CHOPPA-CHOPPA-CHOPPA!
SSSSSSS!
CHIK-CHIK-CHIK!
BBBLUBLE!
TASTE.
YOU CAN STAY.
COLLINSES! TEA ON THE TABLE IN FIVE MINUTES!!!
THIS LOOKS GREAT, DOCTOR!
I AM MERELY A STUDENT IN THE PRESENCE OF CULINARY GREATNESS.
HMPH!
MAXWELL, COMIC AWAY. TIME TO EAT!
YEAH, YEAH...

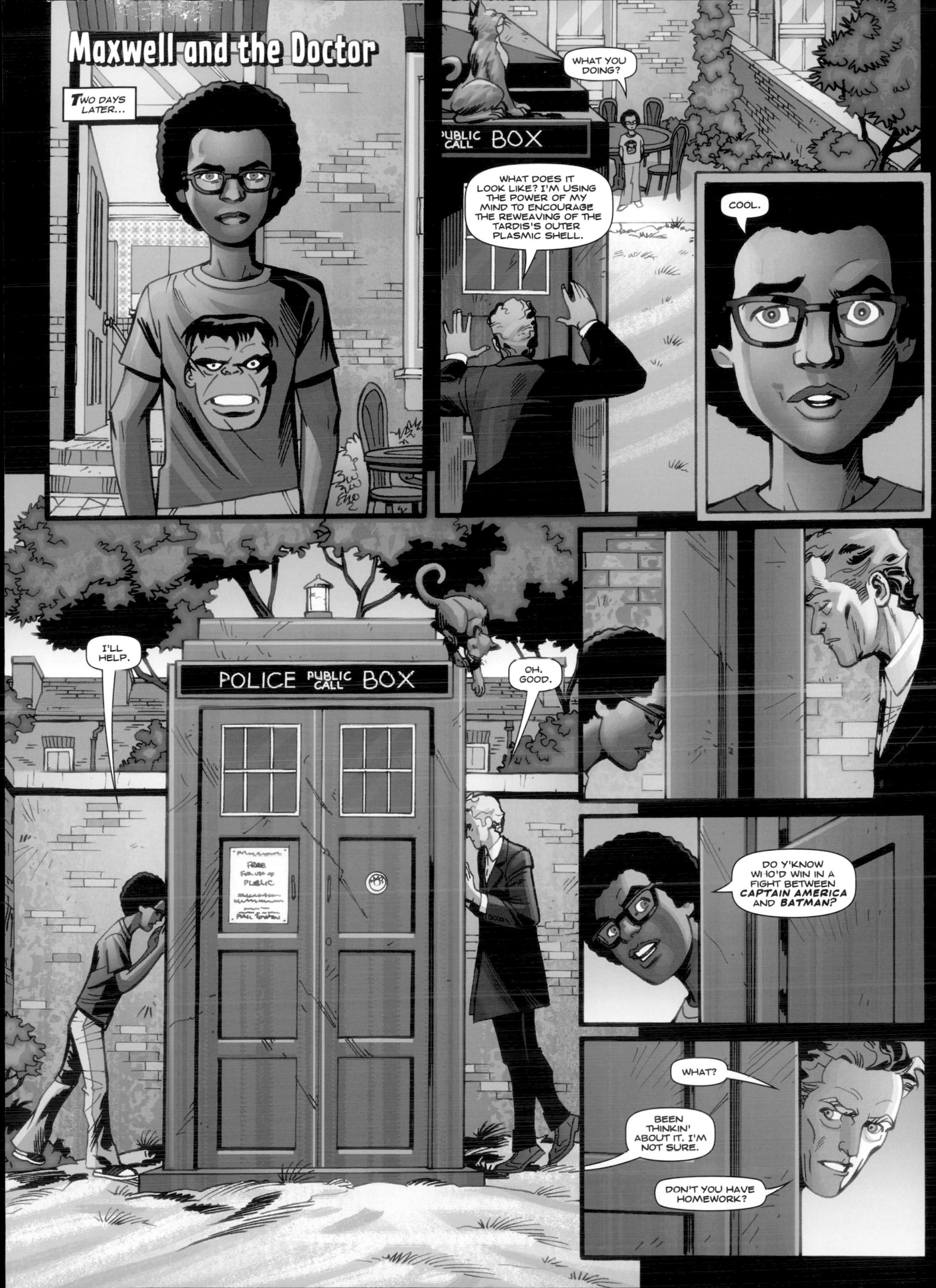
Maxwell and the Doctor
TWO DAYS LATER...
WHAT YOU DOING?
PUBLIC CALL BOX
WHAT DOES IT LOOK LIKE? I'M USING THE POWER OF MY MIND TO ENCOURAGE THE REWEAVING OF THE TARDIS'S OUTER PLASMIC SHELL.
COOL.
I'LL HELP.
POLICE PUBLIC CALL BOX
OH, GOOD.
DO Y'KNOW WHO'D WIN IN A FIGHT BETWEEN CAPTAIN AMERICA AND BATMAN?
WHAT?
BEEN THINKIN' ABOUT IT. I'M NOT SURE.
DON'T YOU HAVE HOMEWORK?

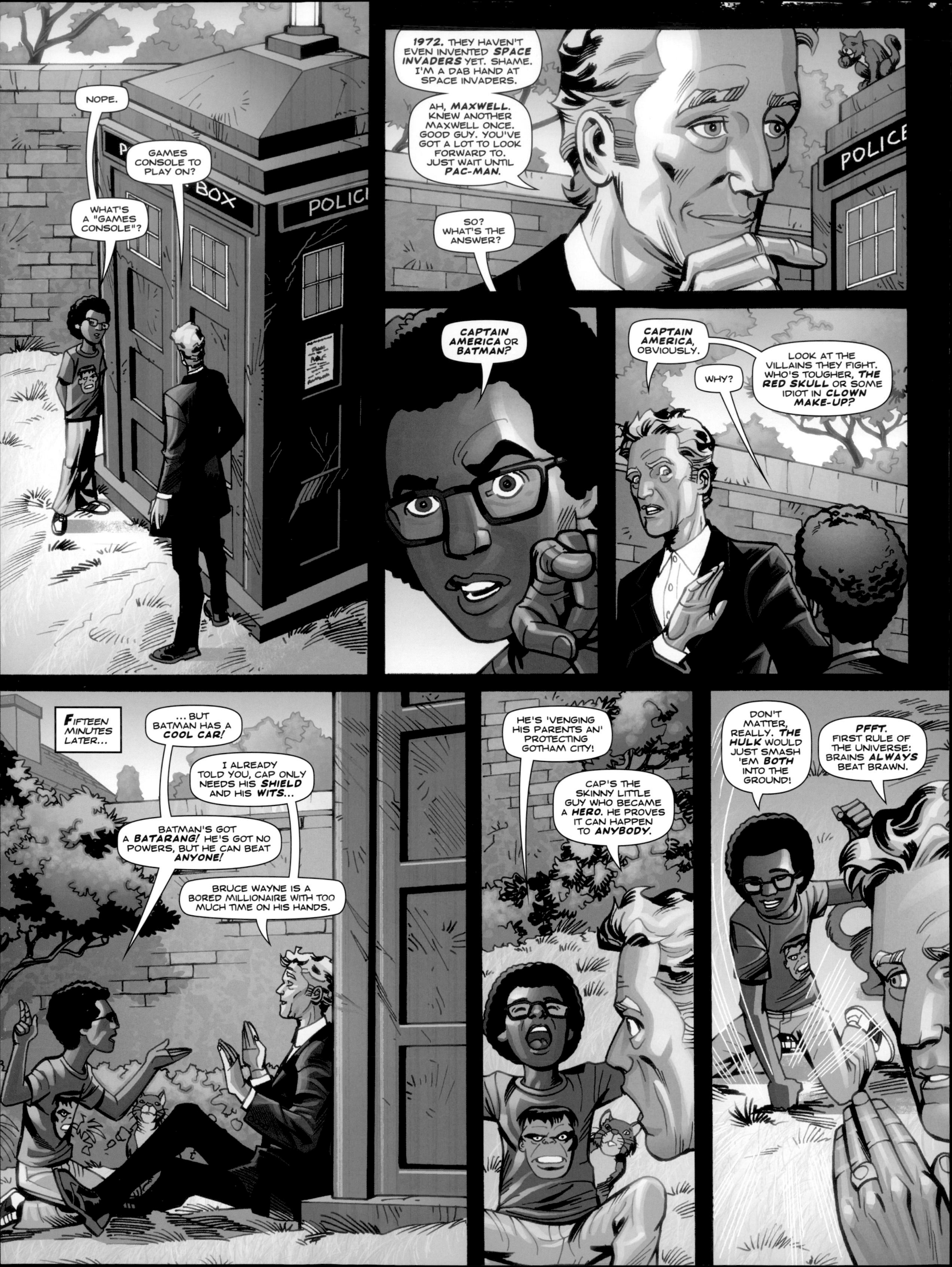
NOPE.
GAMES CONSOLE TO PLAY ON?
WHAT'S A "GAMES CONSOLE"?
POLICE BOX
1972. THEY HAVEN'T EVEN INVENTED SPACE INVADERS YET. SHAME. I'M A DAB HAND AT SPACE INVADERS.
AH, MAXWELL. KNEW ANOTHER MAXWELL ONCE. GOOD GUY. YOU'VE GOT A LOT TO LOOK FORWARD TO. JUST WAIT UNTIL PAC-MAN.
SO? WHAT'S THE ANSWER?
CAPTAIN AMERICA OR BATMAN?
CAPTAIN AMERICA, OBVIOUSLY.
WHY?
LOOK AT THE VILLAINS THEY FIGHT. WHO'S TOUGHER, THE RED SKULL OR SOME IDIOT IN CLOWN MAKE-UP?
FIFTEEN MINUTES LATER...
... BUT BATMAN HAS A COOL CAR!
I ALREADY TOLD YOU, CAP ONLY NEEDS HIS SHIELD AND HIS WITS...
BATMAN'S GOT A BATARANG! HE'S GOT NO POWERS, BUT HE CAN BEAT ANYONE!
BRUCE WAYNE IS A BORED MILLIONAIRE WITH TOO MUCH TIME ON HIS HANDS.
HE'S 'VENGING HIS PARENTS AN' PROTECTING GOTHAM CITY!
CAP'S THE SKINNY LITTLE GUY WHO BECAME A HERO. HE PROVES IT CAN HAPPEN TO ANYBODY.
DON'T MATTER, REALLY. THE HULK WOULD JUST SMASH 'EM BOTH INTO THE GROUND!
PFFT. FIRST RULE OF THE UNIVERSE: BRAINS ALWAYS BEAT BRAWN.

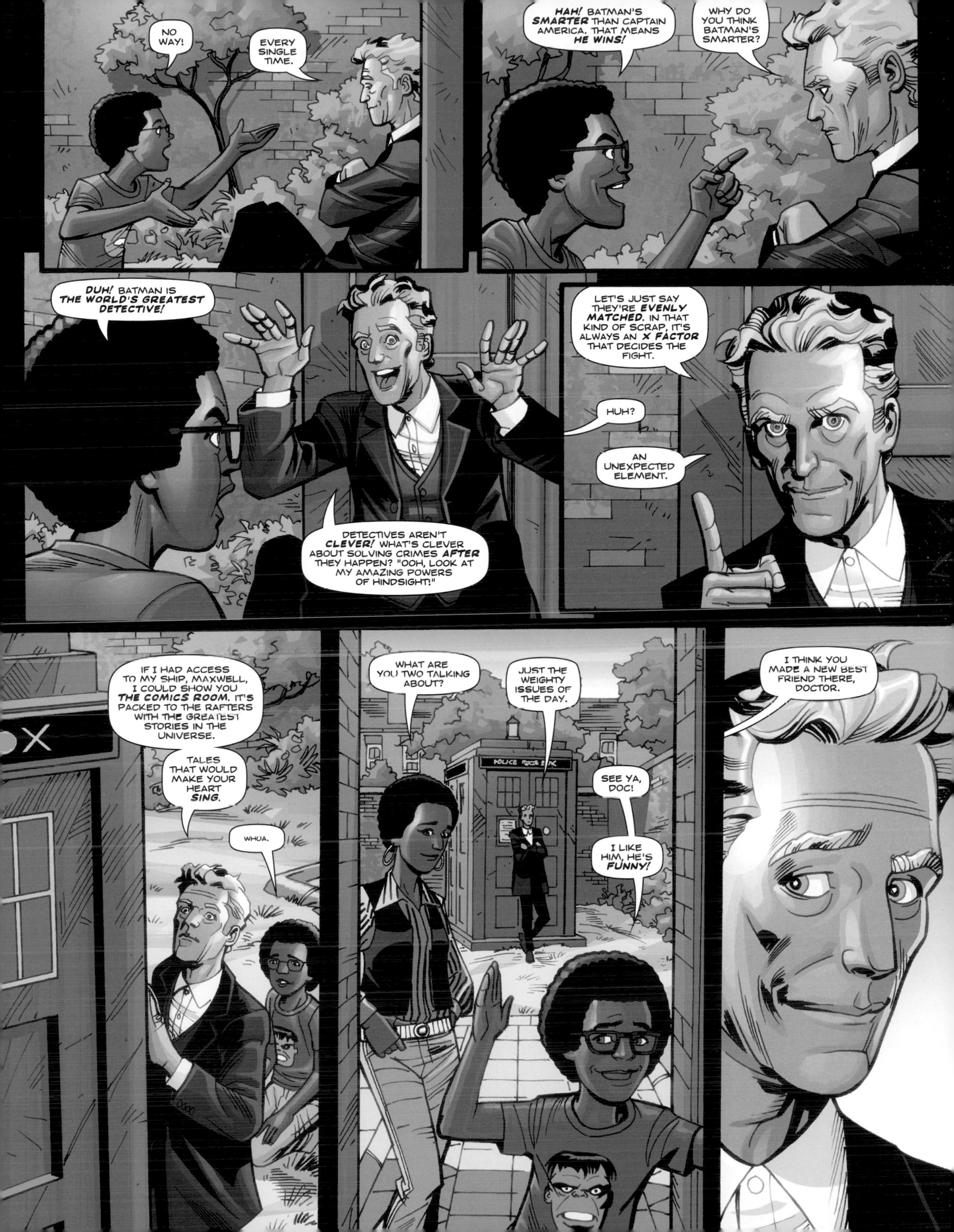
NO WAY!
EVERY SINGLE TIME.
HAH! BATMAN'S SMARTER THAN CAPTAIN AMERICA. THAT MEANS HE WINS!
WHY DO YOU THINK BATMAN'S SMARTER?
DUH! BATMAN IS THE WORLD'S GREATEST DETECTIVE!
DETECTIVES AREN'T CLEVER! WHAT'S CLEVER ABOUT SOLVING CRIMES AFTER THEY HAPPEN? "OOH, LOOK AT MY AMAZING POWERS OF HINDSIGHT!"
LET'S JUST SAY THEY'RE EVENLY MATCHED. IN THAT KIND OF SCRAP, IT'S ALWAYS AN X FACTOR THAT DECIDES THE FIGHT.
HUH?
AN UNEXPECTED ELEMENT.
IF I HAD ACCESS TO MY SHIP, MAXWELL, I COULD SHOW YOU THE COMICS ROOM. IT'S PACKED TO THE RAFTERS WITH THE GREATEST STORIES IN THE UNIVERSE.
TALES THAT WOULD MAKE YOUR HEART SING.
WHOA.
WHAT ARE YOU TWO TALKING ABOUT?
JUST THE WEIGHTY ISSUES OF THE DAY.
SEE YA, DOC!
I LIKE HIM, HE'S FUNNY!
I THINK YOU MADE A NEW BEST FRIEND THERE, DOCTOR.

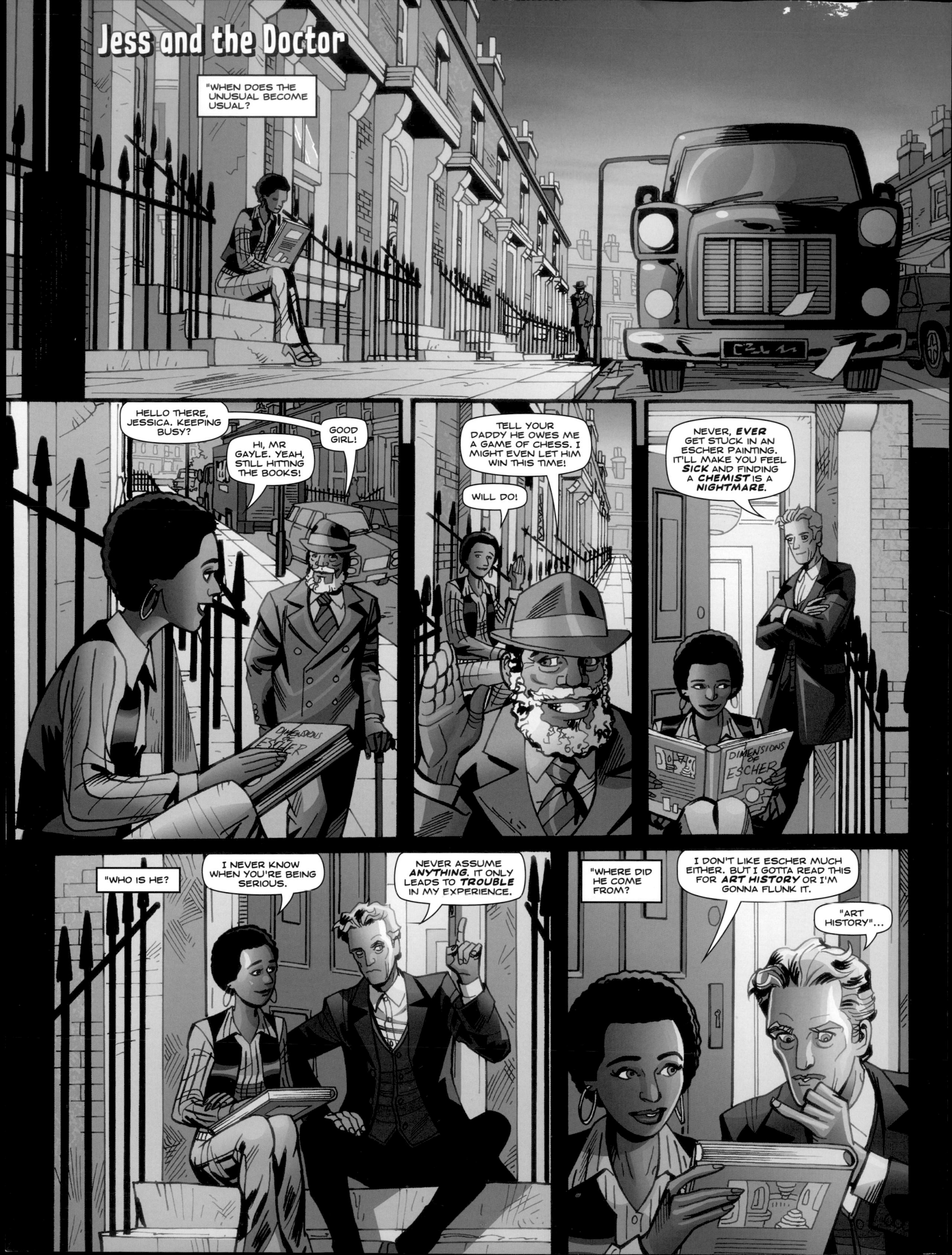
Jess and the Doctor
"WHEN DOES THE UNUSUAL BECOME USUAL?
HELLO THERE, JESSICA. KEEPING BUSY?
HI, MR GAYLE. YEAH, STILL HITTING THE BOOKS!
GOOD GIRL!
TELL YOUR DADDY HE OWES ME A GAME OF CHESS. I MIGHT EVEN LET HIM WIN THIS TIME!
WILL DO!
NEVER, EVER GET STUCK IN AN ESCHER PAINTING. IT'LL MAKE YOU FEEL SICK AND FINDING A CHEMIST IS A NIGHTMARE.
DIMENSIONS OF ESCHER
"WHO IS HE?
I NEVER KNOW WHEN YOU'RE BEING SERIOUS.
NEVER ASSUME ANYTHING. IT ONLY LEADS TO TROUBLE IN MY EXPERIENCE.
"WHERE DID HE COME FROM?
I DON'T LIKE ESCHER MUCH EITHER. BUT I GOTTA READ THIS FOR ART HISTORY OR I'M GONNA FLUNK IT.
"ART HISTORY"...

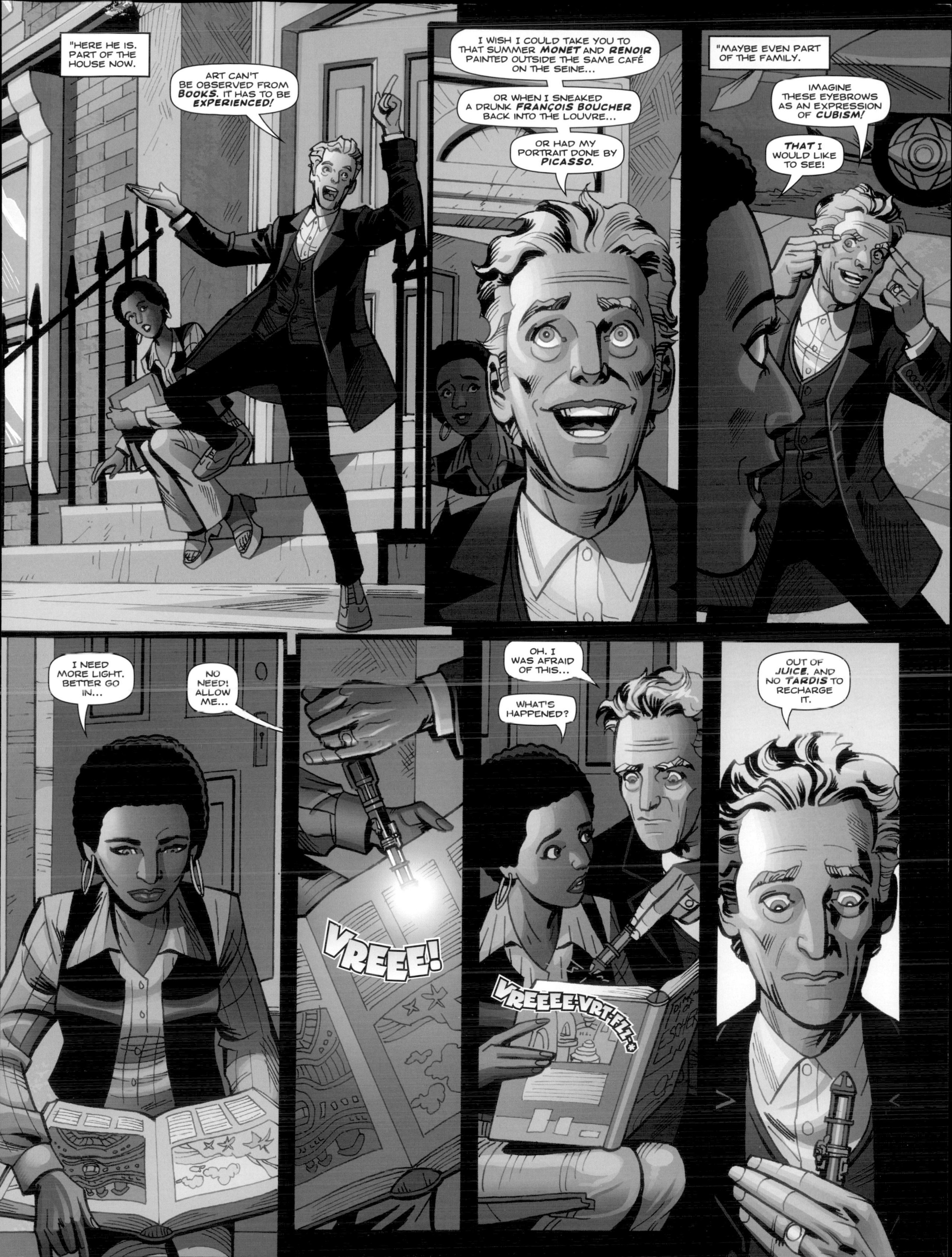
"HERE HE IS. PART OF THE HOUSE NOW.
ART CAN'T BE OBSERVED FROM BOOKS. IT HAS TO BE EXPERIENCED!
I WISH I COULD TAKE YOU TO THAT SUMMER MONET AND RENOIR PAINTED OUTSIDE THE SAME CAFÉ ON THE SEINE...
OR WHEN I SNEAKED A DRUNK FRANÇOIS BOUCHER BACK INTO THE LOUVRE...
OR HAD MY PORTRAIT DONE BY PICASSO.
"MAYBE EVEN PART OF THE FAMILY.
IMAGINE THESE EYEBROWS AS AN EXPRESSION OF CUBISM!
THAT I WOULD LIKE TO SEE!
I NEED MORE LIGHT. BETTER GO IN...
NO NEED! ALLOW ME...
VREEE!
OH. I WAS AFRAID OF THIS...
WHAT'S HAPPENED?
VREEEE-VRT-FZZ*
OUT OF JUICE. AND NO TARDIS TO RECHARGE IT.

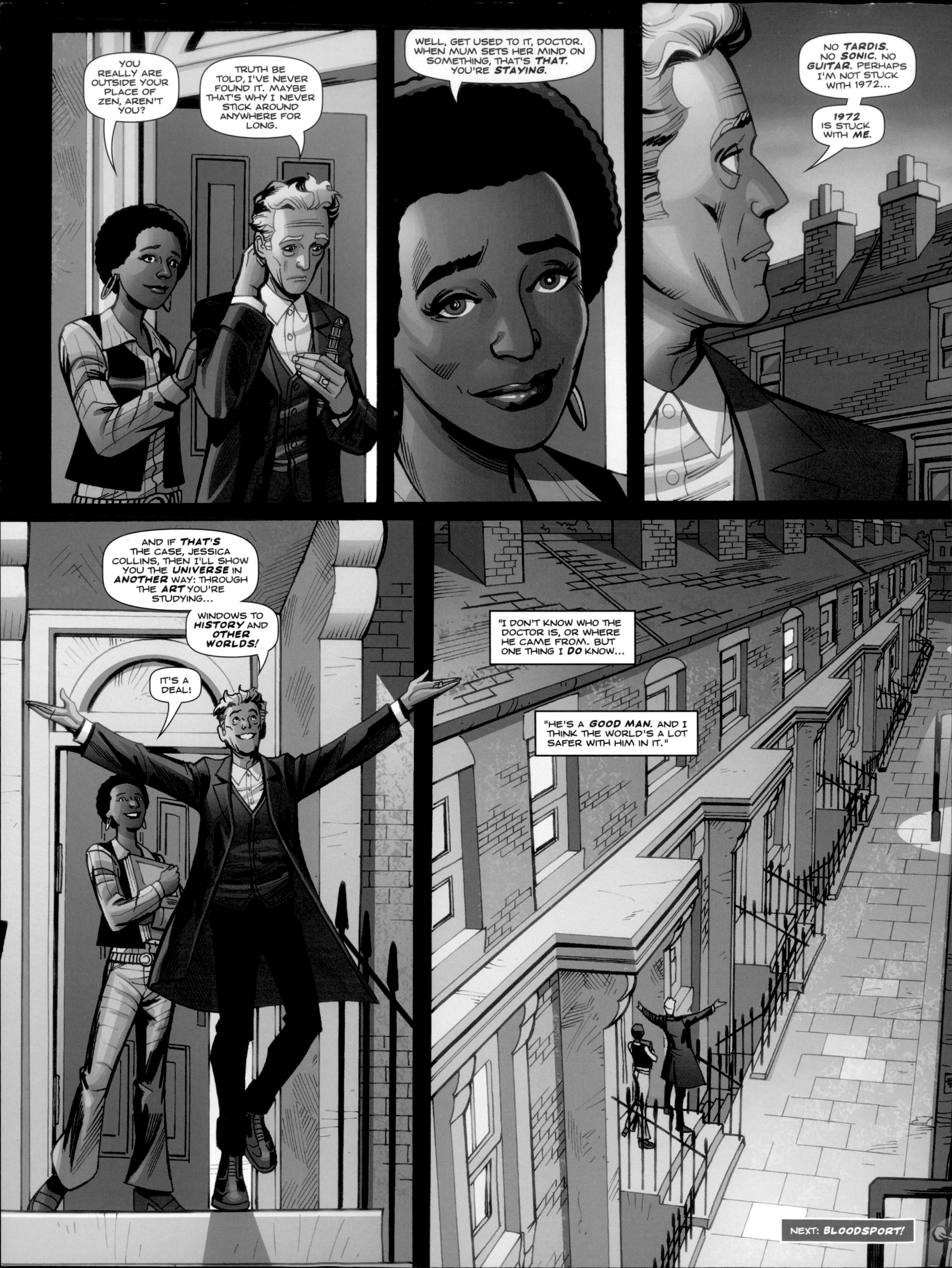
YOU REALLY ARE OUTSIDE YOUR PLACE OF ZEN, AREN'T YOU?
TRUTH BE TOLD, I'VE NEVER FOUND IT. MAYBE THAT'S WHY I NEVER STICK AROUND ANYWHERE FOR LONG.
WELL, GET USED TO IT, DOCTOR. WHEN MUM SETS HER MIND ON SOMETHING, THAT'S THAT. YOU'RE STAYING.
NO TARDIS. NO SONIC. NO GUITAR. PERHAPS I'M NOT STUCK WITH 1972...
1972 IS STUCK WITH ME.
AND IF THAT'S THE CASE, JESSICA COLLINS, THEN I'LL SHOW YOU THE UNIVERSE IN ANOTHER WAY: THROUGH THE ART YOU'RE STUDYING...
WINDOWS TO HISTORY AND OTHER WORLDS!
IT'S A DEAL!
"I DON'T KNOW WHO THE DOCTOR IS, OR WHERE HE CAME FROM. BUT ONE THING I DO KNOW...
"HE'S A GOOD MAN. AND I THINK THE WORLD'S A LOT SAFER WITH HIM IN IT."
NEXT: BLOODSPORT!

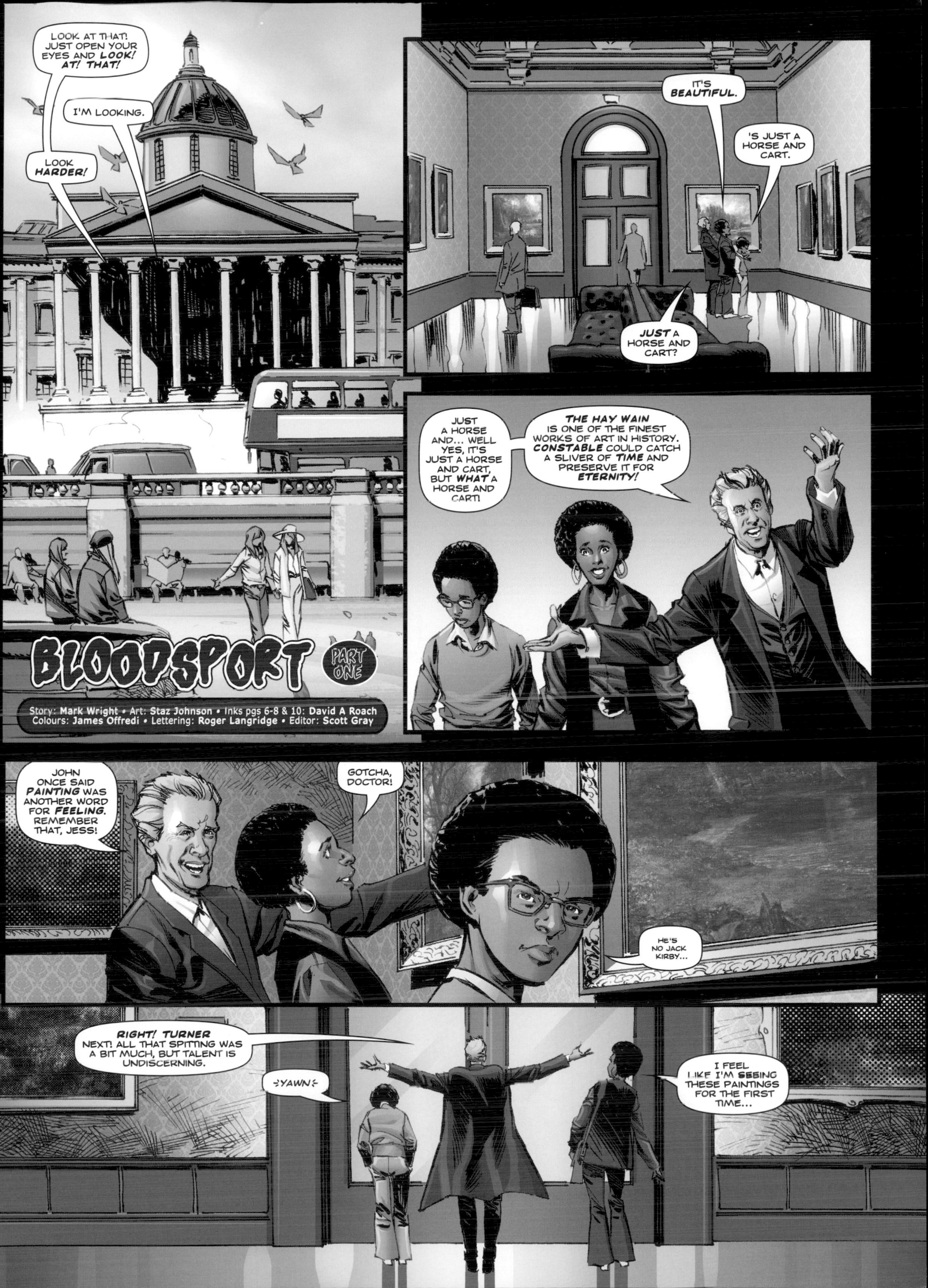
LOOK AT THAT! JUST OPEN YOUR EYES AND LOOK! AT! THAT!
I'M LOOKING.
LOOK HARDER!
IT'S BEAUTIFUL.
'S JUST A HORSE AND CART.
JUST A HORSE AND CART?
BLOODSPORT PART ONE
Story: Mark Wright • Art: Staz Johnson • Inks pgs 6-8 & 10: David A Roach
Colours: James Offredi • Lettering: Roger Langridge • Editor: Scott Gray
JUST A HORSE AND... WELL YES, IT'S JUST A HORSE AND CART, BUT WHAT A HORSE AND CART!
THE HAY WAIN IS ONE OF THE FINEST WORKS OF ART IN HISTORY. CONSTABLE COULD CATCH A SLIVER OF TIME AND PRESERVE IT FOR ETERNITY!
JOHN ONCE SAID PAINTING WAS ANOTHER WORD FOR FEELING. REMEMBER THAT, JESS!
GOTCHA, DOCTOR!
HE'S NO JACK KIRBY...
RIGHT! TURNER NEXT! ALL THAT SPITTING WAS A BIT MUCH, BUT TALENT IS UNDISCERNING.
⁓YAWN⁓
I FEEL LIKE I'M SEEING THESE PAINTINGS FOR THE FIRST TIME...

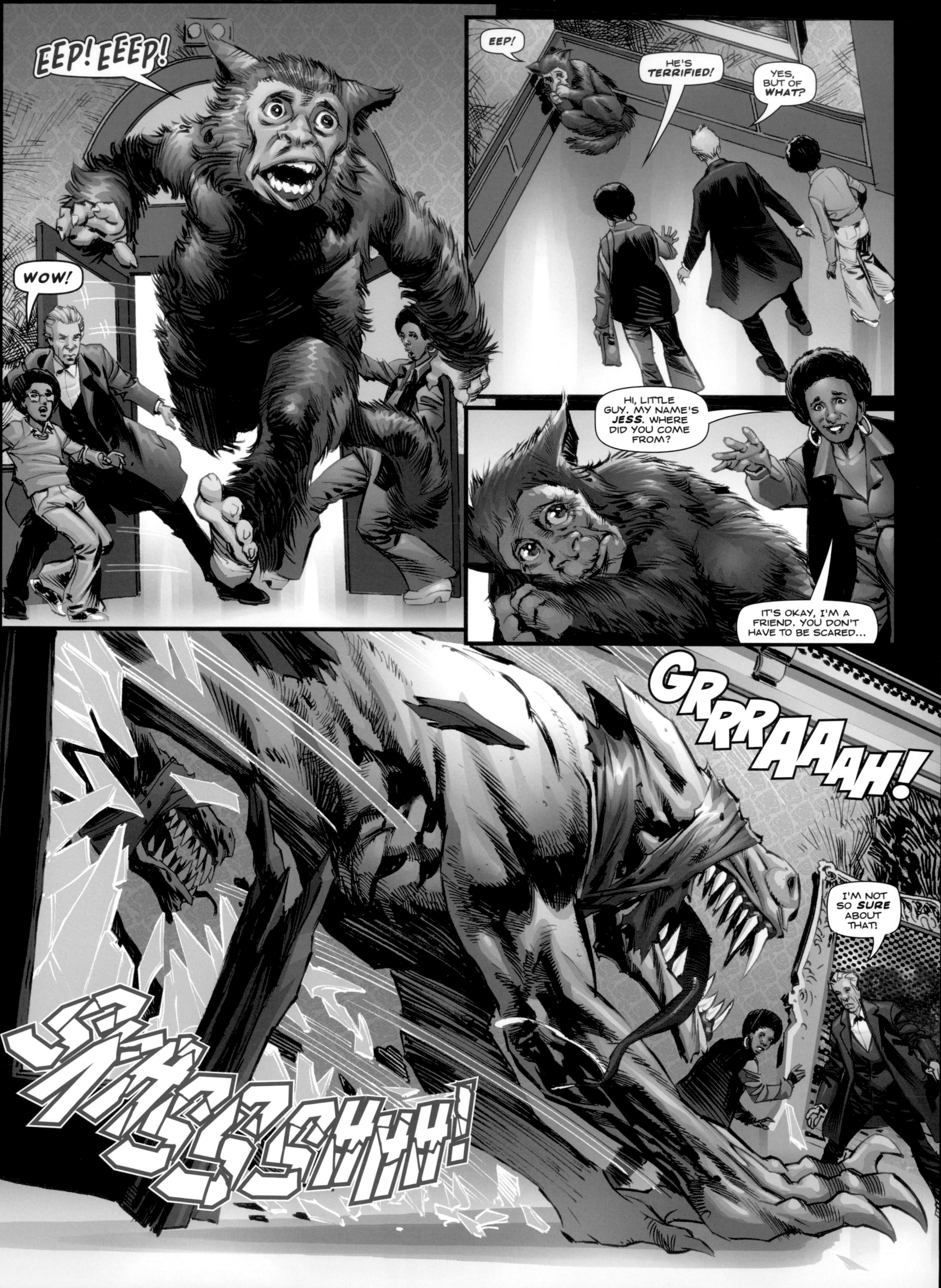
EEP! EEEP!
WOW!
EEP!
HE'S TERRIFIED!
YES, BUT OF WHAT?
HI, LITTLE GUY. MY NAME'S JESS. WHERE DID YOU COME FROM?
IT'S OKAY, I'M A FRIEND. YOU DON'T HAVE TO BE SCARED...
GRRRAAAAH!
I'M NOT SO SURE ABOUT THAT!

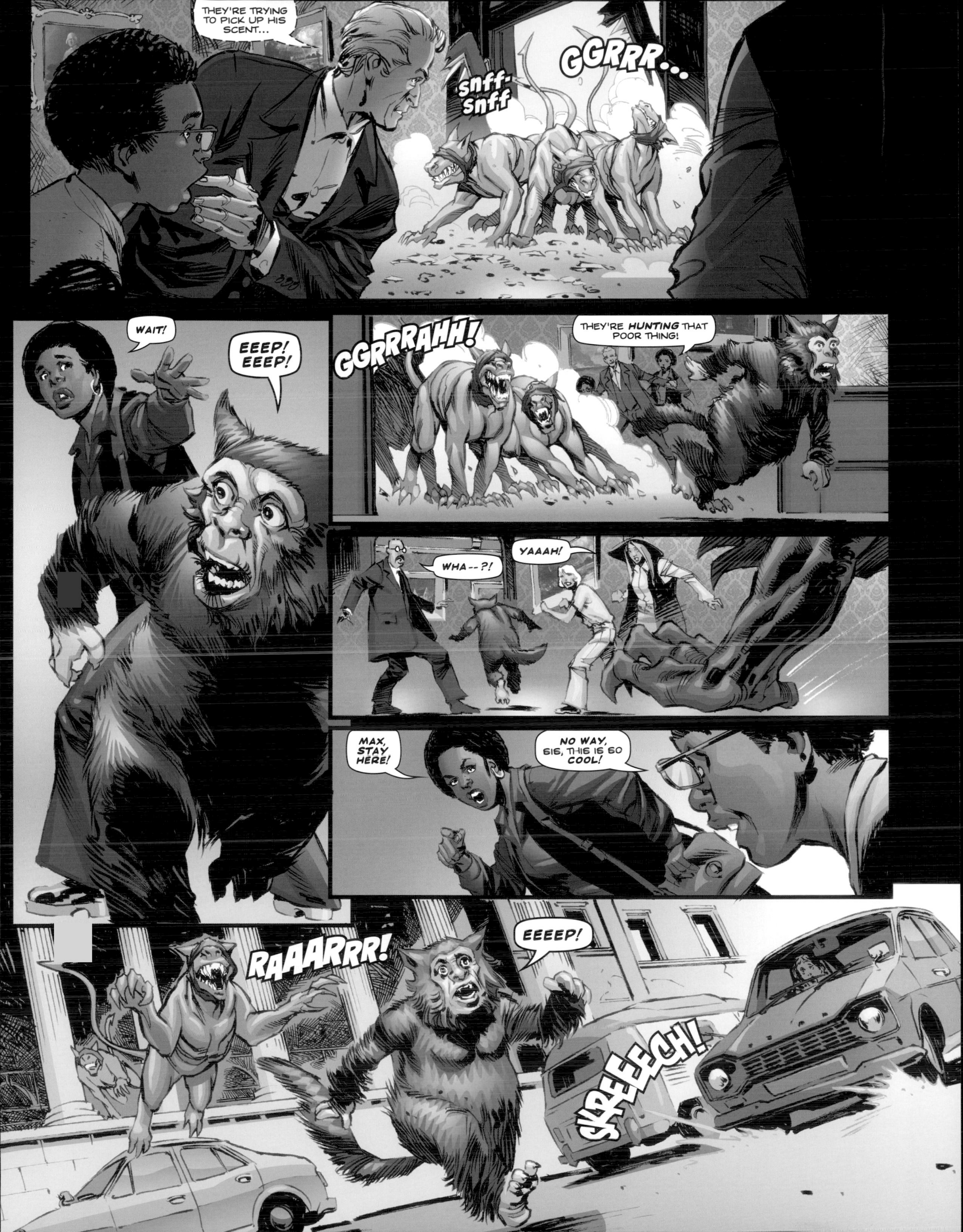
THEY'RE TRYING TO PICK UP HIS SCENT...
snff-snff
GGRRR...
WAIT!
EEEP! EEEP!
GGRRRAHH!
THEY'RE HUNTING THAT POOR THING!
WHA--?!
YAAAH!
MAX, STAY HERE!
NO WAY, SIS, THIS IS SO COOL!
RAAARRR!
EEEEP!
SKREEEECH!

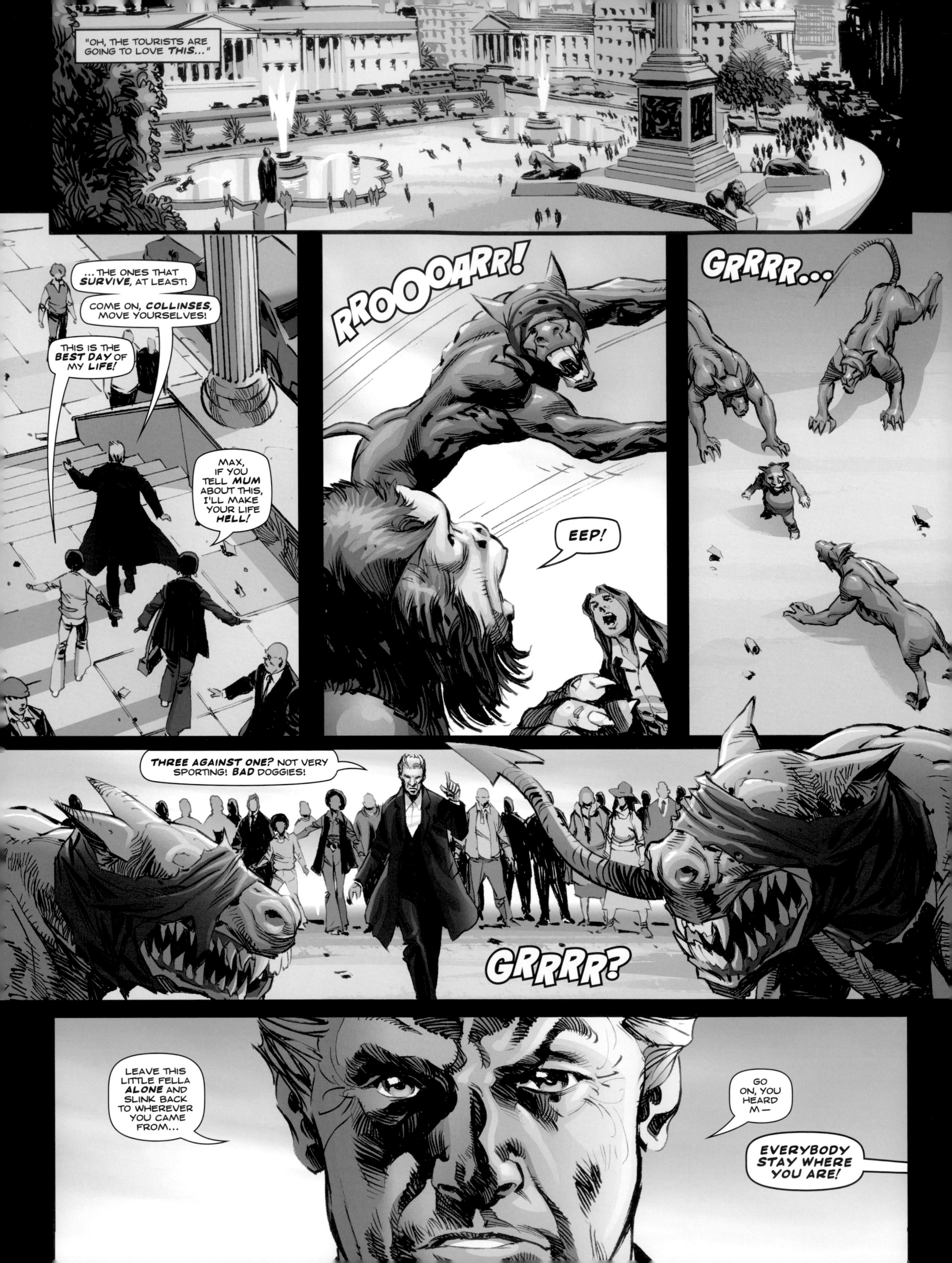
"OH, THE TOURISTS ARE GOING TO LOVE THIS..."
...THE ONES THAT SURVIVE, AT LEAST!
COME ON, COLLINSES, MOVE YOURSELVES!
THIS IS THE BEST DAY OF MY LIFE!
MAX, IF YOU TELL MUM ABOUT THIS, I'LL MAKE YOUR LIFE HELL!
RROOOOARR!
EEP!
GRRRR...
THREE AGAINST ONE? NOT VERY SPORTING! BAD DOGGIES!
GRRRR?
LEAVE THIS LITTLE FELLA ALONE AND SLINK BACK TO WHEREVER YOU CAME FROM...
GO ON, YOU HEARD M—
EVERYBODY STAY WHERE YOU ARE!

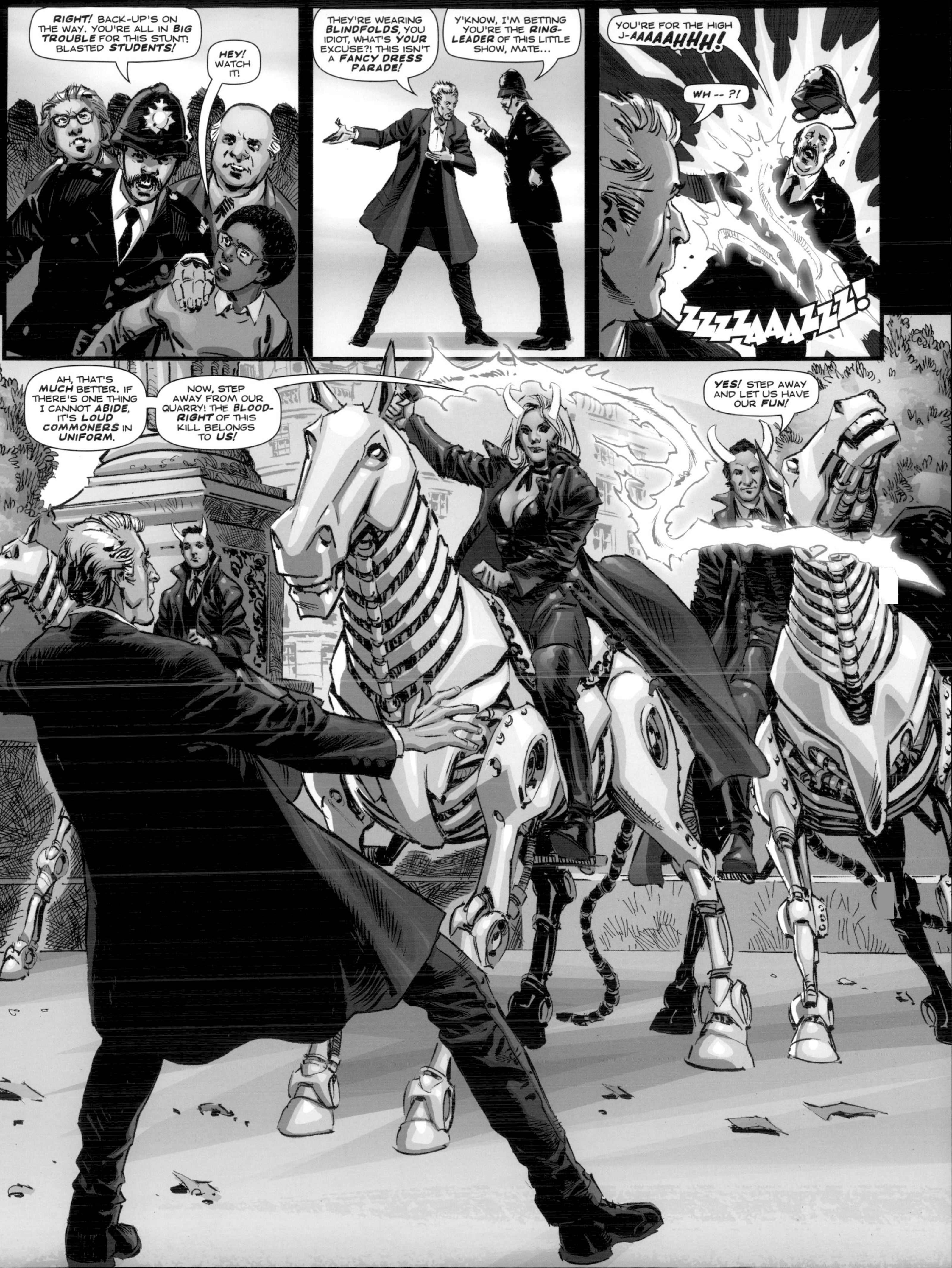
RIGHT! BACK-UP'S ON THE WAY. YOU'RE ALL IN BIG TROUBLE FOR THIS STUNT! BLASTED STUDENTS!
HEY! WATCH IT!
THEY'RE WEARING BLINDFOLDS, YOU IDIOT, WHAT'S YOUR EXCUSE?! THIS ISN'T A FANCY DRESS PARADE!
Y'KNOW, I'M BETTING YOU'RE THE RING-LEADER OF THIS LITTLE SHOW, MATE...
YOU'RE FOR THE HIGH J-AAAAAHHH!
WH -- ?!
ZZZZAAAAZZZZ!
AH, THAT'S MUCH BETTER. IF THERE'S ONE THING I CANNOT ABIDE, IT'S LOUD COMMONERS IN UNIFORM.
NOW, STEP AWAY FROM OUR QUARRY! THE BLOOD-RIGHT OF THIS KILL BELONGS TO US!
YES! STEP AWAY AND LET US HAVE OUR FUN!

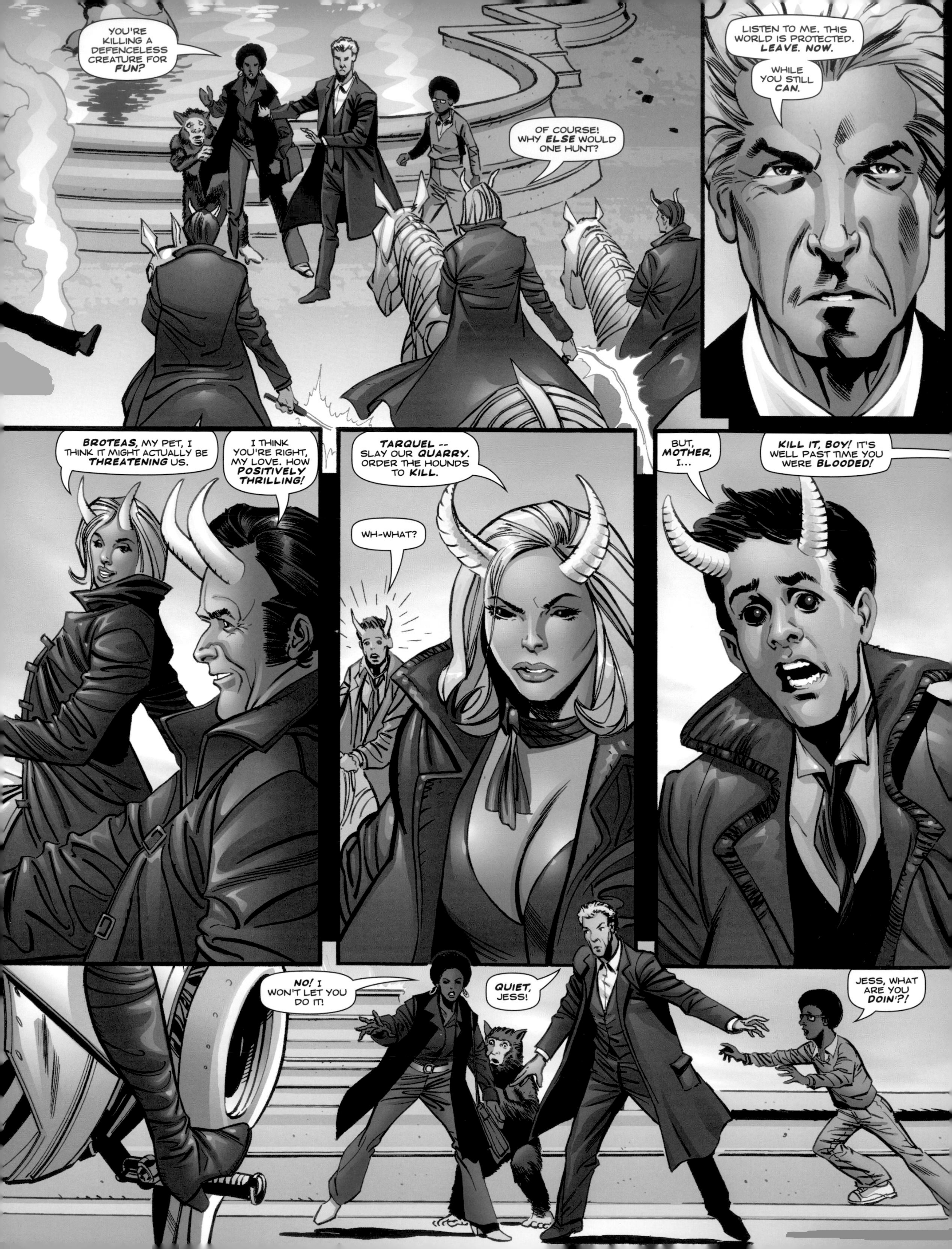
YOU'RE KILLING A DEFENCELESS CREATURE FOR FUN?
OF COURSE! WHY ELSE WOULD ONE HUNT?
LISTEN TO ME. THIS WORLD IS PROTECTED. LEAVE. NOW.
WHILE YOU STILL CAN.
BROTEAS, MY PET, I THINK IT MIGHT ACTUALLY BE THREATENING US.
I THINK YOU'RE RIGHT, MY LOVE. HOW POSITIVELY THRILLING!
TARQUEL -- SLAY OUR QUARRY. ORDER THE HOUNDS TO KILL.
WH-WHAT?
BUT, MOTHER, I...
KILL IT, BOY! IT'S WELL PAST TIME YOU WERE BLOODED!
NO! I WON'T LET YOU DO IT!
QUIET, JESS!
JESS, WHAT ARE YOU DOIN'?!

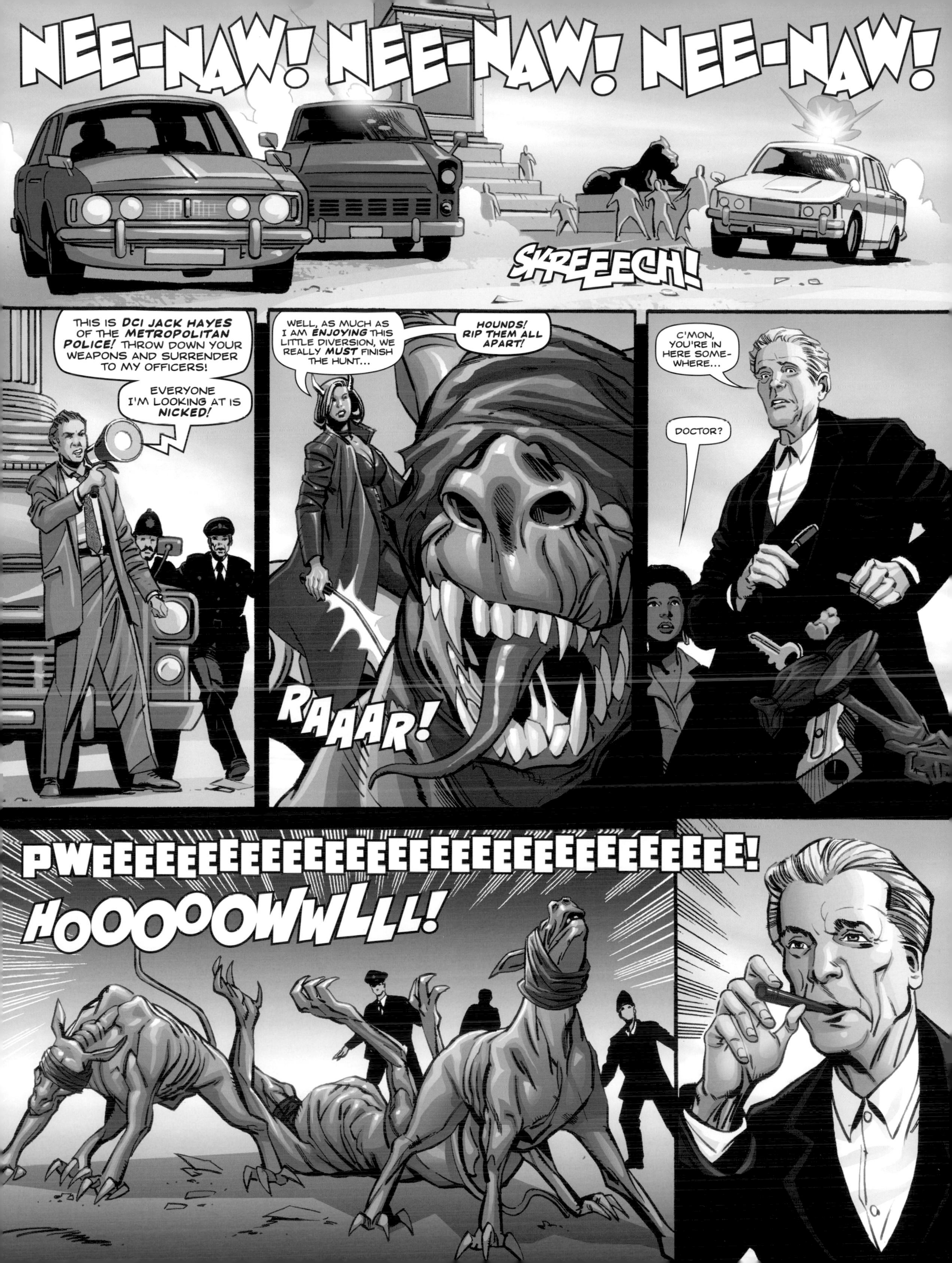

NEE-NAW! NEE-NAW! NEE-NAW!
SKREEECH!
THIS IS DCI JACK HAYES OF THE METROPOLITAN POLICE! THROW DOWN YOUR WEAPONS AND SURRENDER TO MY OFFICERS!
EVERYONE I'M LOOKING AT IS NICKED!
WELL, AS MUCH AS I AM ENJOYING THIS LITTLE DIVERSION, WE REALLY MUST FINISH THE HUNT...
HOUNDS! RIP THEM ALL APART!
RAAAR!
C'MON, YOU'RE IN HERE SOME-WHERE...
DOCTOR?
PWEEEEEEEEEEEEEEEEEEEEEEEEEEEEE!
HOOOOOWWLLL!

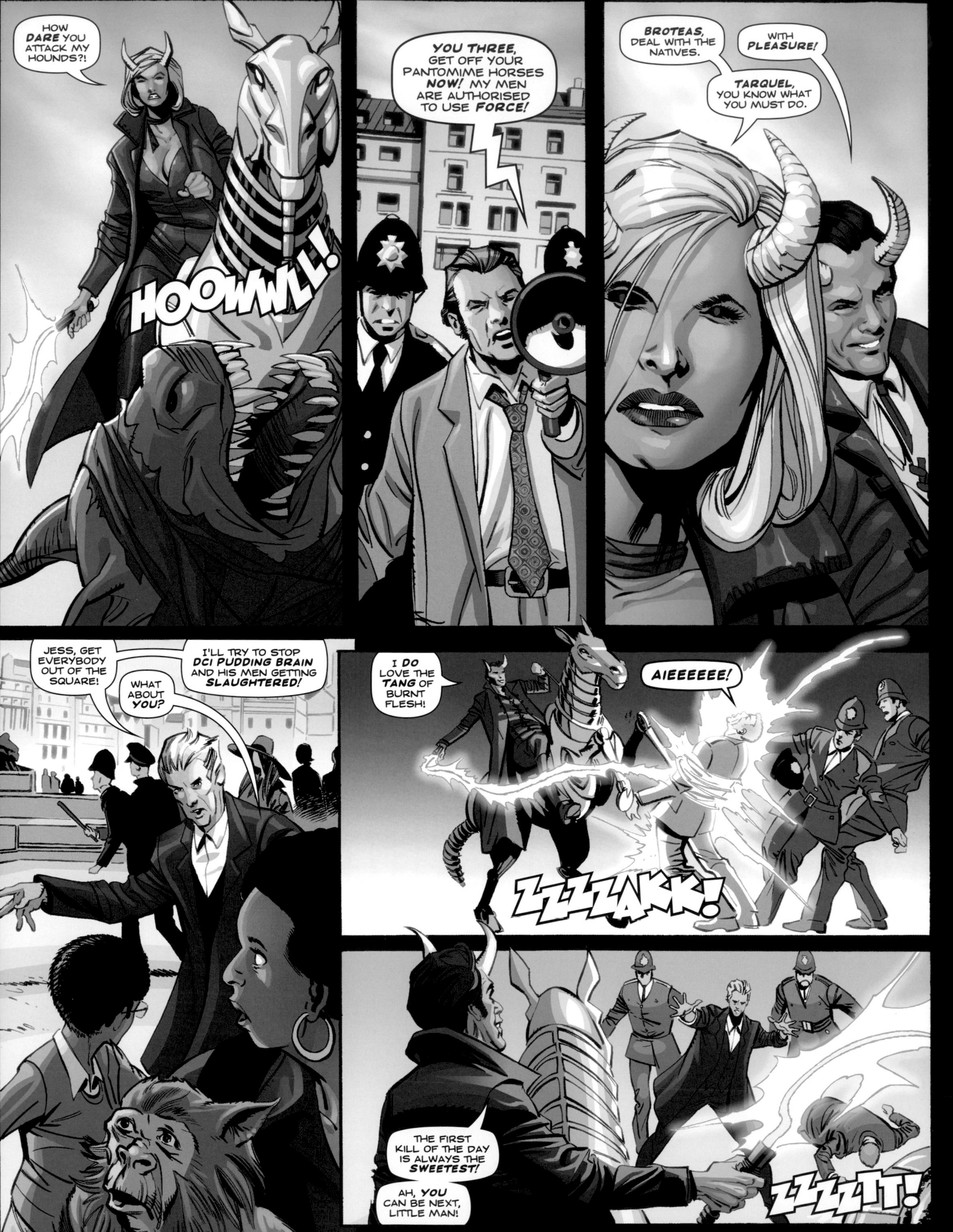

HOW DARE YOU ATTACK MY HOUNDS?!
HOOWWLL!
YOU THREE, GET OFF YOUR PANTOMIME HORSES NOW! MY MEN ARE AUTHORISED TO USE FORCE!
BROTEAS, DEAL WITH THE NATIVES.
WITH PLEASURE!
TARQUEL, YOU KNOW WHAT YOU MUST DO.
JESS, GET EVERYBODY OUT OF THE SQUARE!
WHAT ABOUT YOU?
I'LL TRY TO STOP DCI PUDDING BRAIN AND HIS MEN GETTING SLAUGHTERED!
I DO LOVE THE TANG OF BURNT FLESH!
AIEEEEEE!
ZZZZAKK!
THE FIRST KILL OF THE DAY IS ALWAYS THE SWEETEST!
AH, YOU CAN BE NEXT, LITTLE MAN!
ZZZZTT!

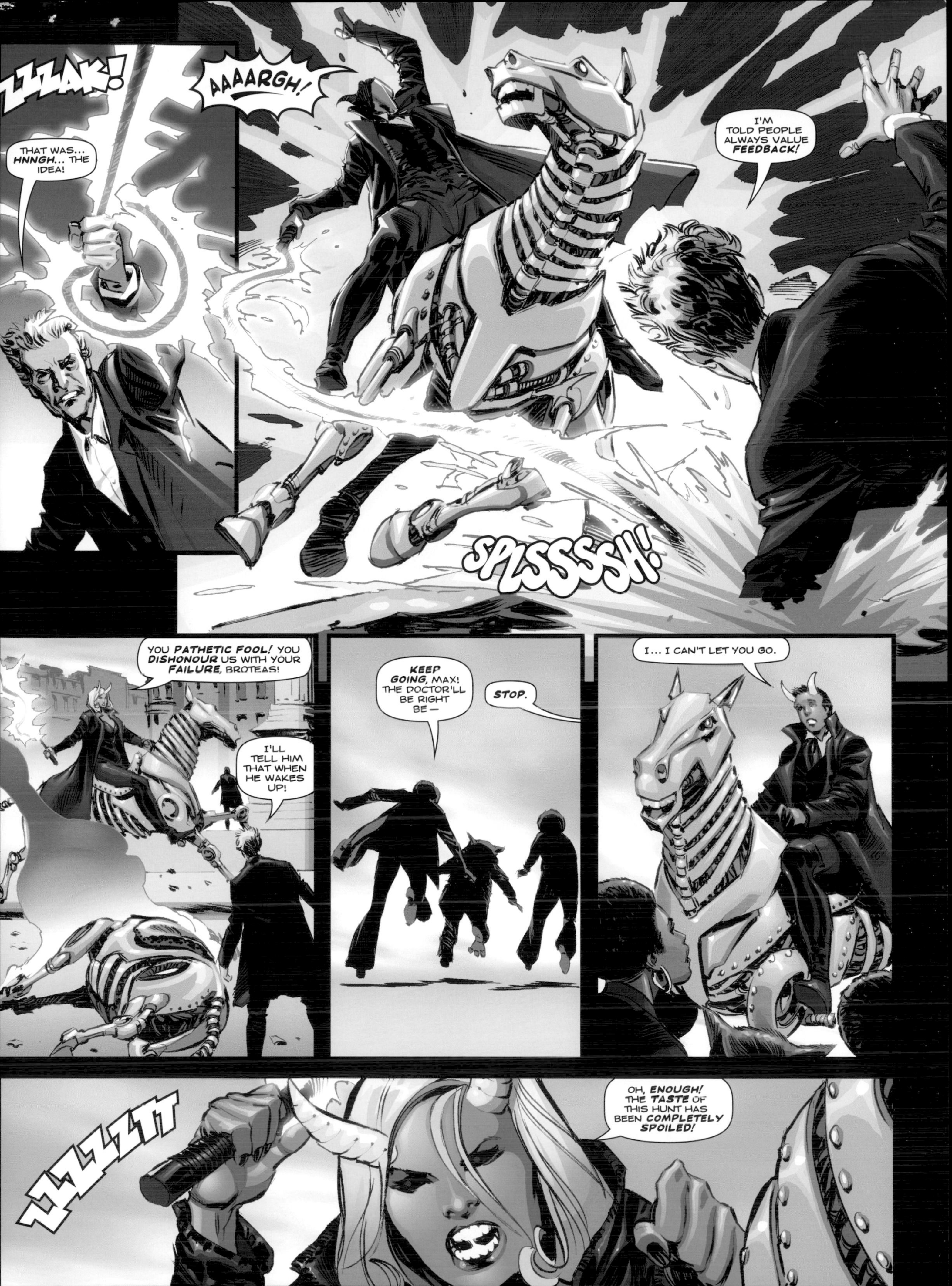
ZZZAK!
AAAARGH!
THAT WAS... HNNGH... THE IDEA!
I'M TOLD PEOPLE ALWAYS VALUE FEEDBACK!
SPLSSSSH!
YOU PATHETIC FOOL! YOU DISHONOUR US WITH YOUR FAILURE, BROTEAS!
I'LL TELL HIM THAT WHEN HE WAKES UP!
KEEP GOING, MAX! THE DOCTOR'LL BE RIGHT BE—
STOP.
I... I CAN'T LET YOU GO.
ZZZZZTT
OH, ENOUGH! THE TASTE OF THIS HUNT HAS BEEN COMPLETELY SPOILED!

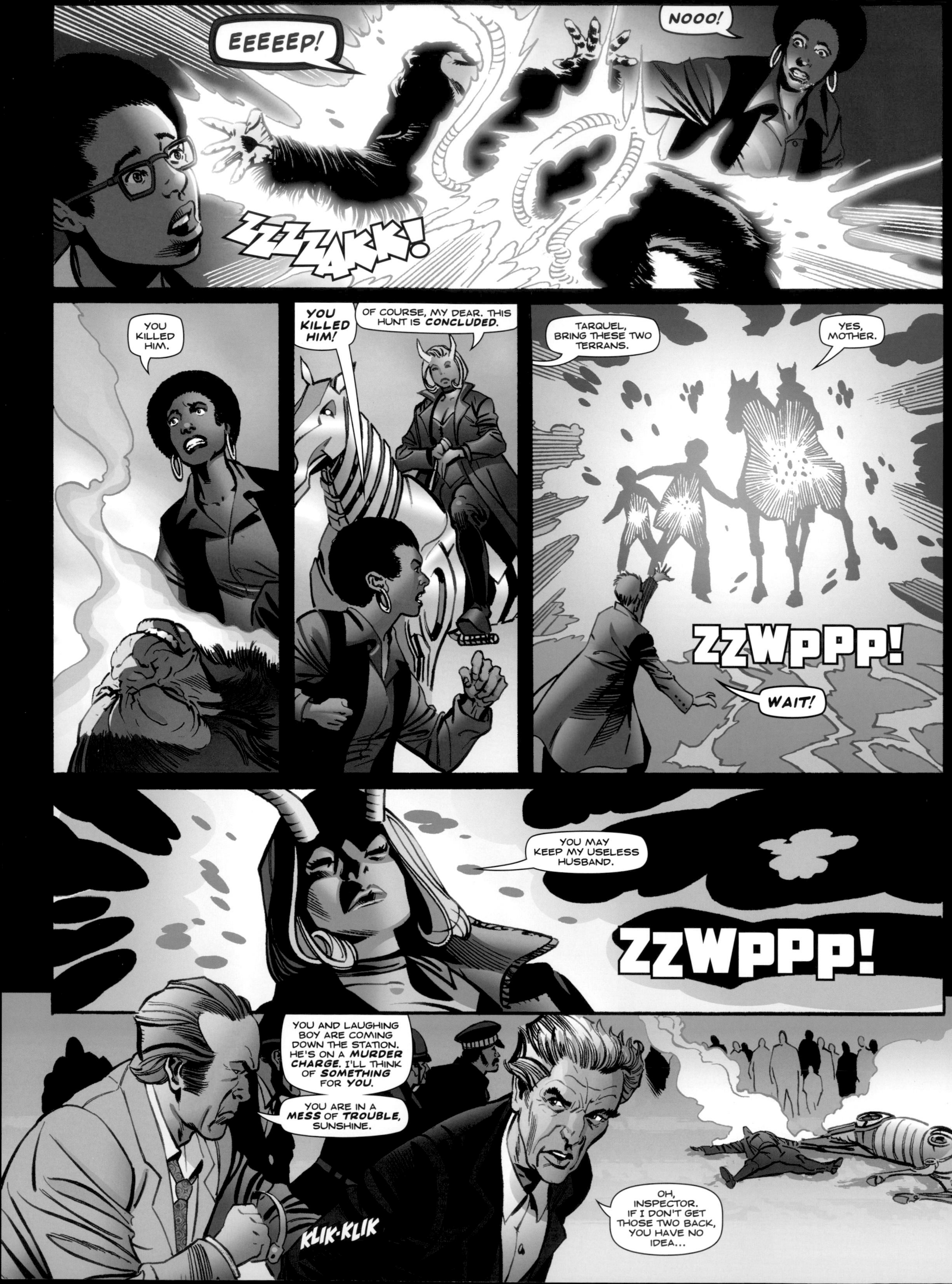
EEEEEP!
NOOO!
ZZZZAKK!
YOU KILLED HIM.
YOU KILLED HIM!
OF COURSE, MY DEAR. THIS HUNT IS CONCLUDED.
TARQUEL, BRING THESE TWO TERRANS.
YES, MOTHER.
ZZWPPP!
WAIT!
YOU MAY KEEP MY USELESS HUSBAND.
ZZWPPP!
YOU AND LAUGHING BOY ARE COMING DOWN THE STATION. HE'S ON A MURDER CHARGE. I'LL THINK OF SOMETHING FOR YOU.
YOU ARE IN A MESS OF TROUBLE, SUNSHINE.
KLIK-KLIK
OH, INSPECTOR. IF I DON'T GET THOSE TWO BACK, YOU HAVE NO IDEA...

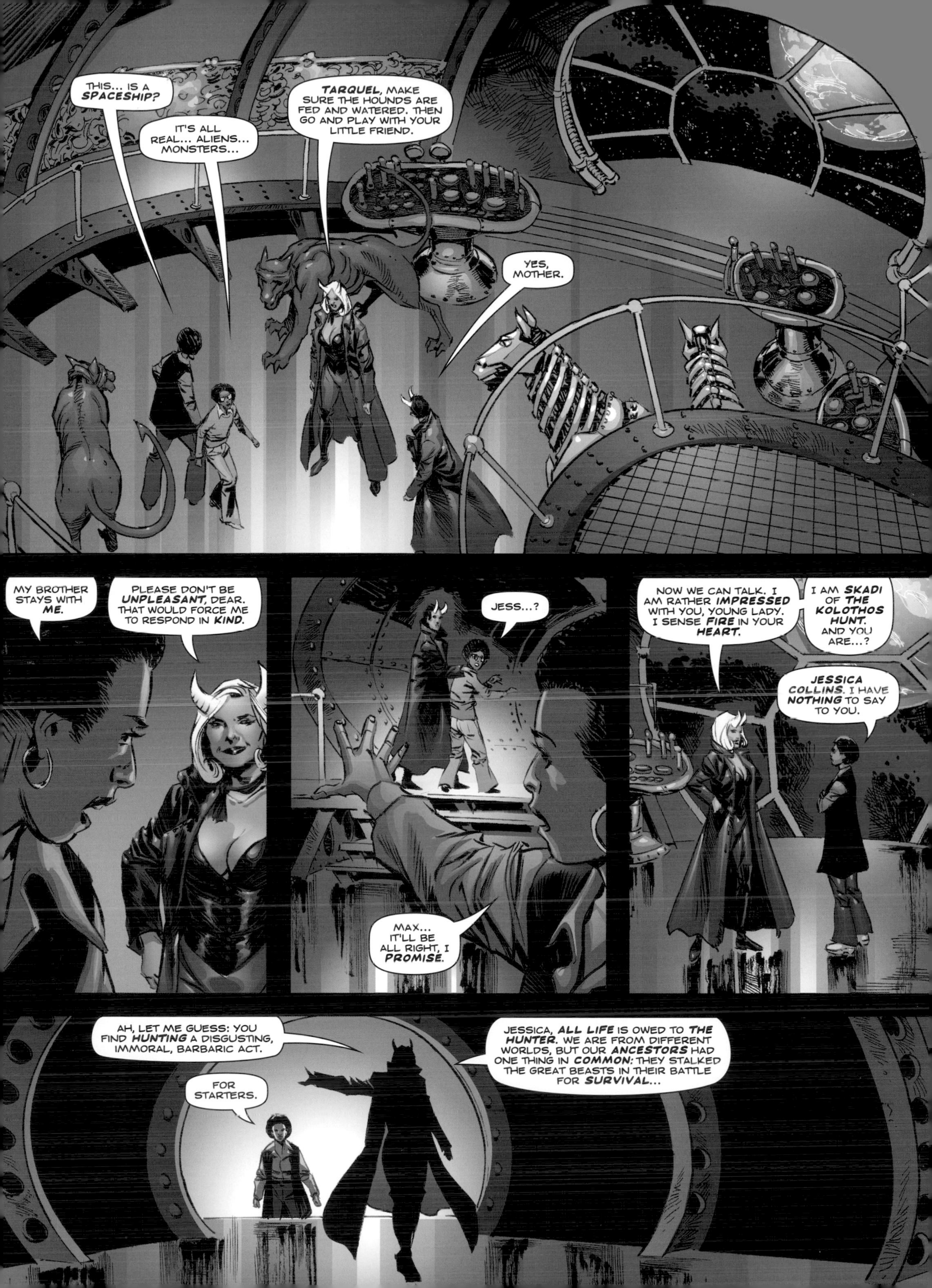
THIS... IS A SPACESHIP?
IT'S ALL REAL... ALIENS... MONSTERS...
TARQUEL, MAKE SURE THE HOUNDS ARE FED AND WATERED. THEN GO AND PLAY WITH YOUR LITTLE FRIEND.
YES, MOTHER.
MY BROTHER STAYS WITH ME.
PLEASE DON'T BE UNPLEASANT, DEAR. THAT WOULD FORCE ME TO RESPOND IN KIND.
JESS...?
MAX... IT'LL BE ALL RIGHT, I PROMISE.
NOW WE CAN TALK. I AM RATHER IMPRESSED WITH YOU, YOUNG LADY. I SENSE FIRE IN YOUR HEART.
I AM SKADI OF THE KOLOTHOS HUNT. AND YOU ARE...?
JESSICA COLLINS. I HAVE NOTHING TO SAY TO YOU.
AH, LET ME GUESS: YOU FIND HUNTING A DISGUSTING, IMMORAL, BARBARIC ACT.
FOR STARTERS.
JESSICA, ALL LIFE IS OWED TO THE HUNTER. WE ARE FROM DIFFERENT WORLDS, BUT OUR ANCESTORS HAD ONE THING IN COMMON: THEY STALKED THE GREAT BEASTS IN THEIR BATTLE FOR SURVIVAL...

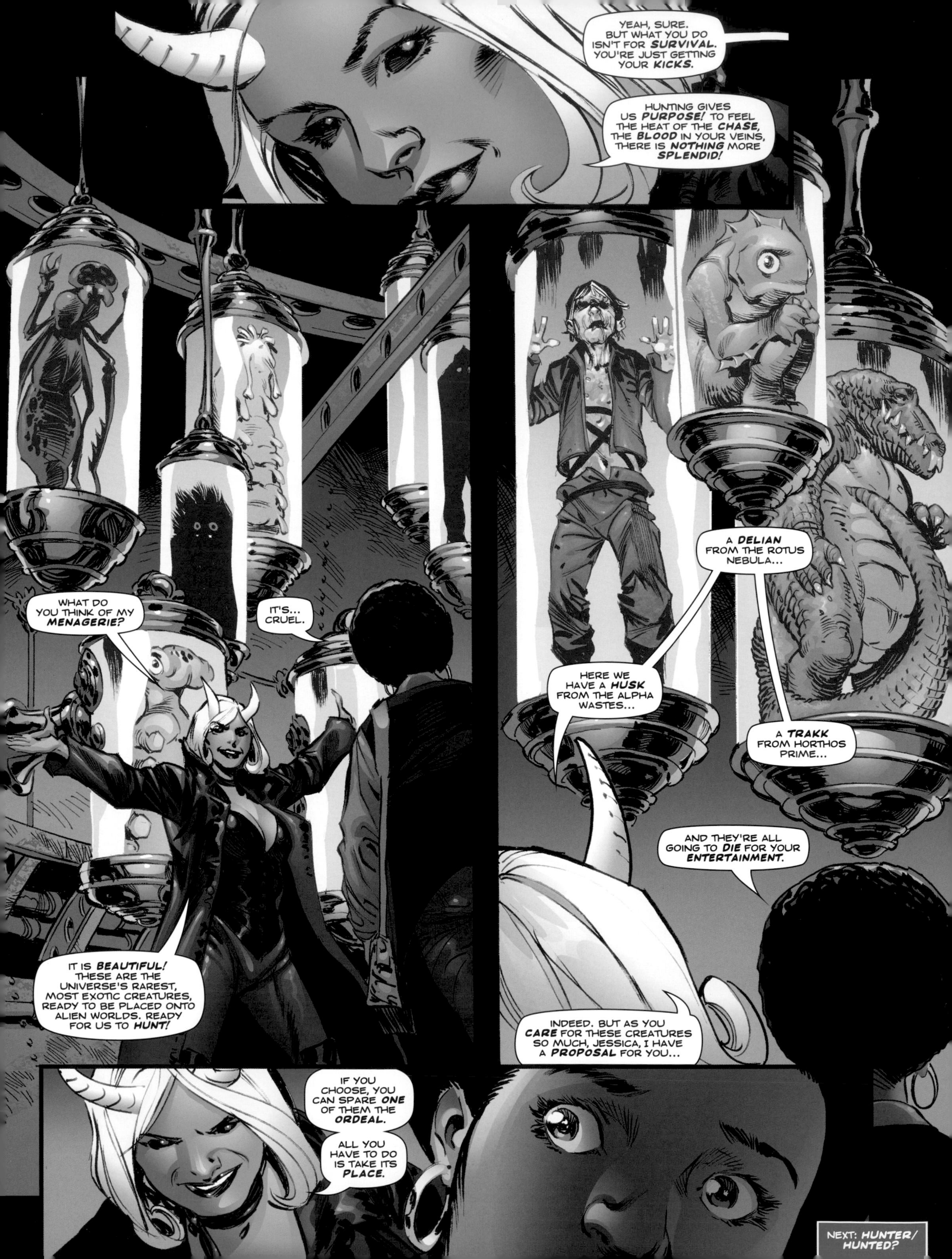
YEAH, SURE. BUT WHAT YOU DO ISN'T FOR SURVIVAL. YOU'RE JUST GETTING YOUR KICKS.
HUNTING GIVES US PURPOSE! TO FEEL THE HEAT OF THE CHASE, THE BLOOD IN YOUR VEINS, THERE IS NOTHING MORE SPLENDID!
WHAT DO YOU THINK OF MY MENAGERIE?
IT'S... CRUEL.
IT IS BEAUTIFUL! THESE ARE THE UNIVERSE'S RAREST, MOST EXOTIC CREATURES, READY TO BE PLACED ONTO ALIEN WORLDS. READY FOR US TO HUNT!
HERE WE HAVE A HUSK FROM THE ALPHA WASTES...
A DELIAN FROM THE ROTUS NEBULA...
A TRAKK FROM HORTHOS PRIME...
AND THEY'RE ALL GOING TO DIE FOR YOUR ENTERTAINMENT.
INDEED. BUT AS YOU CARE FOR THESE CREATURES SO MUCH, JESSICA, I HAVE A PROPOSAL FOR YOU...
IF YOU CHOOSE, YOU CAN SPARE ONE OF THEM THE ORDEAL.
ALL YOU HAVE TO DO IS TAKE ITS PLACE.
NEXT: HUNTER/ HUNTED?

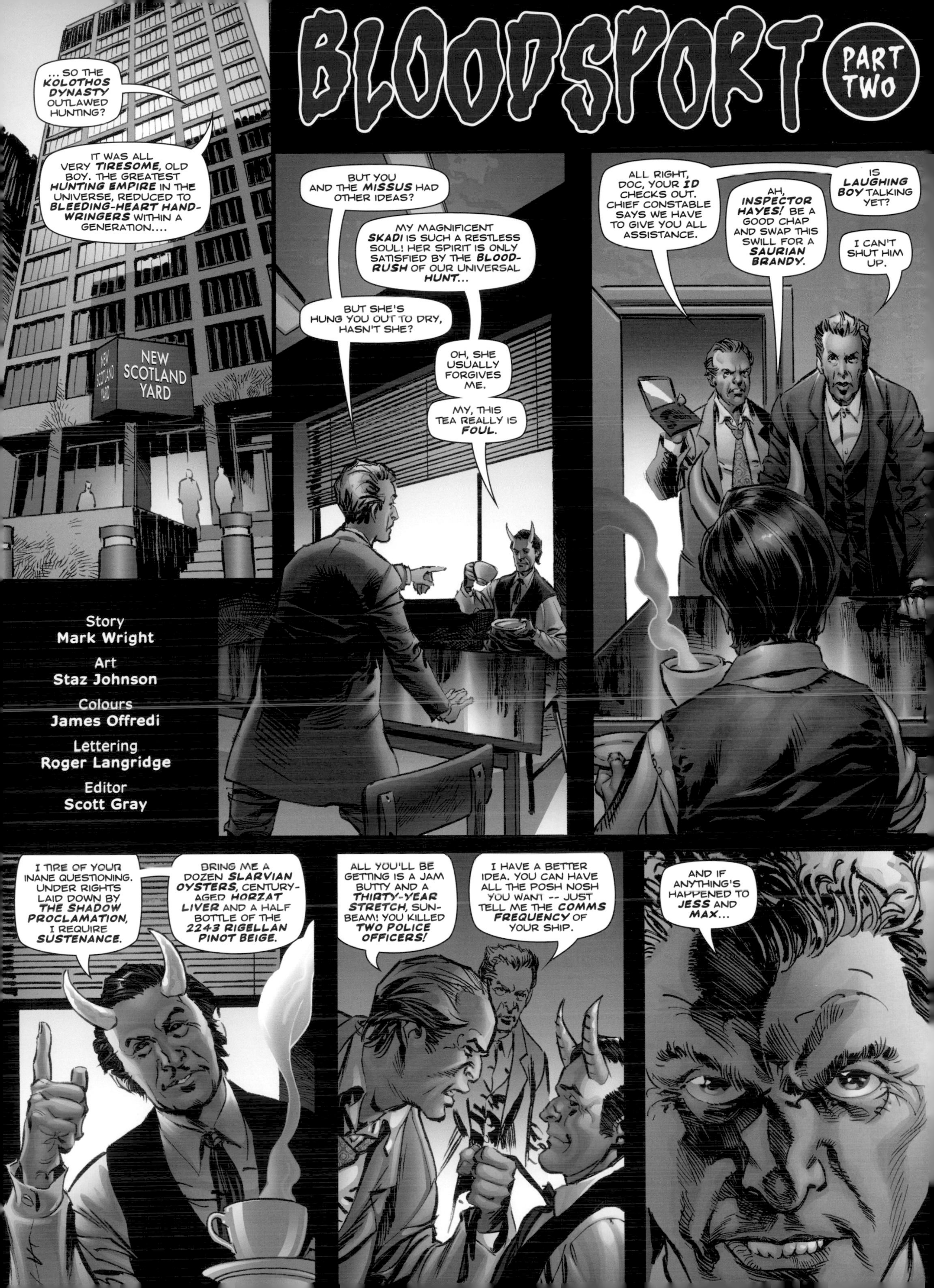
BLOODSPORT
PART TWO
... SO THE KOLOTHOS DYNASTY OUTLAWED HUNTING?
IT WAS ALL VERY TIRESOME, OLD BOY. THE GREATEST HUNTING EMPIRE IN THE UNIVERSE, REDUCED TO BLEEDING-HEART HAND-WRINGERS WITHIN A GENERATION....
NEW SCOTLAND YARD
NEW SCOTLAND YARD
BUT YOU AND THE MISSUS HAD OTHER IDEAS?
MY MAGNIFICENT SKADI IS SUCH A RESTLESS SOUL! HER SPIRIT IS ONLY SATISFIED BY THE BLOOD-RUSH OF OUR UNIVERSAL HUNT...
BUT SHE'S HUNG YOU OUT TO DRY, HASN'T SHE?
OH, SHE USUALLY FORGIVES ME.
MY, THIS TEA REALLY IS FOUL.
ALL RIGHT, DOC, YOUR ID CHECKS OUT. CHIEF CONSTABLE SAYS WE HAVE TO GIVE YOU ALL ASSISTANCE.
AH, INSPECTOR HAYES! BE A GOOD CHAP AND SWAP THIS SWILL FOR A SAURIAN BRANDY.
IS LAUGHING BOY TALKING YET?
I CAN'T SHUT HIM UP.
Story
Mark Wright
Art
Staz Johnson
Colours
James Offredi
Lettering
Roger Langridge
Editor
Scott Gray
I TIRE OF YOUR INANE QUESTIONING. UNDER RIGHTS LAID DOWN BY THE SHADOW PROCLAMATION, I REQUIRE SUSTENANCE.
BRING ME A DOZEN SLARVIAN OYSTERS, CENTURY-AGED HORZAT LIVER AND A HALF BOTTLE OF THE 2243 RIGELLAN PINOT BEIGE.
ALL YOU'LL BE GETTING IS A JAM BUTTY AND A THIRTY-YEAR STRETCH, SUN-BEAM! YOU KILLED TWO POLICE OFFICERS!
I HAVE A BETTER IDEA. YOU CAN HAVE ALL THE POSH NOSH YOU WANT -- JUST TELL ME THE COMMS FREQUENCY OF YOUR SHIP.
AND IF ANYTHING'S HAPPENED TO JESS AND MAX...

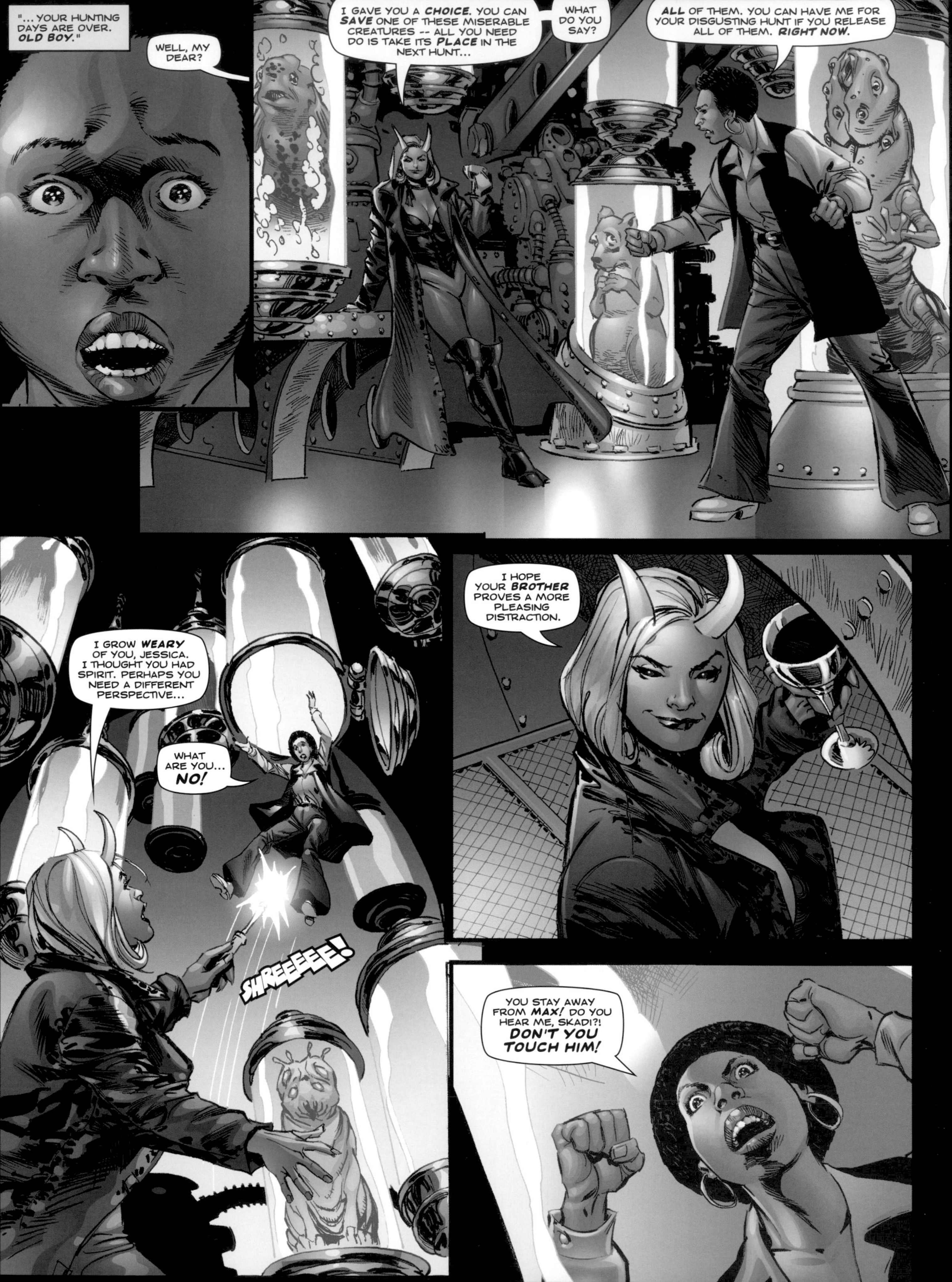
"... YOUR HUNTING DAYS ARE OVER. OLD BOY."
WELL, MY DEAR?
I GAVE YOU A CHOICE. YOU CAN SAVE ONE OF THESE MISERABLE CREATURES -- ALL YOU NEED DO IS TAKE ITS PLACE IN THE NEXT HUNT...
WHAT DO YOU SAY?
ALL OF THEM. YOU CAN HAVE ME FOR YOUR DISGUSTING HUNT IF YOU RELEASE ALL OF THEM. RIGHT NOW.
I GROW WEARY OF YOU, JESSICA. I THOUGHT YOU HAD SPIRIT. PERHAPS YOU NEED A DIFFERENT PERSPECTIVE...
WHAT ARE YOU... NO!
SHREEEEE!
I HOPE YOUR BROTHER PROVES A MORE PLEASING DISTRACTION.
YOU STAY AWAY FROM MAX! DO YOU HEAR ME, SKADI?! DON'T YOU TOUCH HIM!

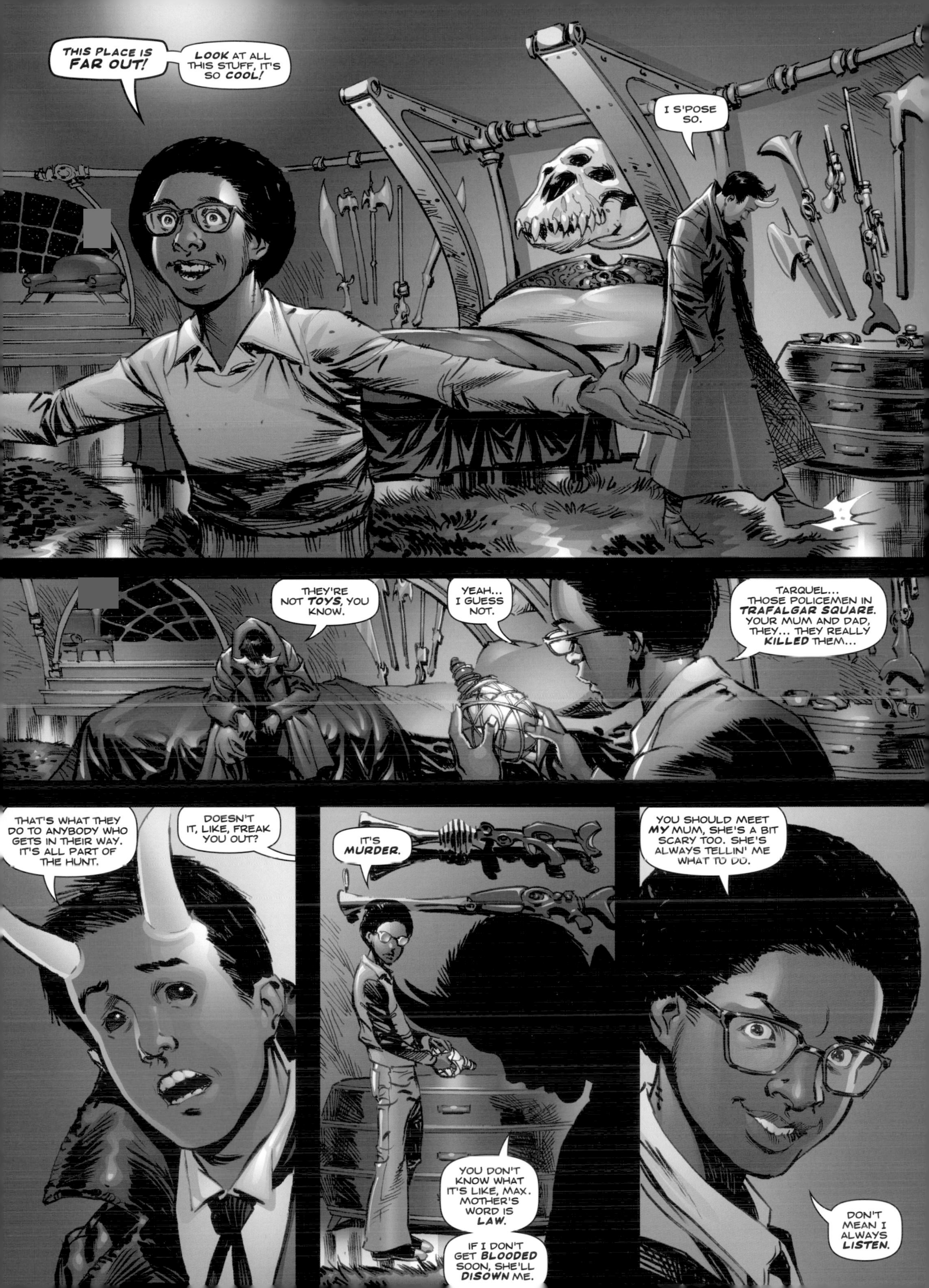
THIS PLACE IS FAR OUT!
LOOK AT ALL THIS STUFF, IT'S SO COOL!
I S'POSE SO.
THEY'RE NOT TOYS, YOU KNOW.
YEAH... I GUESS NOT.
TARQUEL... THOSE POLICEMEN IN TRAFALGAR SQUARE. YOUR MUM AND DAD, THEY... THEY REALLY KILLED THEM...
THAT'S WHAT THEY DO TO ANYBODY WHO GETS IN THEIR WAY. IT'S ALL PART OF THE HUNT.
DOESN'T IT, LIKE, FREAK YOU OUT?
IT'S MURDER.
YOU DON'T KNOW WHAT IT'S LIKE, MAX. MOTHER'S WORD IS LAW.
IF I DON'T GET BLOODED SOON, SHE'LL DISOWN ME.
YOU SHOULD MEET MY MUM, SHE'S A BIT SCARY TOO. SHE'S ALWAYS TELLIN' ME WHAT TO DO.
DON'T MEAN I ALWAYS LISTEN.

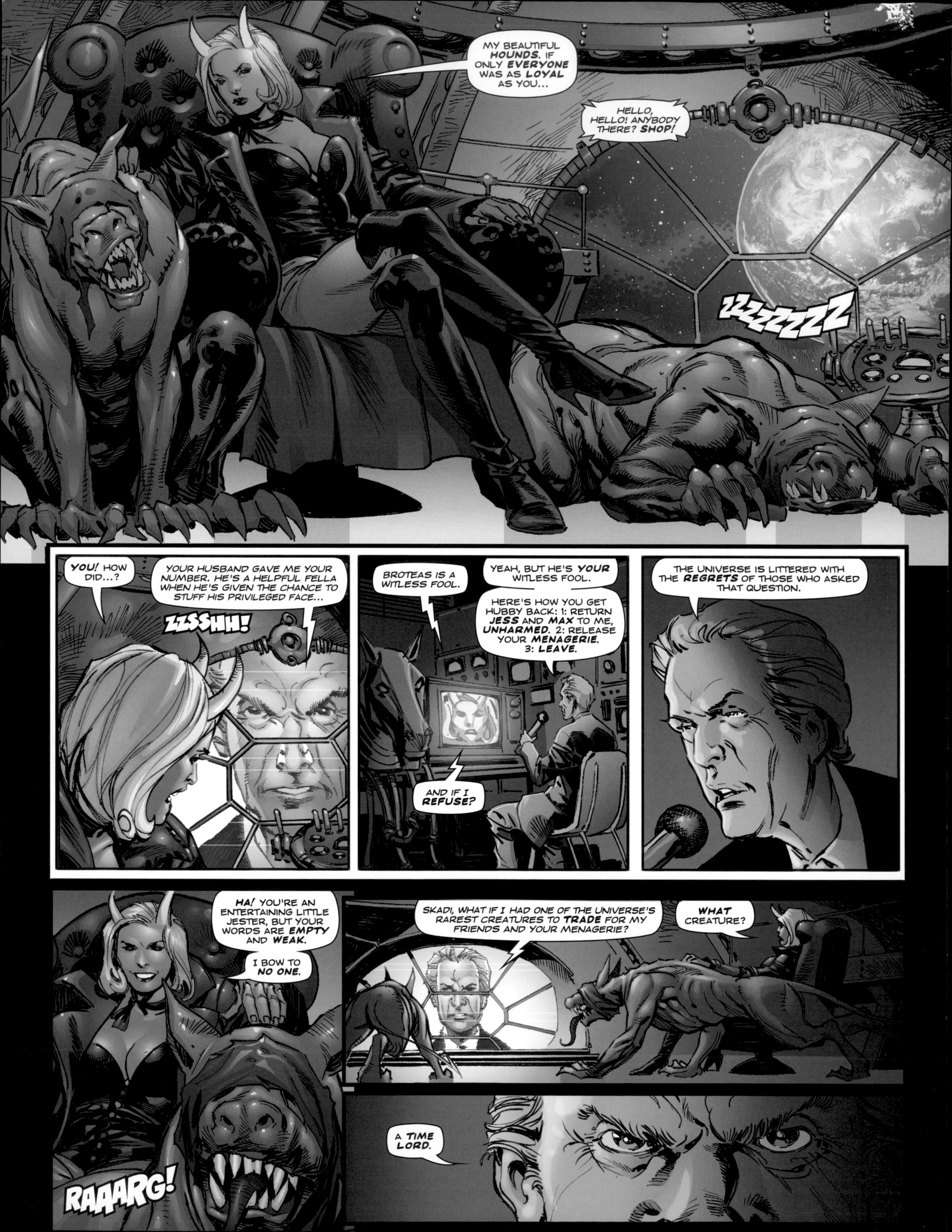
MY BEAUTIFUL HOUNDS. IF ONLY EVERYONE WAS AS LOYAL AS YOU...
HELLO, HELLO! ANYBODY THERE? SHOP!
ZZZZZZZZ
YOU! HOW DID...?
YOUR HUSBAND GAVE ME YOUR NUMBER. HE'S A HELPFUL FELLA WHEN HE'S GIVEN THE CHANCE TO STUFF HIS PRIVILEGED FACE...
ZZSSHH!
BROTEAS IS A WITLESS FOOL.
YEAH, BUT HE'S YOUR WITLESS FOOL.
HERE'S HOW YOU GET HUBBY BACK: 1: RETURN JESS AND MAX TO ME, UNHARMED. 2: RELEASE YOUR MENAGERIE. 3: LEAVE.
AND IF I REFUSE?
THE UNIVERSE IS LITTERED WITH THE REGRETS OF THOSE WHO ASKED THAT QUESTION.
HA! YOU'RE AN ENTERTAINING LITTLE JESTER, BUT YOUR WORDS ARE EMPTY AND WEAK.
I BOW TO NO ONE.
RAAARG!
SKADI, WHAT IF I HAD ONE OF THE UNIVERSE'S RAREST CREATURES TO TRADE FOR MY FRIENDS AND YOUR MENAGERIE?
WHAT CREATURE?
A TIME LORD.

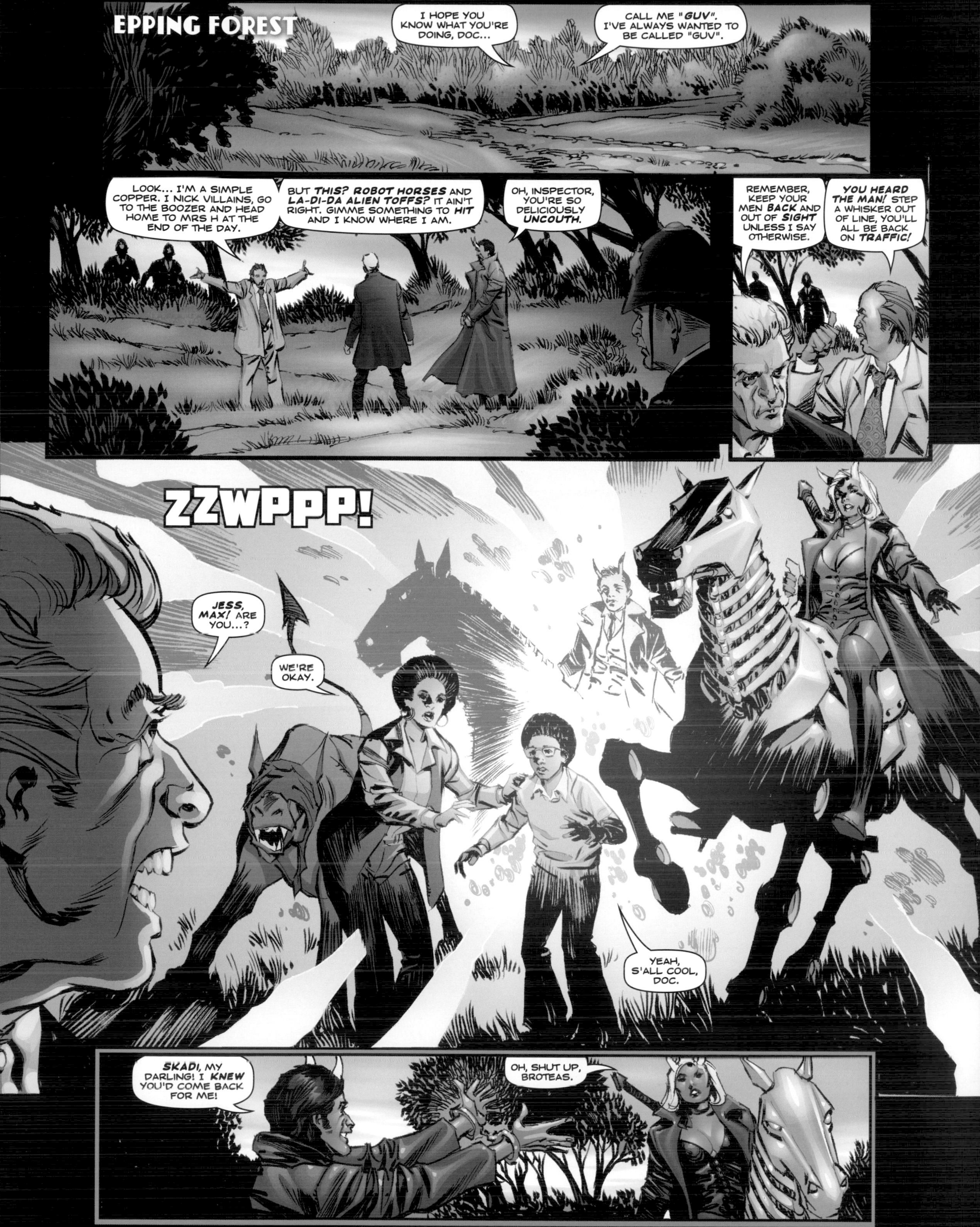
EPPING FOREST
I HOPE YOU KNOW WHAT YOU'RE DOING, DOC...
CALL ME "GUV". I'VE ALWAYS WANTED TO BE CALLED "GUV".
LOOK... I'M A SIMPLE COPPER. I NICK VILLAINS, GO TO THE BOOZER AND HEAD HOME TO MRS H AT THE END OF THE DAY.
BUT THIS? ROBOT HORSES AND LA-DI-DA ALIEN TOFFS? IT AIN'T RIGHT. GIMME SOMETHING TO HIT AND I KNOW WHERE I AM.
OH, INSPECTOR, YOU'RE SO DELICIOUSLY UNCOUTH.
REMEMBER, KEEP YOUR MEN BACK AND OUT OF SIGHT UNLESS I SAY OTHERWISE.
YOU HEARD THE MAN! STEP A WHISKER OUT OF LINE, YOU'LL ALL BE BACK ON TRAFFIC!
ZZWPPPP!
JESS, MAX! ARE YOU...?
WE'RE OKAY.
YEAH, S'ALL COOL, DOC.
SKADI, MY DARLING! I KNEW YOU'D COME BACK FOR ME!
OH, SHUT UP, BROTEAS.

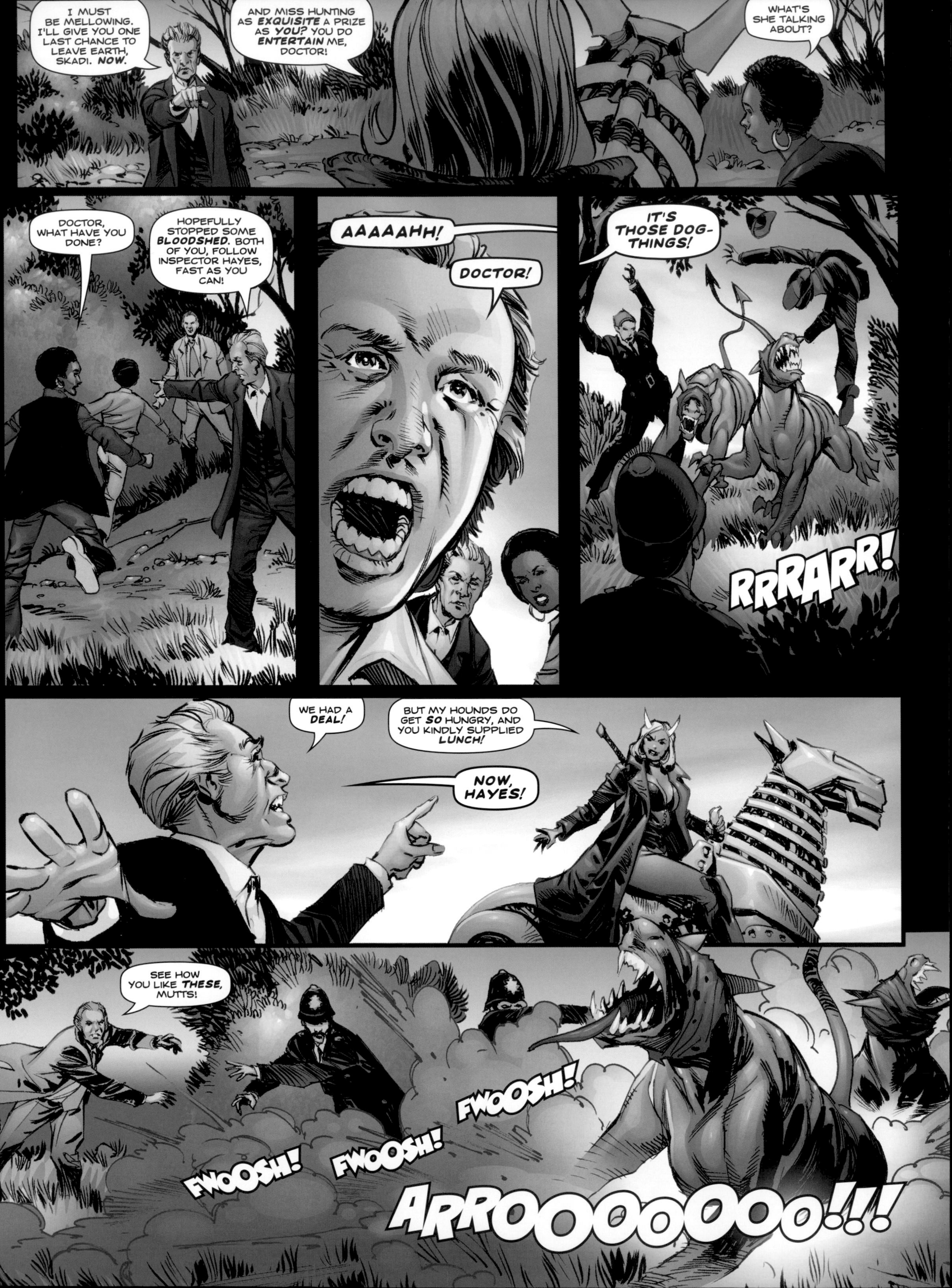
I MUST BE MELLOWING. I'LL GIVE YOU ONE LAST CHANCE TO LEAVE EARTH, SKADI. NOW.
AND MISS HUNTING AS EXQUISITE A PRIZE AS YOU? YOU DO ENTERTAIN ME, DOCTOR!
WHAT'S SHE TALKING ABOUT?
DOCTOR, WHAT HAVE YOU DONE?
HOPEFULLY STOPPED SOME BLOODSHED. BOTH OF YOU, FOLLOW INSPECTOR HAYES, FAST AS YOU CAN!
AAAAAHH!
DOCTOR!
IT'S THOSE DOG-THINGS!
RRRARR!
WE HAD A DEAL!
BUT MY HOUNDS DO GET SO HUNGRY, AND YOU KINDLY SUPPLIED LUNCH!
NOW, HAYES!
SEE HOW YOU LIKE THESE, MUTTS!
FWOOSH!
FWOOSH!
FWOOSH!
ARROOOOOOOO!!!

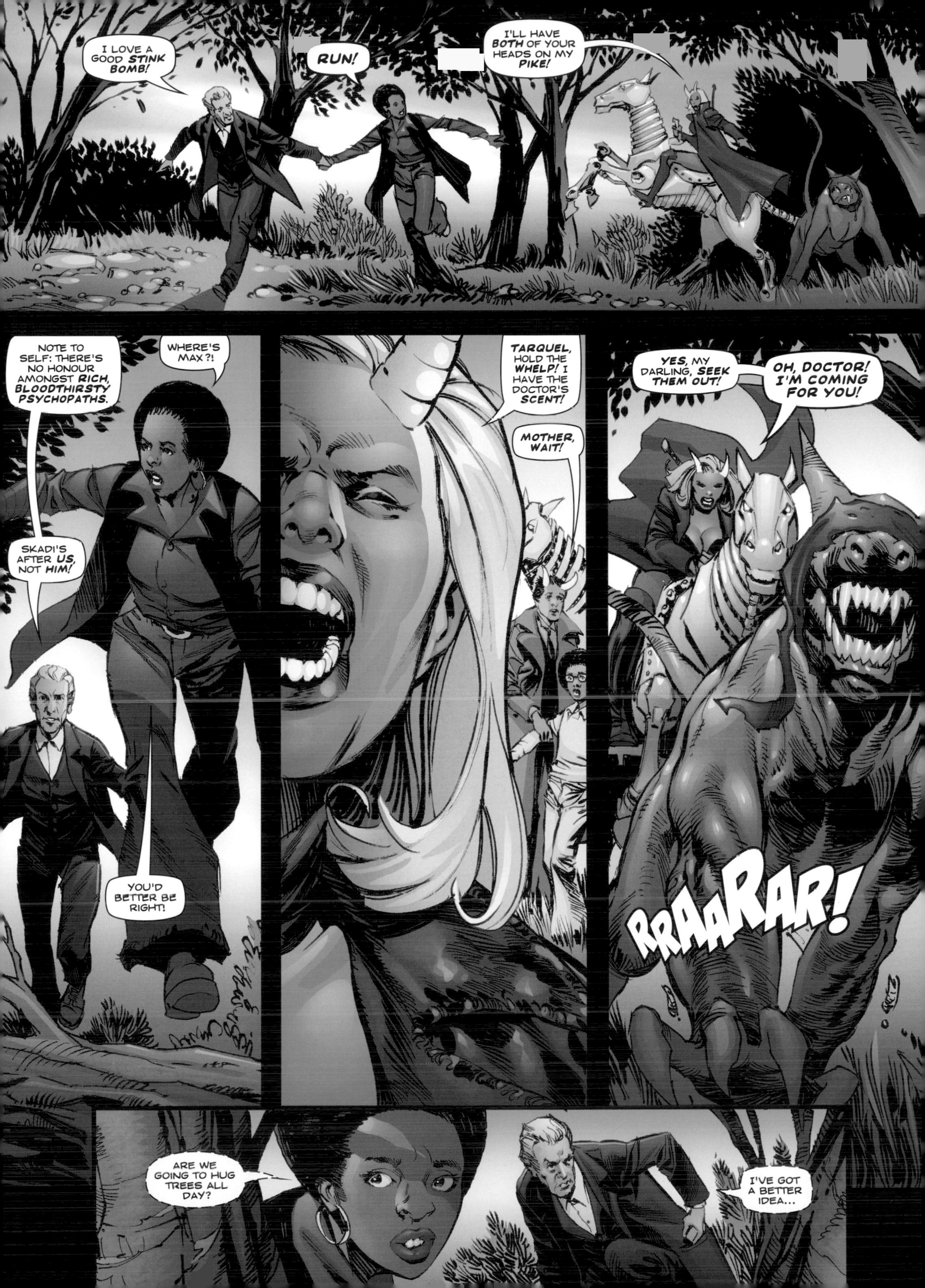
I LOVE A GOOD STINK BOMB!
RUN!
I'LL HAVE BOTH OF YOUR HEADS ON MY PIKE!
NOTE TO SELF: THERE'S NO HONOUR AMONGST RICH, BLOODTHIRSTY PSYCHOPATHS.
WHERE'S MAX?!
SKADI'S AFTER US, NOT HIM!
YOU'D BETTER BE RIGHT!
TARQUEL, HOLD THE WHELP! I HAVE THE DOCTOR'S SCENT!
MOTHER, WAIT!
YES, MY DARLING, SEEK THEM OUT!
OH, DOCTOR! I'M COMING FOR YOU!
RRAARAR!
ARE WE GOING TO HUG TREES ALL DAY?
I'VE GOT A BETTER IDEA...

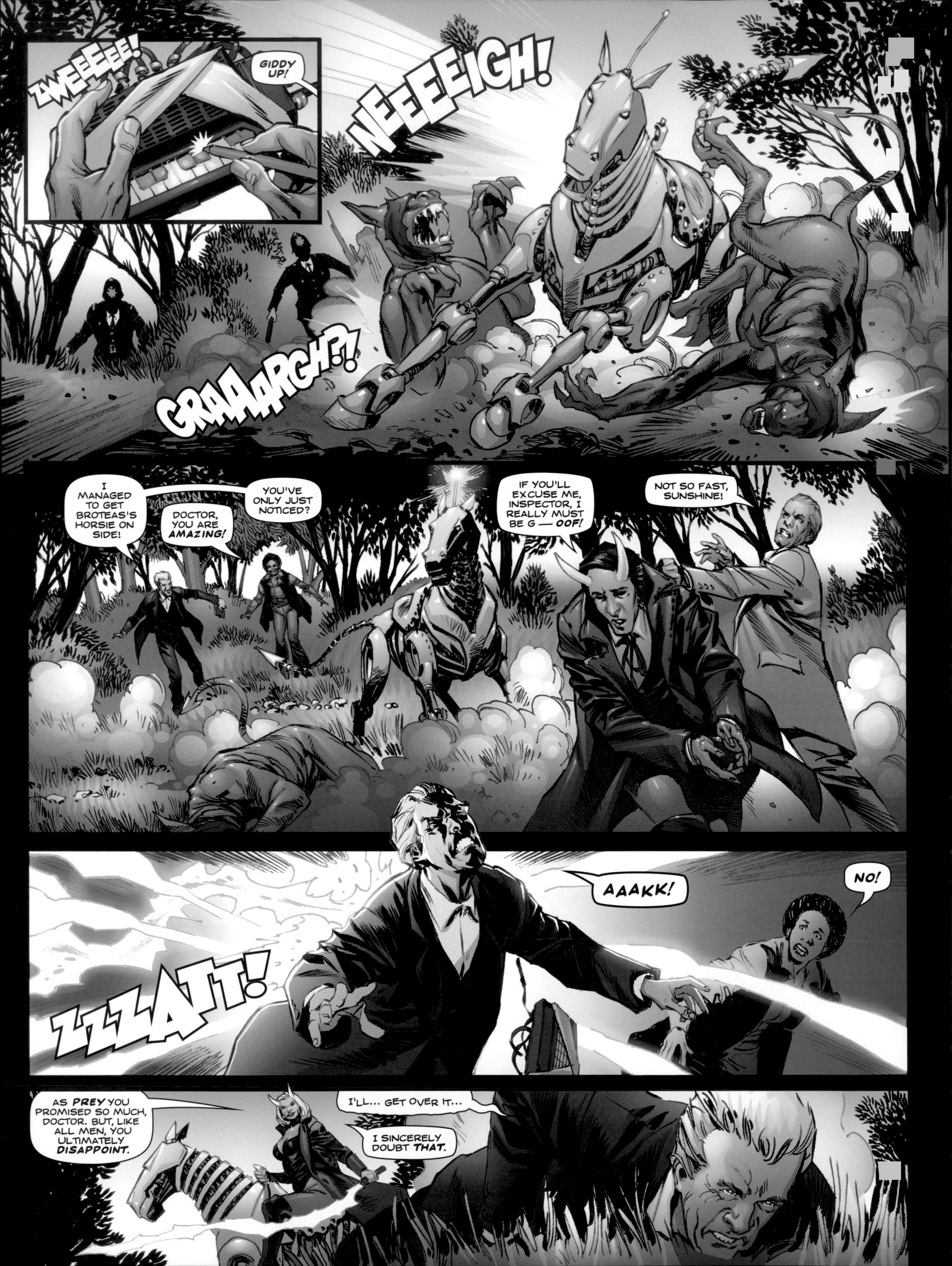

ZWEEEEE!
GIDDY UP!
NEEEEIGH!
GRAAARGH?!
I MANAGED TO GET BROTEAS'S HORSIE ON SIDE!
YOU'VE ONLY JUST NOTICED?
DOCTOR, YOU ARE AMAZING!
IF YOU'LL EXCUSE ME, INSPECTOR, I REALLY MUST BE G — OOF!
NOT SO FAST, SUNSHINE!
AAAKK!
NO!
ZZZATT!
AS PREY YOU PROMISED SO MUCH, DOCTOR. BUT, LIKE ALL MEN, YOU ULTIMATELY DISAPPOINT.
I'LL... GET OVER IT...
I SINCERELY DOUBT THAT.

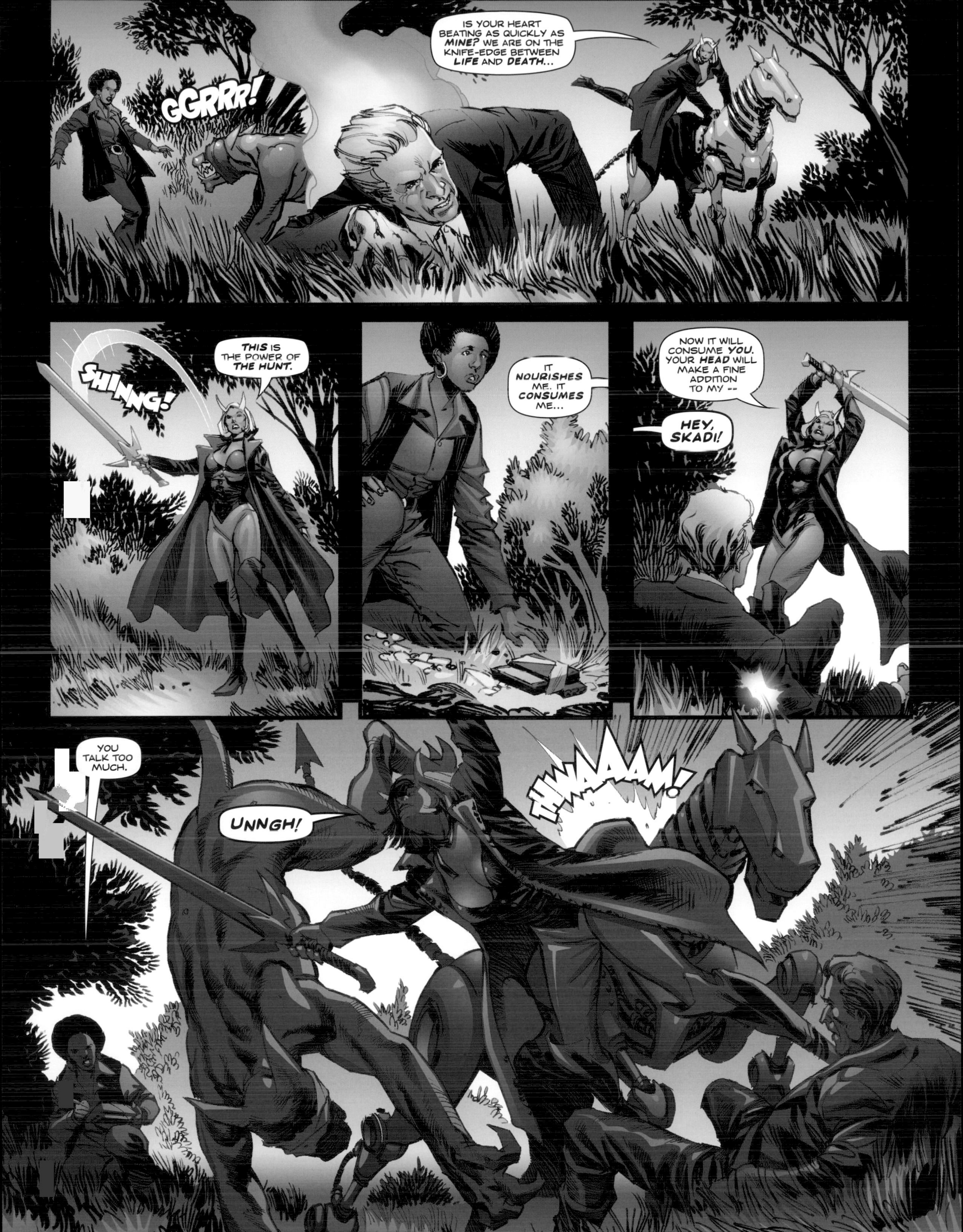
IS YOUR HEART BEATING AS QUICKLY AS MINE? WE ARE ON THE KNIFE-EDGE BETWEEN LIFE AND DEATH...
GGRRR!
SHINNG!
THIS IS THE POWER OF THE HUNT.
IT NOURISHES ME. IT CONSUMES ME...
NOW IT WILL CONSUME YOU. YOUR HEAD WILL MAKE A FINE ADDITION TO MY --
HEY, SKADI!
YOU TALK TOO MUCH.
THWAAAM!
UNNGH!

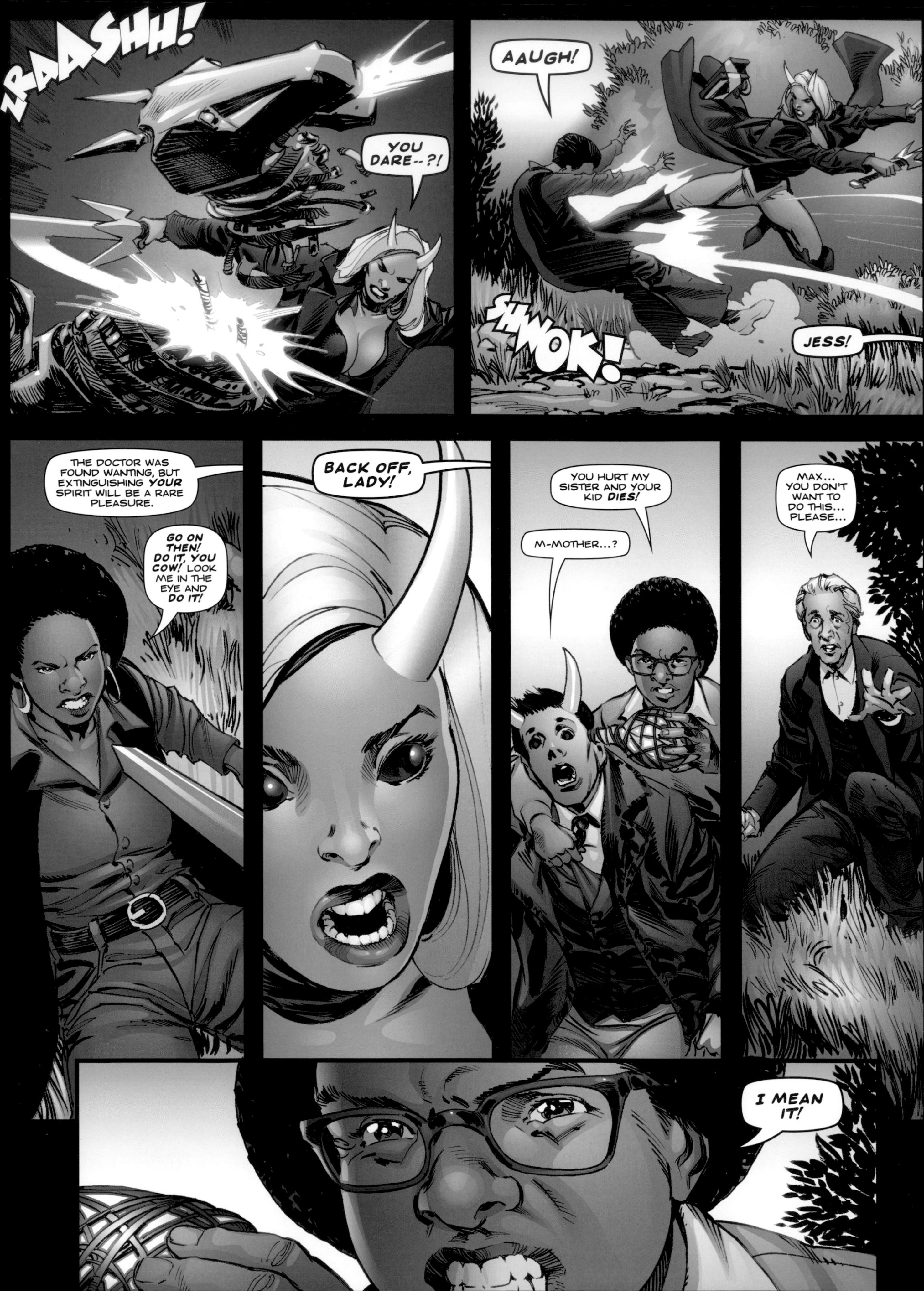
ZRAASHH!
YOU DARE--?!
AAUGH!
SHWOK!
JESS!
THE DOCTOR WAS FOUND WANTING, BUT EXTINGUISHING YOUR SPIRIT WILL BE A RARE PLEASURE.
GO ON THEN! DO IT, YOU COW! LOOK ME IN THE EYE AND DO IT!
BACK OFF, LADY!
YOU HURT MY SISTER AND YOUR KID DIES!
M-MOTHER...?
MAX... YOU DON'T WANT TO DO THIS... PLEASE...
I MEAN IT!

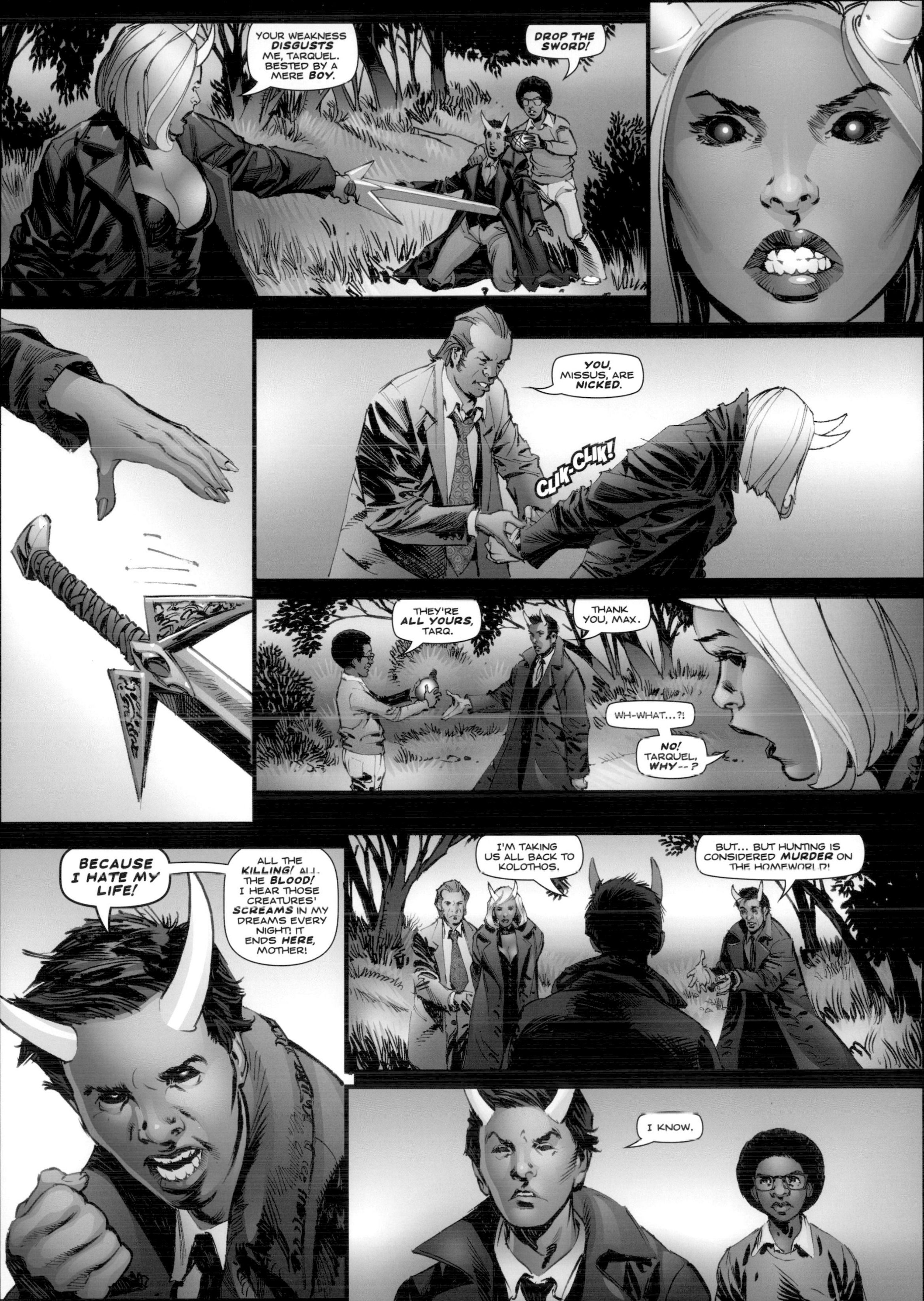
YOUR WEAKNESS DISGUSTS ME, TARQUEL. BESTED BY A MERE BOY.
DROP THE SWORD!
YOU, MISSUS, ARE NICKED.
CLIK-CLIK!
THEY'RE ALL YOURS, TARQ.
THANK YOU, MAX.
WH-WHAT...?!
NO! TARQUEL, WHY--?
BECAUSE I HATE MY LIFE!
ALL THE KILLING! ALL THE BLOOD! I HEAR THOSE CREATURES' SCREAMS IN MY DREAMS EVERY NIGHT! IT ENDS HERE, MOTHER!
I'M TAKING US ALL BACK TO KOLOTHOS.
BUT... BUT HUNTING IS CONSIDERED MURDER ON THE HOMEWORLD!
I KNOW.

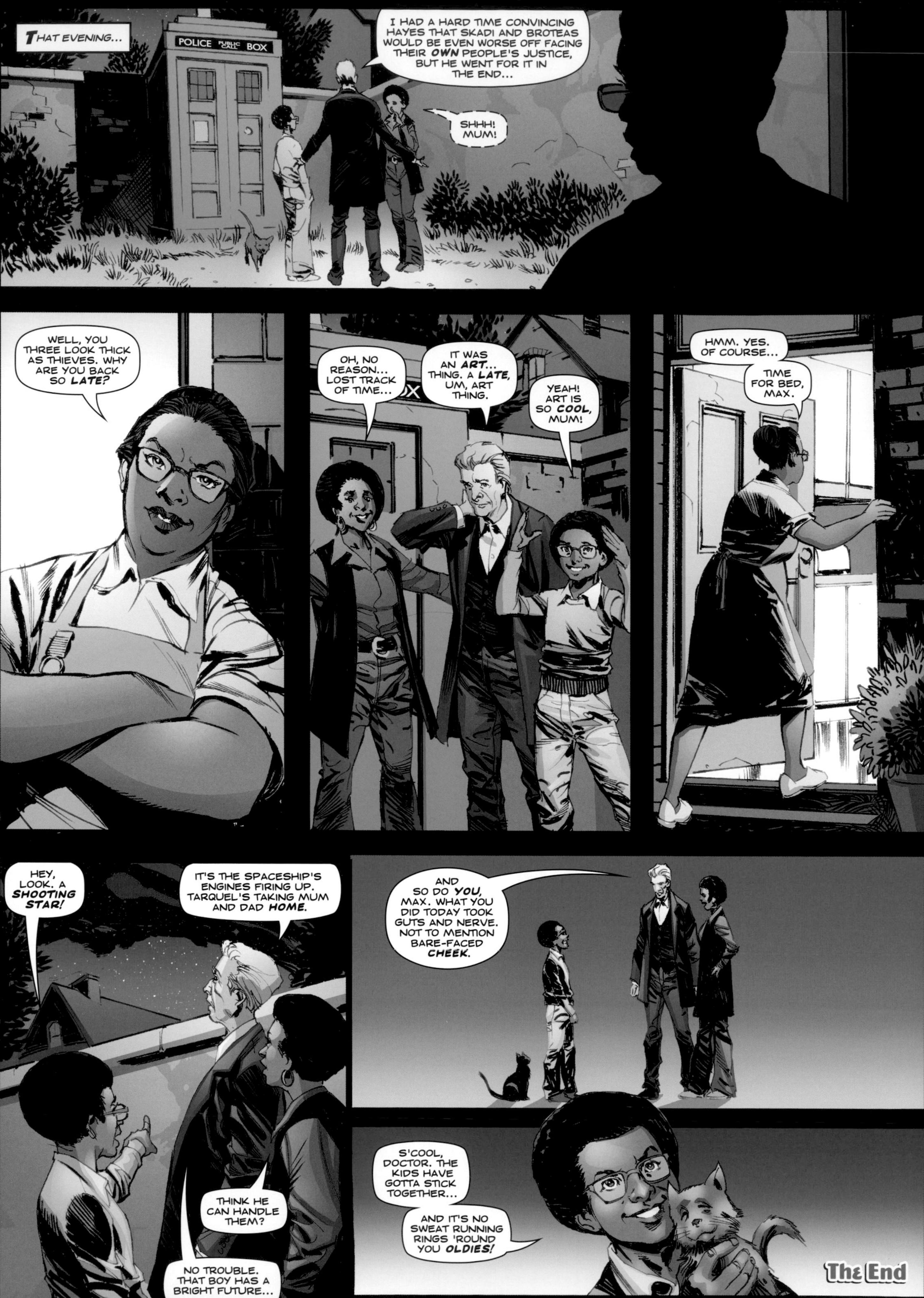
THAT EVENING...
POLICE PUBLIC CALL BOX
I HAD A HARD TIME CONVINCING HAYES THAT SKADI AND BROTEAS WOULD BE EVEN WORSE OFF FACING THEIR OWN PEOPLE'S JUSTICE, BUT HE WENT FOR IT IN THE END...
SHHH! MUM!
WELL, YOU THREE LOOK THICK AS THIEVES. WHY ARE YOU BACK SO LATE?
OH, NO REASON... LOST TRACK OF TIME...
IT WAS AN ART... THING. A LATE, UM, ART THING.
YEAH! ART IS SO COOL, MUM!
HMM. YES. OF COURSE...
TIME FOR BED, MAX.
HEY, LOOK. A SHOOTING STAR!
IT'S THE SPACESHIP'S ENGINES FIRING UP. TARQUEL'S TAKING MUM AND DAD HOME.
THINK HE CAN HANDLE THEM?
NO TROUBLE. THAT BOY HAS A BRIGHT FUTURE...
AND SO DO YOU, MAX. WHAT YOU DID TODAY TOOK GUTS AND NERVE. NOT TO MENTION BARE-FACED CHEEK.
S'COOL, DOCTOR. THE KIDS HAVE GOTTA STICK TOGETHER...
AND IT'S NO SWEAT RUNNING RINGS 'ROUND YOU OLDIES!
The End

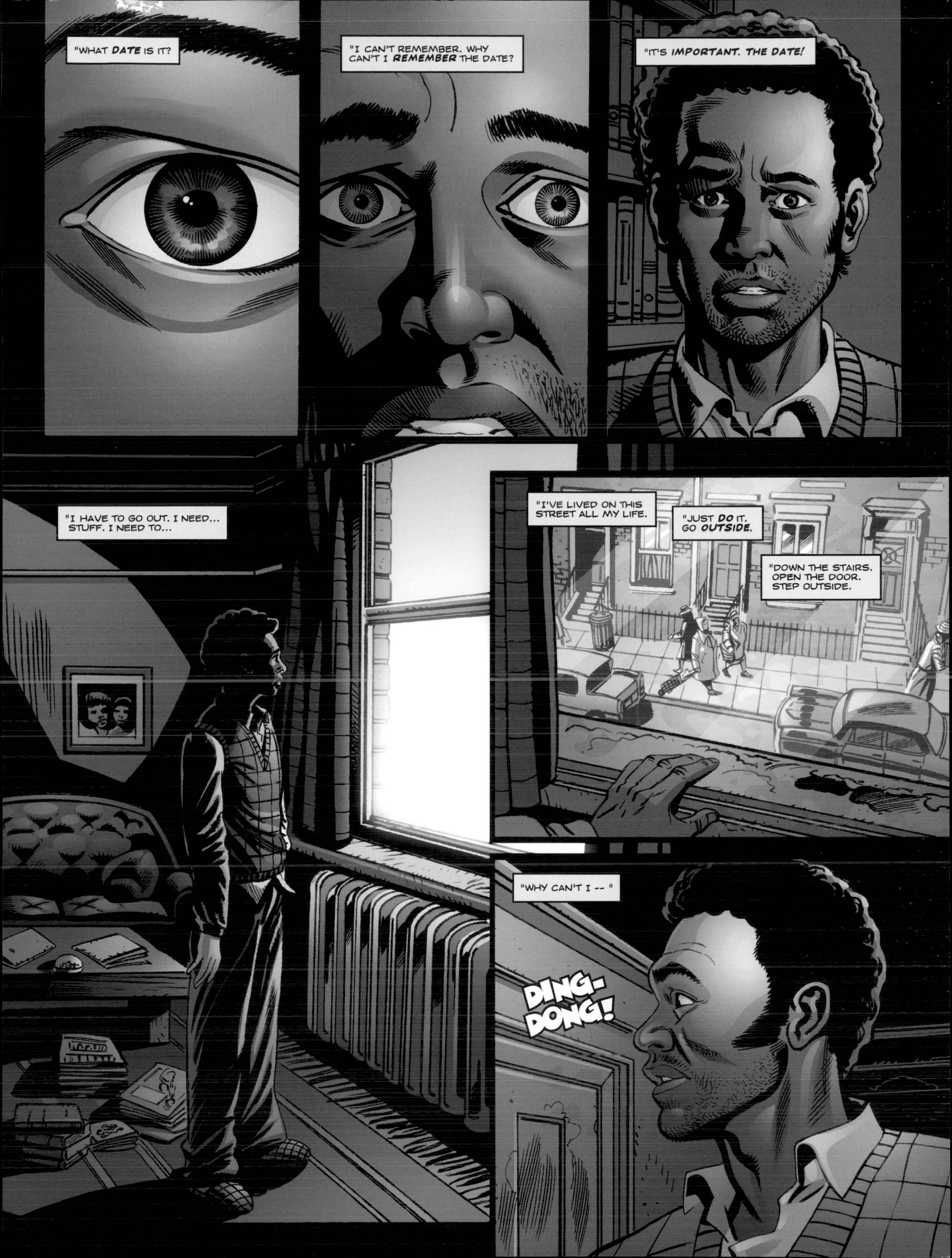
"WHAT DATE IS IT?
"I CAN'T REMEMBER. WHY CAN'T I REMEMBER THE DATE?
"IT'S IMPORTANT. THE DATE!
"I HAVE TO GO OUT. I NEED... STUFF. I NEED TO...
"I'VE LIVED ON THIS STREET ALL MY LIFE.
"JUST DO IT. GO OUTSIDE.
"DOWN THE STAIRS. OPEN THE DOOR. STEP OUTSIDE.
"WHY CAN'T I -- "
DING-DONG!

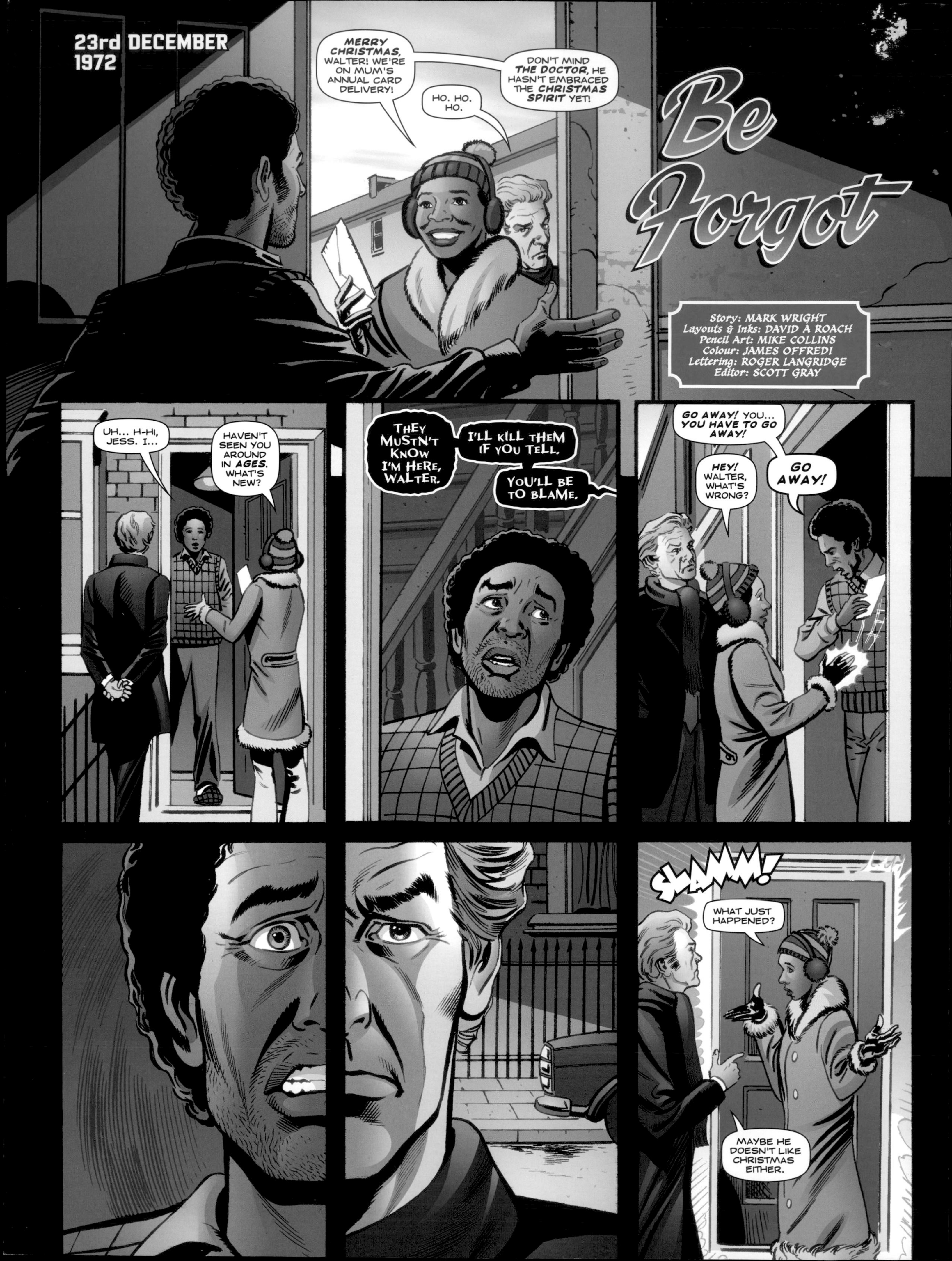

23rd DECEMBER 1972
MERRY CHRISTMAS, WALTER! WE'RE ON MUM'S ANNUAL CARD DELIVERY!
HO. HO. HO.
DON'T MIND THE DOCTOR, HE HASN'T EMBRACED THE CHRISTMAS SPIRIT YET!
Be Forgot
Story: MARK WRIGHT
Layouts & Inks: DAVID A ROACH
Pencil Art: MIKE COLLINS
Colour: JAMES OFFREDI
Lettering: ROGER LANGRIDGE
Editor: SCOTT GRAY
UH... H-HI, JESS. I...
HAVEN'T SEEN YOU AROUND IN AGES. WHAT'S NEW?
THEY MUSTN'T KNOW I'M HERE, WALTER.
I'LL KILL THEM IF YOU TELL.
YOU'LL BE TO BLAME.
GO AWAY! YOU... YOU HAVE TO GO AWAY!
HEY! WALTER, WHAT'S WRONG?
GO AWAY!
SLAMM!
WHAT JUST HAPPENED?
MAYBE HE DOESN'T LIKE CHRISTMAS EITHER.

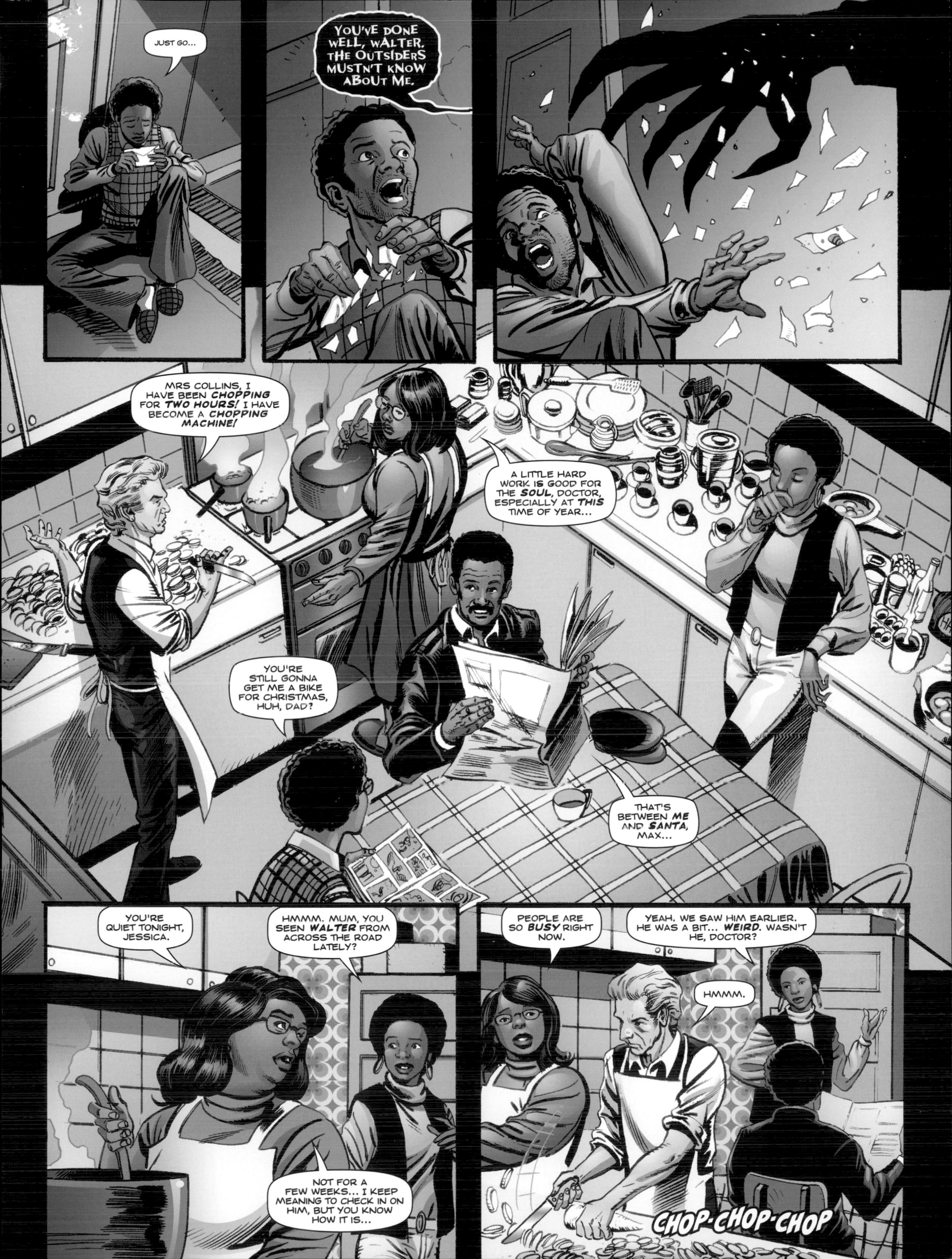
JUST GO...
YOU'VE DONE WELL, WALTER. THE OUTSIDERS MUSTN'T KNOW ABOUT ME.
MRS COLLINS, I HAVE BEEN CHOPPING FOR TWO HOURS! I HAVE BECOME A CHOPPING MACHINE!
A LITTLE HARD WORK IS GOOD FOR THE SOUL, DOCTOR, ESPECIALLY AT THIS TIME OF YEAR...
YOU'RE STILL GONNA GET ME A BIKE FOR CHRISTMAS, HUH, DAD?
THAT'S BETWEEN ME AND SANTA, MAX...
YOU'RE QUIET TONIGHT, JESSICA.
HMMM. MUM, YOU SEEN WALTER FROM ACROSS THE ROAD LATELY?
NOT FOR A FEW WEEKS... I KEEP MEANING TO CHECK IN ON HIM, BUT YOU KNOW HOW IT IS...
PEOPLE ARE SO BUSY RIGHT NOW.
YEAH. WE SAW HIM EARLIER. HE WAS A BIT... WEIRD. WASN'T HE, DOCTOR?
HMMM.
CHOP-CHOP-CHOP

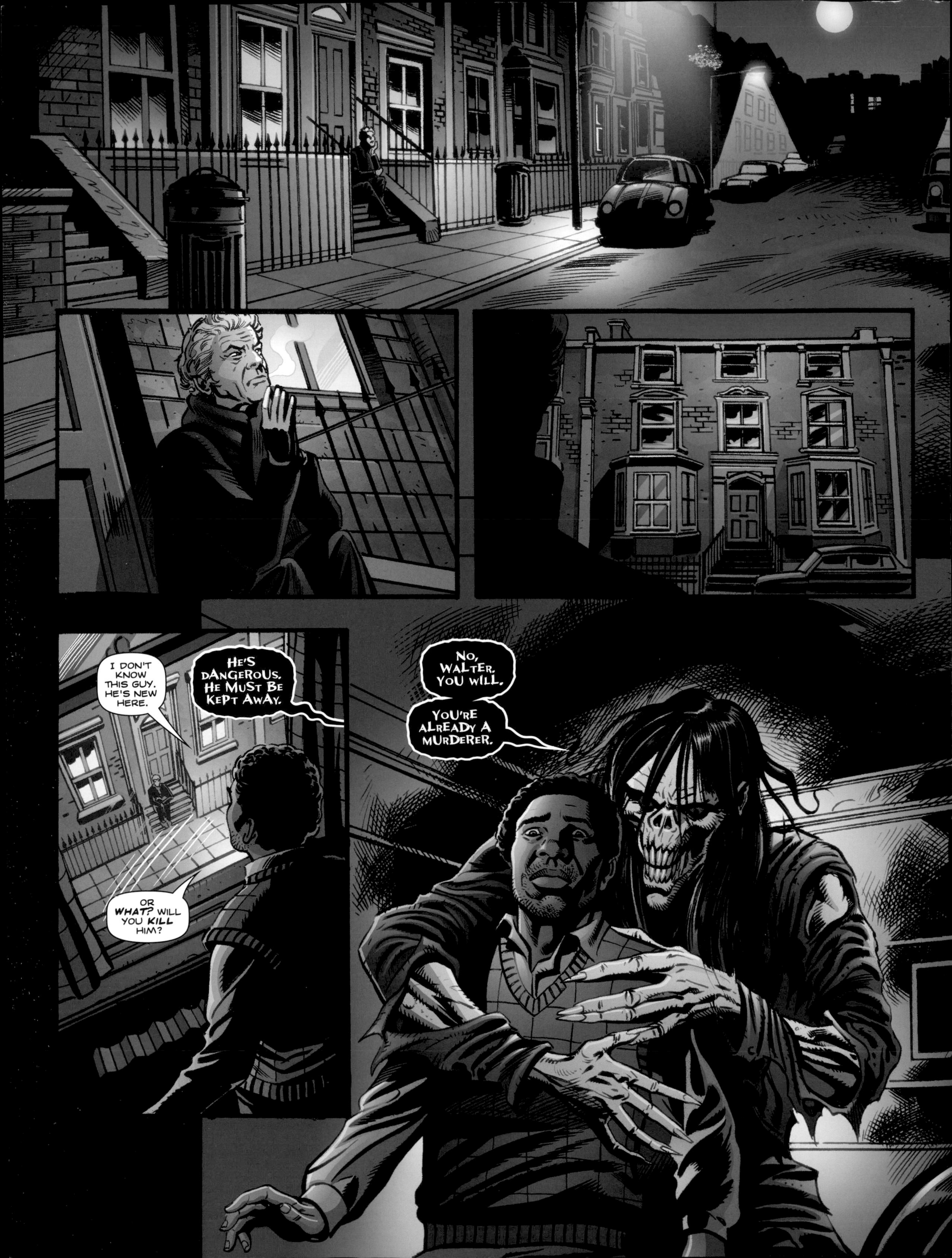
I DON'T KNOW THIS GUY. HE'S NEW HERE.
HE'S DANGEROUS. HE MUST BE KEPT AWAY.
OR WHAT? WILL YOU KILL HIM?
NO, WALTER. YOU WILL.
YOU'RE ALREADY A MURDERER.

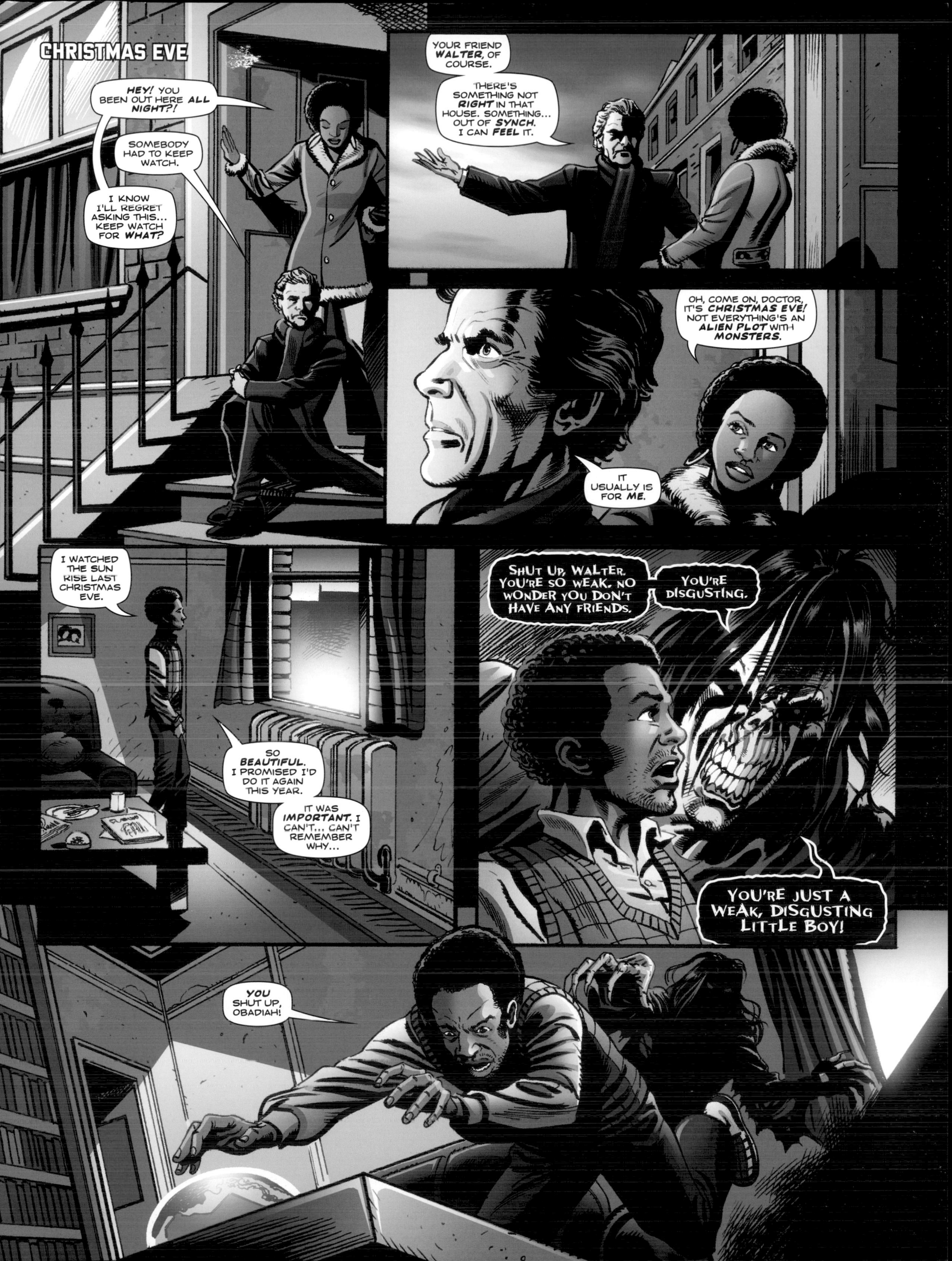
CHRISTMAS EVE
HEY! YOU BEEN OUT HERE ALL NIGHT?!
SOMEBODY HAD TO KEEP WATCH.
I KNOW I'LL REGRET ASKING THIS... KEEP WATCH FOR WHAT?
YOUR FRIEND WALTER, OF COURSE.
THERE'S SOMETHING NOT RIGHT IN THAT HOUSE. SOMETHING... OUT OF SYNCH. I CAN FEEL IT.
OH, COME ON, DOCTOR, IT'S CHRISTMAS EVE! NOT EVERYTHING'S AN ALIEN PLOT WITH MONSTERS.
IT USUALLY IS FOR ME.
I WATCHED THE SUN RISE LAST CHRISTMAS EVE.
SO BEAUTIFUL. I PROMISED I'D DO IT AGAIN THIS YEAR.
IT WAS IMPORTANT. I CAN'T... CAN'T REMEMBER WHY...
SHUT UP, WALTER. YOU'RE SO WEAK. NO WONDER YOU DON'T HAVE ANY FRIENDS.
YOU'RE DISGUSTING.
YOU'RE JUST A WEAK, DISGUSTING LITTLE BOY!
YOU SHUT UP, OBADIAH!

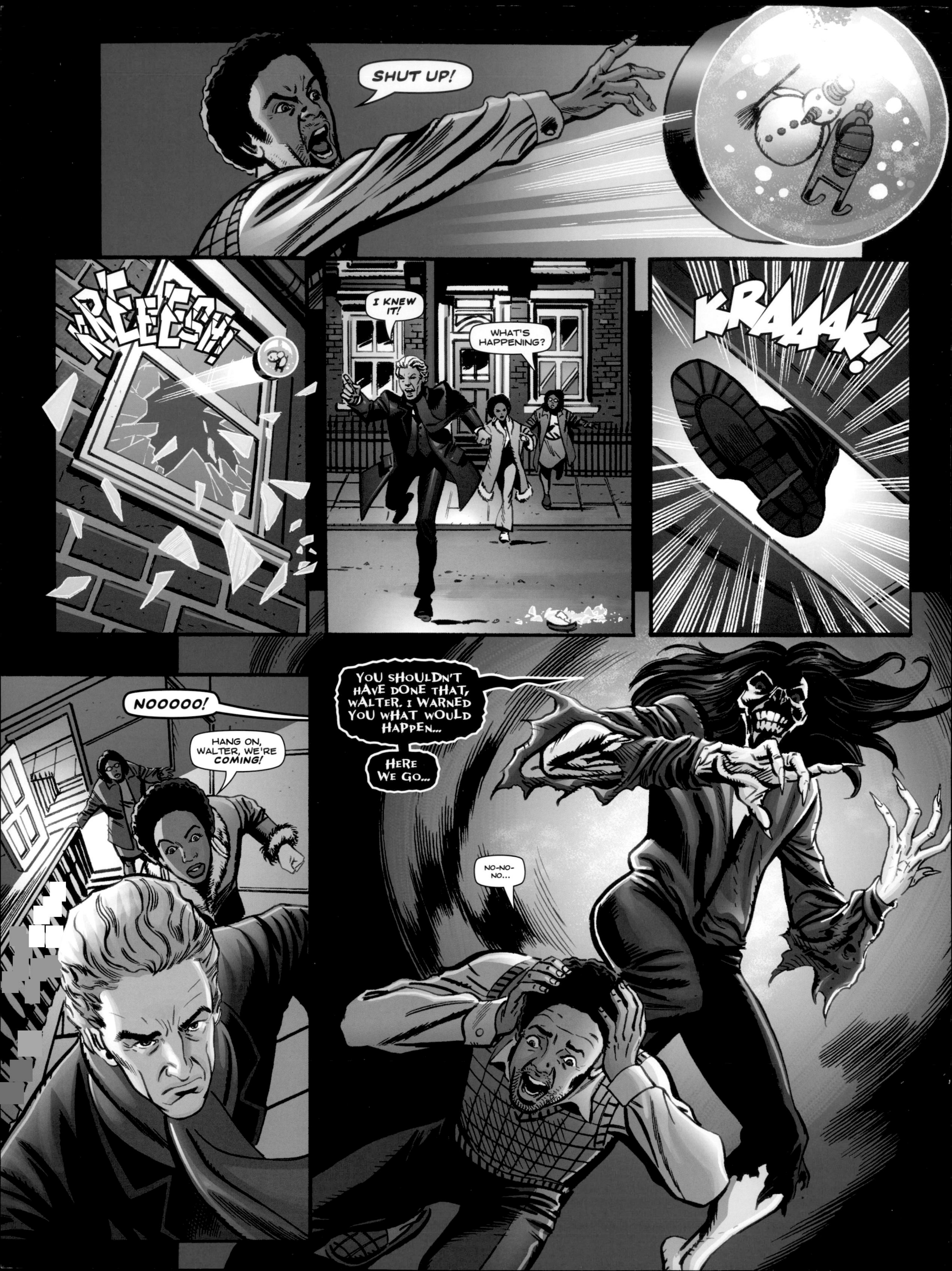

SHUT UP!
KREEESH!
I KNEW IT!
WHAT'S HAPPENING?
KRAAAK!
NOOOOO!
HANG ON, WALTER, WE'RE COMING!
YOU SHOULDN'T HAVE DONE THAT, WALTER. I WARNED YOU WHAT WOULD HAPPEN...
HERE WE GO...
NO-NO-NO...

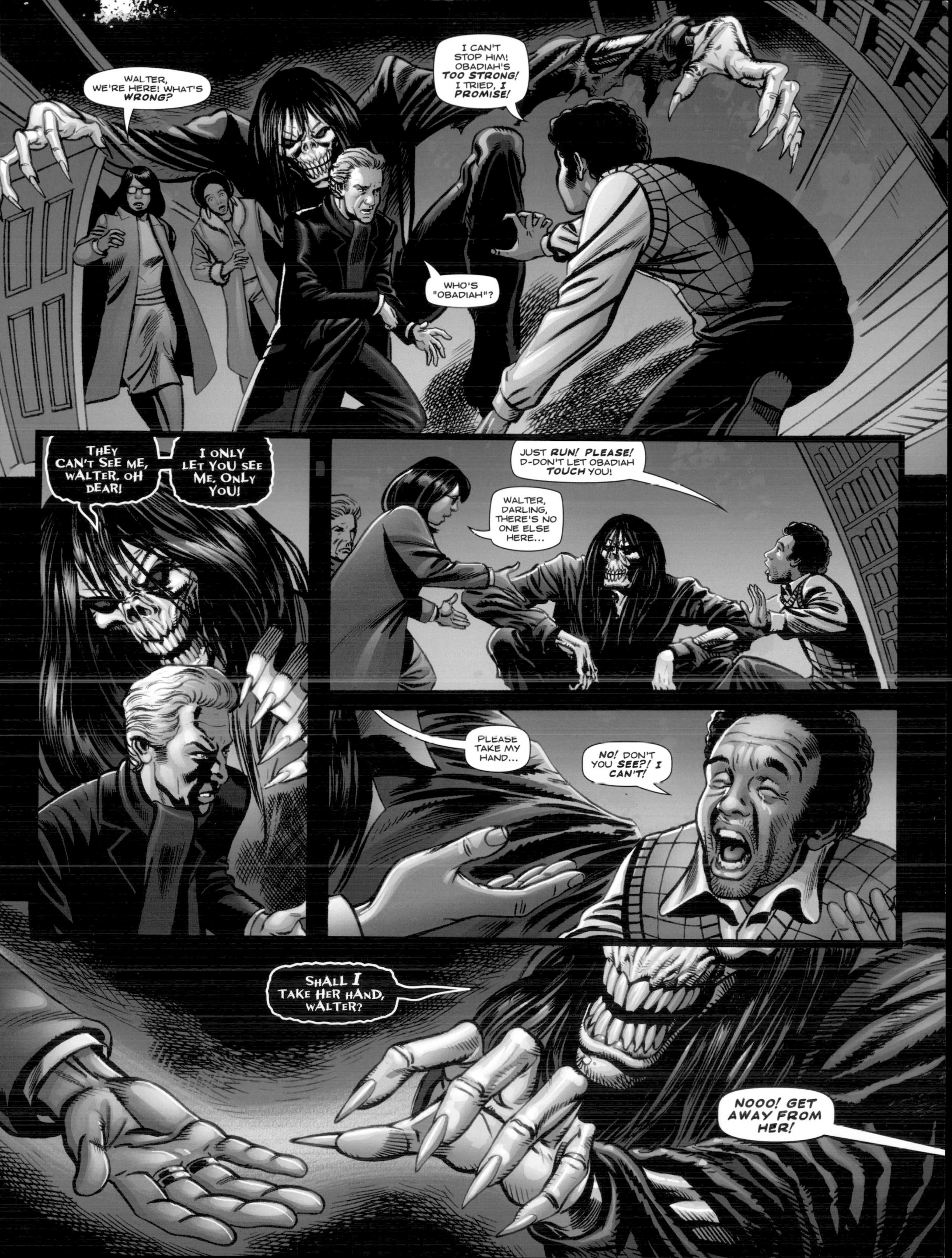
WALTER, WE'RE HERE! WHAT'S WRONG?
I CAN'T STOP HIM! OBADIAH'S TOO STRONG! I TRIED, I PROMISE!
WHO'S "OBADIAH"?
THEY CAN'T SEE ME, WALTER. OH DEAR!
I ONLY LET YOU SEE ME. ONLY YOU!
JUST RUN! PLEASE! D-DON'T LET OBADIAH TOUCH YOU!
WALTER, DARLING, THERE'S NO ONE ELSE HERE...
PLEASE TAKE MY HAND...
NO! DON'T YOU SEE?! I CAN'T!
SHALL I TAKE HER HAND, WALTER?
NOOO! GET AWAY FROM HER!

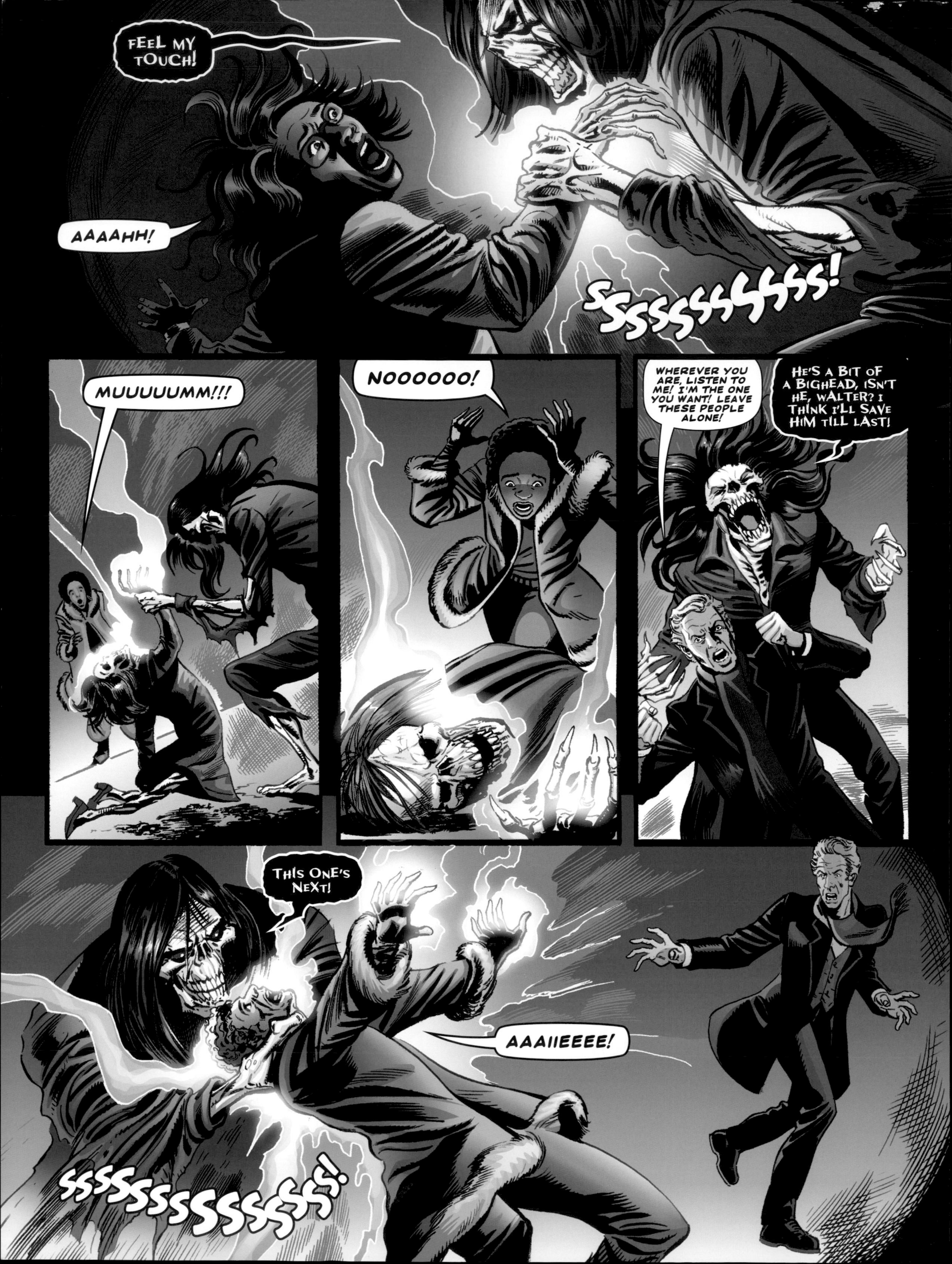
FEEL MY TOUCH!
AAAAHH!
SSSSSSSSSSS!
MUUUUUMM!!!
NOOOOOO!
WHEREVER YOU ARE, LISTEN TO ME! I'M THE ONE YOU WANT! LEAVE THESE PEOPLE ALONE!
HE'S A BIT OF A BIGHEAD, ISN'T HE, WALTER? I THINK I'LL SAVE HIM TILL LAST!
THIS ONE'S NEXT!
AAAIIEEEE!
SSSSSSSSSSSSSS!

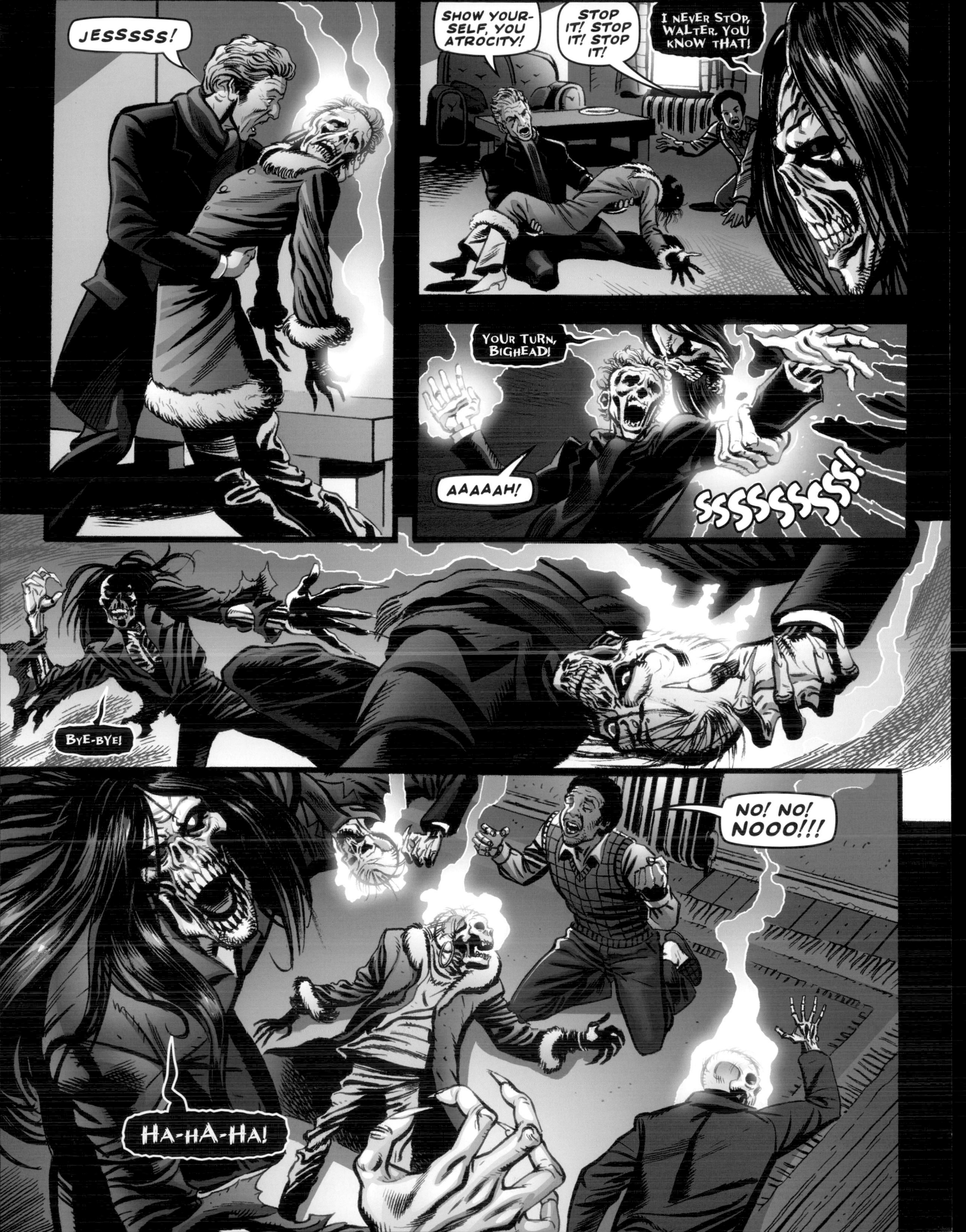

JESSSSS!
SHOW YOURSELF, YOU ATROCITY!
STOP IT! STOP IT! STOP IT!
I NEVER STOP, WALTER. YOU KNOW THAT!
YOUR TURN, BIGHEAD!
AAAAAH!
SSSSSSSSS!
BYE-BYE!
NO! NO! NOOO!!!
HA-HA-HA!

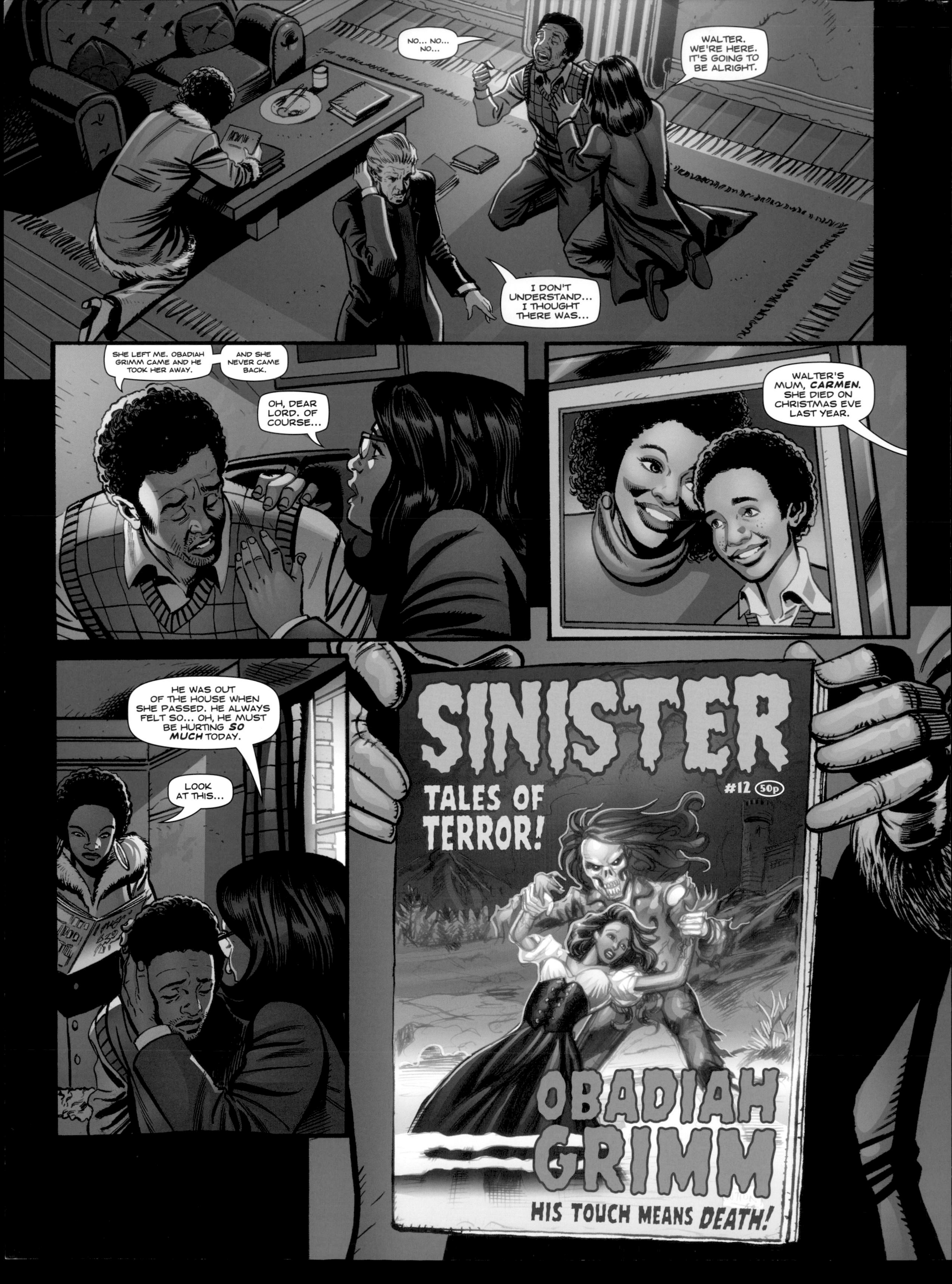
NO... NO... NO...
WALTER. WE'RE HERE. IT'S GOING TO BE ALRIGHT.
I DON'T UNDERSTAND... I THOUGHT THERE WAS...
SHE LEFT ME. OBADIAH GRIMM CAME AND HE TOOK HER AWAY.
AND SHE NEVER CAME BACK.
OH, DEAR LORD. OF COURSE...
WALTER'S MUM, CARMEN. SHE DIED ON CHRISTMAS EVE LAST YEAR.
HE WAS OUT OF THE HOUSE WHEN SHE PASSED. HE ALWAYS FELT SO... OH, HE MUST BE HURTING SO MUCH TODAY.
LOOK AT THIS...
SINISTER
TALES OF TERROR!
#12 50p
OBADIAH GRIMM
HIS TOUCH MEANS DEATH!

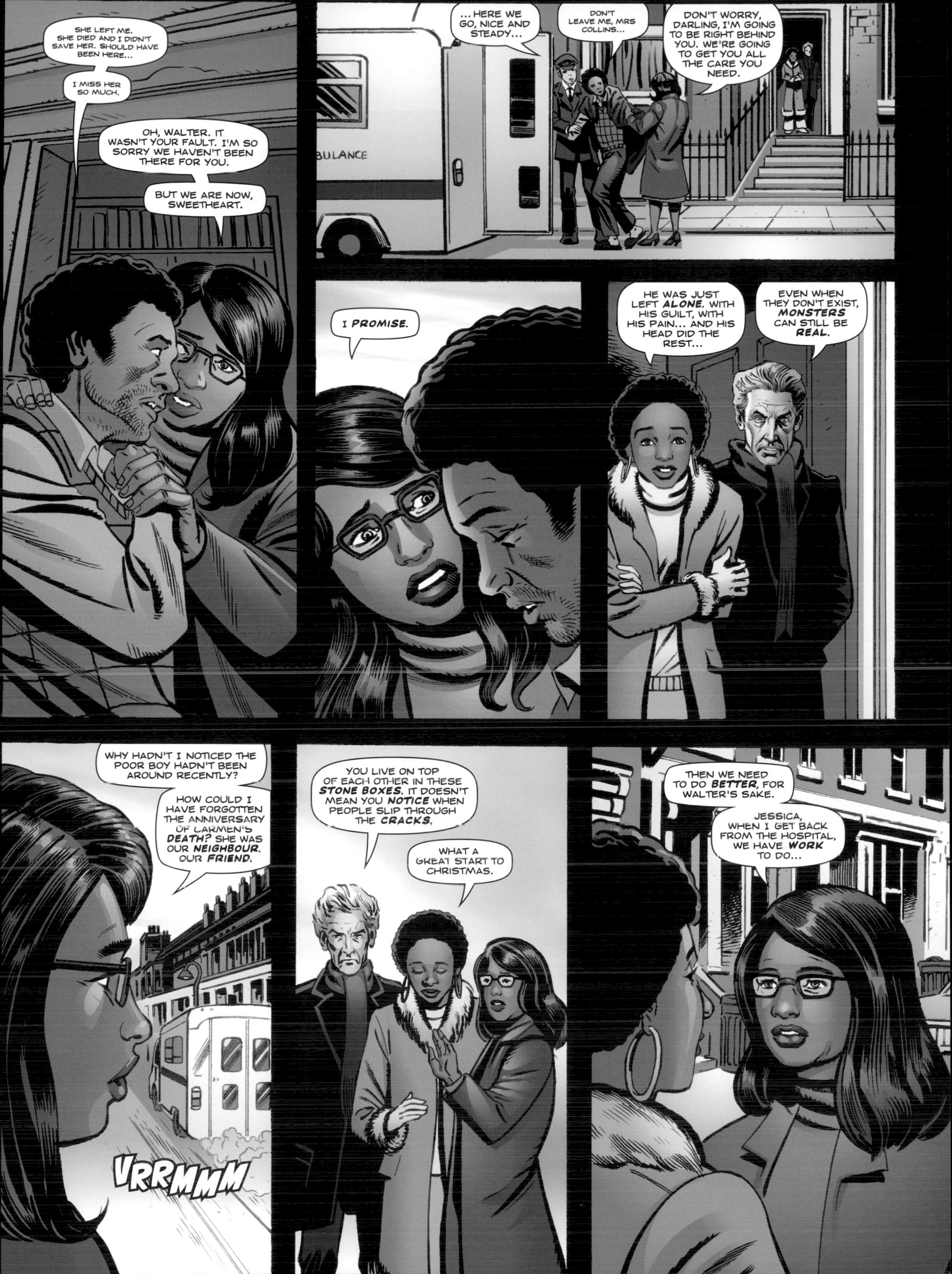
SHE LEFT ME. SHE DIED AND I DIDN'T SAVE HER. SHOULD HAVE BEEN HERE...
I MISS HER SO MUCH.
OH, WALTER. IT WASN'T YOUR FAULT. I'M SO SORRY WE HAVEN'T BEEN THERE FOR YOU.
BUT WE ARE NOW, SWEETHEART.
...HERE WE GO, NICE AND STEADY...
DON'T LEAVE ME, MRS COLLINS...
DON'T WORRY, DARLING, I'M GOING TO BE RIGHT BEHIND YOU. WE'RE GOING TO GET YOU ALL THE CARE YOU NEED.
BULANCE
I PROMISE.
HE WAS JUST LEFT ALONE. WITH HIS GUILT, WITH HIS PAIN... AND HIS HEAD DID THE REST...
EVEN WHEN THEY DON'T EXIST, MONSTERS CAN STILL BE REAL.
WHY HADN'T I NOTICED THE POOR BOY HADN'T BEEN AROUND RECENTLY?
HOW COULD I HAVE FORGOTTEN THE ANNIVERSARY OF CARMEN'S DEATH? SHE WAS OUR NEIGHBOUR. OUR FRIEND.
VRRMMM
YOU LIVE ON TOP OF EACH OTHER IN THESE STONE BOXES. IT DOESN'T MEAN YOU NOTICE WHEN PEOPLE SLIP THROUGH THE CRACKS.
WHAT A GREAT START TO CHRISTMAS.
THEN WE NEED TO DO BETTER, FOR WALTER'S SAKE.
JESSICA, WHEN I GET BACK FROM THE HOSPITAL, WE HAVE WORK TO DO...

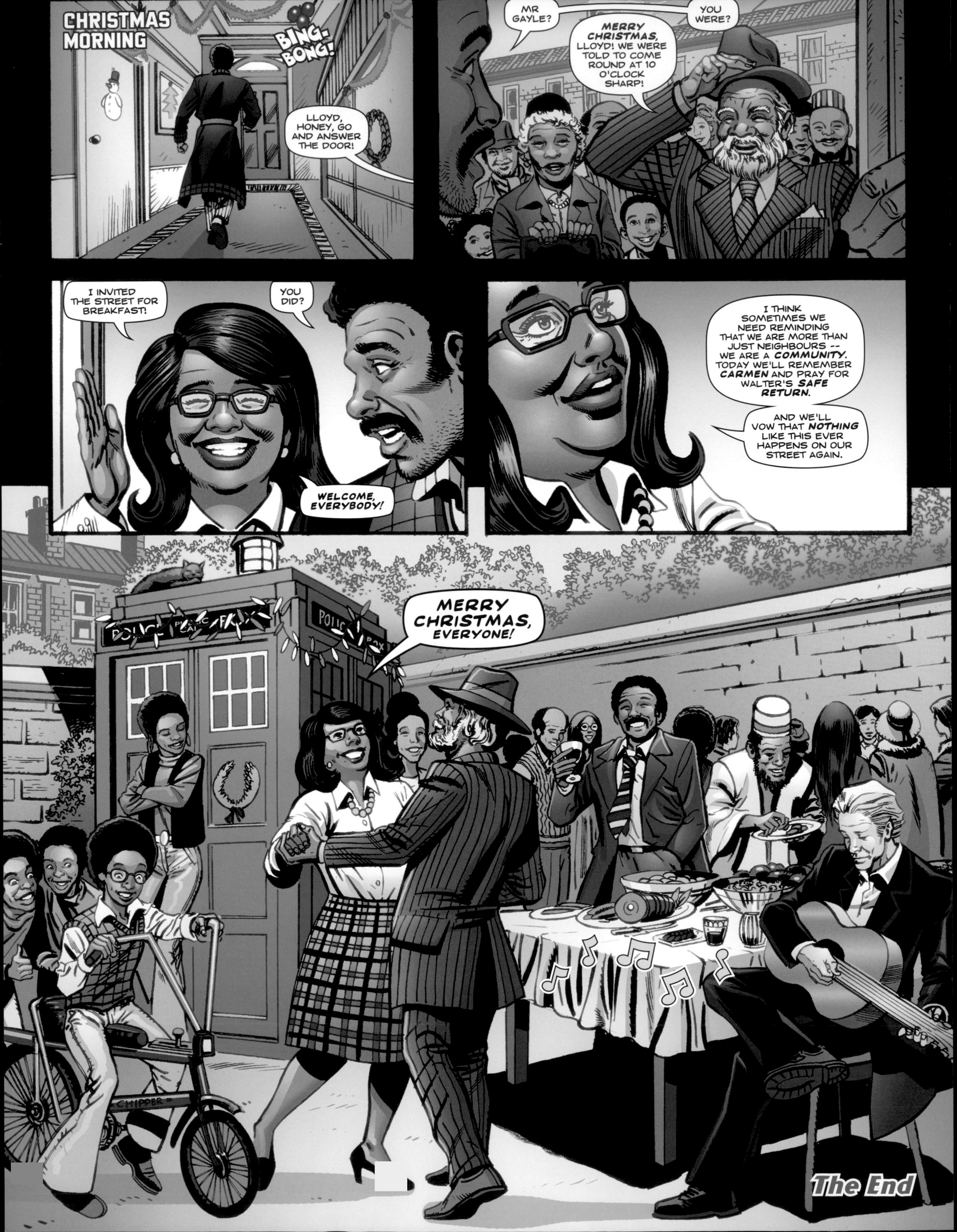
CHRISTMAS MORNING
BING-BONG!
LLOYD, HONEY, GO AND ANSWER THE DOOR!
MR GAYLE?
YOU WERE?
MERRY CHRISTMAS, LLOYD! WE WERE TOLD TO COME ROUND AT 10 O'CLOCK SHARP!
I INVITED THE STREET FOR BREAKFAST!
YOU DID?
WELCOME, EVERYBODY!
I THINK SOMETIMES WE NEED REMINDING THAT WE ARE MORE THAN JUST NEIGHBOURS -- WE ARE A COMMUNITY. TODAY WE'LL REMEMBER CARMEN AND PRAY FOR WALTER'S SAFE RETURN.
AND WE'LL VOW THAT NOTHING LIKE THIS EVER HAPPENS ON OUR STREET AGAIN.
MERRY CHRISTMAS, EVERYONE!
The End

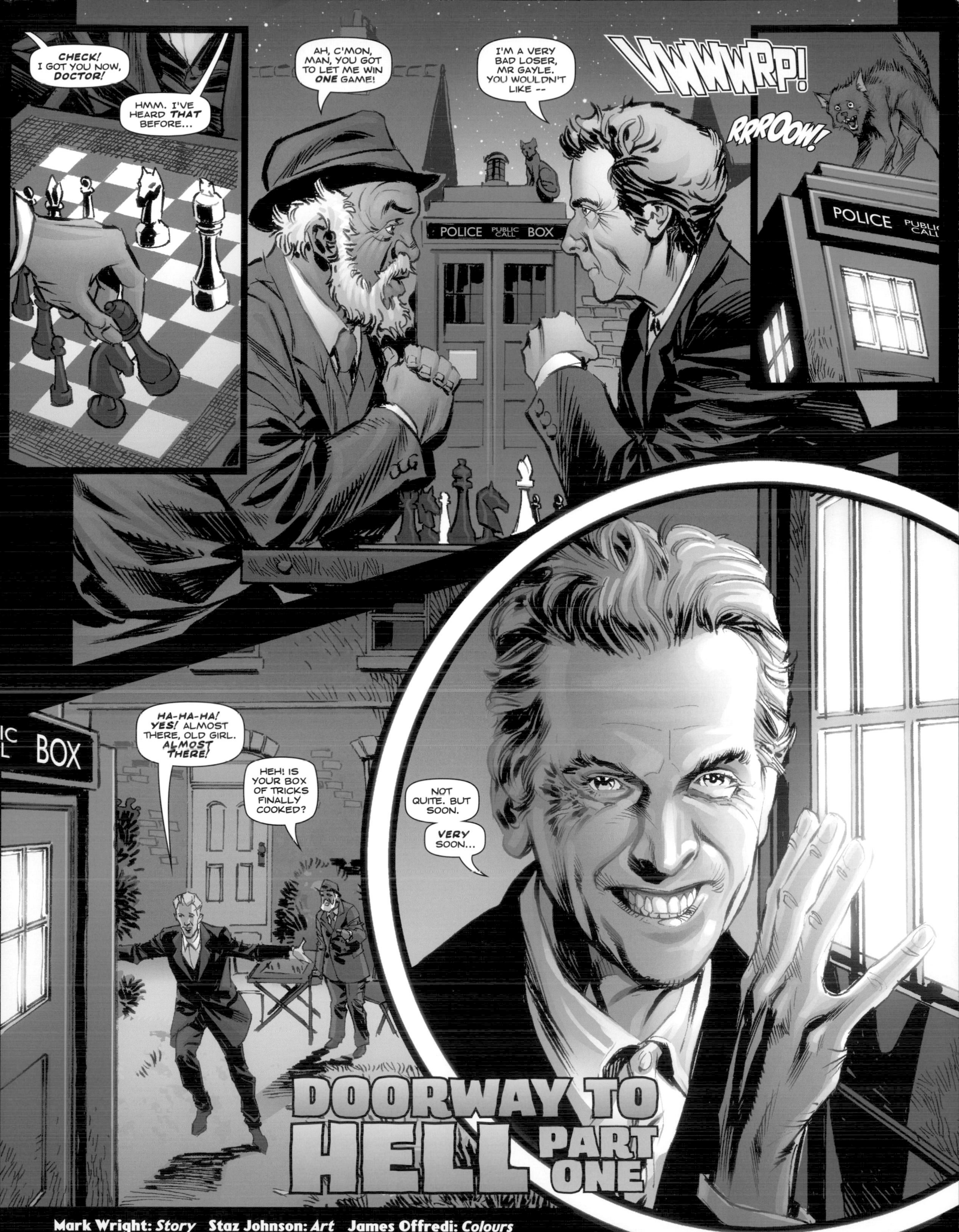
CHECK! I GOT YOU NOW, DOCTOR!
HMM. I'VE HEARD THAT BEFORE...
AH, C'MON, MAN, YOU GOT TO LET ME WIN ONE GAME!
I'M A VERY BAD LOSER, MR GAYLE. YOU WOULDN'T LIKE --
POLICE PUBLIC CALL BOX
VWWWRP!
RRROOW!
HA-HA-HA! YES! ALMOST THERE, OLD GIRL. ALMOST THERE!
HEH! IS YOUR BOX OF TRICKS FINALLY COOKED?
NOT QUITE. BUT SOON.
VERY SOON...
DOORWAY TO HELL PART ONE

**Mark Wright:** *Story* **Staz Johnson:** *Art* **James Offredi:** *Colours*
**Roger Langridge:** *Lettering* **Scott Gray:** *Editor*

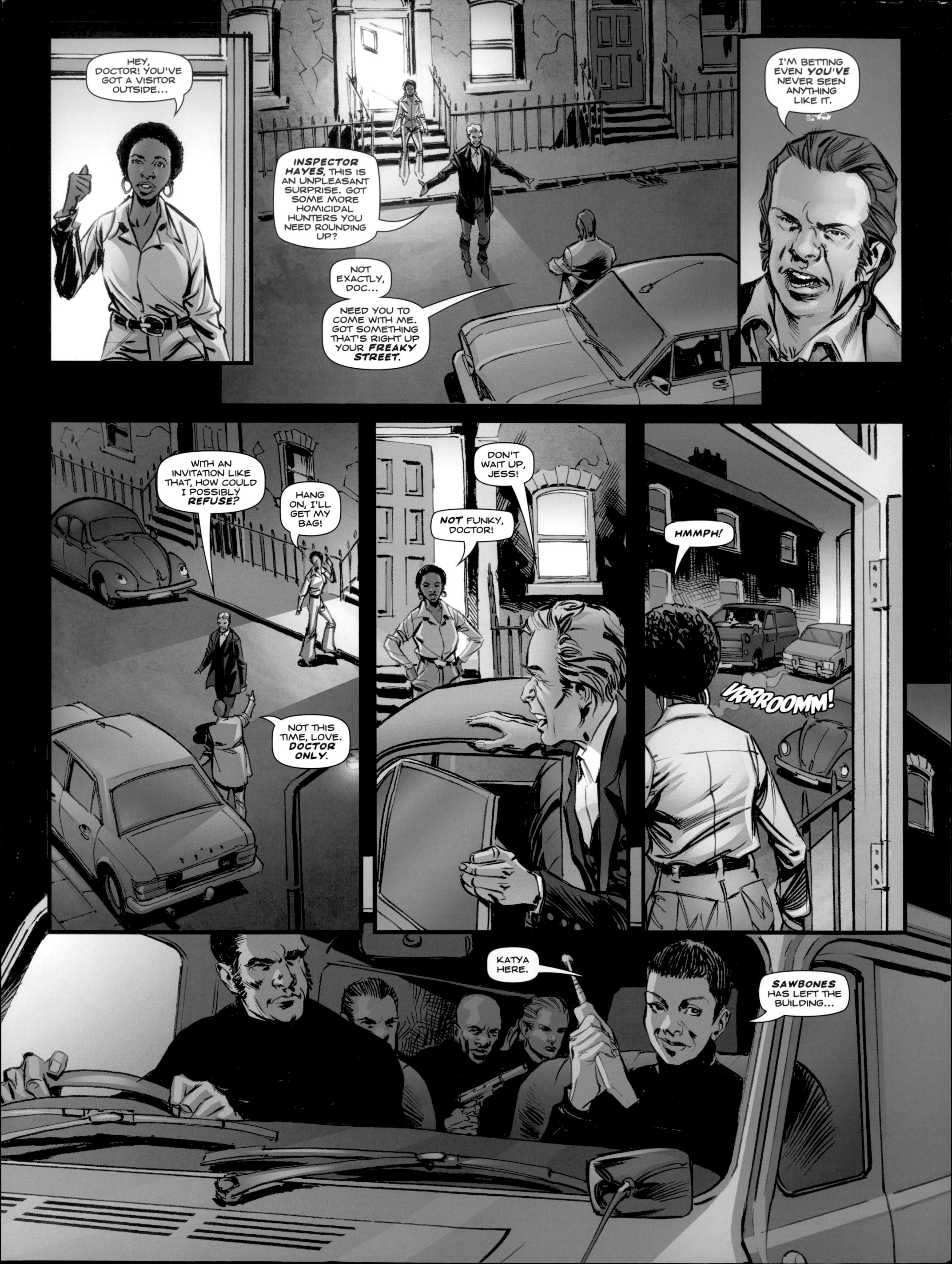
HEY, DOCTOR! YOU'VE GOT A VISITOR OUTSIDE...
INSPECTOR HAYES, THIS IS AN UNPLEASANT SURPRISE. GOT SOME MORE HOMICIDAL HUNTERS YOU NEED ROUNDING UP?
NOT EXACTLY, DOC...
NEED YOU TO COME WITH ME. GOT SOMETHING THAT'S RIGHT UP YOUR FREAKY STREET.
I'M BETTING EVEN YOU'VE NEVER SEEN ANYTHING LIKE IT.
WITH AN INVITATION LIKE THAT, HOW COULD I POSSIBLY REFUSE?
HANG ON, I'LL GET MY BAG!
NOT THIS TIME, LOVE. DOCTOR ONLY.
DON'T WAIT UP, JESS!
NOT FUNKY, DOCTOR!
HMMPH!
VRRROOMM!
KATYA HERE.
SAWBONES HAS LEFT THE BUILDING...

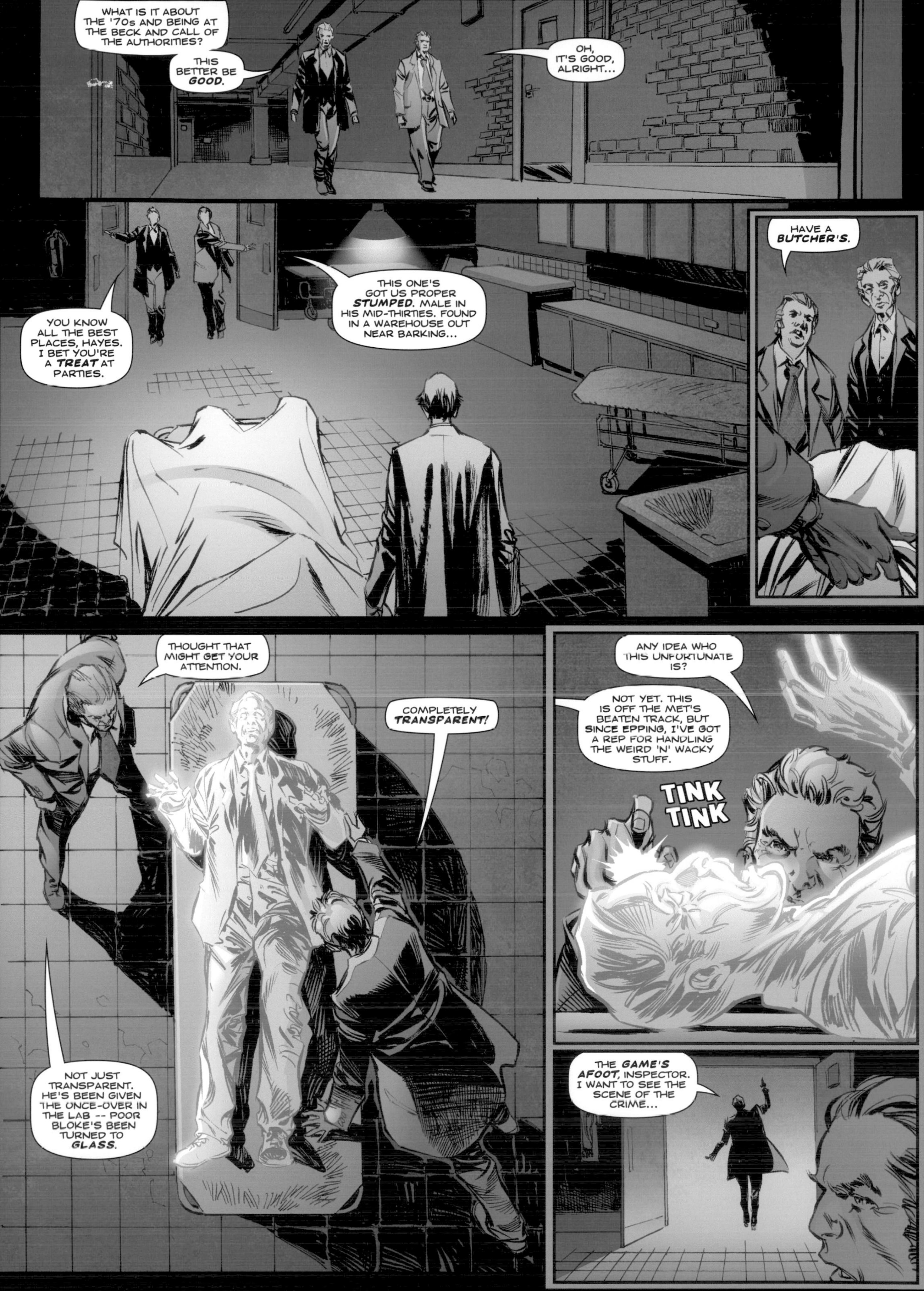
WHAT IS IT ABOUT THE '70s AND BEING AT THE BECK AND CALL OF THE AUTHORITIES?
THIS BETTER BE GOOD.
OH, IT'S GOOD, ALRIGHT...
YOU KNOW ALL THE BEST PLACES, HAYES. I BET YOU'RE A TREAT AT PARTIES.
THIS ONE'S GOT US PROPER STUMPED. MALE IN HIS MID-THIRTIES. FOUND IN A WAREHOUSE OUT NEAR BARKING...
HAVE A BUTCHER'S.
THOUGHT THAT MIGHT GET YOUR ATTENTION.
COMPLETELY TRANSPARENT!
NOT JUST TRANSPARENT. HE'S BEEN GIVEN THE ONCE-OVER IN THE LAB -- POOR BLOKE'S BEEN TURNED TO GLASS.
ANY IDEA WHO THIS UNFORTUNATE IS?
NOT YET. THIS IS OFF THE MET'S BEATEN TRACK, BUT SINCE EPPING, I'VE GOT A REP FOR HANDLING THE WEIRD 'N' WACKY STUFF.
TINK TINK
THE GAME'S AFOOT, INSPECTOR. I WANT TO SEE THE SCENE OF THE CRIME...

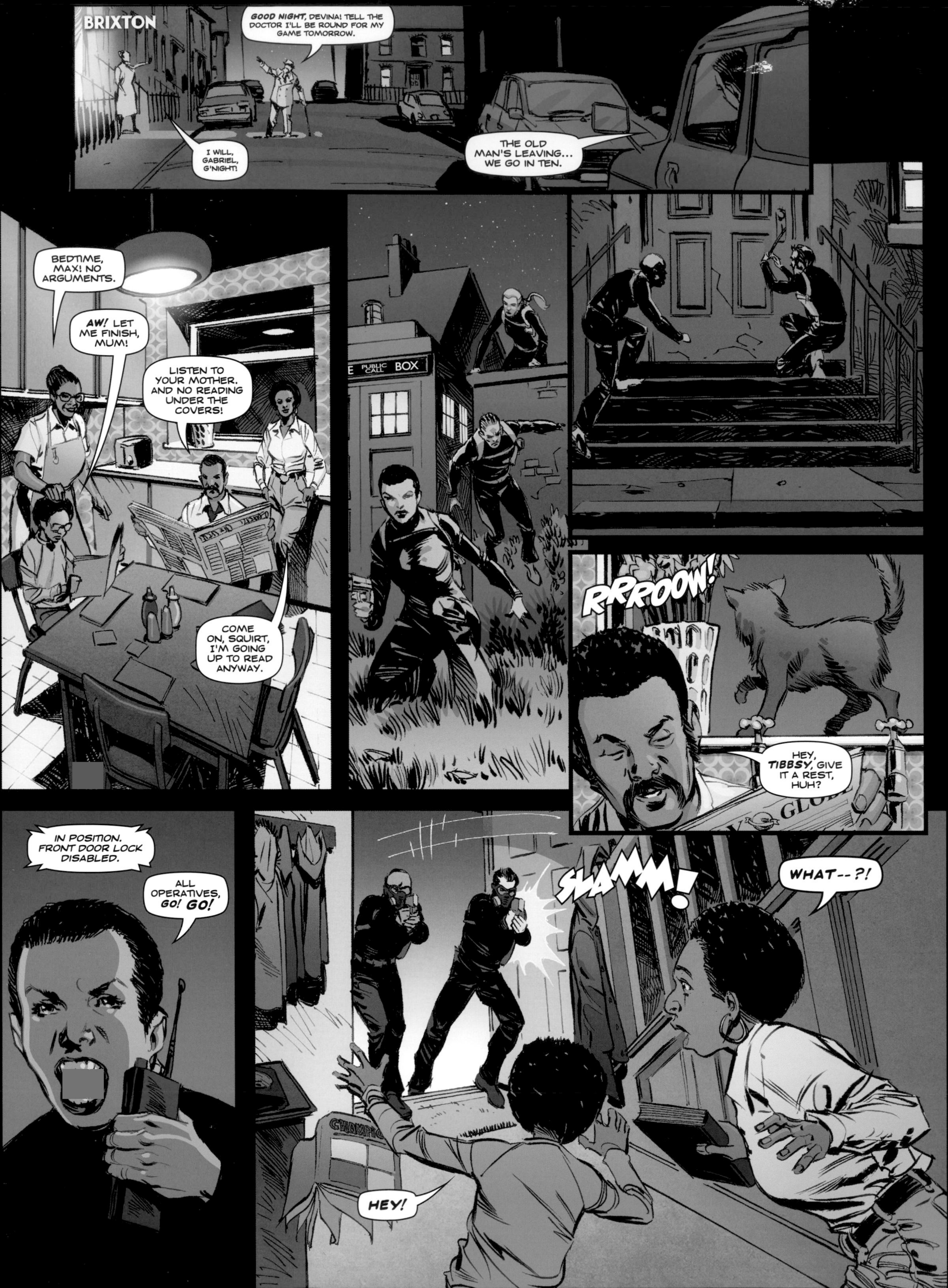
BRIXTON
GOOD NIGHT, DEVINA! TELL THE DOCTOR I'LL BE ROUND FOR MY GAME TOMORROW.
I WILL, GABRIEL, G'NIGHT!
THE OLD MAN'S LEAVING... WE GO IN TEN.
BEDTIME, MAX! NO ARGUMENTS.
AW! LET ME FINISH, MUM!
LISTEN TO YOUR MOTHER. AND NO READING UNDER THE COVERS!
COME ON, SQUIRT, I'M GOING UP TO READ ANYWAY.
PUBLIC CALL BOX
RRROOW!
HEY, TIBBSY, GIVE IT A REST, HUH?
IN POSITION. FRONT DOOR LOCK DISABLED.
ALL OPERATIVES, GO! GO!
SLAMM!
WHAT--?!
HEY!

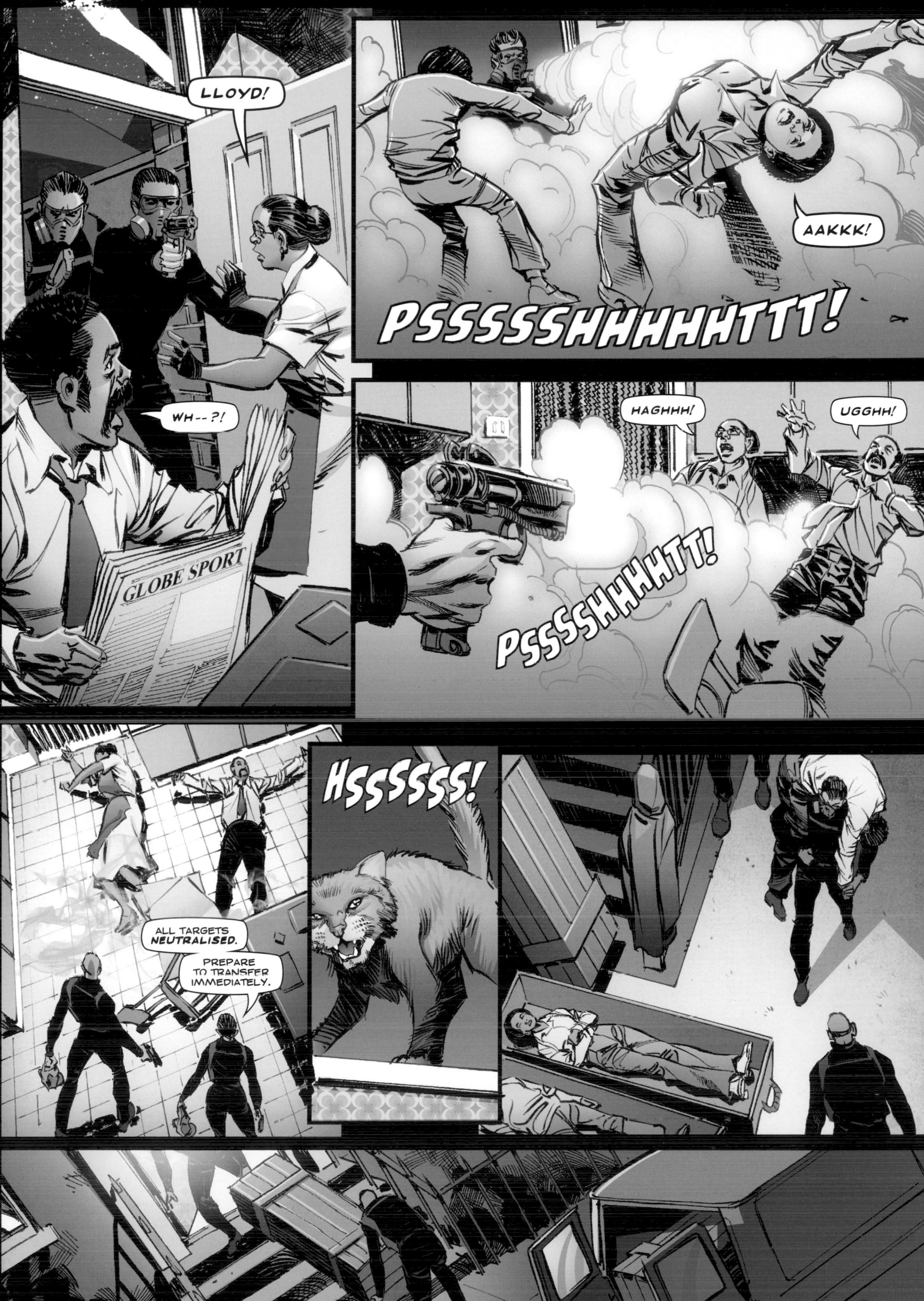
LLOYD!
WH--?!
GLOBE SPORT
AAKKK!
PSSSSSHHHHHTTT!
HAGHHH!
UGGHH!
PSSSSHHHHTT!
ALL TARGETS NEUTRALISED.
PREPARE TO TRANSFER IMMEDIATELY.
HSSSSSS!

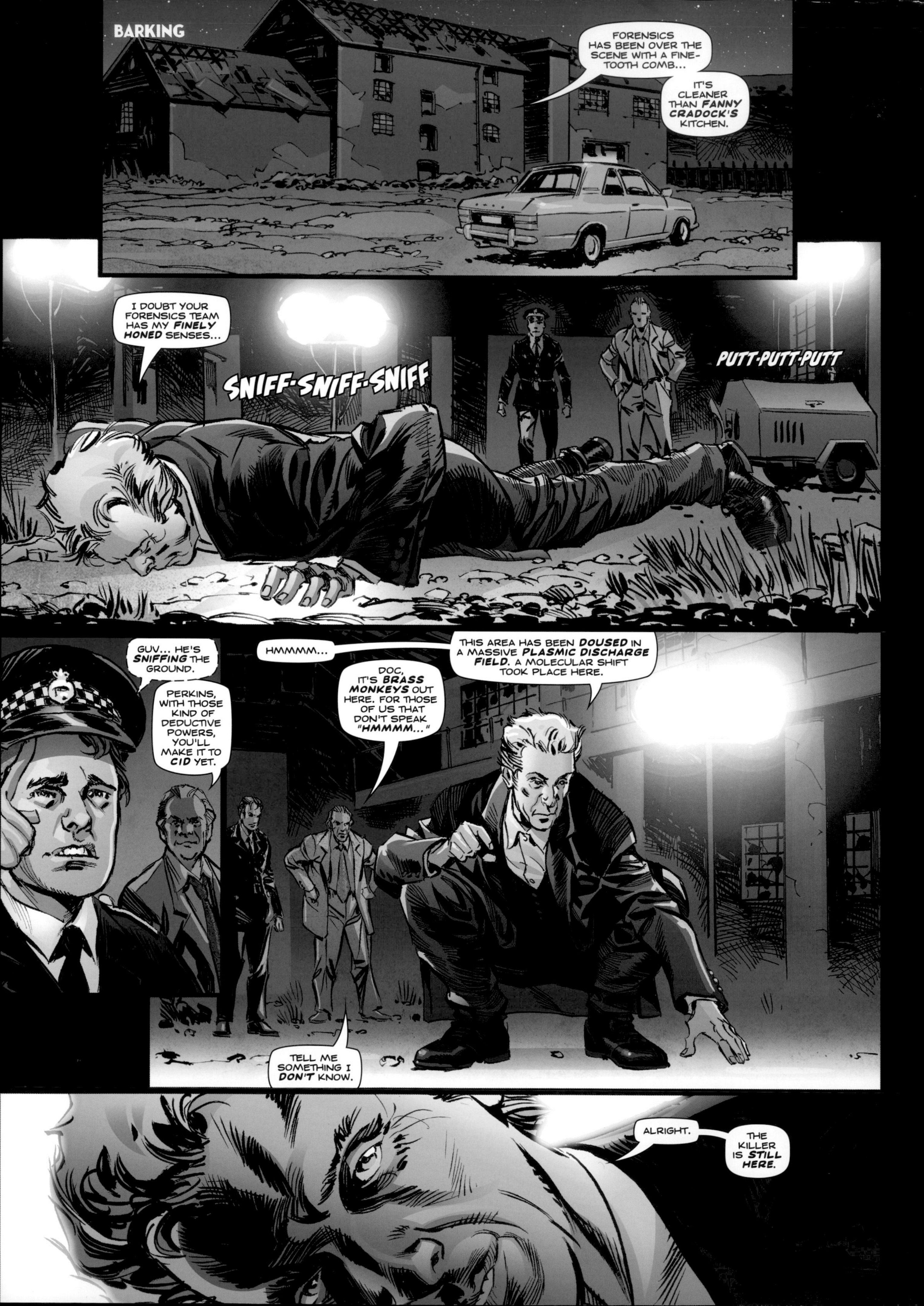

BARKING
FORENSICS HAS BEEN OVER THE SCENE WITH A FINE-TOOTH COMB...
IT'S CLEANER THAN FANNY CRADOCK'S KITCHEN.
I DOUBT YOUR FORENSICS TEAM HAS MY FINELY HONED SENSES...
SNIFF-SNIFF-SNIFF
PUTT-PUTT-PUTT
GUV... HE'S SNIFFING THE GROUND.
PERKINS, WITH THOSE KIND OF DEDUCTIVE POWERS, YOU'LL MAKE IT TO CID YET.
HMMMM...
THIS AREA HAS BEEN DOUSED IN A MASSIVE PLASMIC DISCHARGE FIELD. A MOLECULAR SHIFT TOOK PLACE HERE.
DOC, IT'S BRASS MONKEYS OUT HERE. FOR THOSE OF US THAT DON'T SPEAK "HMMMM..."
TELL ME SOMETHING I DON'T KNOW.
ALRIGHT.
THE KILLER IS STILL HERE.

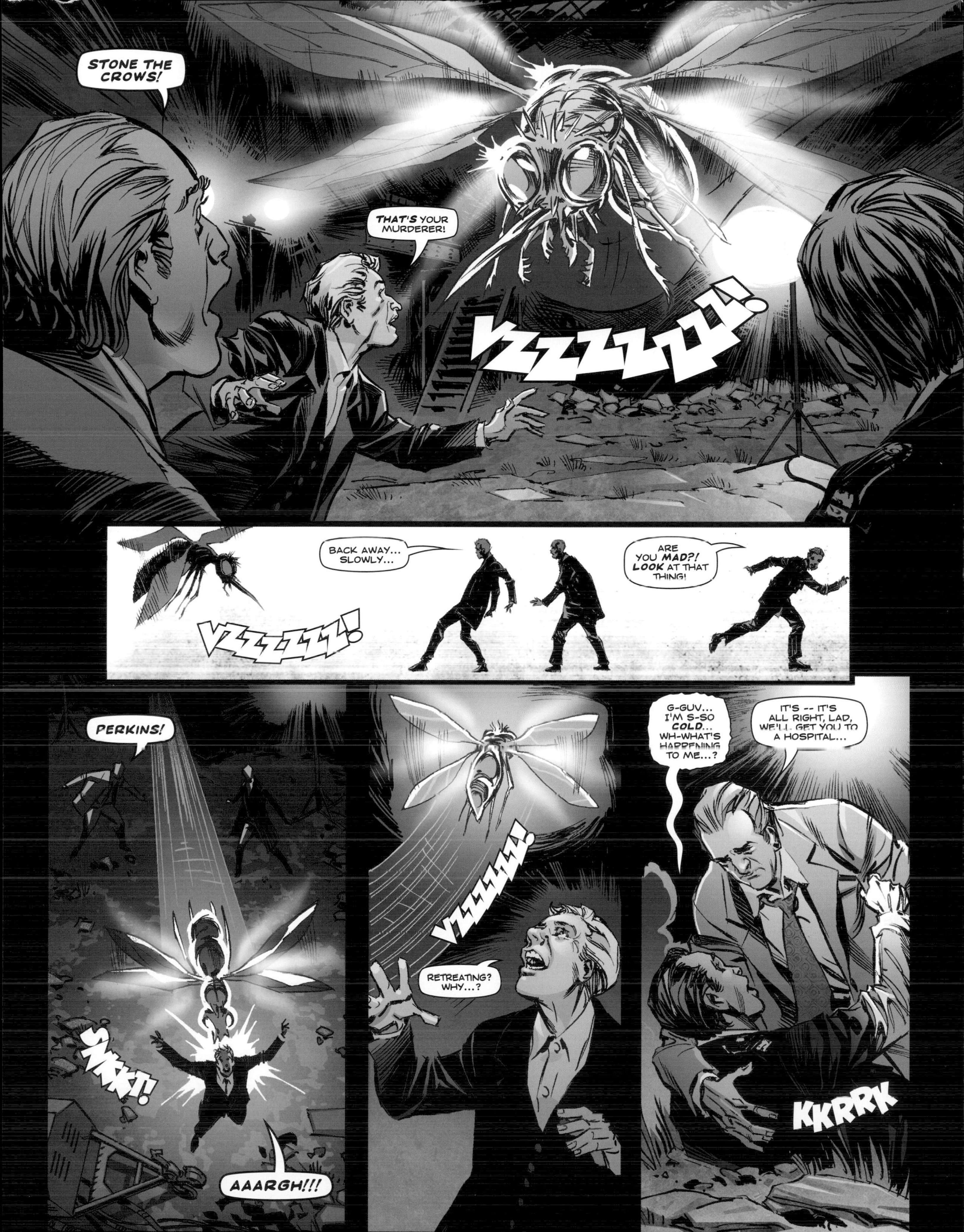
STONE THE CROWS!
THAT'S YOUR MURDERER!
VZZZZZZZ!
BACK AWAY... SLOWLY...
ARE YOU MAD?! LOOK AT THAT THING!
VZZZZZZ!
PERKINS!
SNKKT!
AAARGH!!!
VZZZZZZ!
RETREATING? WHY...?
G-GUV... I'M S-SO COLD... WH-WHAT'S HAPPENING TO ME...?
IT'S -- IT'S ALL RIGHT, LAD, WE'LL GET YOU TO A HOSPITAL...
KKRRK

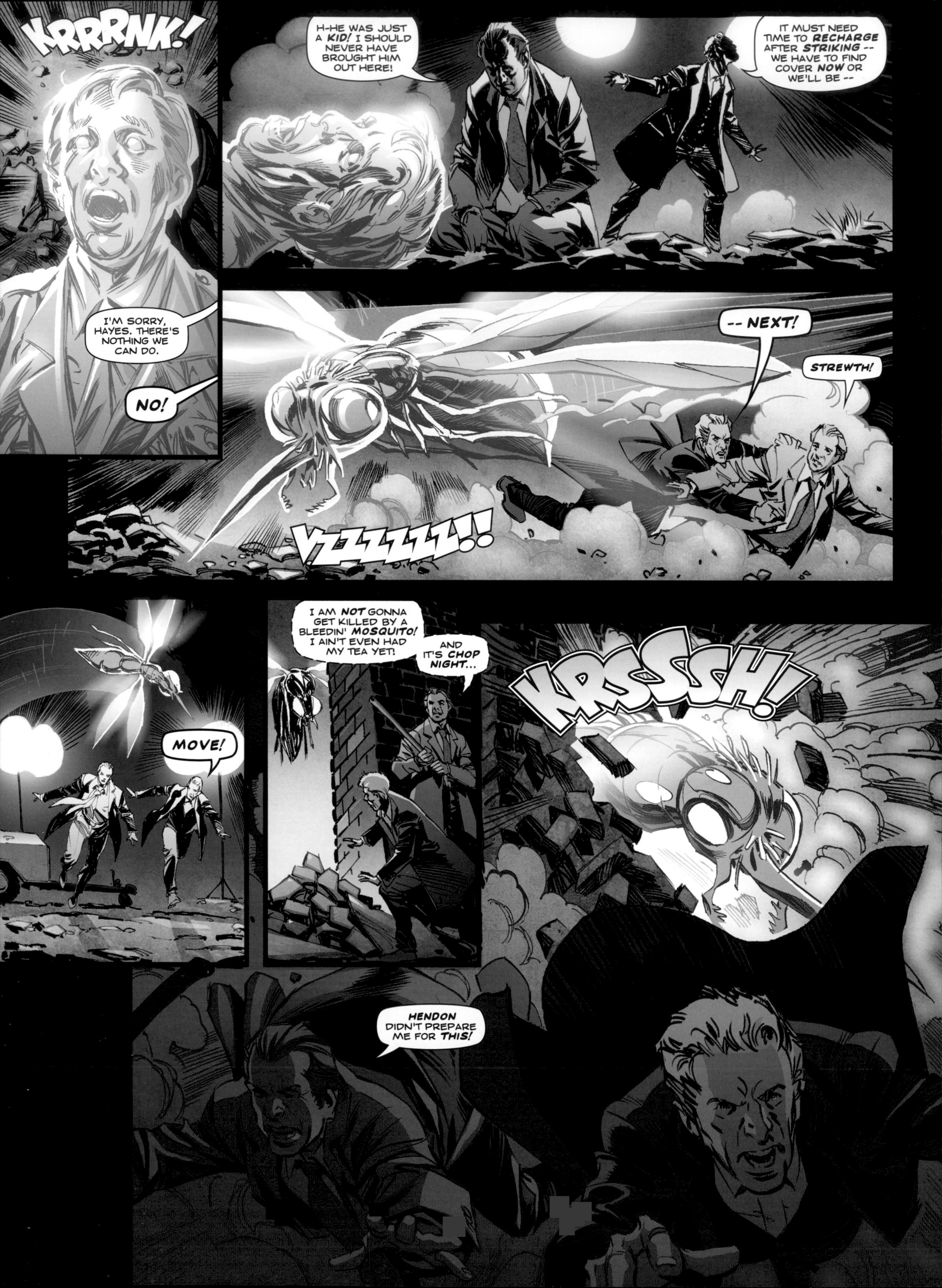
KRRRNK!
H-HE WAS JUST A KID! I SHOULD NEVER HAVE BROUGHT HIM OUT HERE!
IT MUST NEED TIME TO RECHARGE AFTER STRIKING -- WE HAVE TO FIND COVER NOW OR WE'LL BE --
I'M SORRY, HAYES. THERE'S NOTHING WE CAN DO.
NO!
-- NEXT!
STREWTH!
VZZZZZZ!!
MOVE!
I AM NOT GONNA GET KILLED BY A BLEEDIN' MOSQUITO! I AIN'T EVEN HAD MY TEA YET!
AND IT'S CHOP NIGHT...
KRSSSH!
HENDON DIDN'T PREPARE ME FOR THIS!

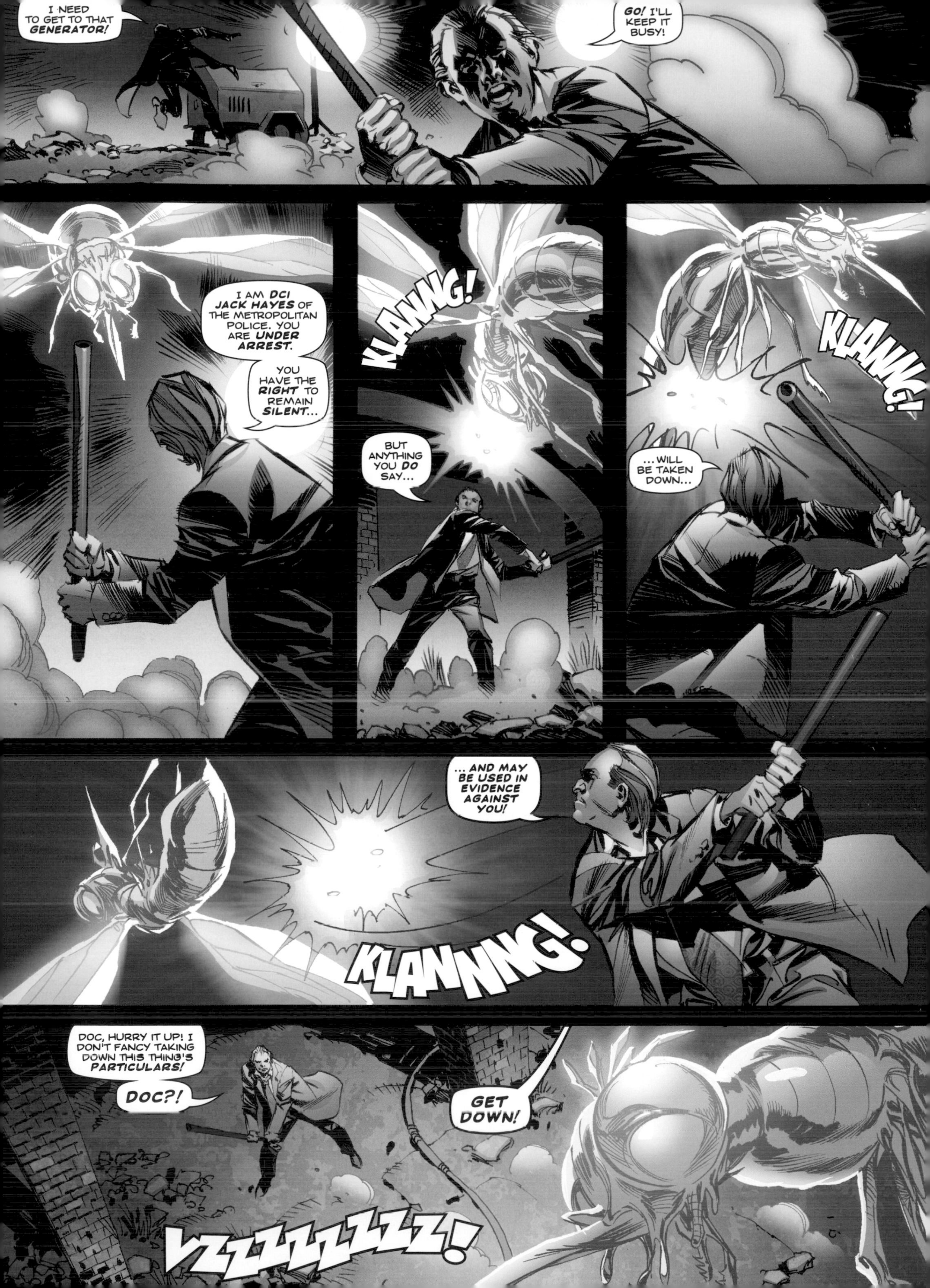

I NEED TO GET TO THAT GENERATOR!
GO! I'LL KEEP IT BUSY!
I AM DCI JACK HAYES OF THE METROPOLITAN POLICE. YOU ARE UNDER ARREST.
YOU HAVE THE RIGHT TO REMAIN SILENT...
KLANNG!
BUT ANYTHING YOU DO SAY...
KLANNG!
...WILL BE TAKEN DOWN...
...AND MAY BE USED IN EVIDENCE AGAINST YOU!
KLANNNG!
DOC, HURRY IT UP! I DON'T FANCY TAKING DOWN THIS THING'S PARTICULARS!
DOC?!
GET DOWN!
VZZZZZZZZZ!

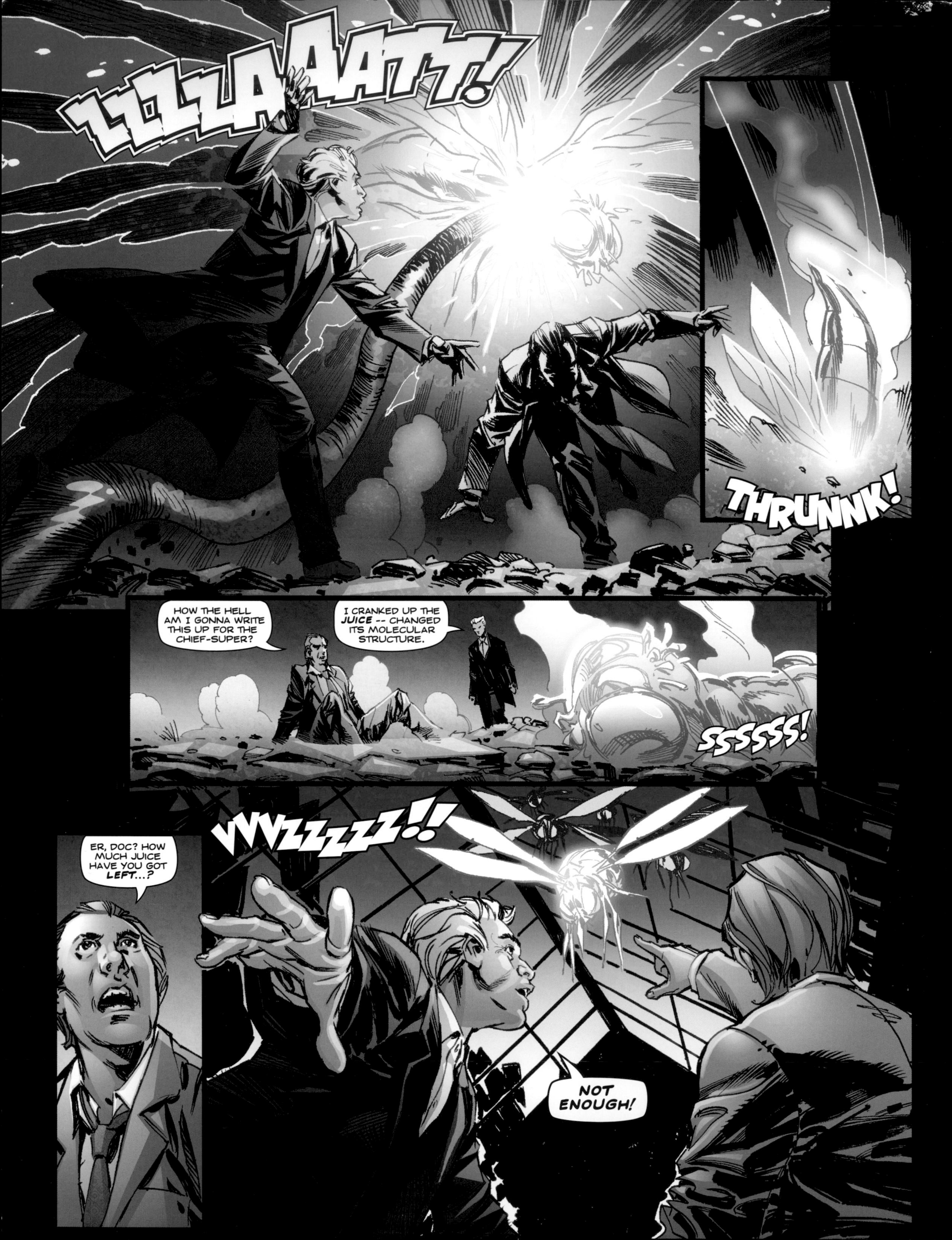
ZZZZAAATT!
THRUNNK!
HOW THE HELL AM I GONNA WRITE THIS UP FOR THE CHIEF-SUPER?
I CRANKED UP THE JUICE -- CHANGED ITS MOLECULAR STRUCTURE.
SSSSSS!
ER, DOC? HOW MUCH JUICE HAVE YOU GOT LEFT...?
VVVZZZZZZ!!
NOT ENOUGH!

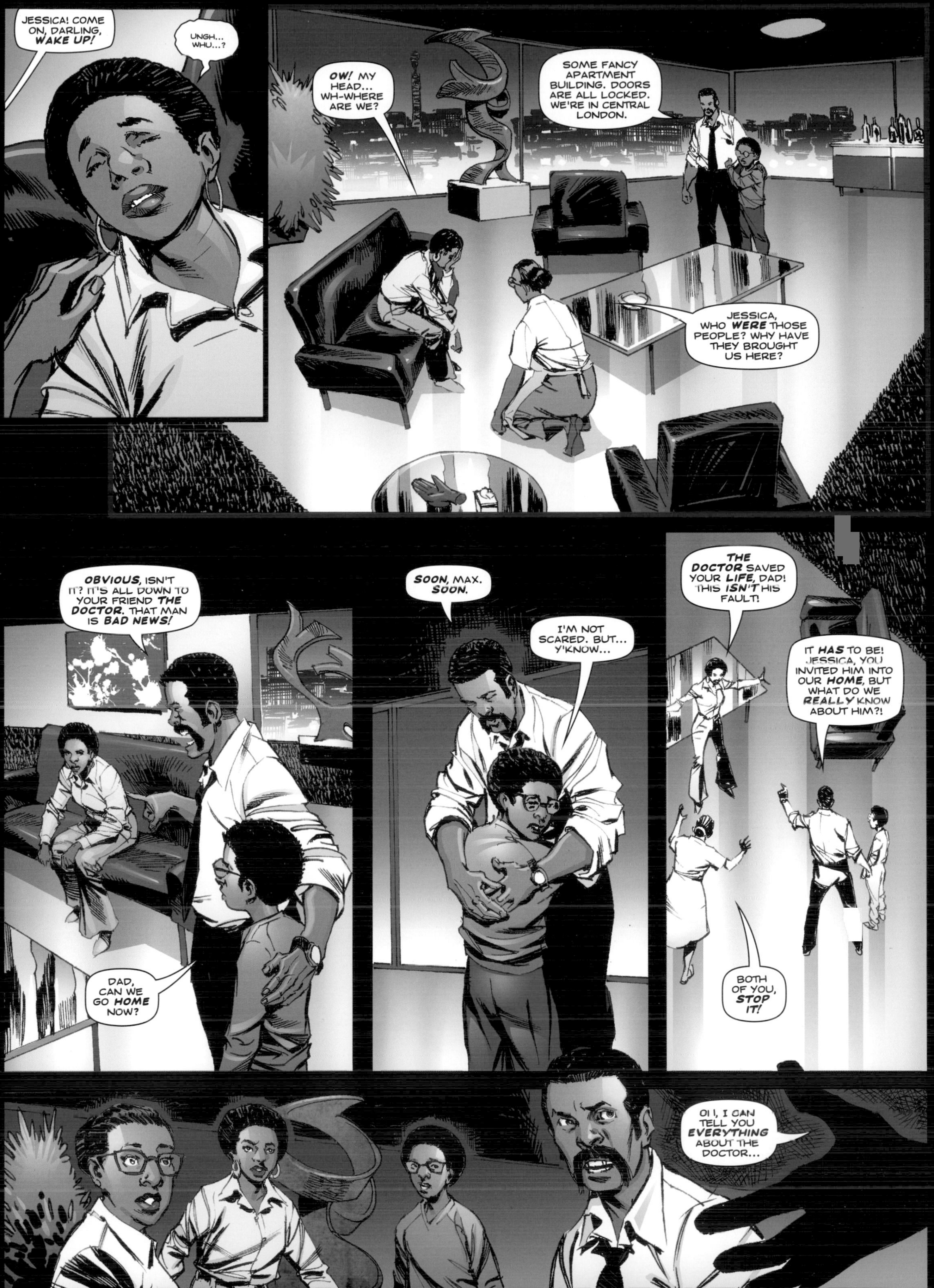
JESSICA! COME ON, DARLING, WAKE UP!
UNGH... WHU...?
OW! MY HEAD... WH-WHERE ARE WE?
SOME FANCY APARTMENT BUILDING. DOORS ARE ALL LOCKED. WE'RE IN CENTRAL LONDON.
JESSICA, WHO WERE THOSE PEOPLE? WHY HAVE THEY BROUGHT US HERE?
OBVIOUS, ISN'T IT? IT'S ALL DOWN TO YOUR FRIEND THE DOCTOR. THAT MAN IS BAD NEWS!
DAD, CAN WE GO HOME NOW?
SOON, MAX. SOON.
I'M NOT SCARED. BUT... Y'KNOW...
THE DOCTOR SAVED YOUR LIFE, DAD! THIS ISN'T HIS FAULT!
IT HAS TO BE! JESSICA, YOU INVITED HIM INTO OUR HOME, BUT WHAT DO WE REALLY KNOW ABOUT HIM?!
BOTH OF YOU, STOP IT!
OI! I CAN TELL YOU EVERYTHING ABOUT THE DOCTOR...

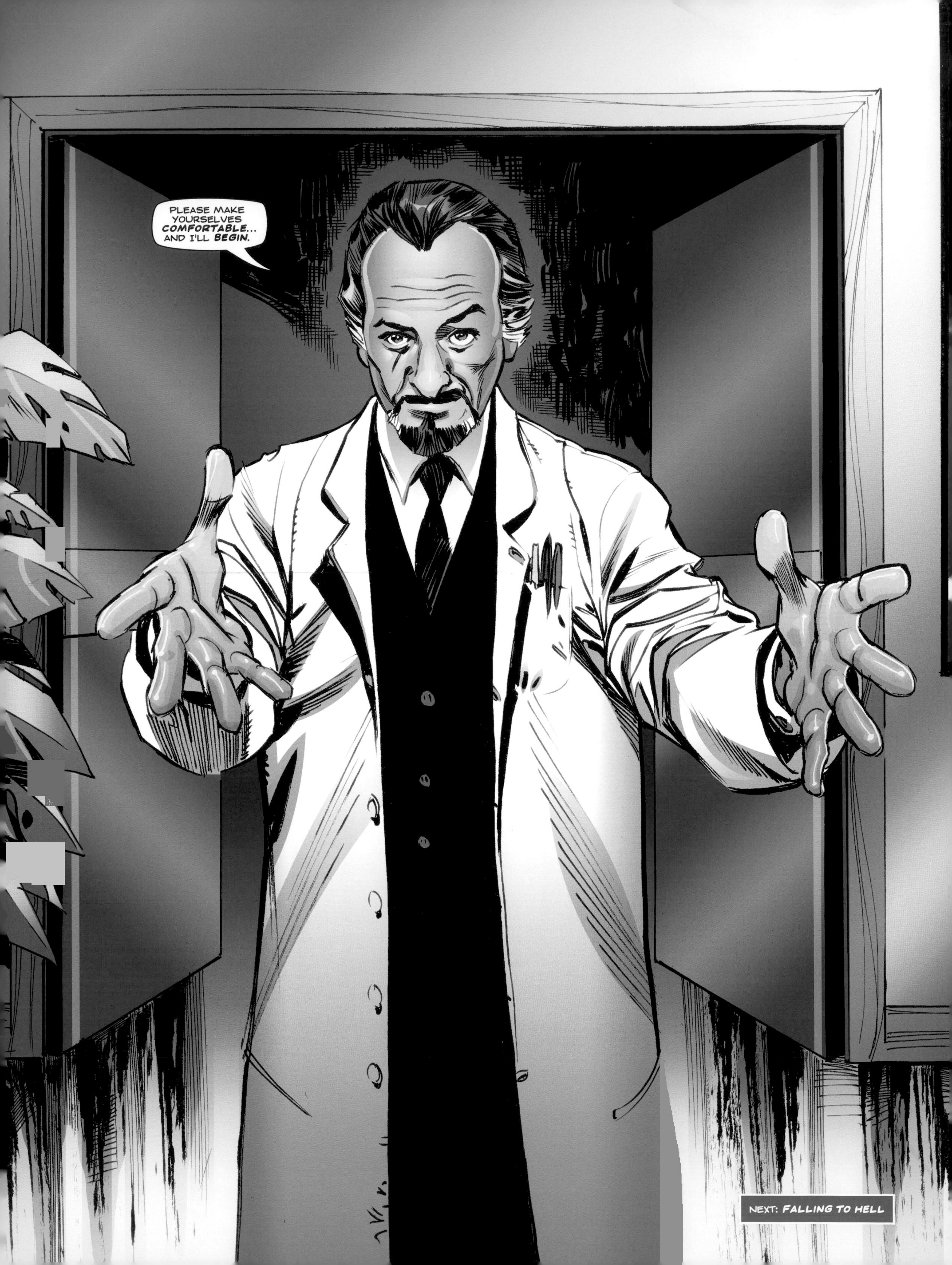
PLEASE MAKE YOURSELVES COMFORTABLE... AND I'LL BEGIN.
NEXT: FALLING TO HELL

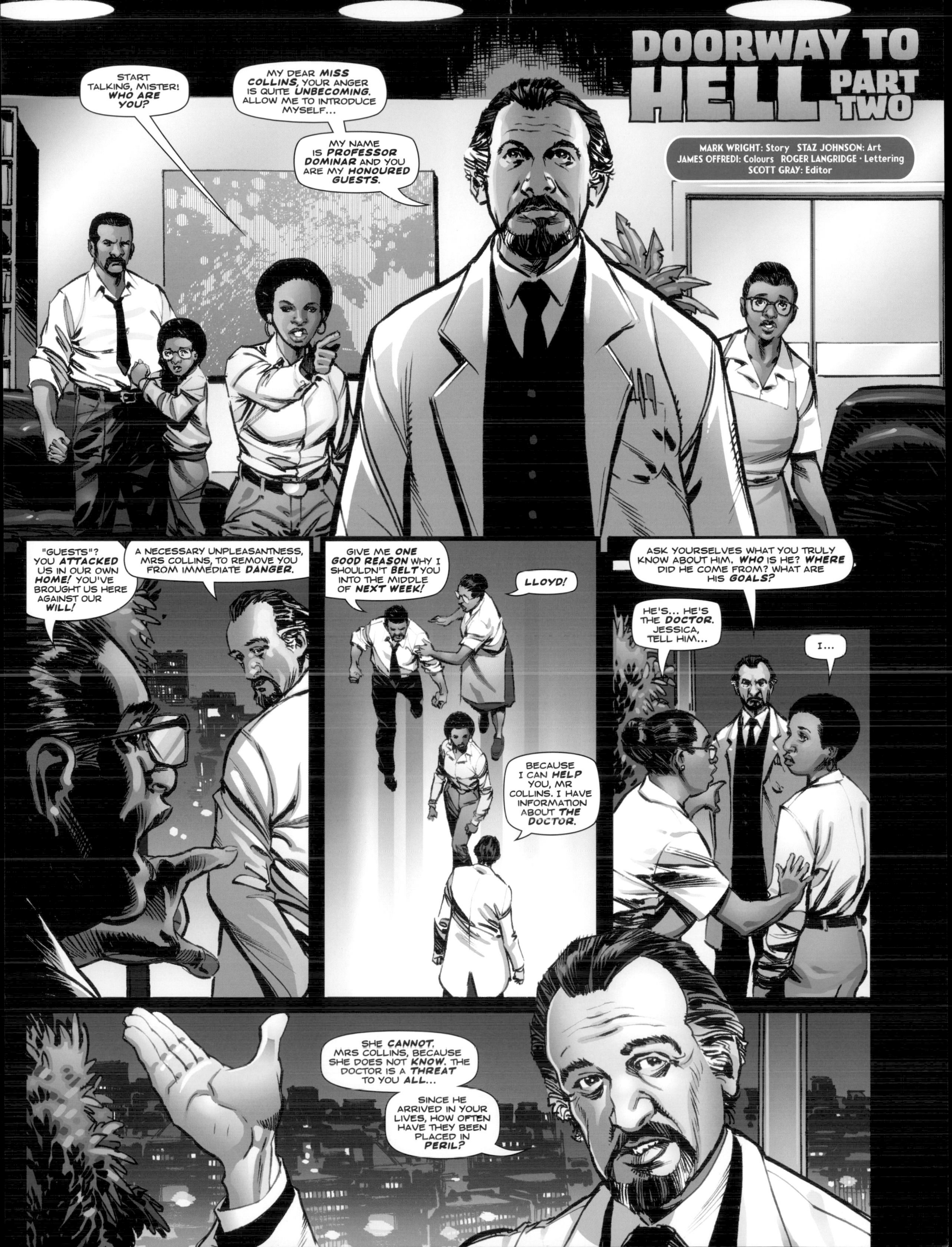
DOORWAY TO HELL PART TWO
MARK WRIGHT: Story STAZ JOHNSON: Art
JAMES OFFREDI: Colours ROGER LANGRIDGE · Lettering
SCOTT GRAY: Editor
START TALKING, MISTER! WHO ARE YOU?
MY DEAR MISS COLLINS, YOUR ANGER IS QUITE UNBECOMING. ALLOW ME TO INTRODUCE MYSELF...
MY NAME IS PROFESSOR DOMINAR AND YOU ARE MY HONOURED GUESTS.
"GUESTS"? YOU ATTACKED US IN OUR OWN HOME! YOU'VE BROUGHT US HERE AGAINST OUR WILL!
A NECESSARY UNPLEASANTNESS, MRS COLLINS, TO REMOVE YOU FROM IMMEDIATE DANGER.
GIVE ME ONE GOOD REASON WHY I SHOULDN'T BELT YOU INTO THE MIDDLE OF NEXT WEEK!
LLOYD!
BECAUSE I CAN HELP YOU, MR COLLINS. I HAVE INFORMATION ABOUT THE DOCTOR.
ASK YOURSELVES WHAT YOU TRULY KNOW ABOUT HIM. WHO IS HE? WHERE DID HE COME FROM? WHAT ARE HIS GOALS?
HE'S... HE'S THE DOCTOR. JESSICA, TELL HIM...
I...
SHE CANNOT, MRS COLLINS, BECAUSE SHE DOES NOT KNOW. THE DOCTOR IS A THREAT TO YOU ALL...
SINCE HE ARRIVED IN YOUR LIVES, HOW OFTEN HAVE THEY BEEN PLACED IN PERIL?

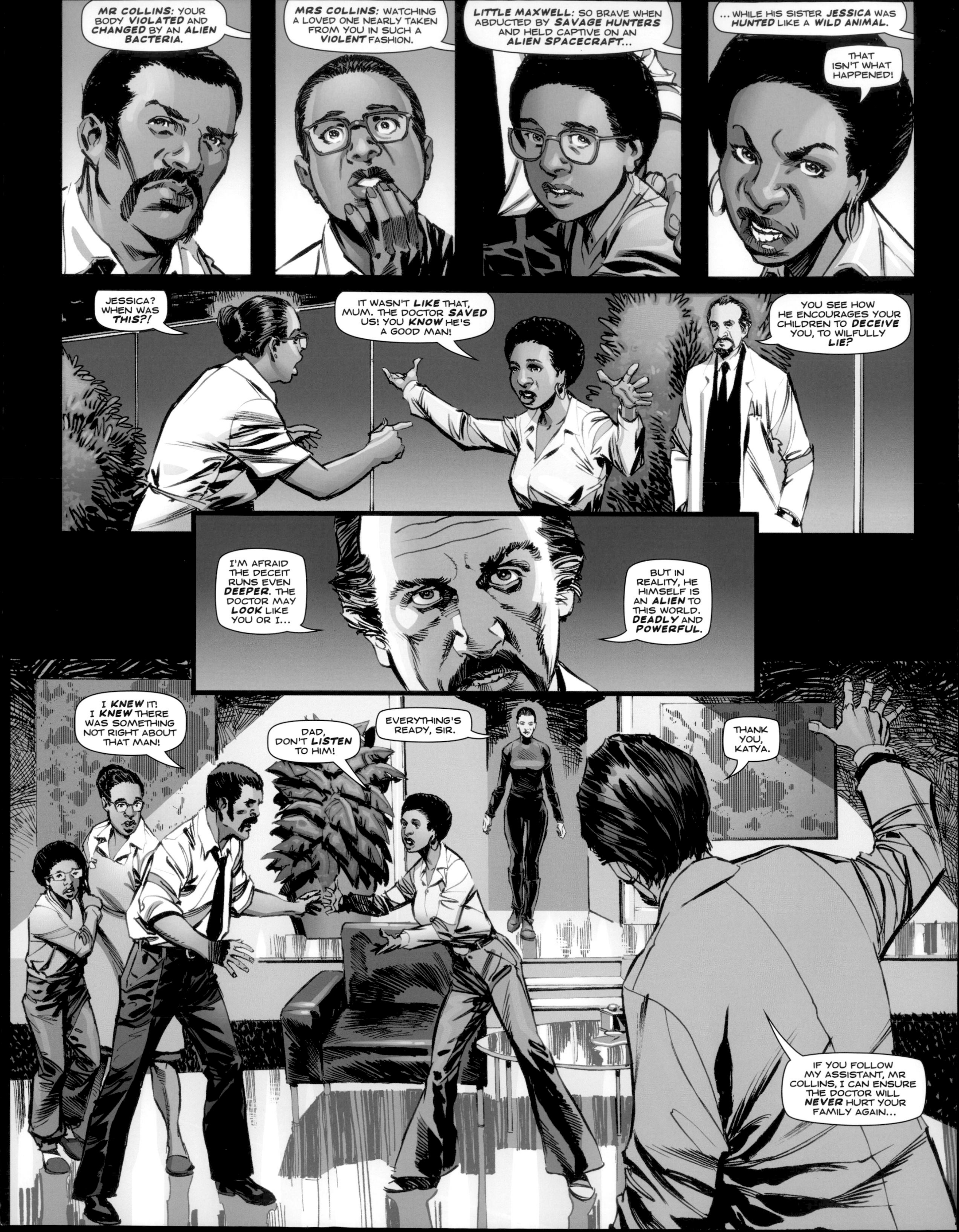
MR COLLINS: YOUR BODY VIOLATED AND CHANGED BY AN ALIEN BACTERIA.
MRS COLLINS: WATCHING A LOVED ONE NEARLY TAKEN FROM YOU IN SUCH A VIOLENT FASHION.
LITTLE MAXWELL: SO BRAVE WHEN ABDUCTED BY SAVAGE HUNTERS AND HELD CAPTIVE ON AN ALIEN SPACECRAFT...
... WHILE HIS SISTER JESSICA WAS HUNTED LIKE A WILD ANIMAL.
THAT ISN'T WHAT HAPPENED!
JESSICA? WHEN WAS THIS?!
IT WASN'T LIKE THAT, MUM. THE DOCTOR SAVED US! YOU KNOW HE'S A GOOD MAN!
YOU SEE HOW HE ENCOURAGES YOUR CHILDREN TO DECEIVE YOU, TO WILFULLY LIE?
I'M AFRAID THE DECEIT RUNS EVEN DEEPER. THE DOCTOR MAY LOOK LIKE YOU OR I...
BUT IN REALITY, HE HIMSELF IS AN ALIEN TO THIS WORLD. DEADLY AND POWERFUL.
I KNEW IT! I KNEW THERE WAS SOMETHING NOT RIGHT ABOUT THAT MAN!
DAD, DON'T LISTEN TO HIM!
EVERYTHING'S READY, SIR.
THANK YOU, KATYA.
IF YOU FOLLOW MY ASSISTANT, MR COLLINS, I CAN ENSURE THE DOCTOR WILL NEVER HURT YOUR FAMILY AGAIN...

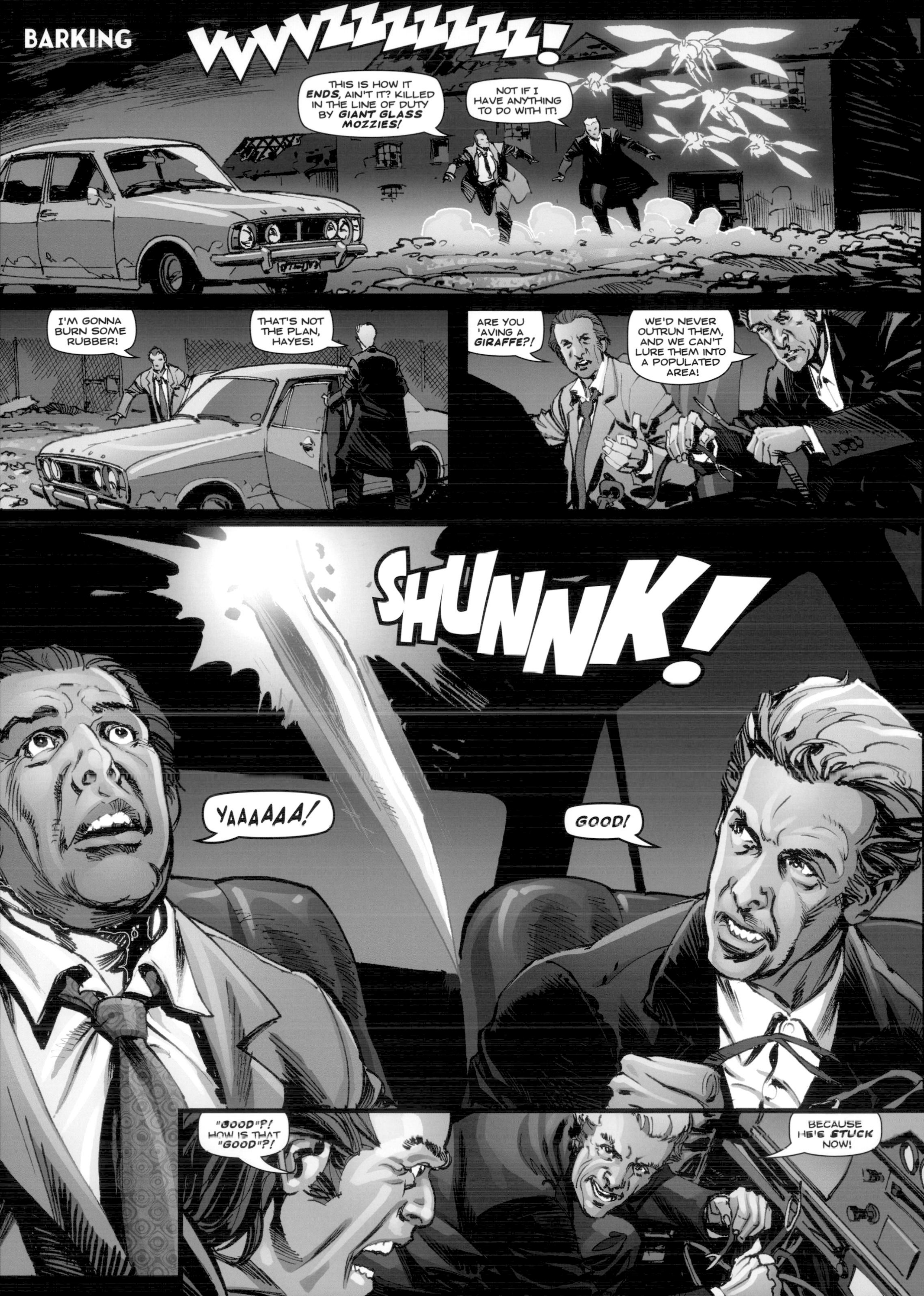
WWZZZZZZZZ!
THIS IS HOW IT ENDS, AIN'T IT? KILLED IN THE LINE OF DUTY BY GIANT GLASS MOZZIES!
NOT IF I HAVE ANYTHING TO DO WITH IT!
I'M GONNA BURN SOME RUBBER!
THAT'S NOT THE PLAN, HAYES!
ARE YOU 'AVING A GIRAFFE?!
WE'D NEVER OUTRUN THEM, AND WE CAN'T LURE THEM INTO A POPULATED AREA!
SHUNNK!
YAAAAAA!
GOOD!
"GOOD"?! HOW IS THAT "GOOD"?!
BECAUSE HE'S STUCK NOW!

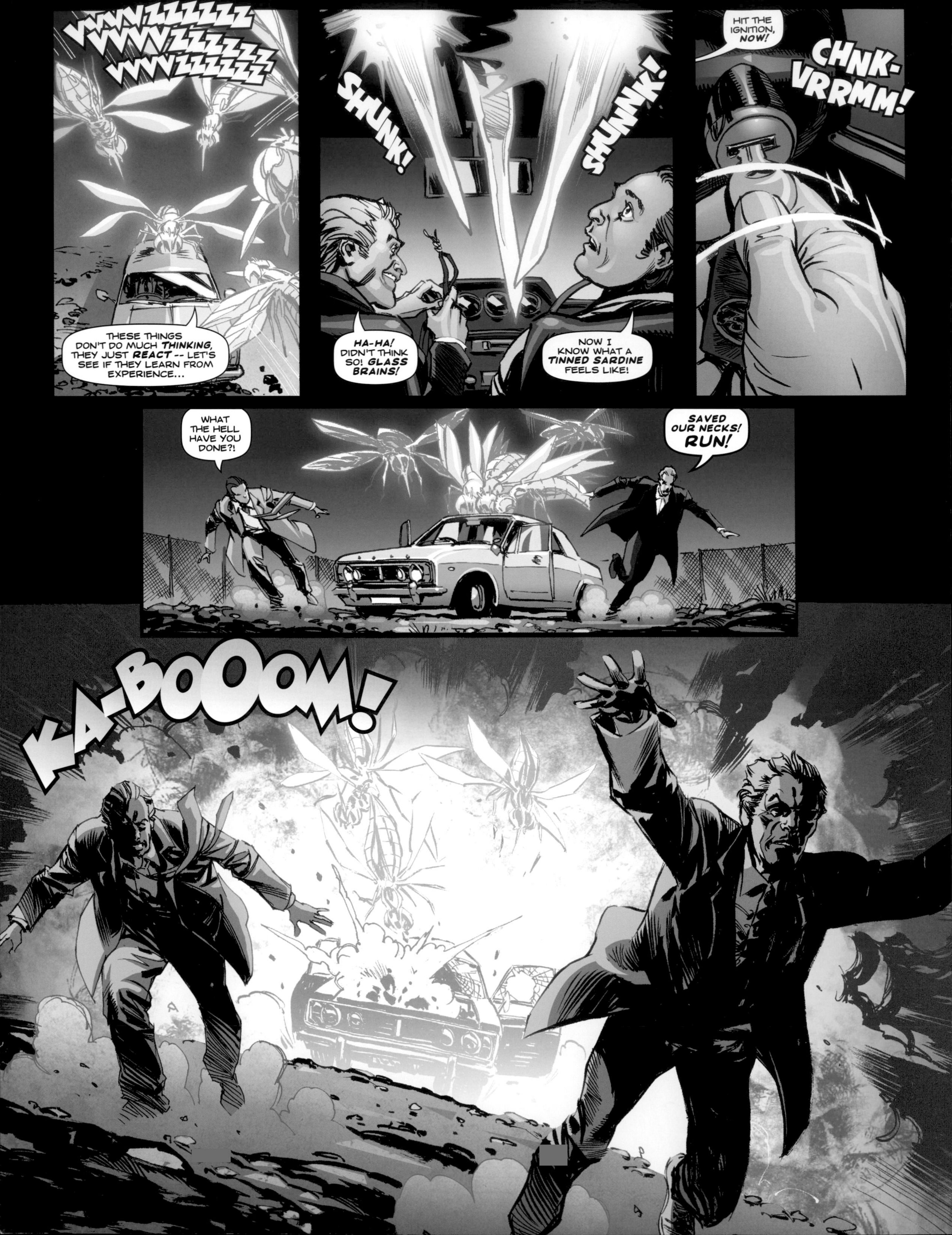
VVVVZZZZZZZ
VVVVZZZZZZZ
VVVVZZZZZZZ
THESE THINGS DON'T DO MUCH THINKING, THEY JUST REACT -- LET'S SEE IF THEY LEARN FROM EXPERIENCE...
SHUNK!
SHUNK!
HA-HA! DIDN'T THINK SO! GLASS BRAINS!
NOW I KNOW WHAT A TINNED SARDINE FEELS LIKE!
HIT THE IGNITION, NOW!
CHNK-VRRMM!
WHAT THE HELL HAVE YOU DONE?!
SAVED OUR NECKS! RUN!
KA-BOOOOM!

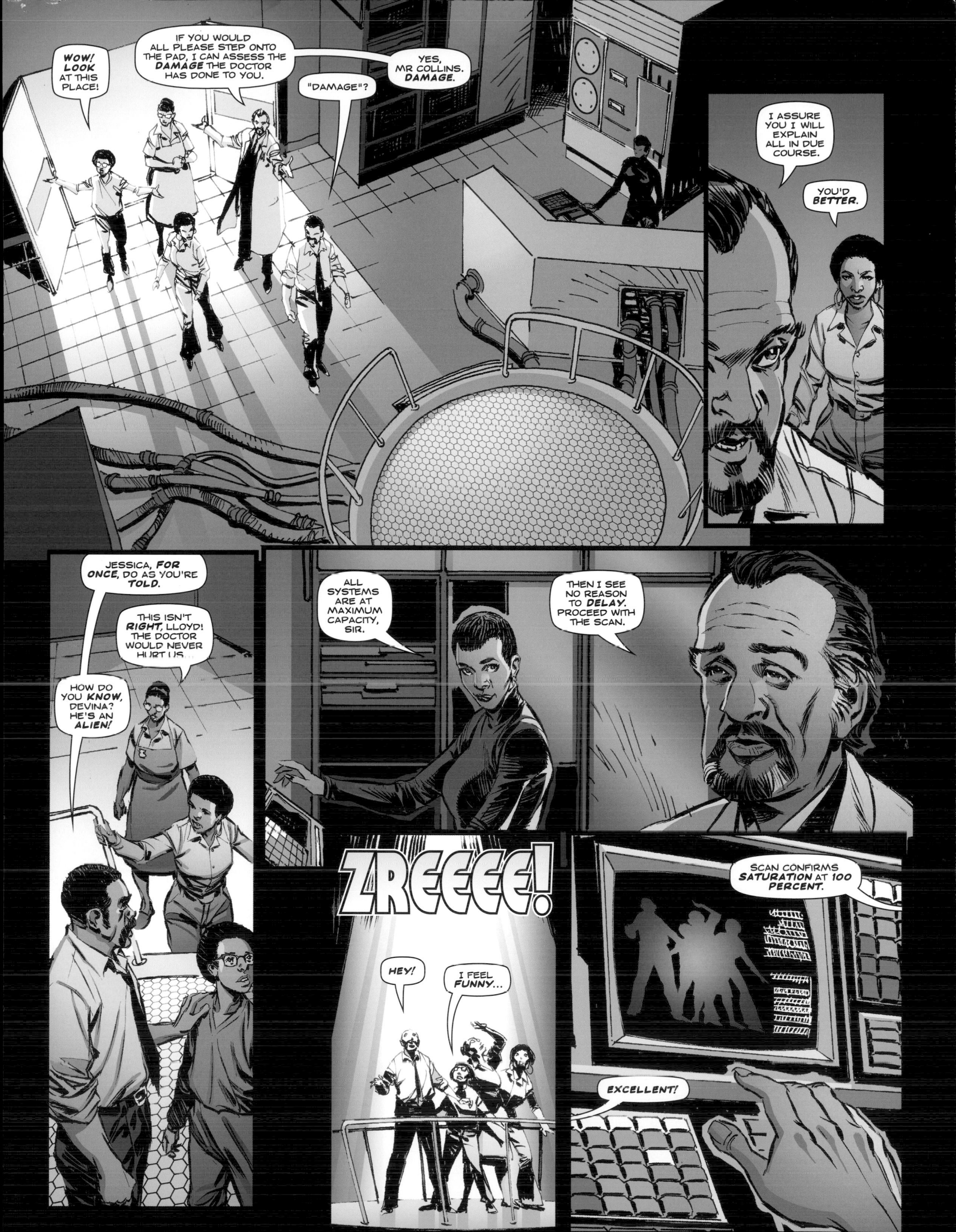

WOW! LOOK AT THIS PLACE!
IF YOU WOULD ALL PLEASE STEP ONTO THE PAD, I CAN ASSESS THE DAMAGE THE DOCTOR HAS DONE TO YOU.
"DAMAGE"?
YES, MR COLLINS. DAMAGE.
I ASSURE YOU I WILL EXPLAIN ALL IN DUE COURSE.
YOU'D BETTER.
JESSICA, FOR ONCE, DO AS YOU'RE TOLD.
THIS ISN'T RIGHT, LLOYD! THE DOCTOR WOULD NEVER HURT US...
HOW DO YOU KNOW, DEVINA? HE'S AN ALIEN!
ALL SYSTEMS ARE AT MAXIMUM CAPACITY, SIR.
THEN I SEE NO REASON TO DELAY. PROCEED WITH THE SCAN.
ZREEEE!
HEY!
I FEEL FUNNY...
SCAN CONFIRMS SATURATION AT 100 PERCENT.
EXCELLENT!

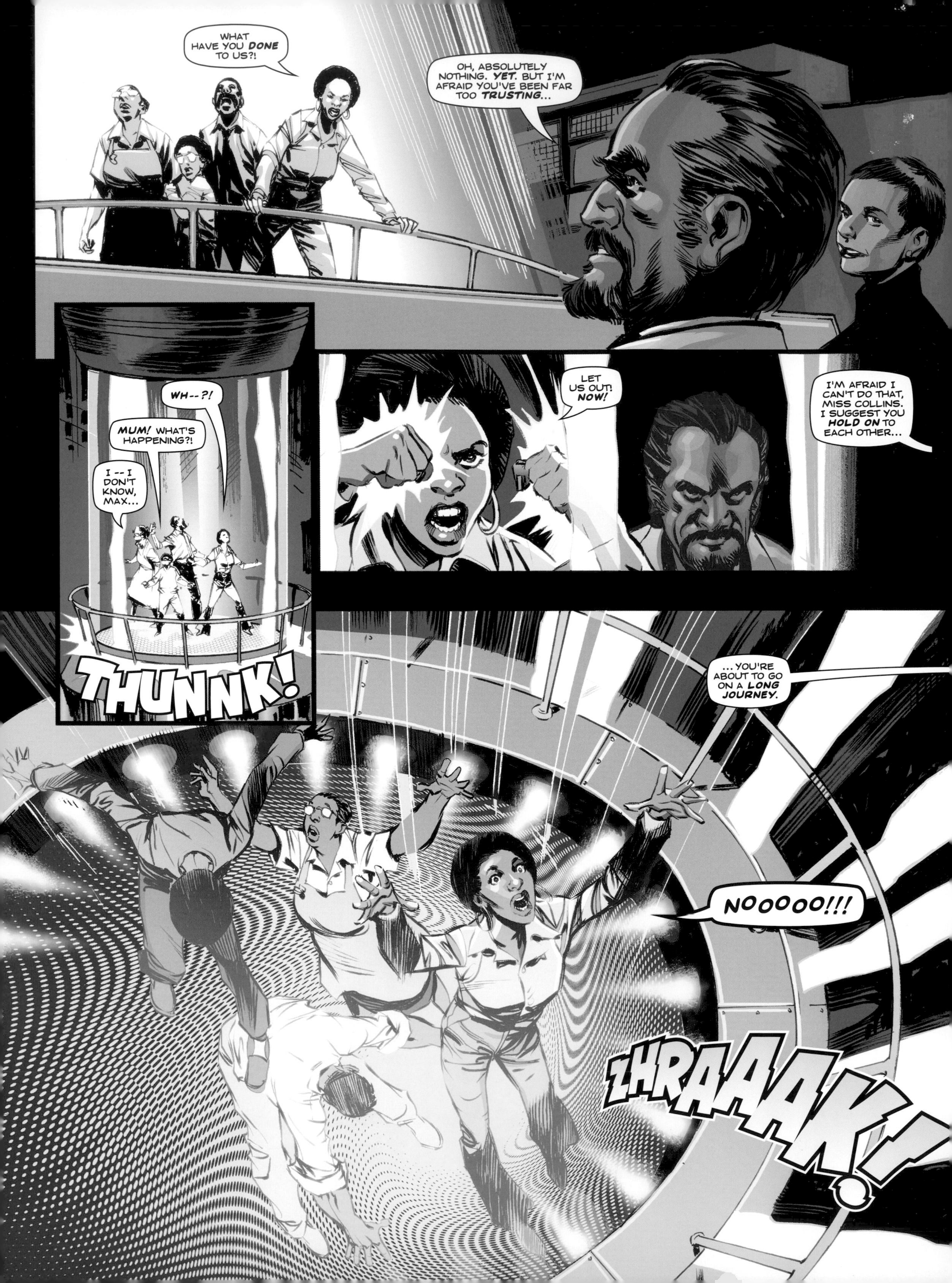
WHAT HAVE YOU DONE TO US?!
OH, ABSOLUTELY NOTHING. YET. BUT I'M AFRAID YOU'VE BEEN FAR TOO TRUSTING...
WH--?!
MUM! WHAT'S HAPPENING?!
I -- I DON'T KNOW, MAX...
THUNNK!
LET US OUT! NOW!
I'M AFRAID I CAN'T DO THAT, MISS COLLINS. I SUGGEST YOU HOLD ON TO EACH OTHER...
...YOU'RE ABOUT TO GO ON A LONG JOURNEY.
NOOOOO!!!
ZHRAAAK!!

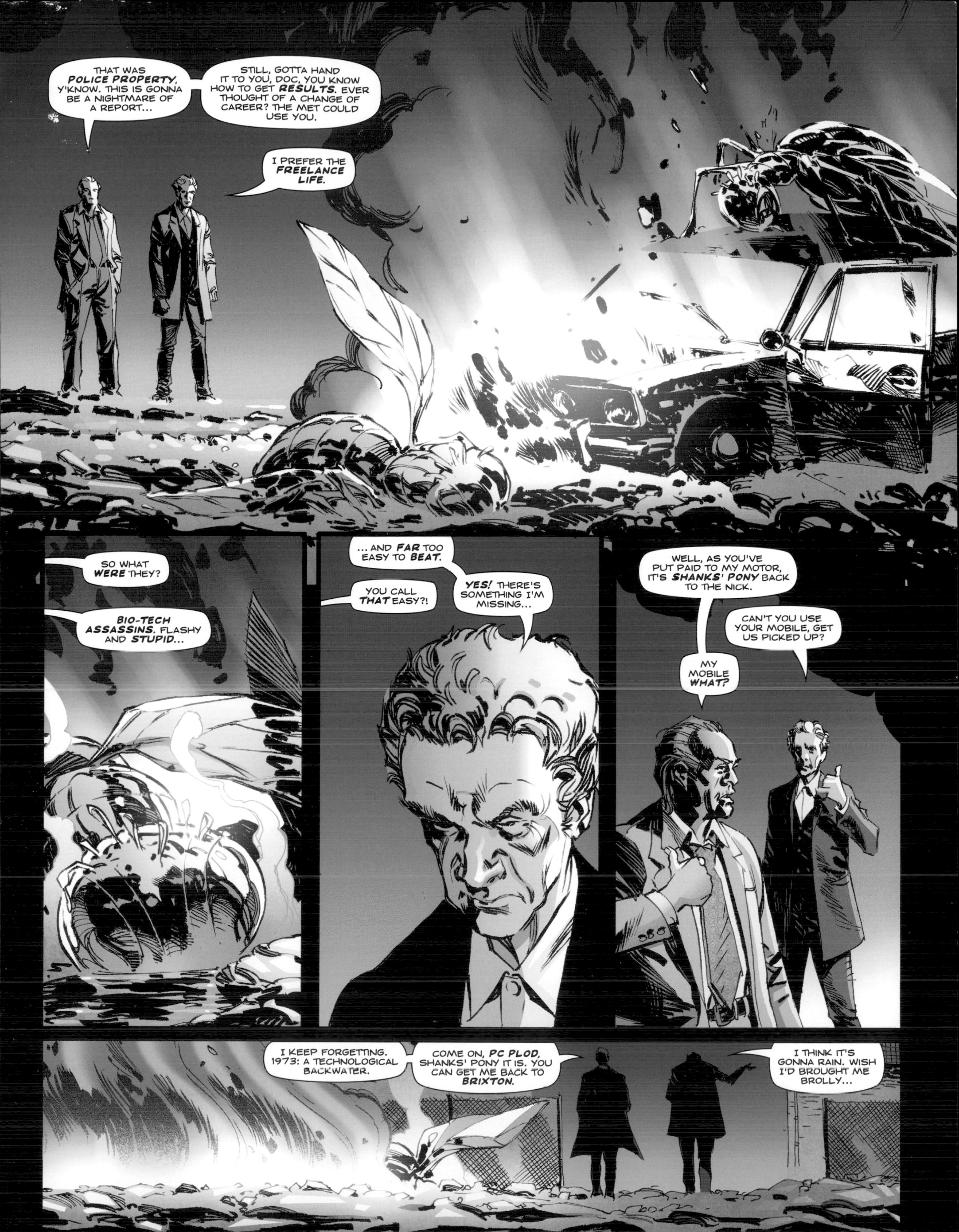
THAT WAS POLICE PROPERTY, Y'KNOW. THIS IS GONNA BE A NIGHTMARE OF A REPORT...
STILL, GOTTA HAND IT TO YOU, DOC, YOU KNOW HOW TO GET RESULTS. EVER THOUGHT OF A CHANGE OF CAREER? THE MET COULD USE YOU.
I PREFER THE FREELANCE LIFE.
SO WHAT WERE THEY?
BIO-TECH ASSASSINS. FLASHY AND STUPID...
...AND FAR TOO EASY TO BEAT.
YOU CALL THAT EASY?!
YES! THERE'S SOMETHING I'M MISSING...
WELL, AS YOU'VE PUT PAID TO MY MOTOR, IT'S SHANKS' PONY BACK TO THE NICK.
CAN'T YOU USE YOUR MOBILE, GET US PICKED UP?
MY MOBILE WHAT?
I KEEP FORGETTING. 1973: A TECHNOLOGICAL BACKWATER.
COME ON, PC PLOD, SHANKS' PONY IT IS. YOU CAN GET ME BACK TO BRIXTON.
I THINK IT'S GONNA RAIN. WISH I'D BROUGHT ME BROLLY...

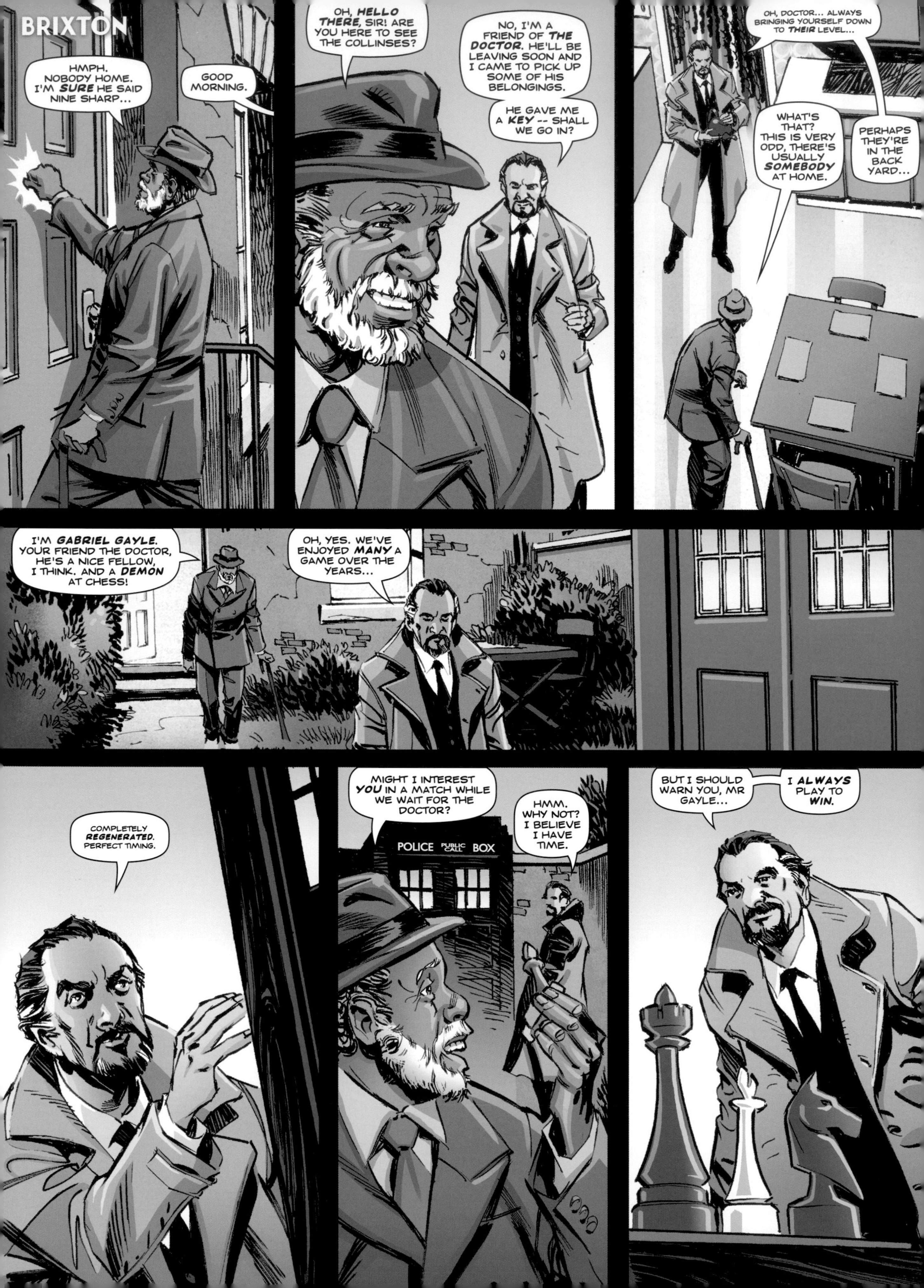
BRIXTON
HMPH. NOBODY HOME. I'M SURE HE SAID NINE SHARP...
GOOD MORNING.
OH, HELLO THERE, SIR! ARE YOU HERE TO SEE THE COLLINSES?
NO, I'M A FRIEND OF THE DOCTOR. HE'LL BE LEAVING SOON AND I CAME TO PICK UP SOME OF HIS BELONGINGS.
HE GAVE ME A KEY -- SHALL WE GO IN?
OH, DOCTOR... ALWAYS BRINGING YOURSELF DOWN TO THEIR LEVEL...
WHAT'S THAT? THIS IS VERY ODD, THERE'S USUALLY SOMEBODY AT HOME.
PERHAPS THEY'RE IN THE BACK YARD...
I'M GABRIEL GAYLE. YOUR FRIEND THE DOCTOR, HE'S A NICE FELLOW, I THINK. AND A DEMON AT CHESS!
OH, YES. WE'VE ENJOYED MANY A GAME OVER THE YEARS...
COMPLETELY REGENERATED. PERFECT TIMING.
MIGHT I INTEREST YOU IN A MATCH WHILE WE WAIT FOR THE DOCTOR?
POLICE PUBLIC CALL BOX
HMM. WHY NOT? I BELIEVE I HAVE TIME.
BUT I SHOULD WARN YOU, MR GAYLE...
I ALWAYS PLAY TO WIN.

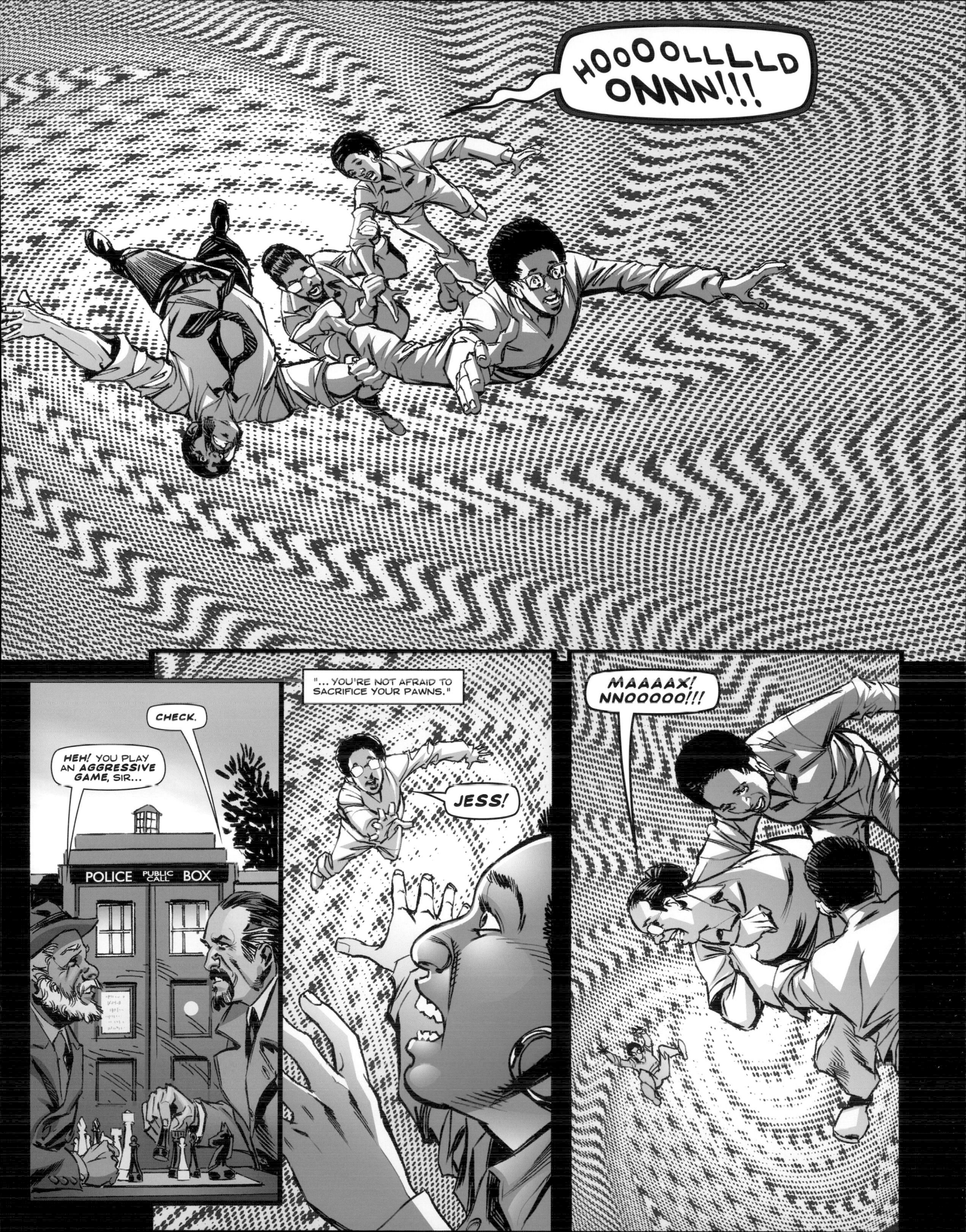
HOOOOLLLLLD ONNN!!!
HEH! YOU PLAY AN AGGRESSIVE GAME, SIR...
CHECK.
POLICE PUBLIC CALL BOX
"... YOU'RE NOT AFRAID TO SACRIFICE YOUR PAWNS."
JESS!
MAAAAX! NNOOOOO!!!

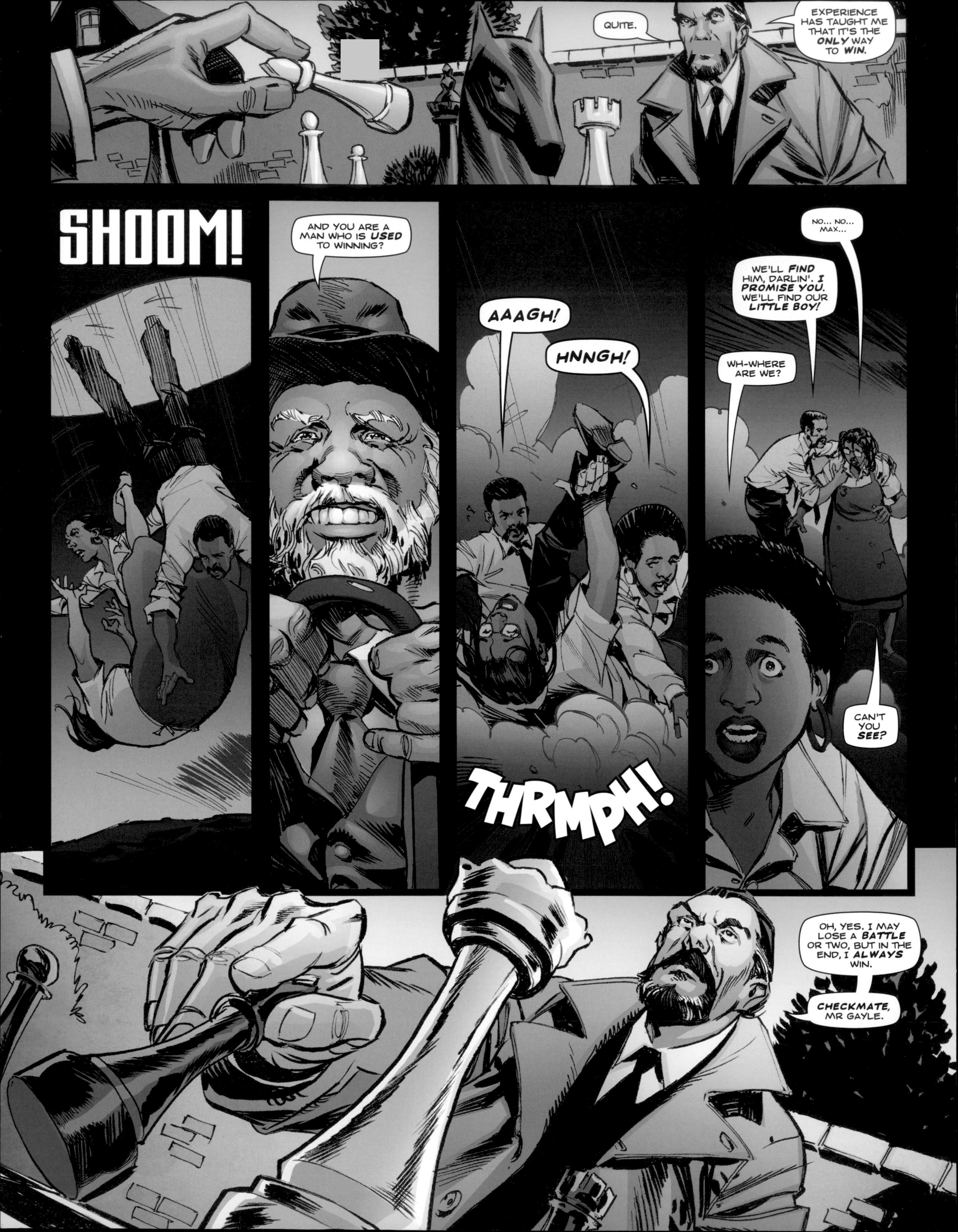
QUITE.
EXPERIENCE HAS TAUGHT ME THAT IT'S THE *ONLY* WAY TO *WIN*.
SHOOM!
AND YOU ARE A MAN WHO IS *USED* TO WINNING?
AAAGH!
HNNGH!
THRMPH!
NO... NO... MAX...
WE'LL *FIND* HIM, DARLIN'. *I PROMISE YOU*. WE'LL FIND OUR *LITTLE BOY!*
WH-WHERE ARE WE?
CAN'T YOU *SEE?*
OH, YES. I MAY LOSE A *BATTLE* OR TWO, BUT IN THE END, I *ALWAYS* WIN.
*CHECKMATE*, MR GAYLE.

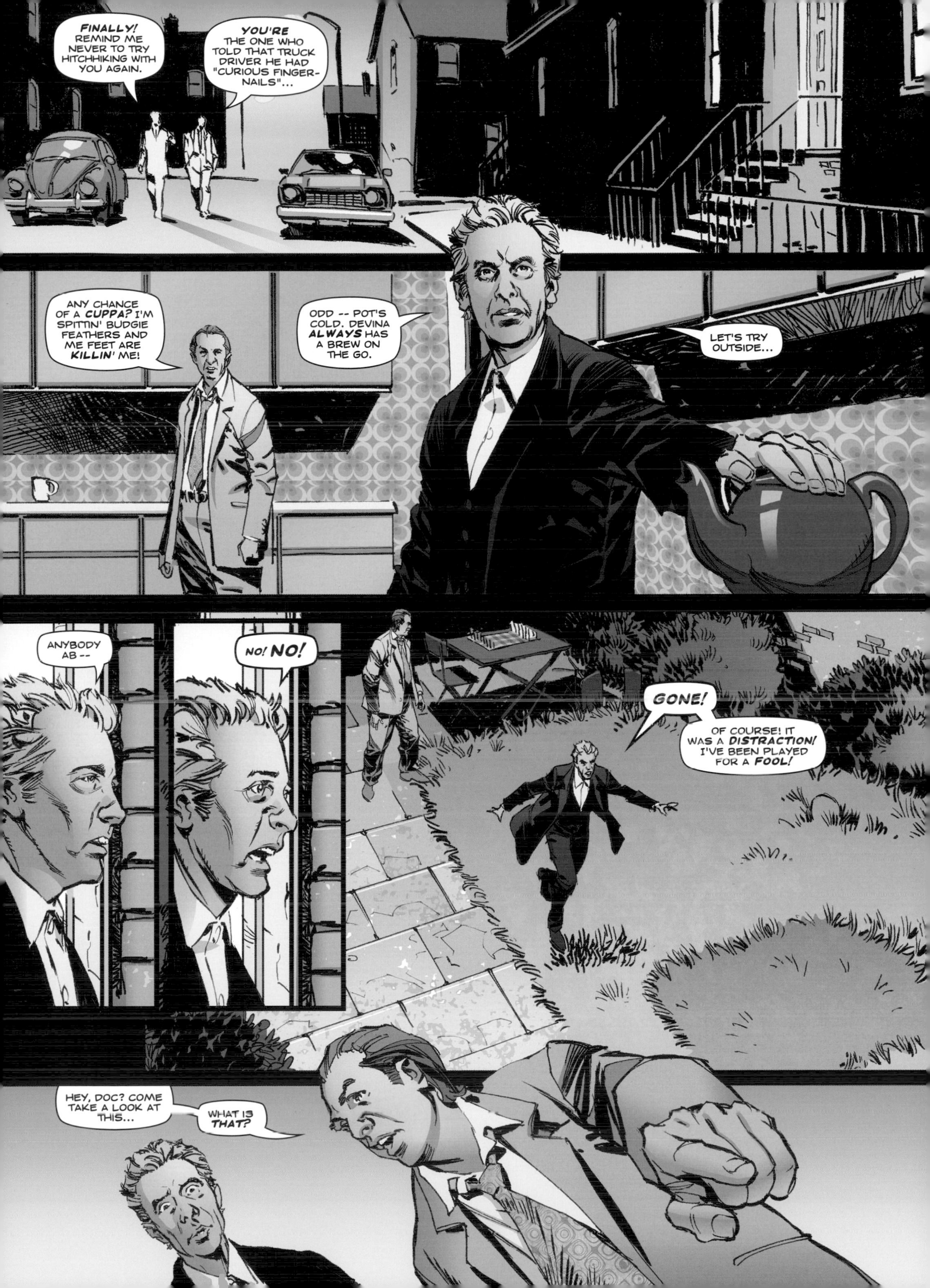
FINALLY! REMIND ME NEVER TO TRY HITCHHIKING WITH YOU AGAIN.
YOU'RE THE ONE WHO TOLD THAT TRUCK DRIVER HE HAD "CURIOUS FINGER-NAILS"...
ANY CHANCE OF A CUPPA? I'M SPITTIN' BUDGIE FEATHERS AND ME FEET ARE KILLIN' ME!
ODD -- POT'S COLD. DEVINA ALWAYS HAS A BREW ON THE GO.
LET'S TRY OUTSIDE...
ANYBODY AB --
NO! NO!
GONE!
OF COURSE! IT WAS A DISTRACTION! I'VE BEEN PLAYED FOR A FOOL!
HEY, DOC? COME TAKE A LOOK AT THIS...
WHAT IS THAT?

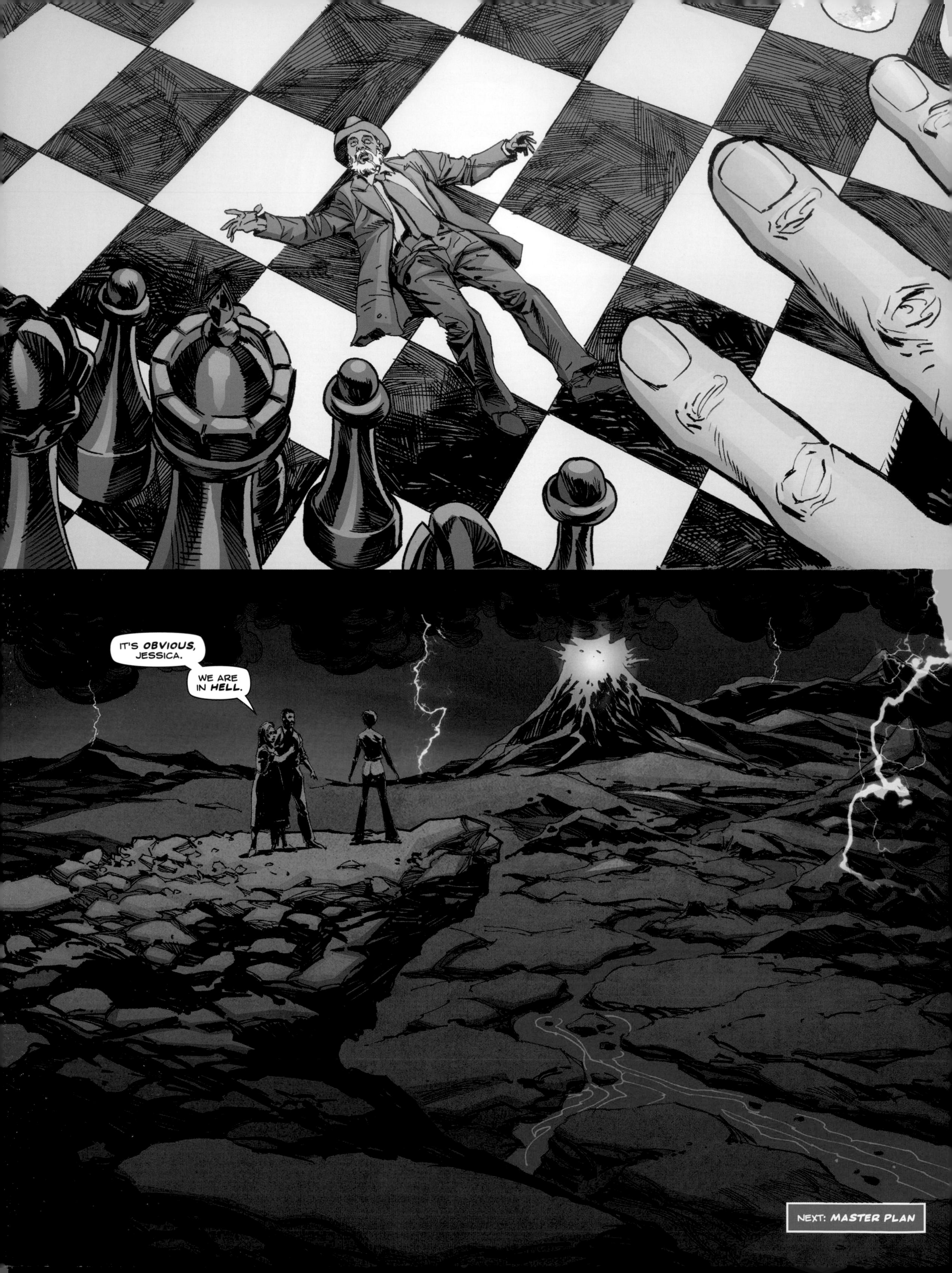

IT'S *OBVIOUS*, JESSICA.
WE ARE IN *HELL*.
NEXT: *MASTER PLAN*

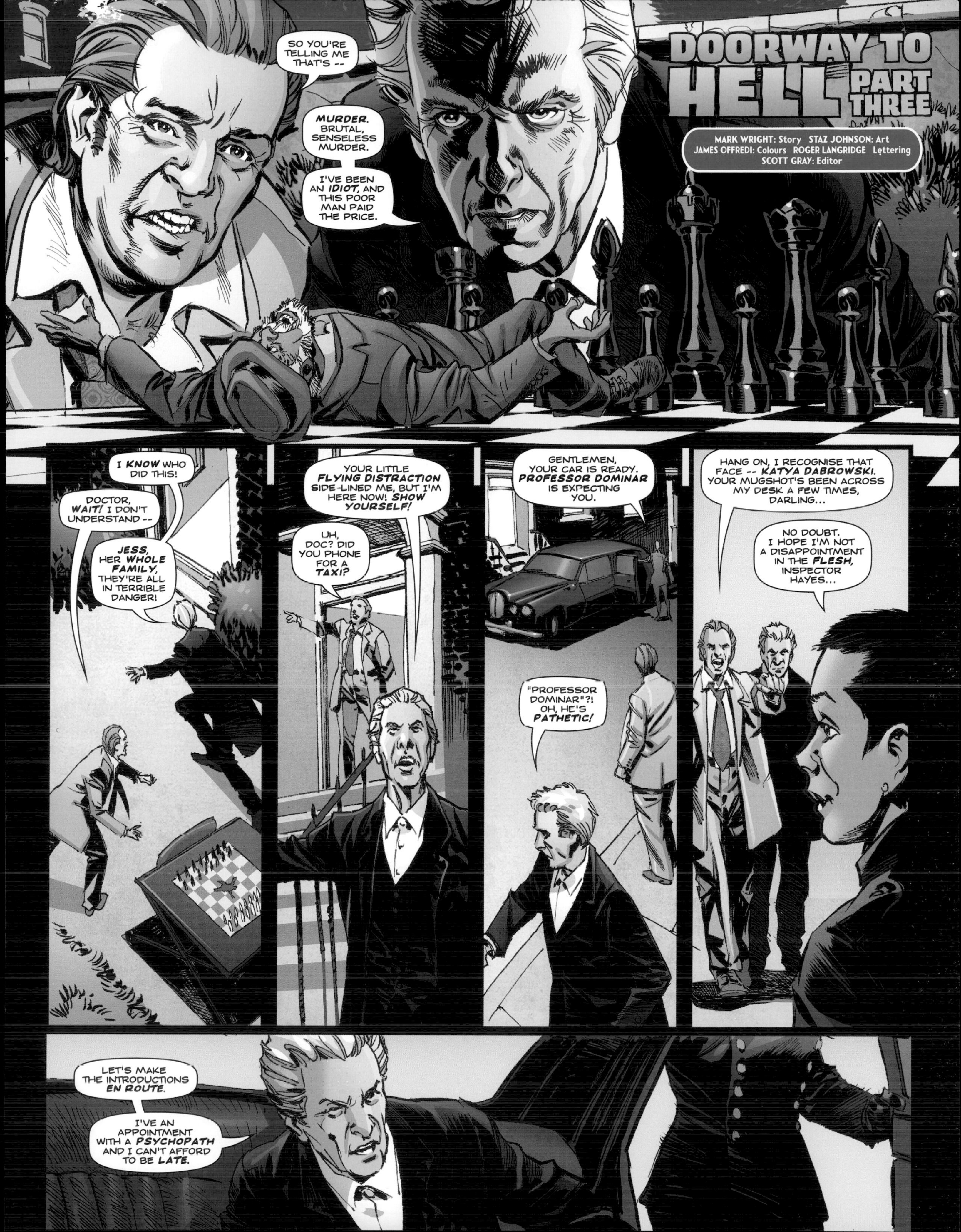
DOORWAY TO HELL PART THREE
MARK WRIGHT: Story STAZ JOHNSON: Art
JAMES OFFREDI: Colours ROGER LANGRIDGE Lettering
SCOTT GRAY: Editor
SO YOU'RE TELLING ME THAT'S --
MURDER. BRUTAL, SENSELESS MURDER.
I'VE BEEN AN IDIOT, AND THIS POOR MAN PAID THE PRICE.
I KNOW WHO DID THIS!
DOCTOR, WAIT! I DON'T UNDERSTAND --
JESS, HER WHOLE FAMILY, THEY'RE ALL IN TERRIBLE DANGER!
YOUR LITTLE FLYING DISTRACTION SIDE-LINED ME, BUT I'M HERE NOW! SHOW YOURSELF!
UH, DOC? DID YOU PHONE FOR A TAXI?
GENTLEMEN, YOUR CAR IS READY. PROFESSOR DOMINAR IS EXPECTING YOU.
"PROFESSOR DOMINAR"?! OH, HE'S PATHETIC!
HANG ON, I RECOGNISE THAT FACE -- KATYA DABROWSKI. YOUR MUGSHOT'S BEEN ACROSS MY DESK A FEW TIMES, DARLING...
NO DOUBT. I HOPE I'M NOT A DISAPPOINTMENT IN THE FLESH, INSPECTOR HAYES...
LET'S MAKE THE INTRODUCTIONS EN ROUTE.
I'VE AN APPOINTMENT WITH A PSYCHOPATH AND I CAN'T AFFORD TO BE LATE.

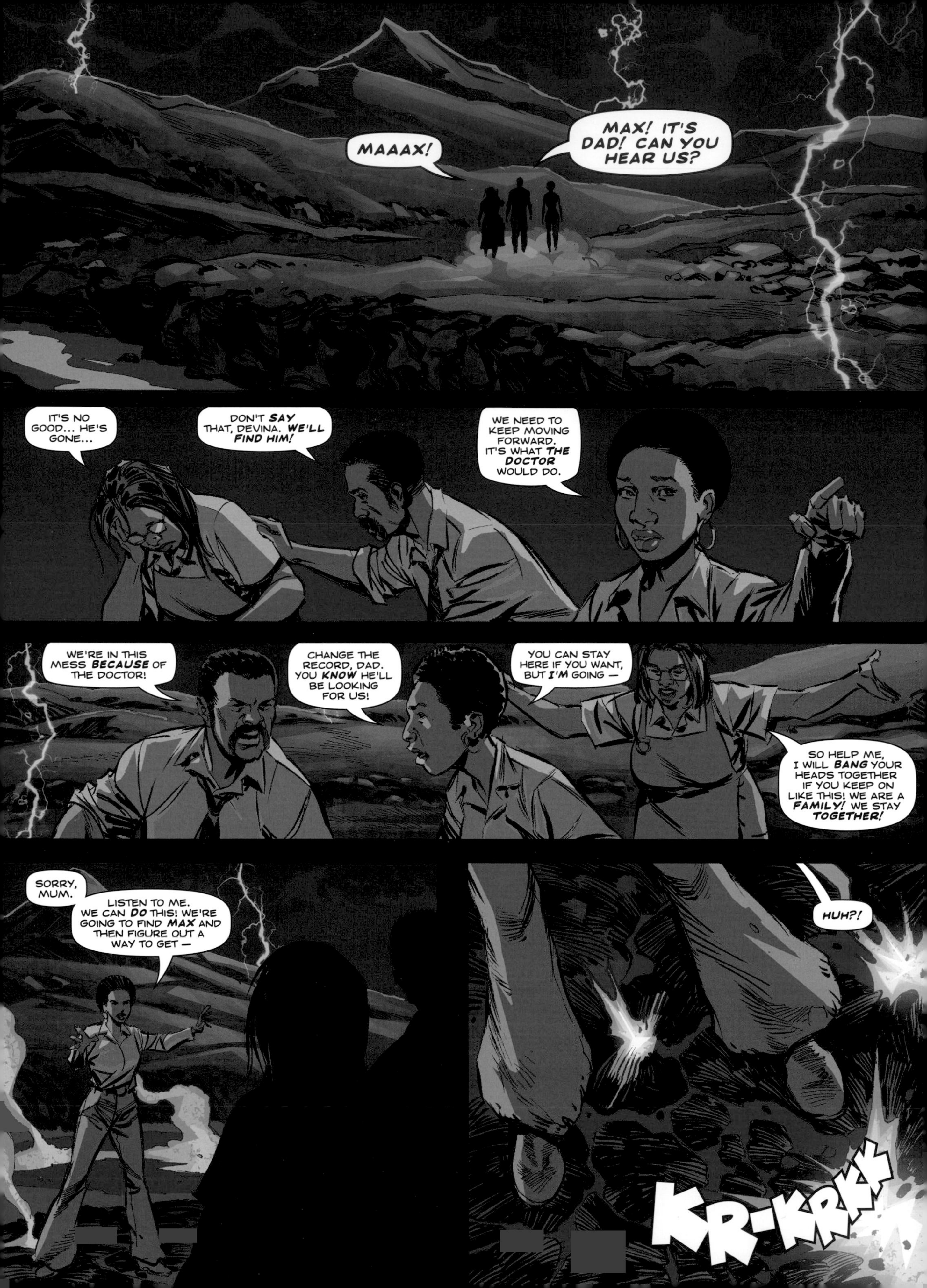
MAAAX!
MAX! IT'S DAD! CAN YOU HEAR US?
IT'S NO GOOD... HE'S GONE...
DON'T SAY THAT, DEVINA. WE'LL FIND HIM!
WE NEED TO KEEP MOVING FORWARD. IT'S WHAT THE DOCTOR WOULD DO.
WE'RE IN THIS MESS BECAUSE OF THE DOCTOR!
CHANGE THE RECORD, DAD. YOU KNOW HE'LL BE LOOKING FOR US!
YOU CAN STAY HERE IF YOU WANT, BUT I'M GOING —
SO HELP ME, I WILL BANG YOUR HEADS TOGETHER IF YOU KEEP ON LIKE THIS! WE ARE A FAMILY! WE STAY TOGETHER!
SORRY, MUM.
LISTEN TO ME. WE CAN DO THIS! WE'RE GOING TO FIND MAX AND THEN FIGURE OUT A WAY TO GET —
HUH?!
KR-KRKK

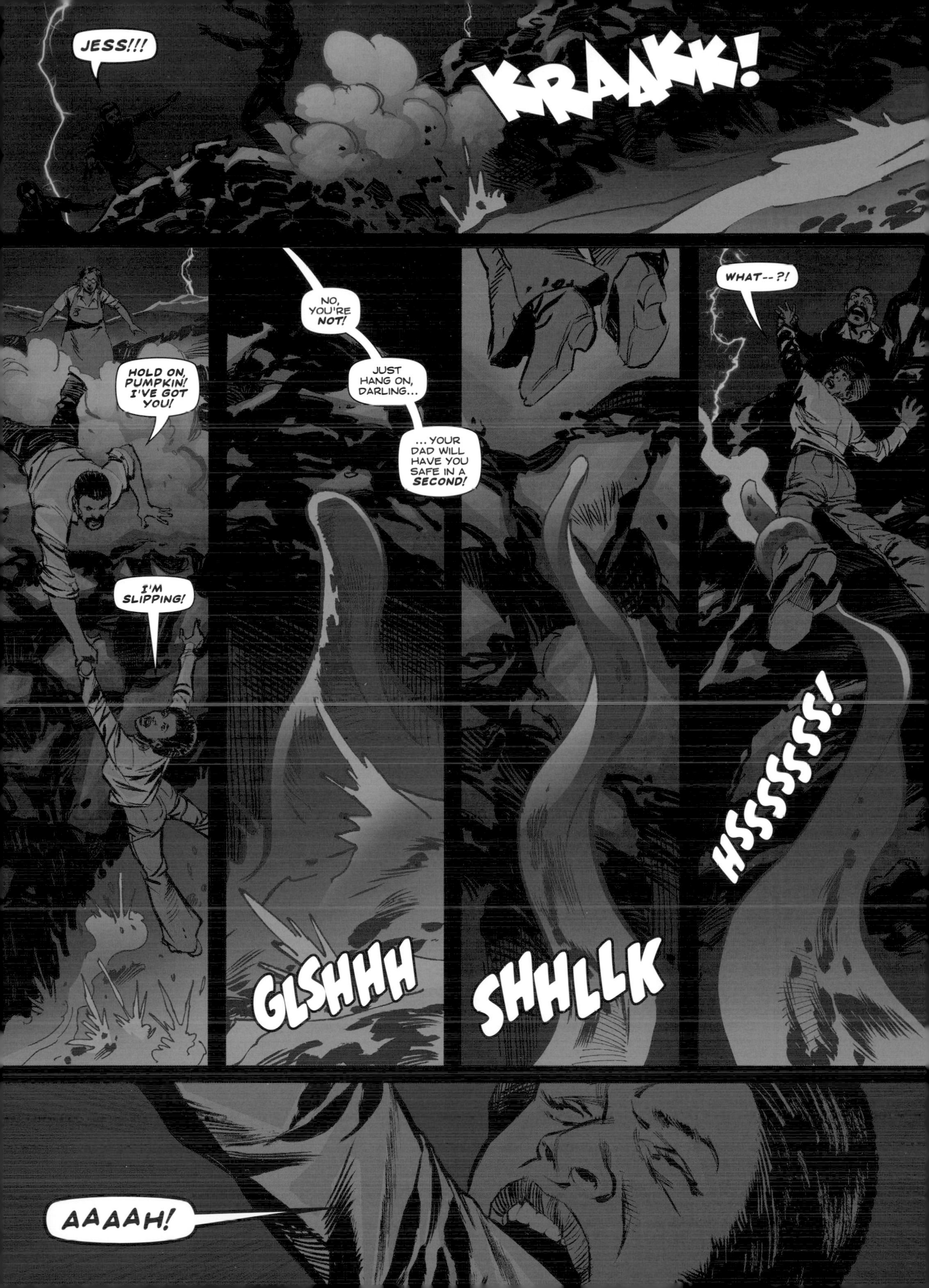
JESS!!!
KRAAKK!
HOLD ON, PUMPKIN! I'VE GOT YOU!
I'M SLIPPING!
NO, YOU'RE NOT!
JUST HANG ON, DARLING...
...YOUR DAD WILL HAVE YOU SAFE IN A SECOND!
GLSHHH
SHHLLK
WHAT--?!
HSSSSSSS!
AAAAH!

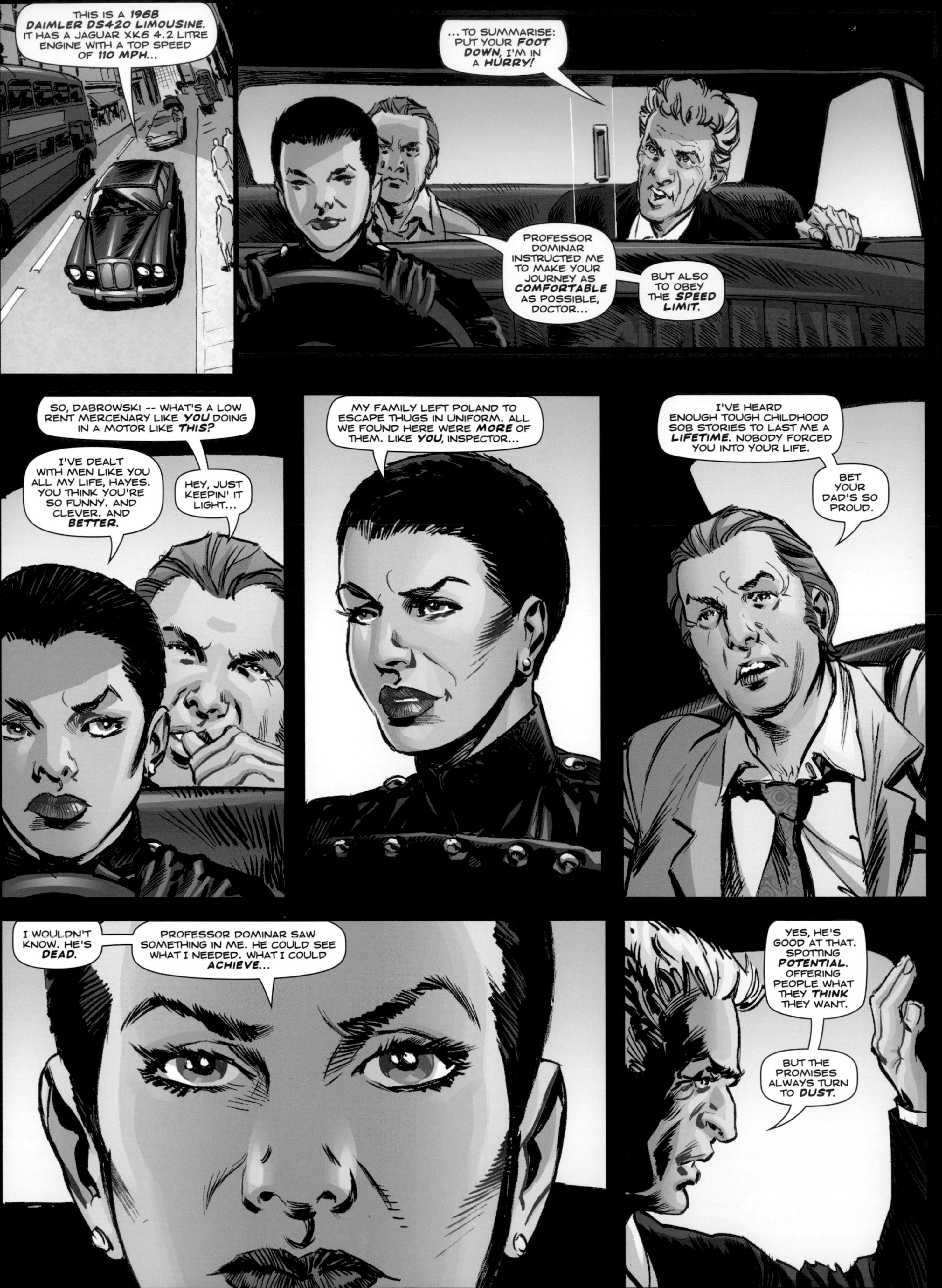
THIS IS A 1968 DAIMLER DS420 LIMOUSINE. IT HAS A JAGUAR XK6 4.2 LITRE ENGINE WITH A TOP SPEED OF 110 MPH...
...TO SUMMARISE: PUT YOUR FOOT DOWN, I'M IN A HURRY!
PROFESSOR DOMINAR INSTRUCTED ME TO MAKE YOUR JOURNEY AS COMFORTABLE AS POSSIBLE, DOCTOR...
BUT ALSO TO OBEY THE SPEED LIMIT.
SO, DABROWSKI -- WHAT'S A LOW RENT MERCENARY LIKE YOU DOING IN A MOTOR LIKE THIS?
I'VE DEALT WITH MEN LIKE YOU ALL MY LIFE, HAYES. YOU THINK YOU'RE SO FUNNY. AND CLEVER. AND BETTER.
HEY, JUST KEEPIN' IT LIGHT...
MY FAMILY LEFT POLAND TO ESCAPE THUGS IN UNIFORM. ALL WE FOUND HERE WERE MORE OF THEM. LIKE YOU, INSPECTOR...
I'VE HEARD ENOUGH TOUGH CHILDHOOD SOB STORIES TO LAST ME A LIFETIME. NOBODY FORCED YOU INTO YOUR LIFE.
BET YOUR DAD'S SO PROUD.
I WOULDN'T KNOW. HE'S DEAD.
PROFESSOR DOMINAR SAW SOMETHING IN ME. HE COULD SEE WHAT I NEEDED. WHAT I COULD ACHIEVE...
YES, HE'S GOOD AT THAT. SPOTTING POTENTIAL. OFFERING PEOPLE WHAT THEY THINK THEY WANT.
BUT THE PROMISES ALWAYS TURN TO DUST.

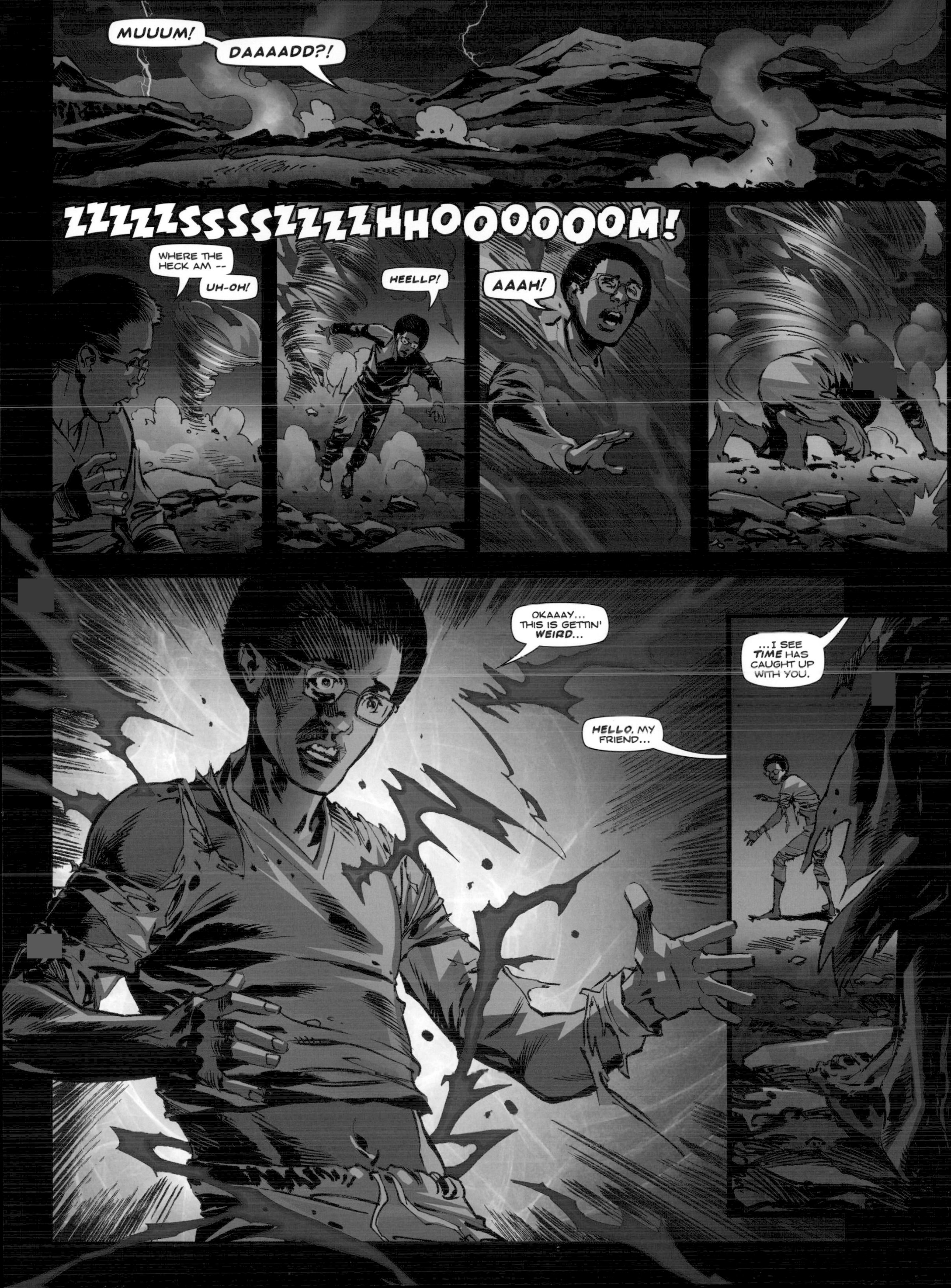
MUUUM!
DAAAADD?!
ZZZZZSSSSZZZZZHHOOOOOOM!
WHERE THE HECK AM --
UH-OH!
HEELLP!
AAAH!
OKAAAY... THIS IS GETTIN' WEIRD...
HELLO, MY FRIEND...
...I SEE TIME HAS CAUGHT UP WITH YOU.

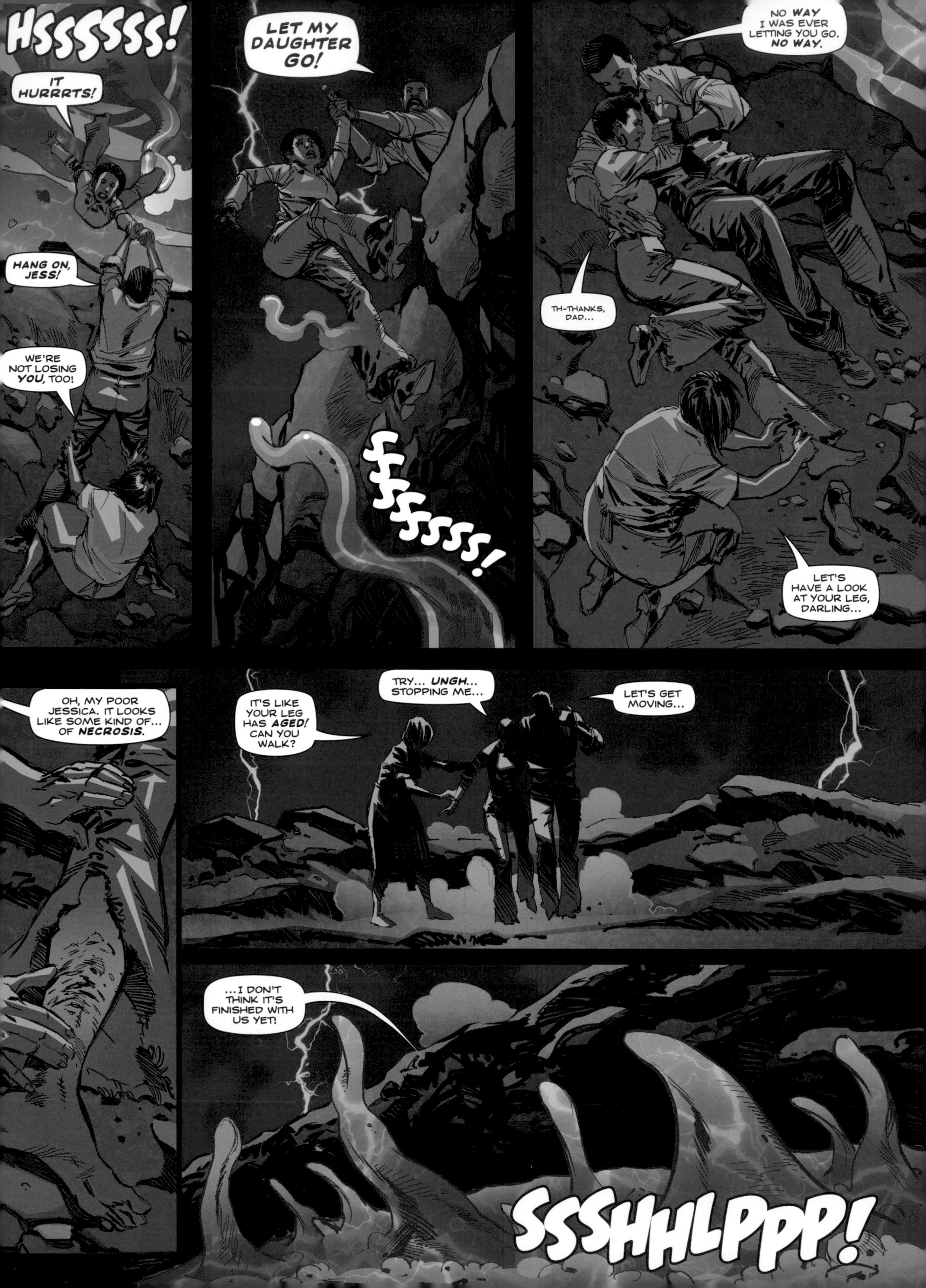
HSSSSSS!
IT HURRRTS!
HANG ON, JESS!
WE'RE NOT LOSING YOU, TOO!
LET MY DAUGHTER GO!
SSSSSSS!
NO WAY I WAS EVER LETTING YOU GO. NO WAY.
TH-THANKS, DAD...
LET'S HAVE A LOOK AT YOUR LEG, DARLING...
OH, MY POOR JESSICA. IT LOOKS LIKE SOME KIND OF... OF NECROSIS.
IT'S LIKE YOUR LEG HAS AGED! CAN YOU WALK?
TRY... UNGH... STOPPING ME...
LET'S GET MOVING...
...I DON'T THINK IT'S FINISHED WITH US YET!
SSSHHLPPP!

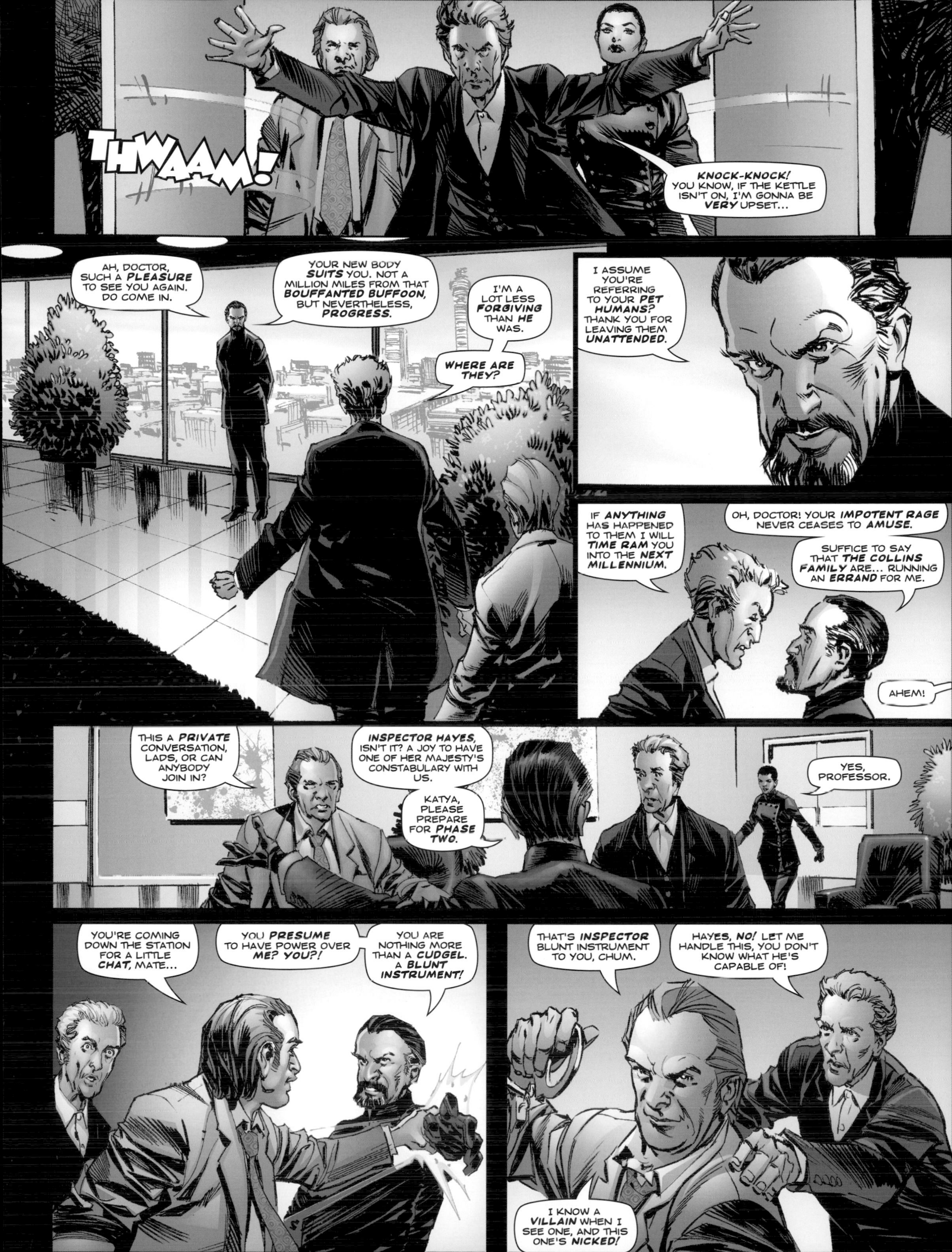
THWAAM!
KNOCK-KNOCK! YOU KNOW, IF THE KETTLE ISN'T ON, I'M GONNA BE VERY UPSET...
AH, DOCTOR, SUCH A PLEASURE TO SEE YOU AGAIN. DO COME IN.
YOUR NEW BODY SUITS YOU. NOT A MILLION MILES FROM THAT BOUFFANTED BUFFOON, BUT NEVERTHELESS, PROGRESS.
I'M A LOT LESS FORGIVING THAN HE WAS.
WHERE ARE THEY?
I ASSUME YOU'RE REFERRING TO YOUR PET HUMANS? THANK YOU FOR LEAVING THEM UNATTENDED.
IF ANYTHING HAS HAPPENED TO THEM I WILL TIME RAM YOU INTO THE NEXT MILLENNIUM.
OH, DOCTOR! YOUR IMPOTENT RAGE NEVER CEASES TO AMUSE.
SUFFICE TO SAY THAT THE COLLINS FAMILY ARE... RUNNING AN ERRAND FOR ME.
AHEM!
THIS A PRIVATE CONVERSATION, LADS, OR CAN ANYBODY JOIN IN?
INSPECTOR HAYES, ISN'T IT? A JOY TO HAVE ONE OF HER MAJESTY'S CONSTABULARY WITH US.
KATYA, PLEASE PREPARE FOR PHASE TWO.
YES, PROFESSOR.
YOU'RE COMING DOWN THE STATION FOR A LITTLE CHAT, MATE...
YOU PRESUME TO HAVE POWER OVER ME? YOU?!
YOU ARE NOTHING MORE THAN A CUDGEL. A BLUNT INSTRUMENT!
THAT'S INSPECTOR BLUNT INSTRUMENT TO YOU, CHUM.
HAYES, NO! LET ME HANDLE THIS, YOU DON'T KNOW WHAT HE'S CAPABLE OF!
I KNOW A VILLAIN WHEN I SEE ONE, AND THIS ONE'S NICKED!

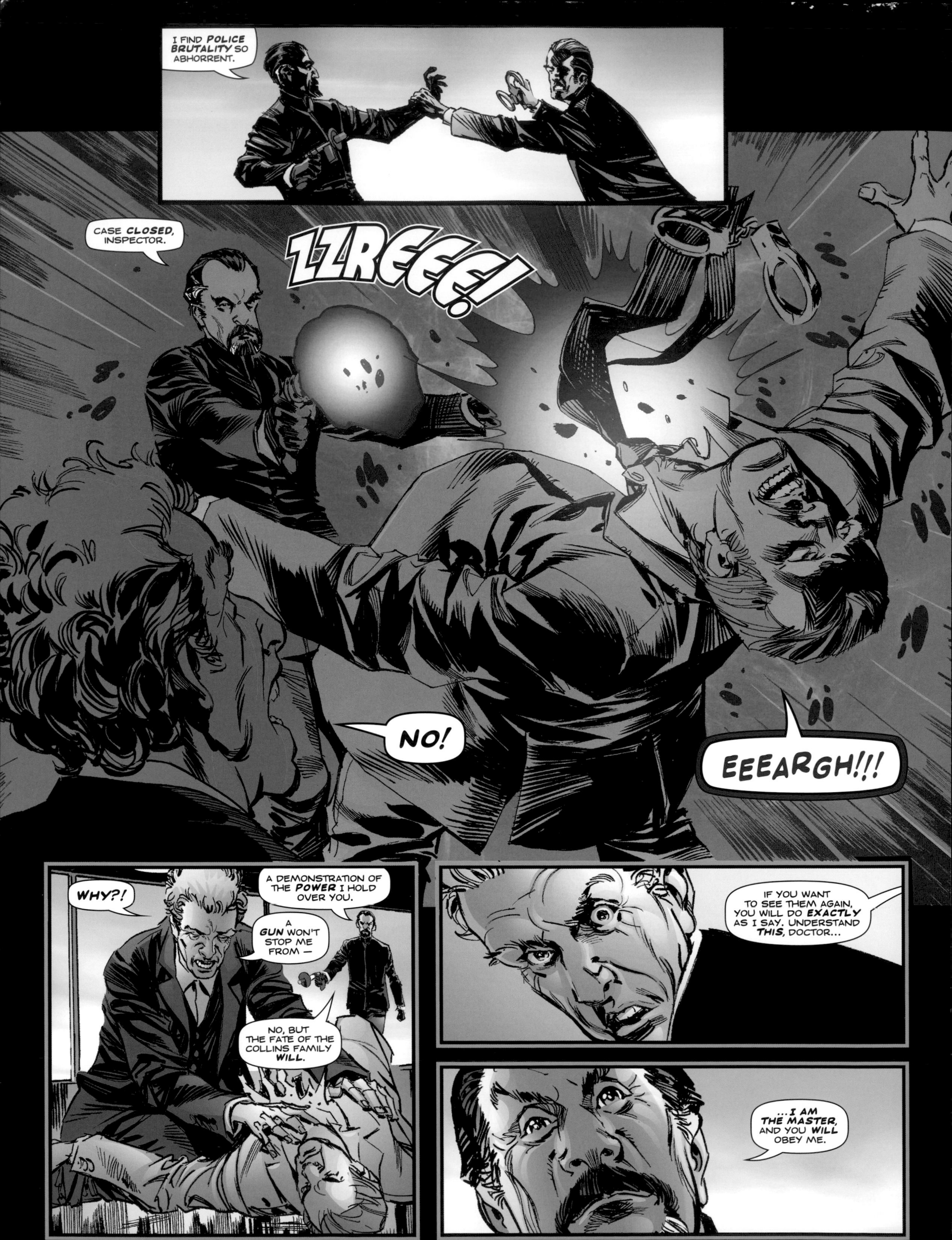

I FIND POLICE BRUTALITY SO ABHORRENT.
CASE CLOSED, INSPECTOR.
ZZREEE!
NO!
EEEARGH!!!
WHY?!
A DEMONSTRATION OF THE POWER I HOLD OVER YOU.
A GUN WON'T STOP ME FROM —
NO, BUT THE FATE OF THE COLLINS FAMILY WILL.
IF YOU WANT TO SEE THEM AGAIN, YOU WILL DO EXACTLY AS I SAY. UNDERSTAND THIS, DOCTOR...
...I AM THE MASTER, AND YOU WILL OBEY ME.

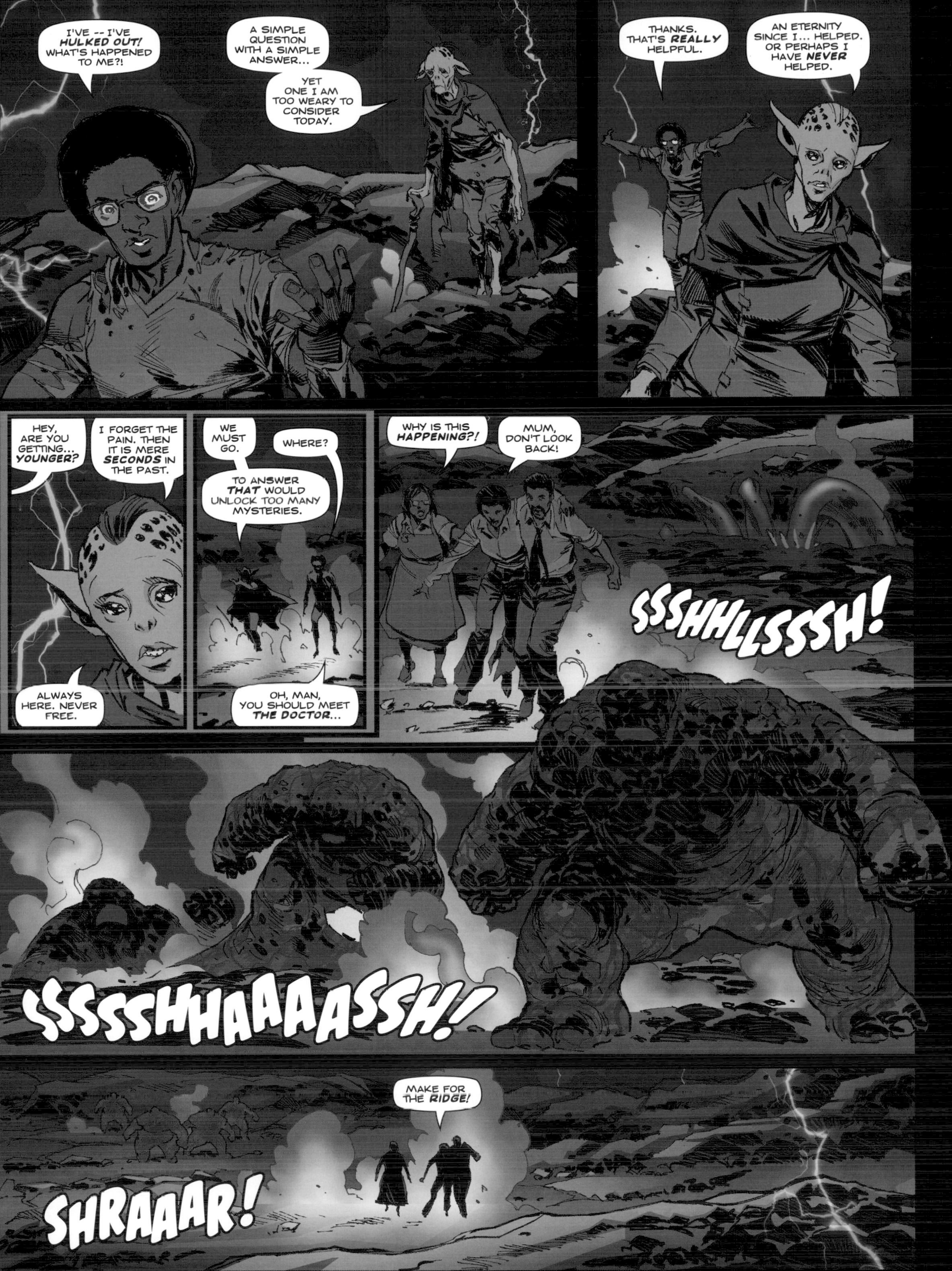

I'VE -- I'VE HULKED OUT! WHAT'S HAPPENED TO ME?!
A SIMPLE QUESTION WITH A SIMPLE ANSWER...
YET ONE I AM TOO WEARY TO CONSIDER TODAY.
THANKS. THAT'S REALLY HELPFUL.
AN ETERNITY SINCE I... HELPED. OR PERHAPS I HAVE NEVER HELPED.
HEY, ARE YOU GETTING... YOUNGER?
I FORGET THE PAIN. THEN IT IS MERE SECONDS IN THE PAST.
ALWAYS HERE. NEVER FREE.
WE MUST GO.
WHERE?
TO ANSWER THAT WOULD UNLOCK TOO MANY MYSTERIES.
OH, MAN, YOU SHOULD MEET THE DOCTOR...
WHY IS THIS HAPPENING?!
MUM, DON'T LOOK BACK!
SSSHHLLSSSH!
SSSSSHHAAAAASSH!
MAKE FOR THE RIDGE!
SHRAAAR!

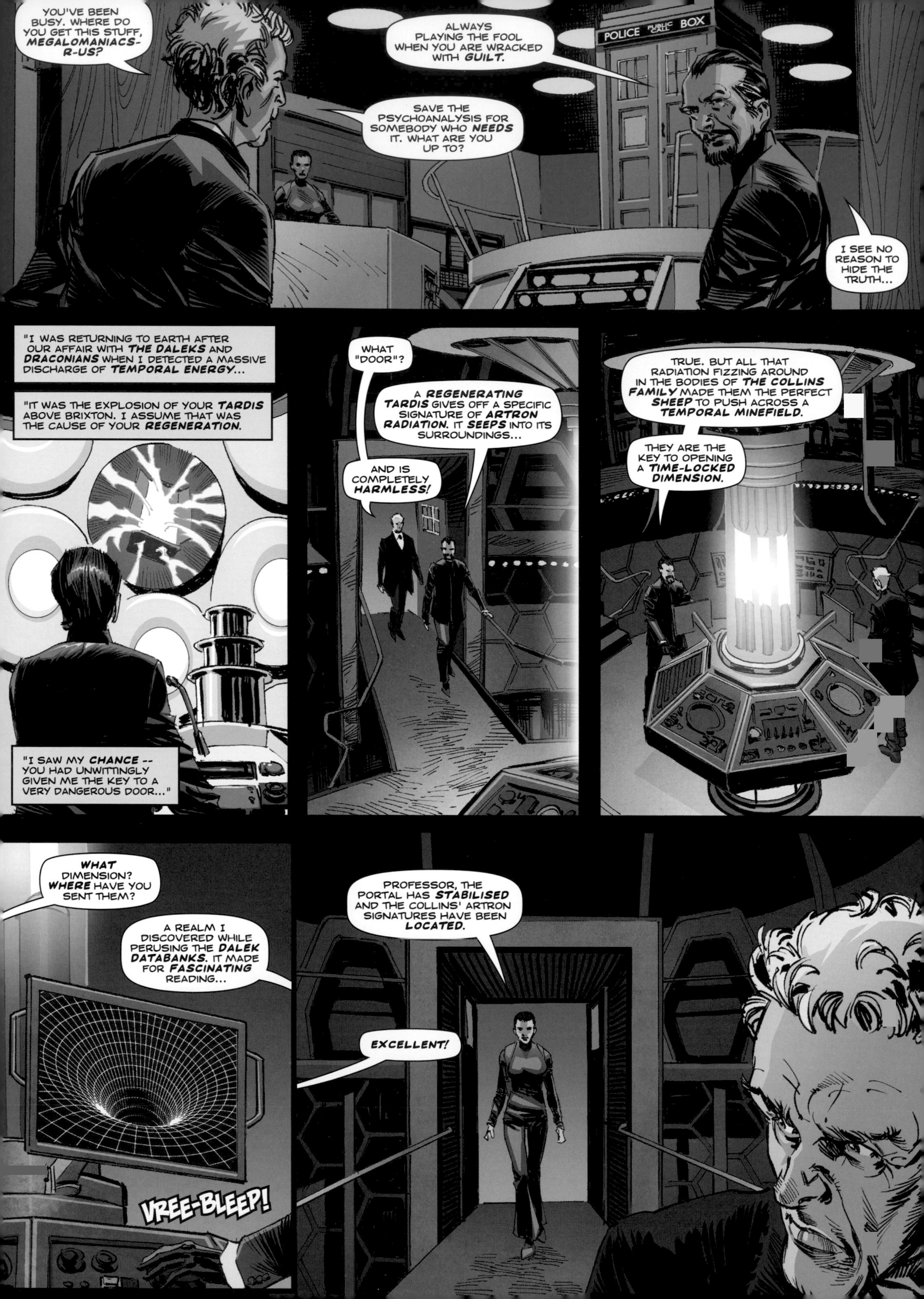
YOU'VE BEEN BUSY. WHERE DO YOU GET THIS STUFF, MEGALOMANIACS-R-US?
ALWAYS PLAYING THE FOOL WHEN YOU ARE WRACKED WITH GUILT.
POLICE PUBLIC CALL BOX
SAVE THE PSYCHOANALYSIS FOR SOMEBODY WHO NEEDS IT. WHAT ARE YOU UP TO?
I SEE NO REASON TO HIDE THE TRUTH...
"I WAS RETURNING TO EARTH AFTER OUR AFFAIR WITH THE DALEKS AND DRACONIANS WHEN I DETECTED A MASSIVE DISCHARGE OF TEMPORAL ENERGY...
"IT WAS THE EXPLOSION OF YOUR TARDIS ABOVE BRIXTON. I ASSUME THAT WAS THE CAUSE OF YOUR REGENERATION.
"I SAW MY CHANCE -- YOU HAD UNWITTINGLY GIVEN ME THE KEY TO A VERY DANGEROUS DOOR..."
WHAT "DOOR"?
A REGENERATING TARDIS GIVES OFF A SPECIFIC SIGNATURE OF ARTRON RADIATION. IT SEEPS INTO ITS SURROUNDINGS...
AND IS COMPLETELY HARMLESS!
TRUE. BUT ALL THAT RADIATION FIZZING AROUND IN THE BODIES OF THE COLLINS FAMILY MADE THEM THE PERFECT SHEEP TO PUSH ACROSS A TEMPORAL MINEFIELD.
THEY ARE THE KEY TO OPENING A TIME-LOCKED DIMENSION.
WHAT DIMENSION? WHERE HAVE YOU SENT THEM?
A REALM I DISCOVERED WHILE PERUSING THE DALEK DATABANKS. IT MADE FOR FASCINATING READING...
VREE-BLEEP!
PROFESSOR, THE PORTAL HAS STABILISED AND THE COLLINS' ARTRON SIGNATURES HAVE BEEN LOCATED.
EXCELLENT!

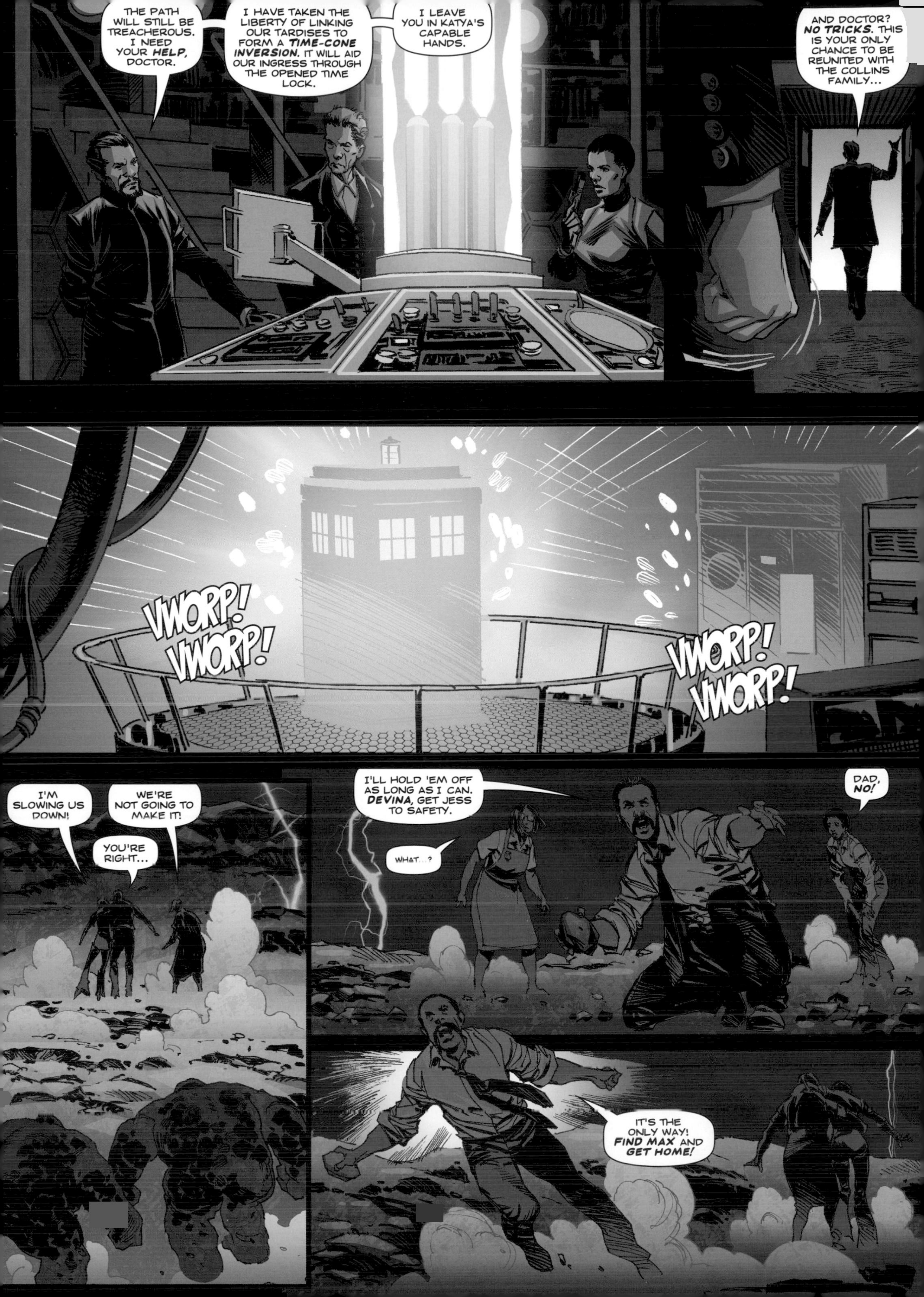
THE PATH WILL STILL BE TREACHEROUS. I NEED YOUR **HELP**, DOCTOR.
I HAVE TAKEN THE LIBERTY OF LINKING OUR TARDISES TO FORM A ***TIME-CONE INVERSION***. IT WILL AID OUR INGRESS THROUGH THE OPENED TIME LOCK.
I LEAVE YOU IN KATYA'S CAPABLE HANDS.
AND DOCTOR? ***NO TRICKS***. THIS IS YOUR ONLY CHANCE TO BE REUNITED WITH THE COLLINS FAMILY...
VWORP! VWORP!
VWORP! VWORP!
I'M SLOWING US DOWN!
WE'RE NOT GOING TO MAKE IT!
YOU'RE RIGHT...
I'LL HOLD 'EM OFF AS LONG AS I CAN. ***DEVINA***, GET JESS TO SAFETY.
WHAT...?
DAD, ***NO!***
IT'S THE ONLY WAY! ***FIND MAX*** AND ***GET HOME!***

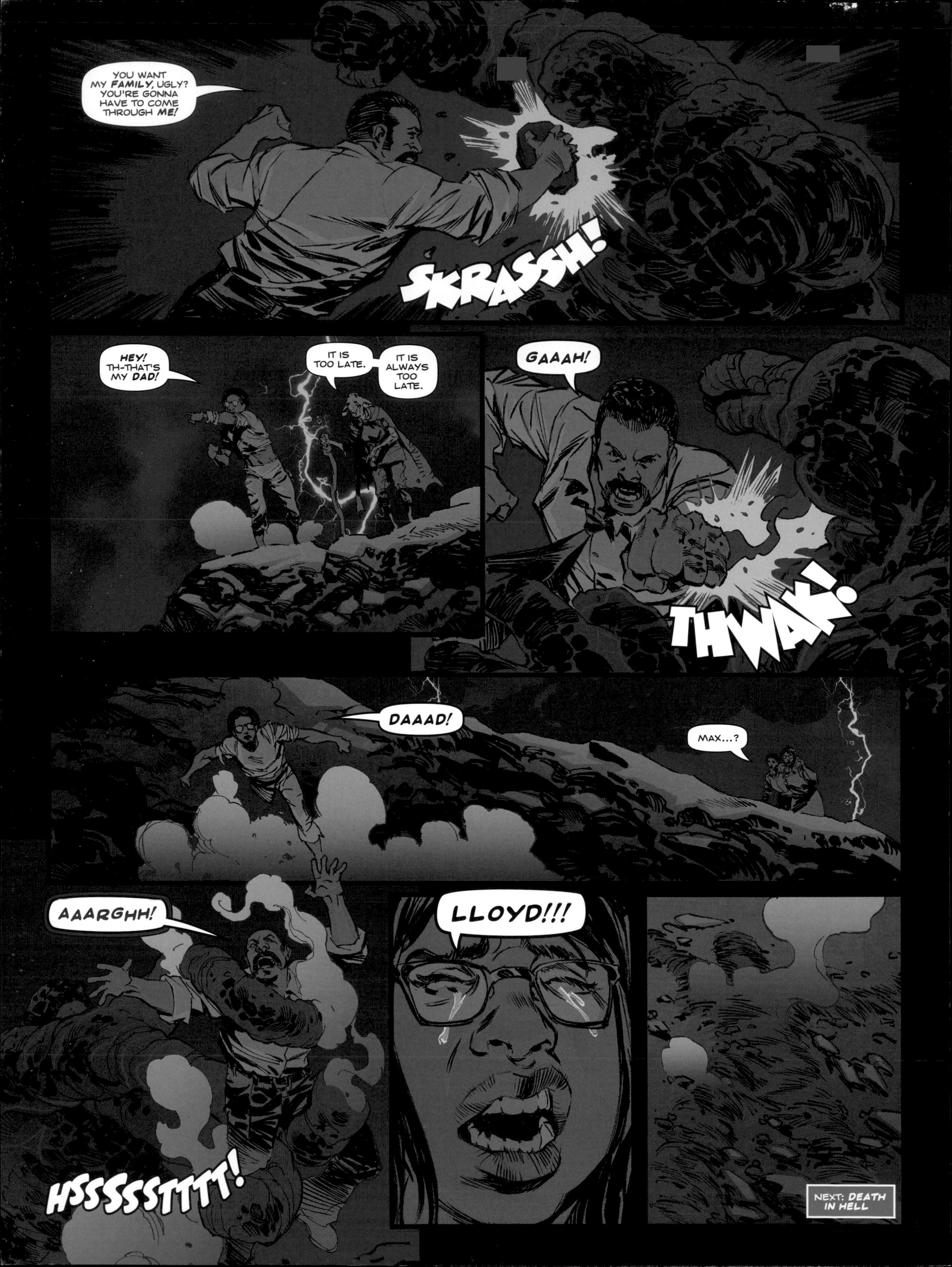
YOU WANT MY FAMILY, UGLY? YOU'RE GONNA HAVE TO COME THROUGH ME!
SKRASSH!
HEY! TH-THAT'S MY DAD!
IT IS TOO LATE.
IT IS ALWAYS TOO LATE.
GAAAH!
THWAK!
DAAAD!
MAX...?
AAARGHH!
HSSSSSTTTT!
LLOYD!!!
NEXT: DEATH IN HELL

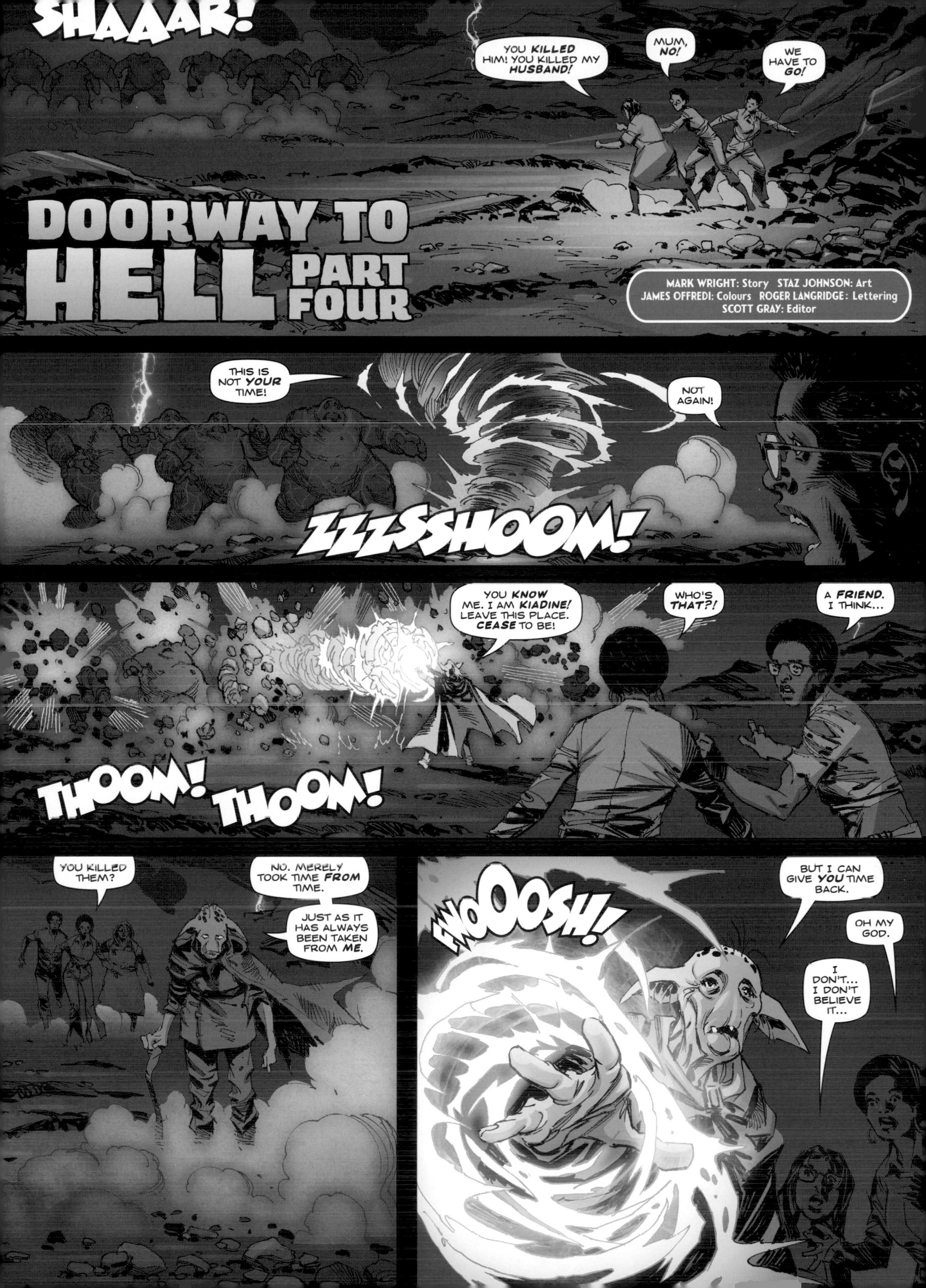
SHAAAR!
YOU KILLED HIM! YOU KILLED MY HUSBAND!
MUM, NO!
WE HAVE TO GO!
DOORWAY TO HELL PART FOUR
MARK WRIGHT: Story STAZ JOHNSON: Art
JAMES OFFREDI: Colours ROGER LANGRIDGE: Lettering
SCOTT GRAY: Editor
THIS IS NOT YOUR TIME!
NOT AGAIN!
ZZZSSHOOM!
YOU KNOW ME. I AM KIADINE! LEAVE THIS PLACE. CEASE TO BE!
WHO'S THAT?!
A FRIEND. I THINK...
THOOM! THOOM!
YOU KILLED THEM?
NO. MERELY TOOK TIME FROM TIME.
JUST AS IT HAS ALWAYS BEEN TAKEN FROM ME.
FWOOOSH!
BUT I CAN GIVE YOU TIME BACK.
OH MY GOD.
I DON'T... I DON'T BELIEVE IT...

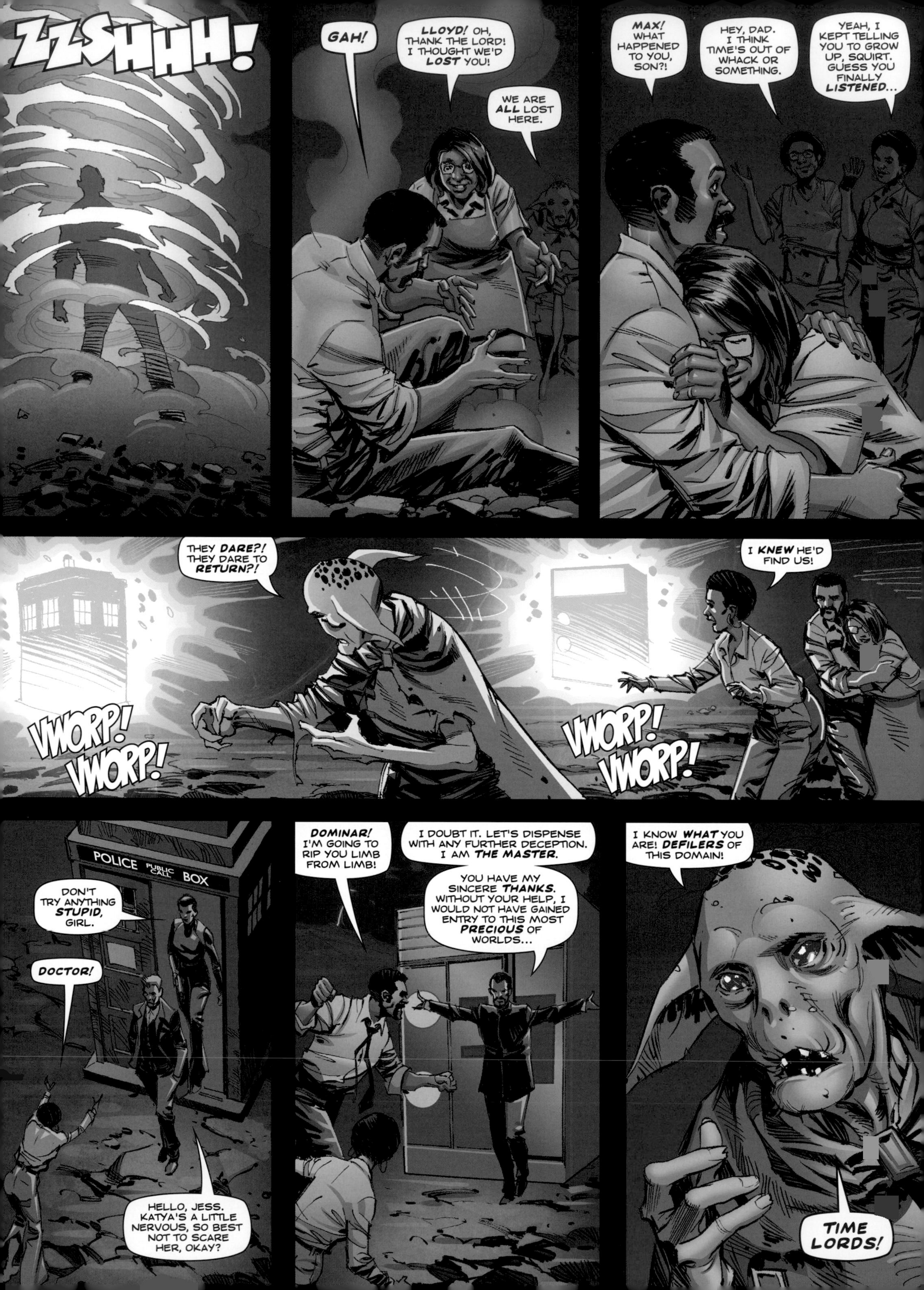

ZZSHHH!
GAH!
LLOYD! OH, THANK THE LORD! I THOUGHT WE'D LOST YOU!
WE ARE ALL LOST HERE.
MAX! WHAT HAPPENED TO YOU, SON?!
HEY, DAD. I THINK TIME'S OUT OF WHACK OR SOMETHING.
YEAH, I KEPT TELLING YOU TO GROW UP, SQUIRT. GUESS YOU FINALLY LISTENED...
THEY DARE?! THEY DARE TO RETURN?!
VWORP! VWORP!
I KNEW HE'D FIND US!
VWORP! VWORP!
POLICE PUBLIC CALL BOX
DON'T TRY ANYTHING STUPID, GIRL.
DOCTOR!
HELLO, JESS. KATYA'S A LITTLE NERVOUS, SO BEST NOT TO SCARE HER, OKAY?
DOMINAR! I'M GOING TO RIP YOU LIMB FROM LIMB!
I DOUBT IT. LET'S DISPENSE WITH ANY FURTHER DECEPTION. I AM THE MASTER.
YOU HAVE MY SINCERE THANKS. WITHOUT YOUR HELP, I WOULD NOT HAVE GAINED ENTRY TO THIS MOST PRECIOUS OF WORLDS...
I KNOW WHAT YOU ARE! DEFILERS OF THIS DOMAIN!
TIME LORDS!

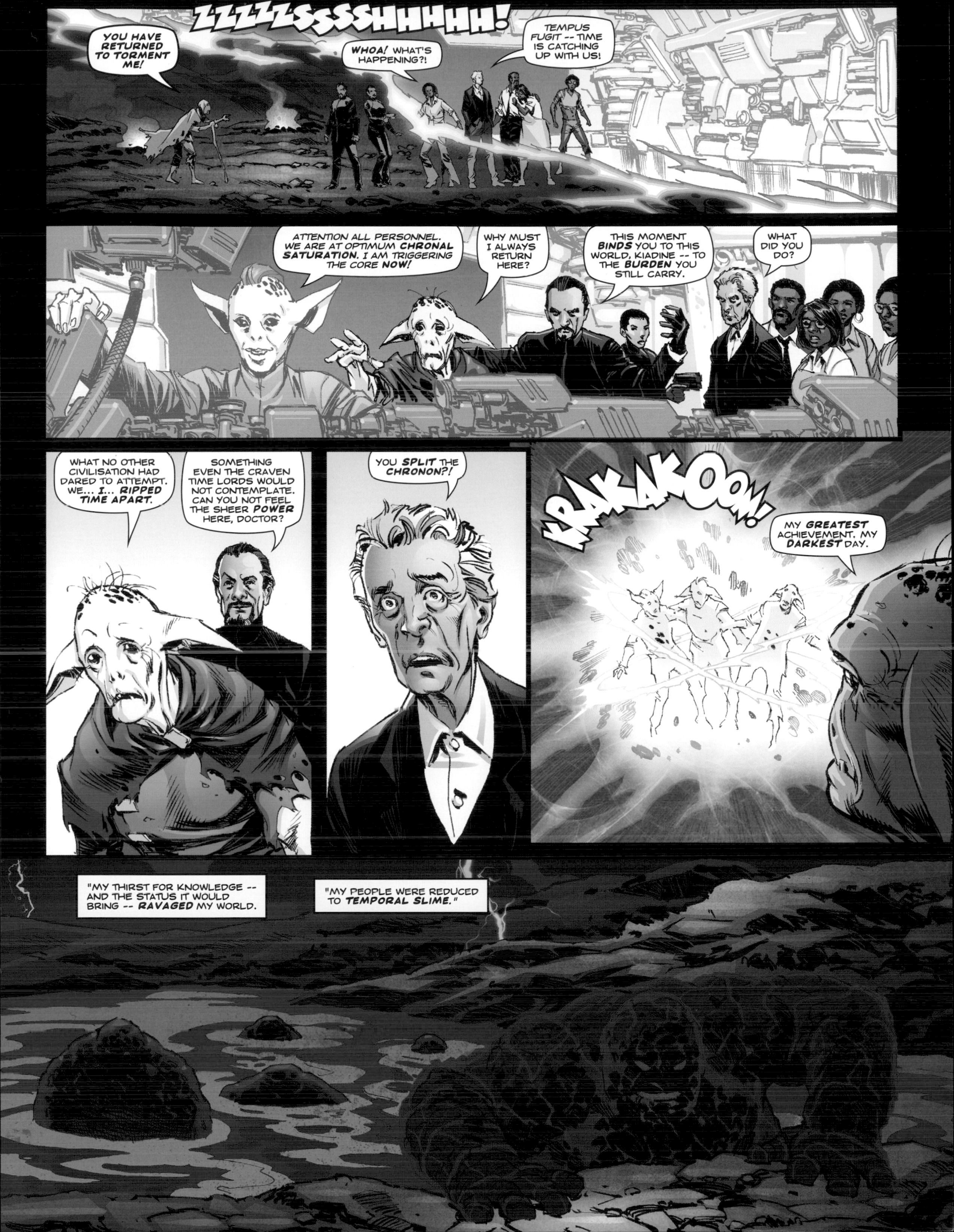
ZZZZZSSSSHHHHH!
YOU HAVE RETURNED TO TORMENT ME!
WHOA! WHAT'S HAPPENING?!
TEMPUS FUGIT -- TIME IS CATCHING UP WITH US!
ATTENTION ALL PERSONNEL. WE ARE AT OPTIMUM CHRONAL SATURATION. I AM TRIGGERING THE CORE NOW!
WHY MUST I ALWAYS RETURN HERE?
THIS MOMENT BINDS YOU TO THIS WORLD, KIADINE -- TO THE BURDEN YOU STILL CARRY.
WHAT DID YOU DO?
WHAT NO OTHER CIVILISATION HAD DARED TO ATTEMPT. WE... I... RIPPED TIME APART.
SOMETHING EVEN THE CRAVEN TIME LORDS WOULD NOT CONTEMPLATE. CAN YOU NOT FEEL THE SHEER POWER HERE, DOCTOR?
YOU SPLIT THE CHRONON?!
KRAKAKOOM!
MY GREATEST ACHIEVEMENT. MY DARKEST DAY.
"MY THIRST FOR KNOWLEDGE -- AND THE STATUS IT WOULD BRING -- RAVAGED MY WORLD.
"MY PEOPLE WERE REDUCED TO TEMPORAL SLIME."

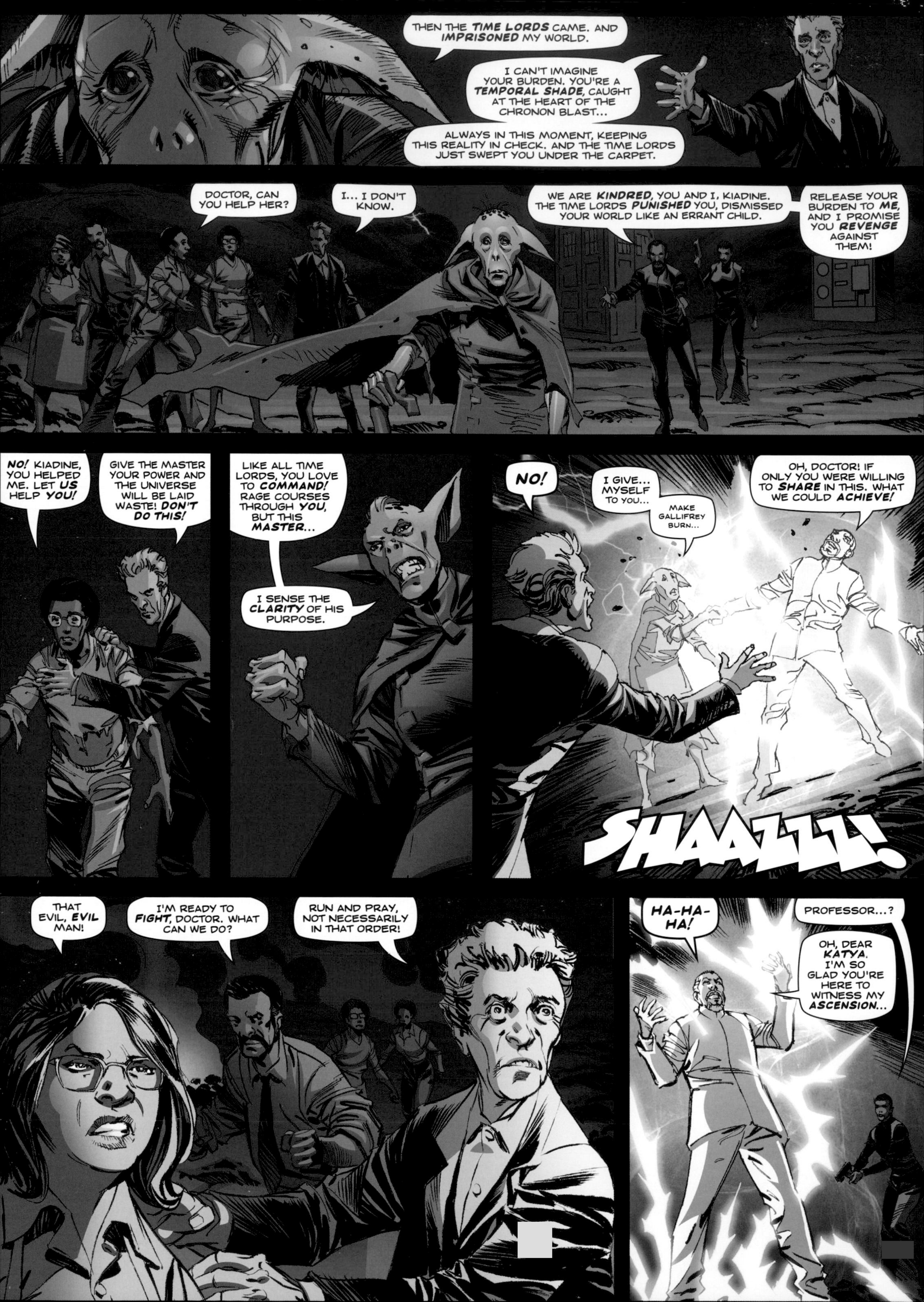
THEN THE TIME LORDS CAME. AND IMPRISONED MY WORLD.
I CAN'T IMAGINE YOUR BURDEN. YOU'RE A TEMPORAL SHADE, CAUGHT AT THE HEART OF THE CHRONON BLAST...
ALWAYS IN THIS MOMENT, KEEPING THIS REALITY IN CHECK. AND THE TIME LORDS JUST SWEPT YOU UNDER THE CARPET.
DOCTOR, CAN YOU HELP HER?
I... I DON'T KNOW.
WE ARE KINDRED, YOU AND I, KIADINE. THE TIME LORDS PUNISHED YOU, DISMISSED YOUR WORLD LIKE AN ERRANT CHILD.
RELEASE YOUR BURDEN TO ME, AND I PROMISE YOU REVENGE AGAINST THEM!
NO! KIADINE, YOU HELPED ME. LET US HELP YOU!
GIVE THE MASTER YOUR POWER AND THE UNIVERSE WILL BE LAID WASTE! DON'T DO THIS!
LIKE ALL TIME LORDS, YOU LOVE TO COMMAND! RAGE COURSES THROUGH YOU, BUT THIS MASTER...
I SENSE THE CLARITY OF HIS PURPOSE.
NO!
I GIVE... MYSELF TO YOU...
MAKE GALLIFREY BURN...
OH, DOCTOR! IF ONLY YOU WERE WILLING TO SHARE IN THIS. WHAT WE COULD ACHIEVE!
SHAAZZZ!
THAT EVIL, EVIL MAN!
I'M READY TO FIGHT, DOCTOR. WHAT CAN WE DO?
RUN AND PRAY, NOT NECESSARILY IN THAT ORDER!
HA-HA-HA!
PROFESSOR...?
OH, DEAR KATYA. I'M SO GLAD YOU'RE HERE TO WITNESS MY ASCENSION...

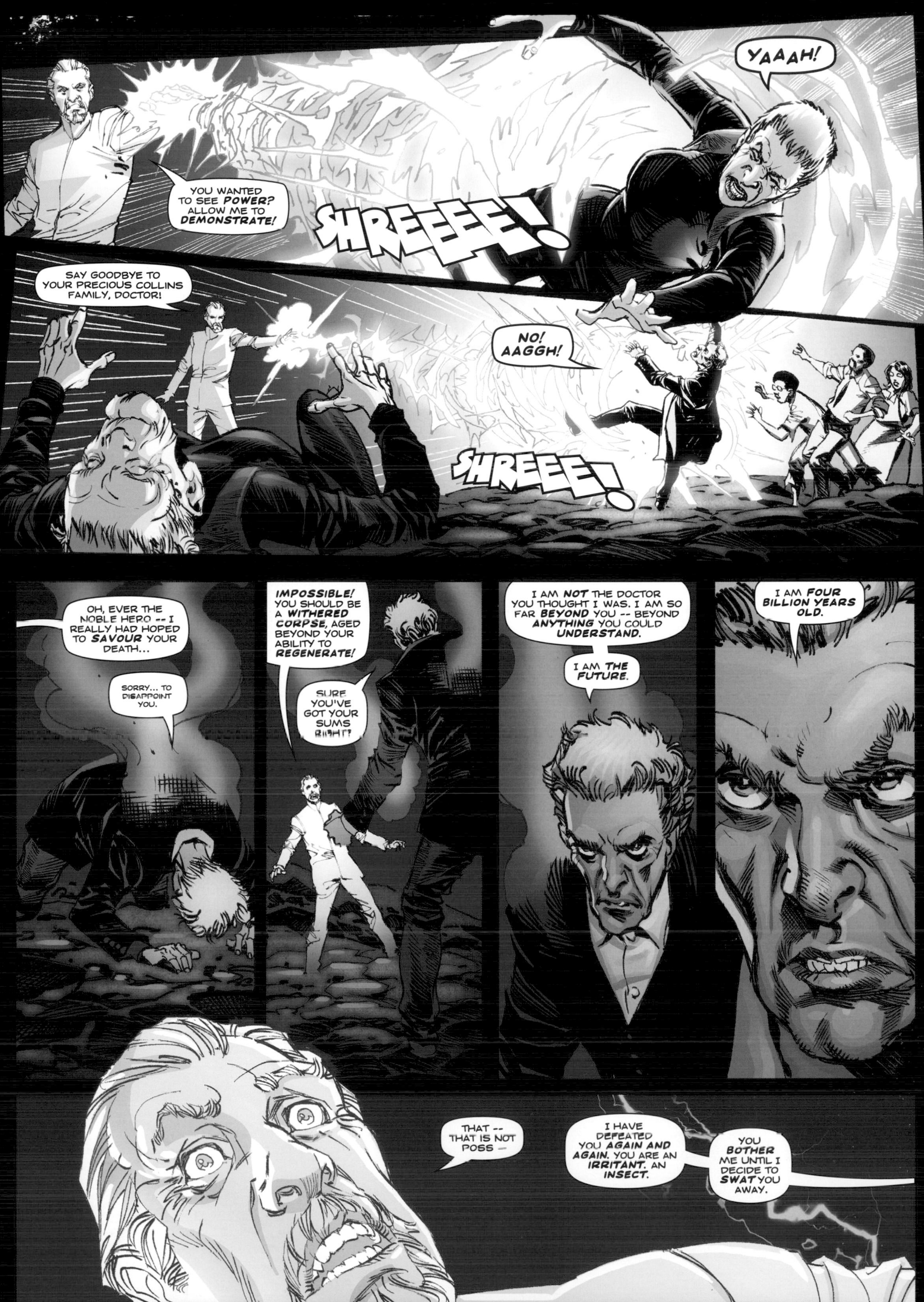
YAAAH!
YOU WANTED TO SEE POWER? ALLOW ME TO DEMONSTRATE!
SHREEEE!
SAY GOODBYE TO YOUR PRECIOUS COLLINS FAMILY, DOCTOR!
NO! AAGGH!
SHREEE!
OH, EVER THE NOBLE HERO -- I REALLY HAD HOPED TO SAVOUR YOUR DEATH...
SORRY... TO DISAPPOINT YOU.
IMPOSSIBLE! YOU SHOULD BE A WITHERED CORPSE, AGED BEYOND YOUR ABILITY TO REGENERATE!
SURE YOU'VE GOT YOUR SUMS RIGHT?
I AM NOT THE DOCTOR YOU THOUGHT I WAS. I AM SO FAR BEYOND YOU -- BEYOND ANYTHING YOU COULD UNDERSTAND.
I AM THE FUTURE.
I AM FOUR BILLION YEARS OLD.
THAT -- THAT IS NOT POSS --
I HAVE DEFEATED YOU AGAIN AND AGAIN. YOU ARE AN IRRITANT. AN INSECT.
YOU BOTHER ME UNTIL I DECIDE TO SWAT YOU AWAY.

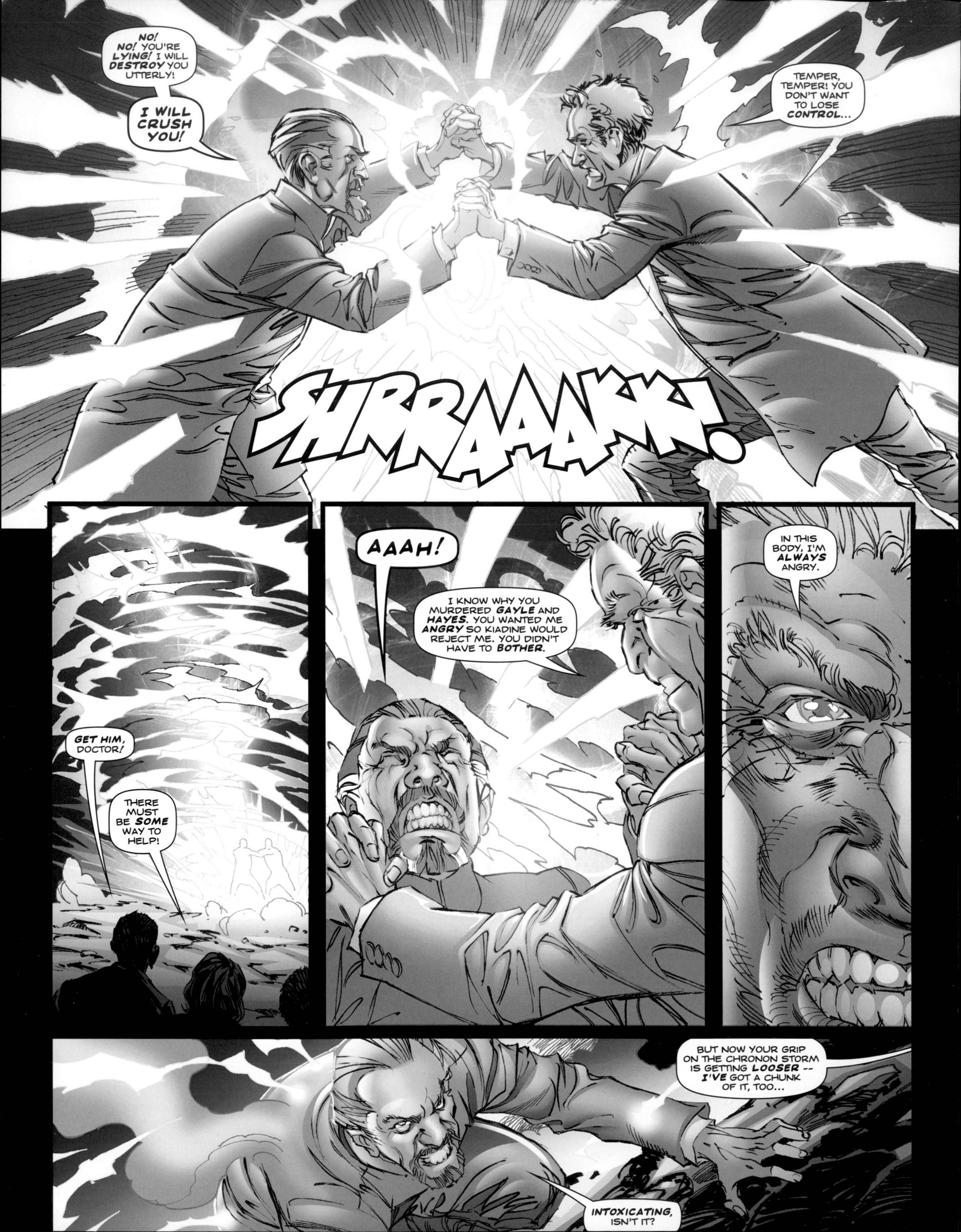
NO! NO! YOU'RE LYING! I WILL DESTROY YOU UTTERLY!
I WILL CRUSH YOU!
TEMPER, TEMPER! YOU DON'T WANT TO LOSE CONTROL...
SHRRAAAKK!
GET HIM, DOCTOR!
THERE MUST BE SOME WAY TO HELP!
AAAH!
I KNOW WHY YOU MURDERED GAYLE AND HAYES. YOU WANTED ME ANGRY SO KIADINE WOULD REJECT ME. YOU DIDN'T HAVE TO BOTHER.
IN THIS BODY, I'M ALWAYS ANGRY.
BUT NOW YOUR GRIP ON THE CHRONON STORM IS GETTING LOOSER -- I'VE GOT A CHUNK OF IT, TOO...
INTOXICATING, ISN'T IT?

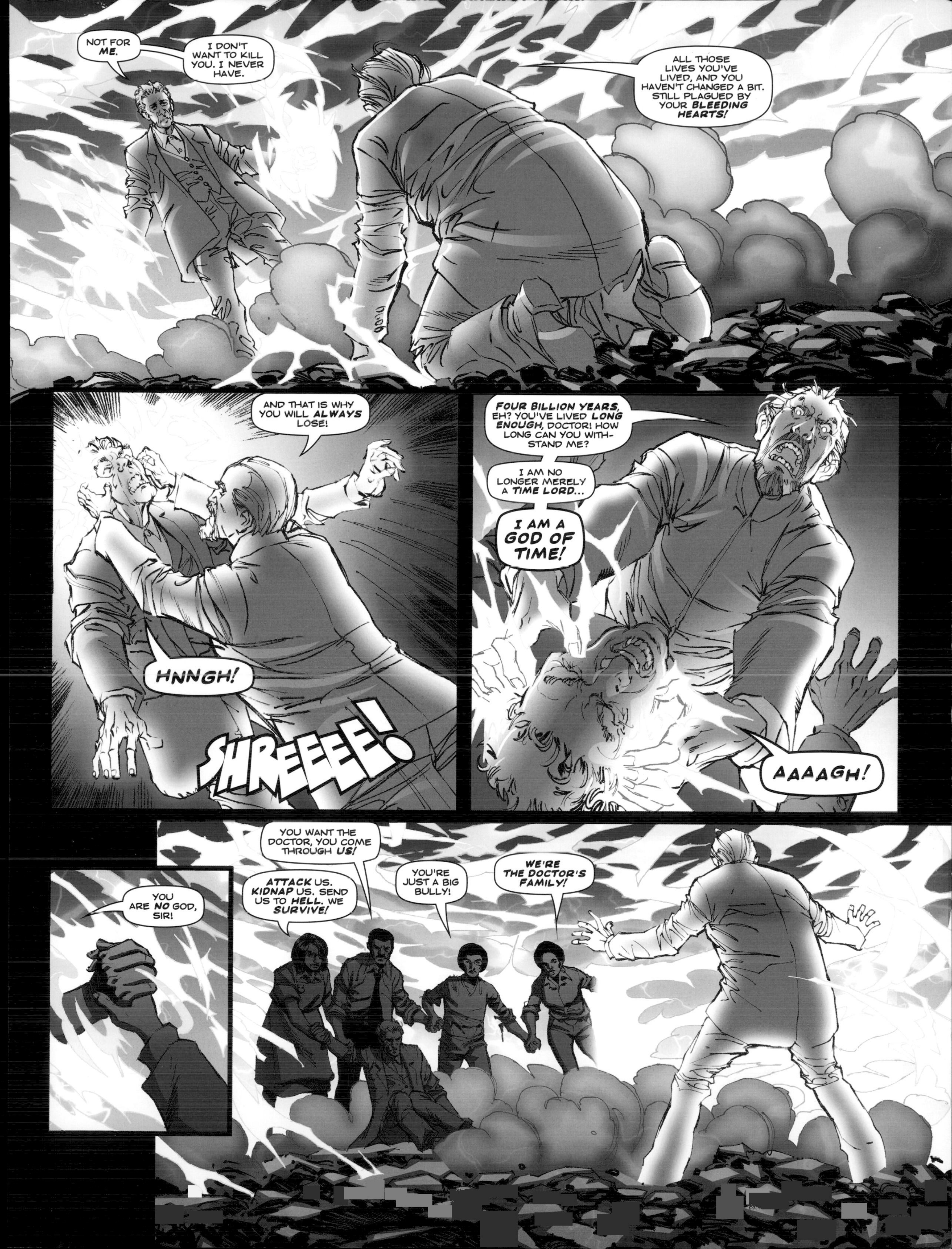
NOT FOR ME.
I DON'T WANT TO KILL YOU. I NEVER HAVE.
ALL THOSE LIVES YOU'VE LIVED, AND YOU HAVEN'T CHANGED A BIT. STILL PLAGUED BY YOUR BLEEDING HEARTS!
AND THAT IS WHY YOU WILL ALWAYS LOSE!
HNNGH!
SHREEEEE!
FOUR BILLION YEARS, EH? YOU'VE LIVED LONG ENOUGH, DOCTOR! HOW LONG CAN YOU WITHSTAND ME?
I AM NO LONGER MERELY A TIME LORD...
I AM A GOD OF TIME!
AAAAGH!
YOU ARE NO GOD, SIR!
ATTACK US. KIDNAP US. SEND US TO HELL. WE SURVIVE!
YOU WANT THE DOCTOR, YOU COME THROUGH US!
YOU'RE JUST A BIG BULLY!
WE'RE THE DOCTOR'S FAMILY!

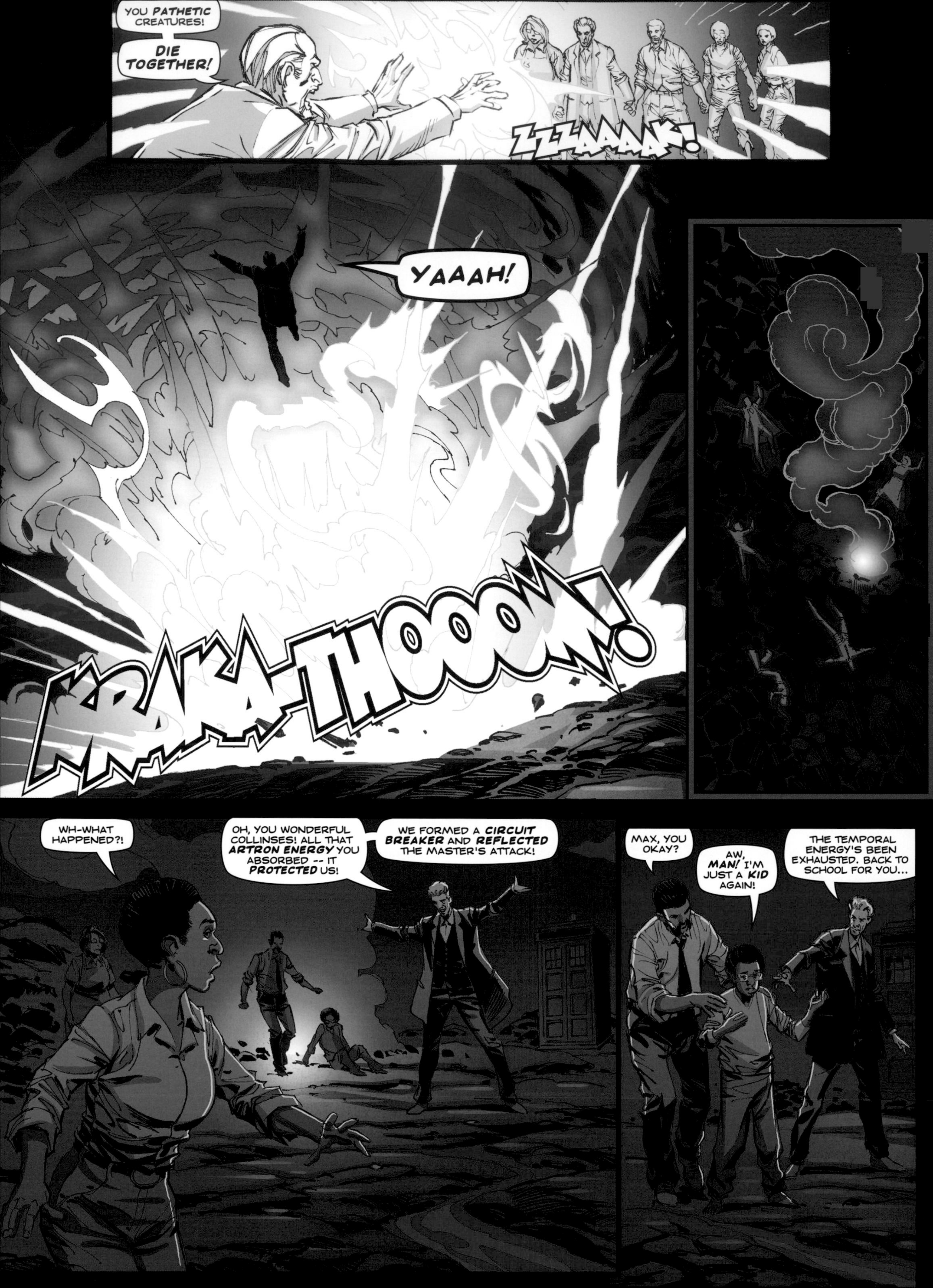

YOU PATHETIC CREATURES!
DIE TOGETHER!
ZZZAAAAK!
YAAAH!
KRAKA-THOOOM!
WH-WHAT HAPPENED?!
OH, YOU WONDERFUL COLLINSES! ALL THAT ARTRON ENERGY YOU ABSORBED -- IT PROTECTED US!
WE FORMED A CIRCUIT BREAKER AND REFLECTED THE MASTER'S ATTACK!
MAX, YOU OKAY?
AW, MAN! I'M JUST A KID AGAIN!
THE TEMPORAL ENERGY'S BEEN EXHAUSTED. BACK TO SCHOOL FOR YOU...

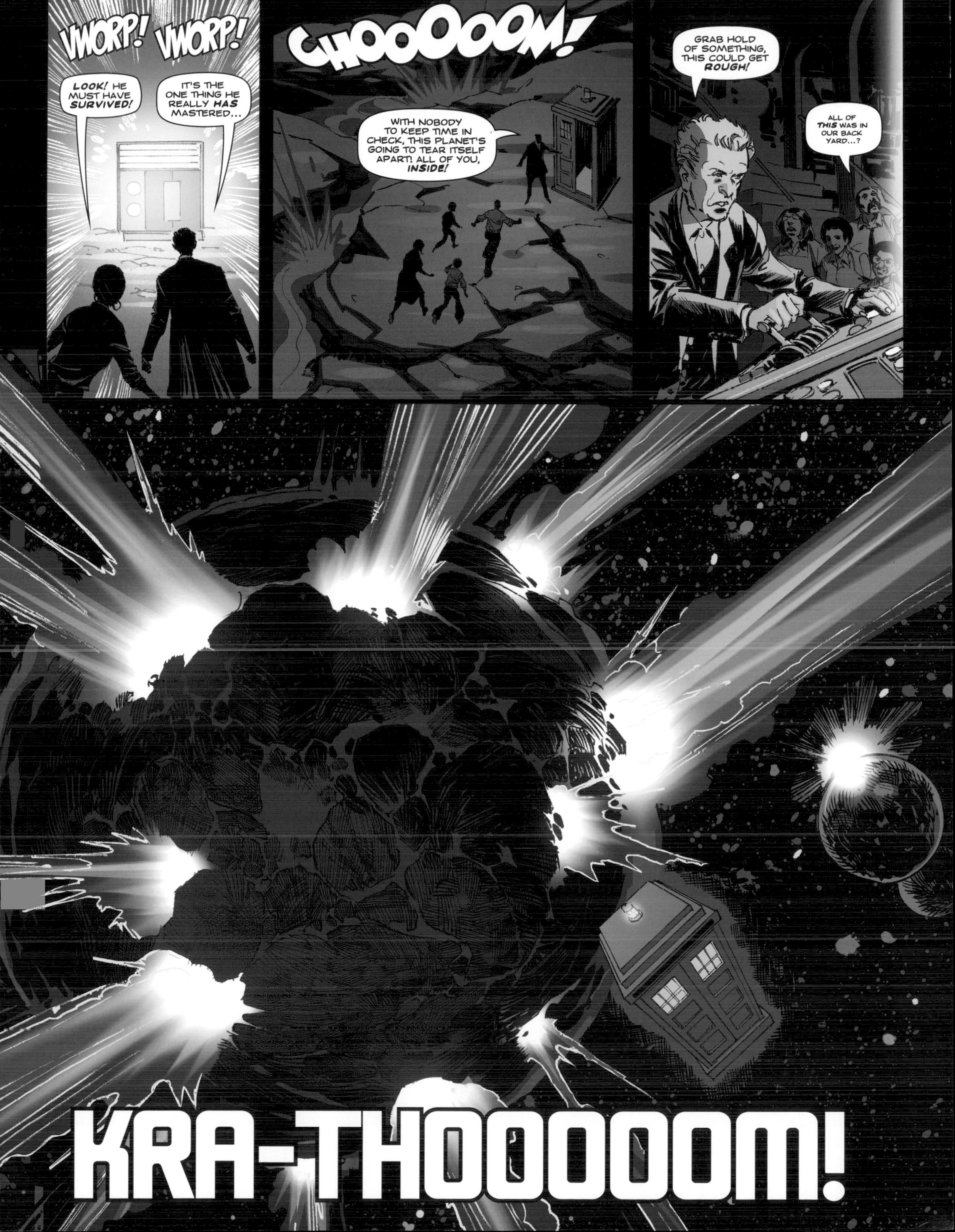
VWORP! VWORP!
LOOK! HE MUST HAVE SURVIVED!
IT'S THE ONE THING HE REALLY HAS MASTERED...
CHOOOOOM!
WITH NOBODY TO KEEP TIME IN CHECK, THIS PLANET'S GOING TO TEAR ITSELF APART! ALL OF YOU, INSIDE!
GRAB HOLD OF SOMETHING, THIS COULD GET ROUGH!
ALL OF THIS WAS IN OUR BACK YARD...?
KRA-THOOOOOOM!

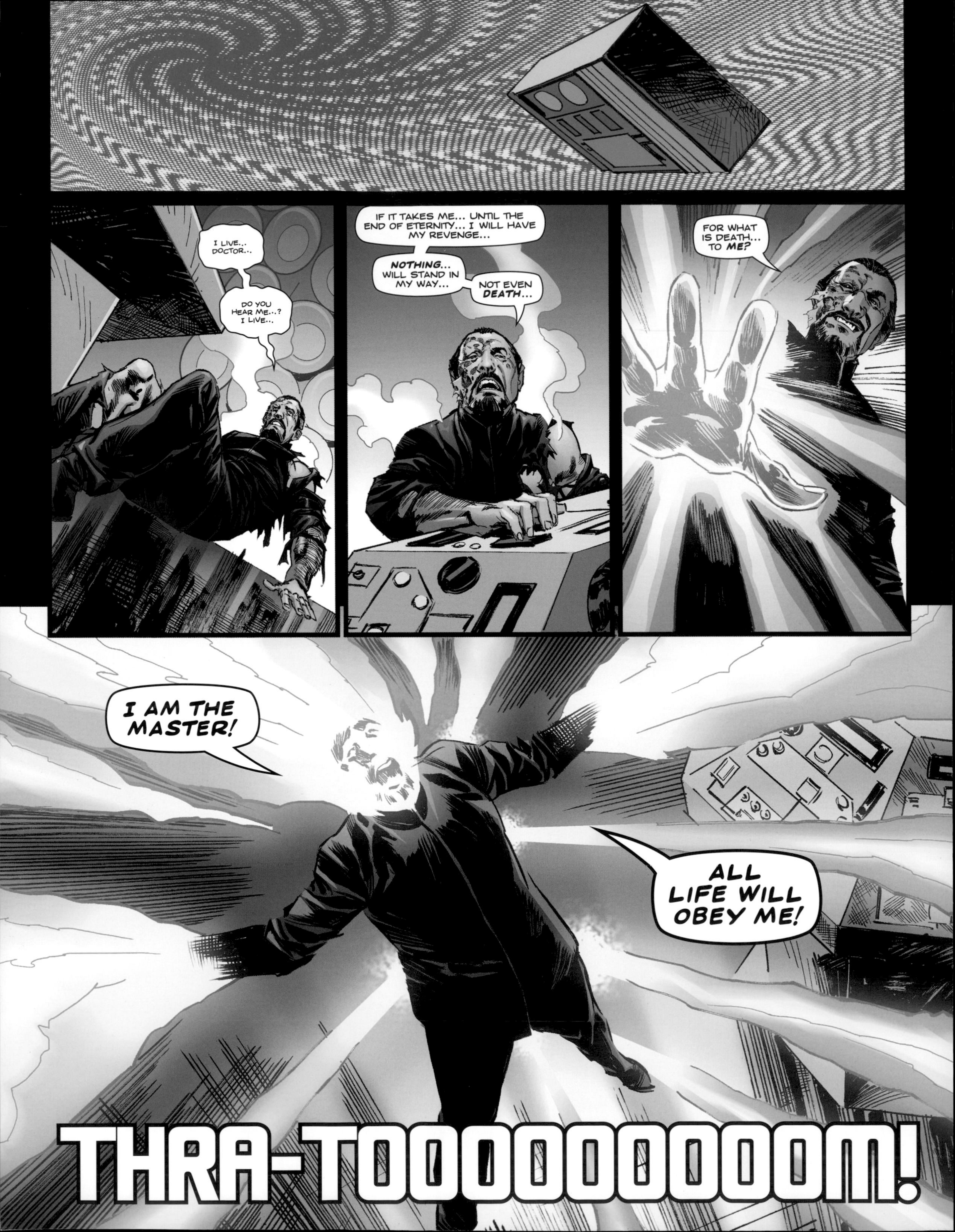
I LIVE... DOCTOR...
DO YOU HEAR ME...? I LIVE...
IF IT TAKES ME... UNTIL THE END OF ETERNITY... I WILL HAVE MY REVENGE...
NOTHING... WILL STAND IN MY WAY...
NOT EVEN DEATH...
FOR WHAT IS DEATH... TO ME?
I AM THE MASTER!
ALL LIFE WILL OBEY ME!
THRA-TOOOOOOOOOOM!

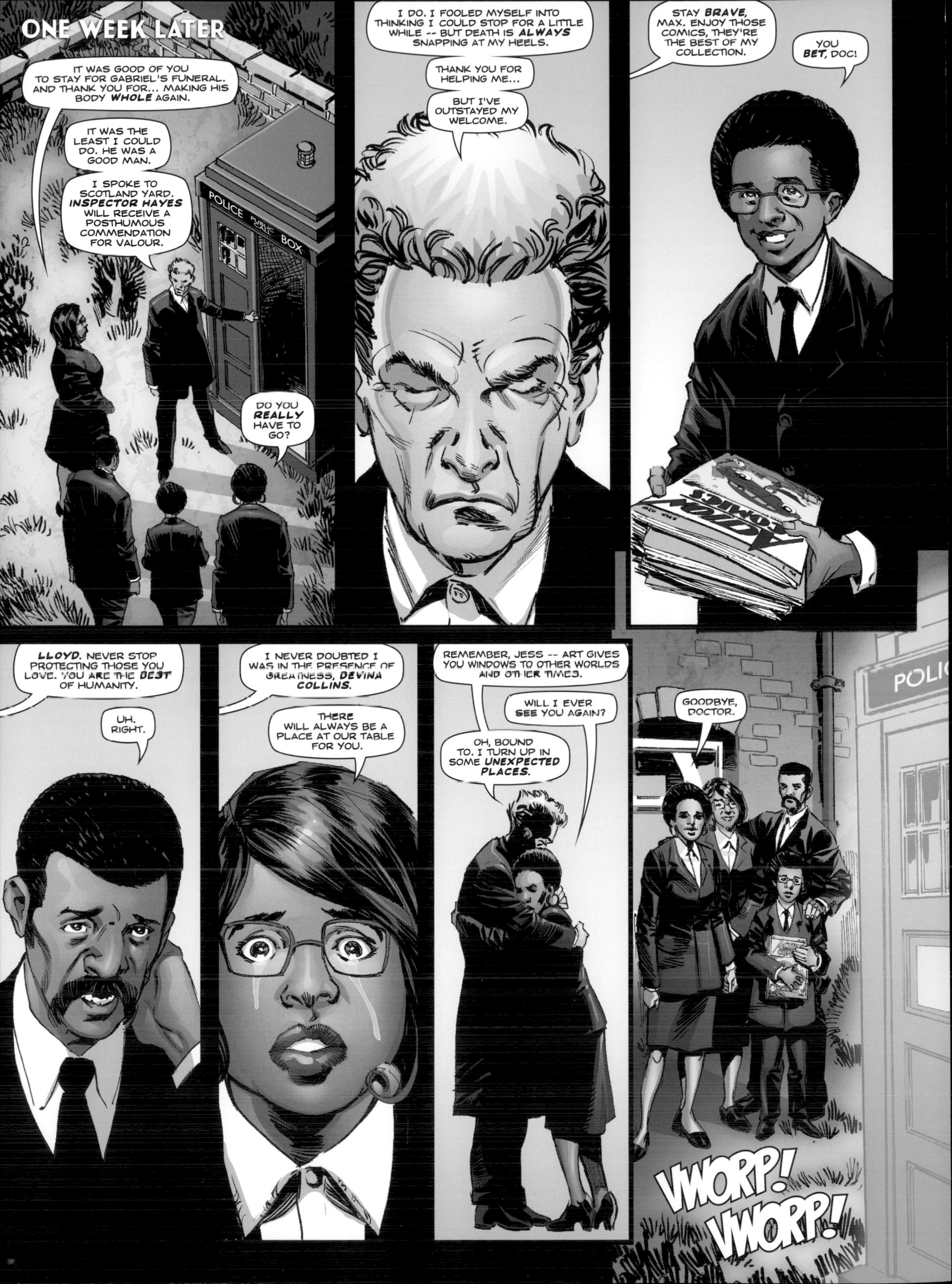
ONE WEEK LATER
IT WAS GOOD OF YOU TO STAY FOR GABRIEL'S FUNERAL. AND THANK YOU FOR... MAKING HIS BODY WHOLE AGAIN.
IT WAS THE LEAST I COULD DO. HE WAS A GOOD MAN.
I SPOKE TO SCOTLAND YARD. INSPECTOR HAYES WILL RECEIVE A POSTHUMOUS COMMENDATION FOR VALOUR.
POLICE PUBLIC CALL BOX
DO YOU REALLY HAVE TO GO?
I DO. I FOOLED MYSELF INTO THINKING I COULD STOP FOR A LITTLE WHILE -- BUT DEATH IS ALWAYS SNAPPING AT MY HEELS.
THANK YOU FOR HELPING ME...
BUT I'VE OUTSTAYED MY WELCOME.
STAY BRAVE, MAX. ENJOY THOSE COMICS, THEY'RE THE BEST OF MY COLLECTION.
YOU BET, DOC!
LLOYD. NEVER STOP PROTECTING THOSE YOU LOVE. YOU ARE THE BEST OF HUMANITY.
UH. RIGHT.
I NEVER DOUBTED I WAS IN THE PRESENCE OF GREATNESS, DEVINA COLLINS.
THERE WILL ALWAYS BE A PLACE AT OUR TABLE FOR YOU.
REMEMBER, JESS -- ART GIVES YOU WINDOWS TO OTHER WORLDS AND OTHER TIMES.
WILL I EVER SEE YOU AGAIN?
OH, BOUND TO. I TURN UP IN SOME UNEXPECTED PLACES.
GOODBYE, DOCTOR.
VWORP! VWORP!

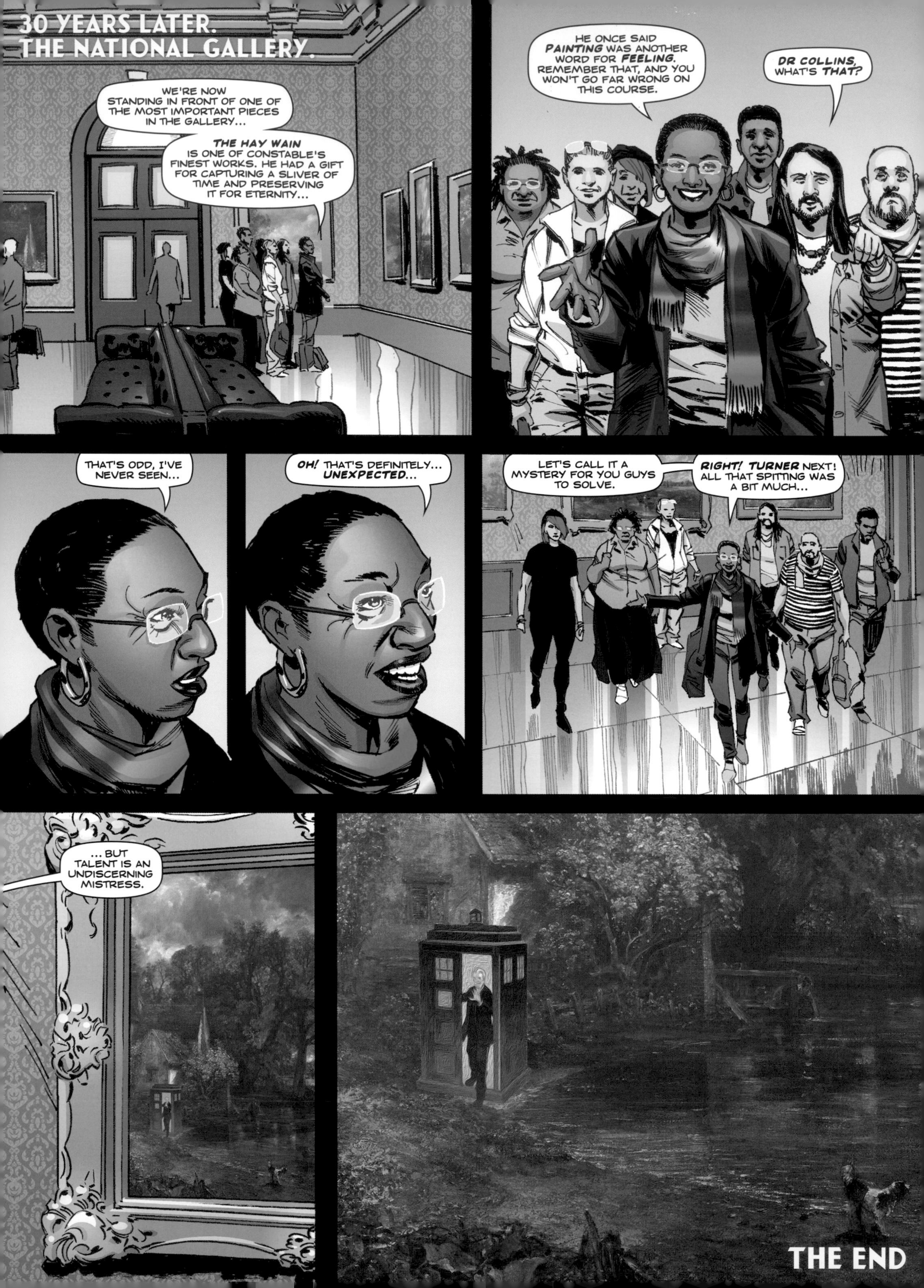
30 YEARS LATER.
THE NATIONAL GALLERY.
WE'RE NOW STANDING IN FRONT OF ONE OF THE MOST IMPORTANT PIECES IN THE GALLERY...
THE HAY WAIN IS ONE OF CONSTABLE'S FINEST WORKS. HE HAD A GIFT FOR CAPTURING A SLIVER OF TIME AND PRESERVING IT FOR ETERNITY...
HE ONCE SAID PAINTING WAS ANOTHER WORD FOR FEELING. REMEMBER THAT, AND YOU WON'T GO FAR WRONG ON THIS COURSE.
DR COLLINS, WHAT'S THAT?
THAT'S ODD, I'VE NEVER SEEN...
OH! THAT'S DEFINITELY... UNEXPECTED...
LET'S CALL IT A MYSTERY FOR YOU GUYS TO SOLVE.
RIGHT! TURNER NEXT! ALL THAT SPITTING WAS A BIT MUCH...
...BUT TALENT IS AN UNDISCERNING MISTRESS.
THE END

# Commentary

## The Pestilent Heart

**Mark Wright** Writer

Despite how it may appear, none of this was planned. Looking at the ongoing development of the **Doctor Who Magazine** comic strip, it might seem that when Jess Collins had her terrifying encounter with the Doctor and Clara in *The Highgate Horror*, her destiny as a companion-in-waiting had already been decided. Far from it – she was originally written as a one-story guest character, never to be seen again. But, as is often the case, Jess just happened to be in the right place at the right time...

By November 2015, after five years as an on/off freelance editorial assistant on **DWM**, I'd recently moved across to editing the *Doctor Who: The Complete History* partwork, a job that still saw me pay a regular monthly visit to the Panini offices in Tunbridge Wells. On the team's daily trip to a local coffee shop, comic strip editor Scott Gray suddenly said, "I think we should make Jess the companion after Clara goes." Scott had seen moments of spark between the Doctor and Jess in *The Highgate Horror*. With Clara being written out of both the TV series and the comic, there was going to be space for a new, original companion while the series was off-air in 2016.

Welcome aboard, Miss Jessica Collins!

At this stage we didn't know exactly when the new TV companion was going to be introduced; at one point, Jess might have only been around for six issues, which influenced Scott's email to me in early December: "It would feel weird to have Jess join the TARDIS at the end of your story and then leave it only four issues later. So instead, how about we strand the Doctor on Earth for a few months? Break the TARDIS so he can't leave?"

That was it – the moment where it all clicked. Within the space of a few emails, we had the 1970s Brixton backdrop, a fully formed family for Jess, and the wheeze of the Doctor effectively living in their back garden while the TARDIS regenerated. There was lots of fun to be had with placing this most alien of Doctors into such a domestic setting. And what a joy to bring Jess' family into being. Lloyd, dependable and protective; Devina, magnificent, a little bit scary but full of so much love and able to get the Doctor eating out of her hand; and cheeky little brother Max. Max became such an integral part of this run, I was taken aback to realise he's only in a handful of panels across all three parts of *The Pestilent Heart*.

Once the family was in place, *The Pestilent Heart* – or 'The Stroke of Pestilence' as it was first known – came together really quickly. I'd lived in Brixton for a few years in the early noughties, so there was a comforting familiarity to setting a story there. The area from the Brixton Underground station, looking up Brixton Hill towards the Ritzy Cinema and Lambeth Town Hall was a part of London I walked through almost every day for three years.

The London Underground has always been a source of fascination, this network spreading like tree roots beneath the city and used to such good effect in *The Web of Fear*. A bit of research gave me a fact that was almost too good to be true: the extension of the Victoria Line to Brixton was completed in 1971. With *The Highgate Horror* being set in early 1972, it gave me a timeline that worked beautifully, with the Doctor arriving back in London in late summer '72 at the start of *The Pestilent Heart*. A whole year of trains thundering in and out of Brixton Underground station... just what might they have disturbed? Connecting that particular line of thought to a previously undiscovered (fictional) plague pit, and with Lloyd Collins working the night shift on the Underground, all the elements were there.

I was thrilled to hear that Mike Collins would be on pencil duties for *The Pestilent Heart*. Mike had drawn my very first

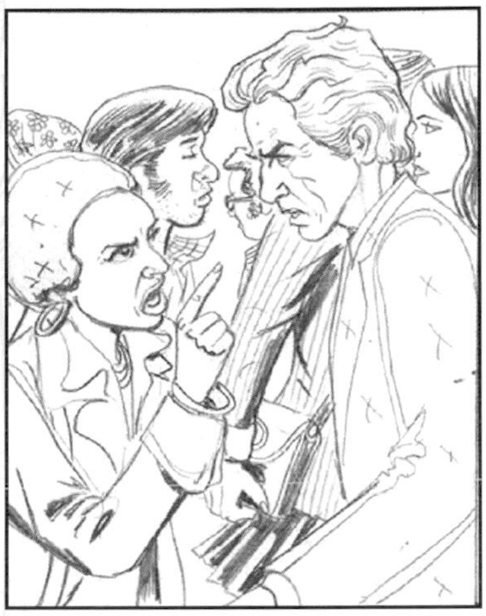

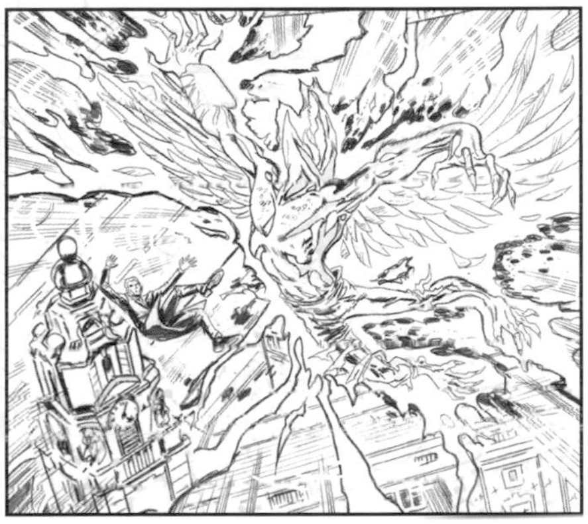

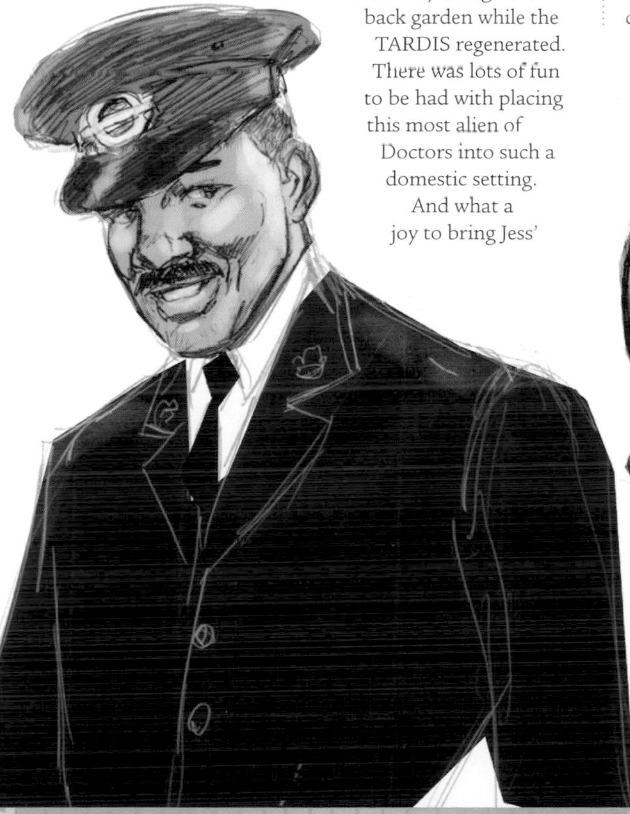

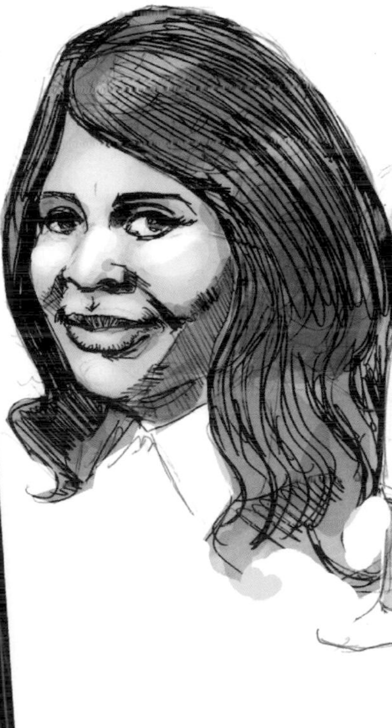

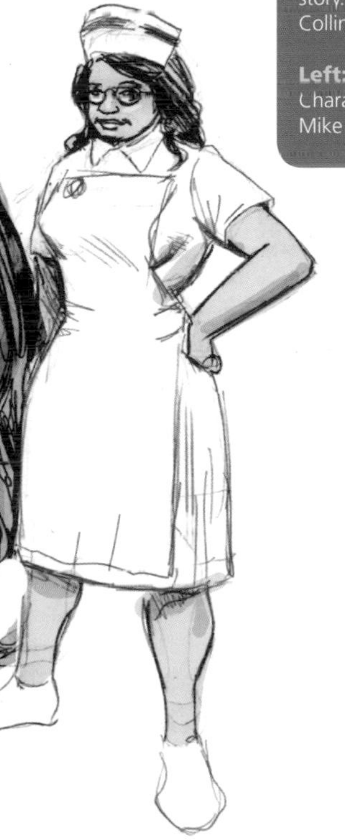

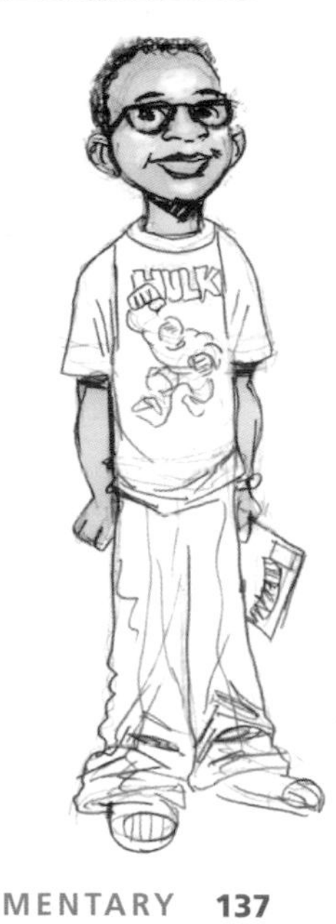

**Above:** Two scenes from the story. Pencil art by Mike Collins.

**Left:** Character sketches by Mike Collins.

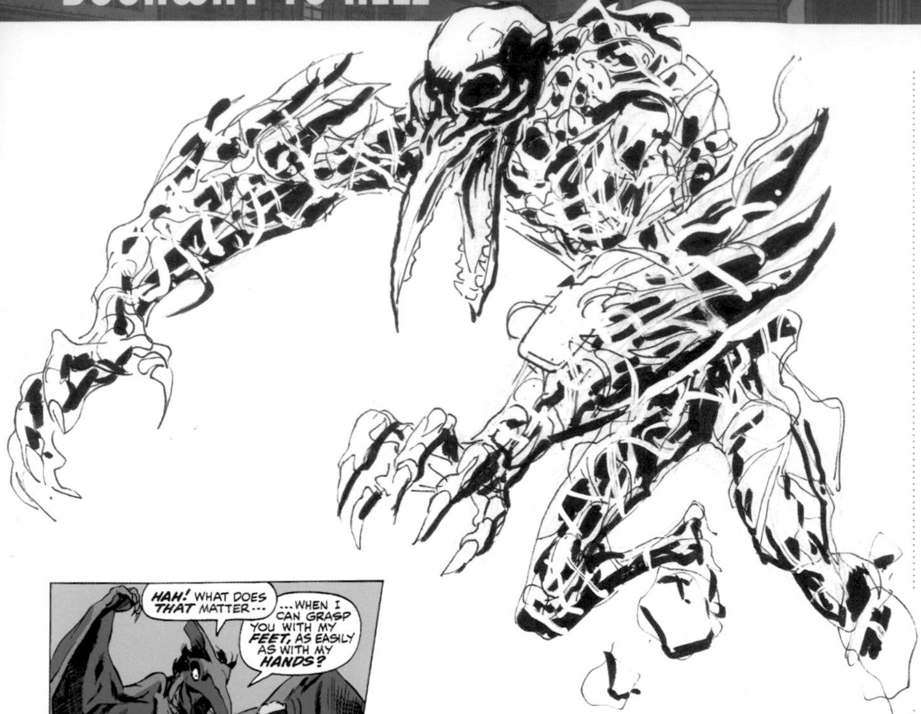

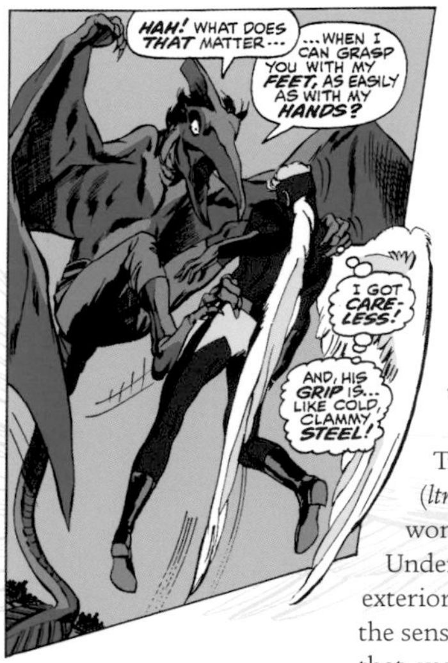
HAH! WHAT DOES THAT MATTER...
...WHEN I CAN GRASP YOU WITH MY FEET, AS EASILY AS WITH MY HANDS?
I GOT CARE-LESS!
AND, HIS GRIP IS... LIKE COLD, CLAMMY STEEL!

**DWM** comic, *Space Invaders!*, and I learnt so much from him then about writing visually. Along with Scott as editor, Mike got me through that first script when my inexperience was screaming at me to run away very quickly in the other direction. I'll always be grateful for that, so I knew I was going to be in safe hands.

A fantastic resource was the London Transport Museum's online photograph collection (*ltmcollection.org/photos/index.html*), which had some wonderfully detailed images of the brand new Brixton Underground station ticket hall, platforms and the entrance exterior from around 1971/72. This really helped me establish the sense of space in the writing – and also to confirm the detail that, yes, there were ticket barriers at Brixton station in 1972. Go and have a look at the website, it's incredible.

Part One was originally a bit angsty and emotional. A note from Scott to make the Doctor a bit more oddball led to his busking on the street outside the station (originally singing Girls Aloud's *Sound of the Underground*). That note really helped anchor things and set the tone in the right direction.

Part Three was the tricky one and had me running head-first into a problem that would return throughout my run – cramming too much action into too few panels. This was my steepest learning curve, and the lesson I'll always remember in any future comic work. Scott sent me off to do a second draft that needed an immense amount of cutting to fit everything in – you can't have a page where the TARDIS explodes above Brixton crammed into seven panels!

I sat at a table in the National Theatre on London's South Bank with my laptop, bashing away, probably looking quite pained. I looked up, and sitting across at the next table was actor Simon Williams, *aka* Group Captain 'Chunky' Gilmore from *Remembrance of the Daleks* and Big Finish's *Counter-Measures* spin-off series. It was a little moment that made me smile and spurred me on to the finish line.

I was able to cut so much from the second draft of Part Three that we were able to put back in a sequence that gave our new regular characters a bit of depth. The flashback to Lloyd and Devina's meeting and journey to England on the Empire Windrush touched on the wider social impact of emigration from the Caribbean to England in the late 1940s. This is *Doctor Who* – we're not going to do detailed social commentary every issue – but I hope we were able to bring this crucial subject out naturally from the story.

**Top:**
A sketch of the Hakaui by Mike Collins.

**Above:**
Sauron from *X-Men* #61. Art by Neal Adams and Tom Palmer. © 2017 Marvel Characters.

## Mike Collins Artist

Scott knows I'm a sucker for history stories and the 70s was the decade I grew up in... I'd previously done a story around the same period (*The Nightmare Game*), although – scarily – that itself was almost 15 years ago!

Mark's script called for a real sense of period detail and is set very clearly in Brixton. One problem we had, ironically, is that we couldn't use real signage for reasons of copyright. I had to be creative in altering brands (British Homes Stores and Dunn & Co became 'Briton House Shop' and 'Dune & Co'). I wallowed deep in the research for this story, making sure clothes, cars and kettles all looked and felt right. About half of the Collins' decor was actually this Collins' childhood kitchen. I even took a trip to London to check out and photograph the Brixton Underground Station that's central to the adventure. Although the frontage is totally different, the ticket hall and access to the tubes is essentially the same. Mark had found a fantastic online resource with period accurate photographs of the London Underground, which surprised people who thought we'd made a mistake in featuring the automatic ticket gates – they really are that old!

There's also, for me, echoes of the Marvel comics I got as a kid, particularly Neal Adams' brief stint on *X-Men* which I'd picked up in 1970/71, mouldering neglected on spinner racks in seaside newsagents. The transformed dad has clear echoes of the X-Men's enemy Sauron. That and Gil Kane's brief run on *Captain Marvel* seared into my brain how exciting comics could be. I appreciate Scott and Mark giving me the chance to wallow in all this glorious 70s fabness...

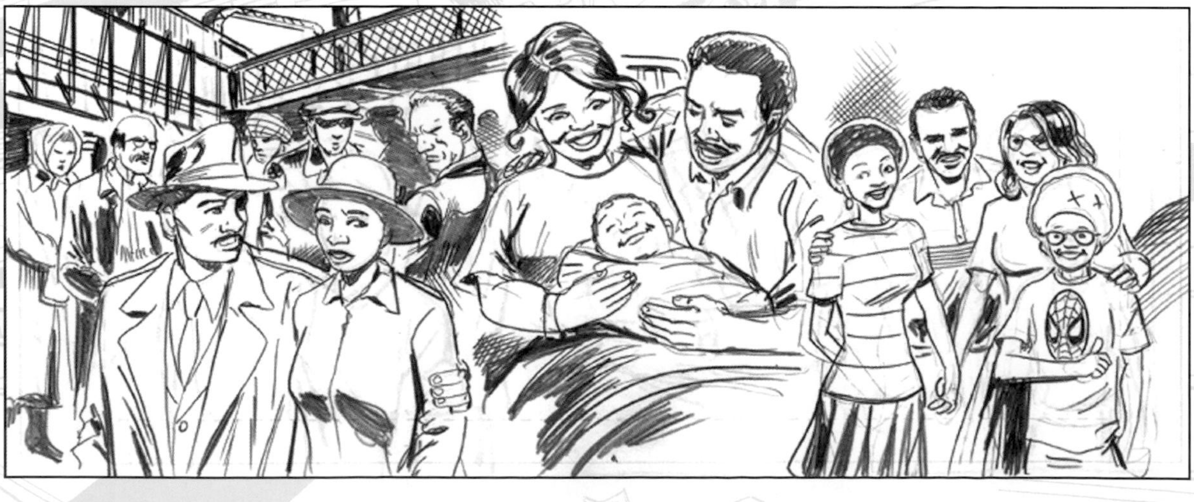

**Right:**
Lloyd remembers his journey from Jamaica to Britain. Pencil art by Mike Collins.

# Moving In

## Mark Wright Writer

I love *Moving In*. It's a contender for my favourite story of my extended residency on the **DWM** comic. Originally it wasn't part of the plan. *The Pestilent Heart* was meant to lead in to the three-part *Bloodsport*, but when I delivered the synopsis to Scott, he had different ideas.

I may be wrong, but I think this is possibly the only time Scott has had a writer on the comic who paid a regular, monthly visit to the Panini office for a whole week at a time. A lot of what came to pass on this was shaped on our lunchtime walks into Tunbridge Wells for coffee. Email is a wonderful thing, but there's no substitute for being able to bat things back and forth in person. It also meant Scott could loom across my desk and ask "Where's my script, Wrighty?!", but I'm accentuating the positives here.

It was on one of these lunchtime walks that *Moving In* came about. My submitted synopsis for *Bloodsport* was good, but there wasn't enough plot to sustain three parts. Scott suggested that *Bloodsport* become a two-parter and we add a one-shot of the Doctor moving into his new Brixton digs. No threats, no monsters, just four vignettes of how this new figure affected each member of the Collins family.

Sometimes an idea comes along that just fizzes with possibilities. This was my chance to flesh out the Collinses further. Looking back over all 11 issues, I think the chance to do *Moving In* stood us in good stead for future instalments, especially *Doorway to Hell*. It gave the readers a reason to care about these characters.

This is probably the smoothest story I've ever written. The synopsis was written one afternoon, a rare instance when everything flowed. The first image I had in my head before one word went on the page was the Doctor and Max standing with their heads against the TARDIS in the back garden. That helped bring Max into focus, and made him click into place in the ongoing story.

The challenge here was having only three pages for each of the individual vignettes, but for once, the space constraints didn't seem to be a problem when I got to the script stage. It was fascinating to see how the Doctor reacted to each of the family, and they to him. Some of it surprised me along the way, especially how the Doctor went out of his way to please Devina. The Twelfth Doctor is the incarnation that makes you go to him, so it was fun to turn that on its head a bit and have him trying to make Devina happy, knowing full well she was the guv'nor in this house.

We also get two new characters introduced – Tibbsy the cat, and sweet old Mr Gayle from up the road. As a cat-lover, I wish I could have done more with Tibbsy; a new, deadly adversary for the Doctor, but space issues made it impractical. I like that he's there, though, always popping up in a scene, curled up on top of the TARDIS. And Mr Gayle came from a request from Scott to have some supporting characters, people who could be in peril, who could die. That extended to the family – as non-TV series characters, any one of them could meet a terrible end.

But for now, we were in our safe space. The Collins house is like the bridge of the *Enterprise*, the flight deck of the *Liberator*, a surrogate TARDIS. We want it to be familiar, the place we retreat to in times of crisis (and again, this was important for this arc's finale) Mike Collins had done a top job of establishing the house in *The Pestilent Heart* – the kitchen was spot-on, helped out by James Offredi's always breathtaking colour work. John Ross took this a step further. He made that back garden feel real and solid; crucial for a space where a lot of scenes over the coming months would take place. That first panel of the Doctor atop the TARDIS still makes me grin – so stylised with such depth. That extended throughout the next 12 pages, into the kitchen and out onto the front steps.

One thing Scott observed about *Moving In* was that the Doctor was *enjoying* himself. This isn't an exile; he knows the TARDIS will regenerate and his time with the Collinses is finite. He has tricked himself into thinking he can stay for a while...

Oh, and did you spot the *Castrovalva* gag?

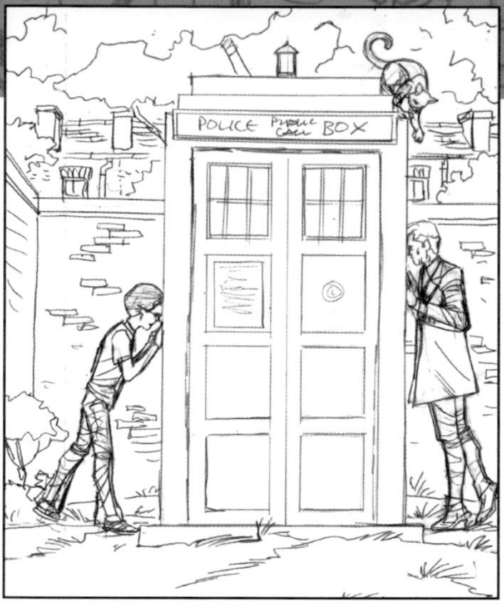
POLICE
BOX

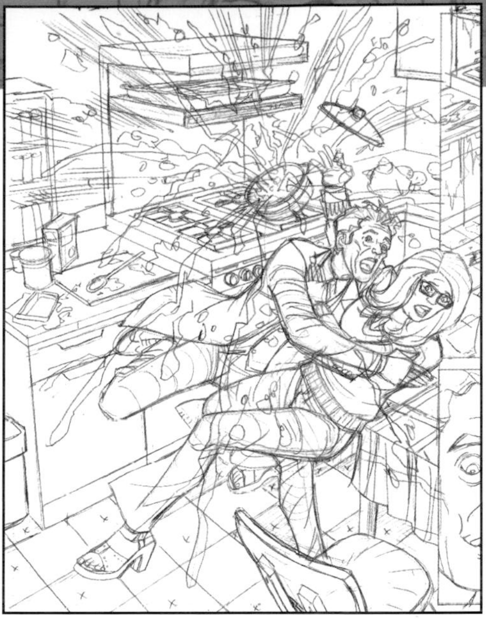

**Top left:**
Max helps the Doctor with the TARDIS. Pencil art by John Ross.

**Above:**
Disaster in Devina's kitchen! Pencil art by John Ross.

**Below:**
Tibbsy attacks! Pencil art by John Ross.

## John Ross Artist

When I initially scanned through the script for *Moving In*, a few things struck me straight off: first, it was a great read (I particularly liked the idea of exploring each of the characters' relationship with the Doctor). Second, there was little to no action (anyone who's familiar with the magazines I've worked on will know that I mostly do all-out action stuff with not so much emphasis on the peaceful human interaction side of things). Third, it might be a bit of a challenge holding the readers' interest over 12 pages where there are no monsters, aliens, exotic locations (much as I love Brixton), life-threatening scenarios and the usual *Who*-type drama.

In the process of laying the strip out, I quickly realised it wasn't going to be that much of a challenge after all. Mark had done a brilliant job of adding something to each of the character sections that was visually interesting, and the interplay between the characters was beautifully written (with lots of detail on body language, expressions and ideas for 'camera' angles). I couldn't have been happier to work on this. I haven't had the opportunity for a long time to focus to this degree on 'just' character stuff and it is something I'm really into; taking a script, dragging the emotion out of it and splattering it onto a page. Creating body language and expression and, of course, extreme dynamics where appropriate.

So, having said all of that, the strip pretty much drew itself. The highlights for me included getting to see James Offredi's colours, particularly the opening panel on page 1 which bowled me over (lovely choice of palette), getting to draw Lloyd as the birdman (even though it was only in flashback), and Devina's many moods and

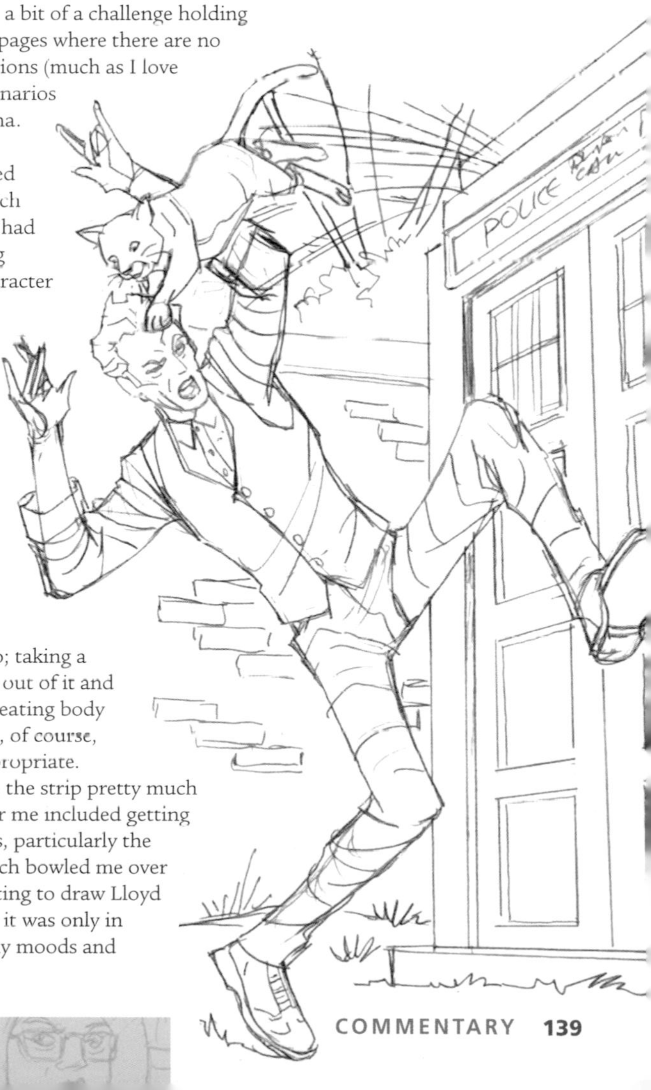
POLICE

expressions (I unashamedly enjoyed wrecking her kitchen!). The scene between Maxwell and the Doctor was fantastic to visualise. Mark had really thought everything through, down to the cat in the background and its reaction to events.

Really enjoyed this one, although, true to form, I made things slightly harder for myself than they needed to be: on page 12, panel 5, I had a finished pencilled image I was happy with... only to discover after I'd finished inking it that I had the dimensions of the stairs wrong and had to re-draw that entire section of the whole building with all those stairs and railings. That'll teach me to use what I've drawn on previous pages as reference!

**Below:** Staz Johnson's pencil art for Skadi and Max, and the climactic action scene in Part Two.

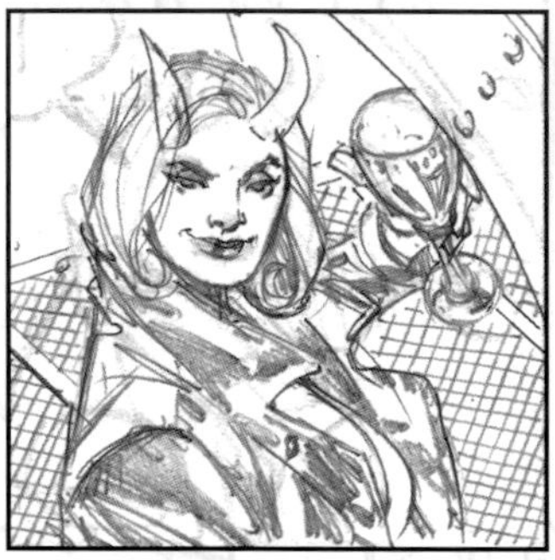

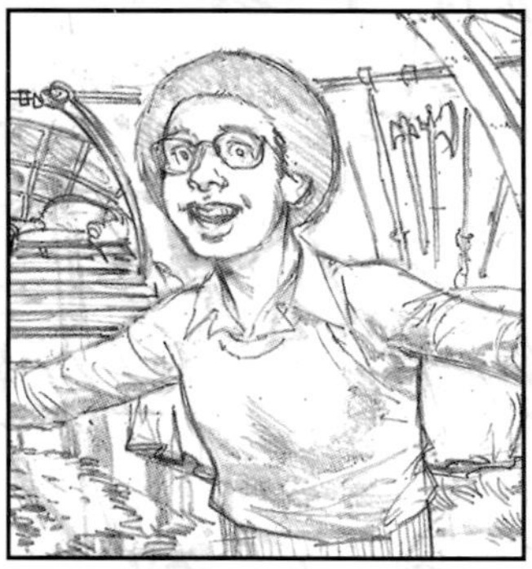

## Bloodsport

### Mark Wright Writer

After getting *The Pestilent Heart* up and running, the realities of doing a longer run on the **DWM** strip hit home – you have to generate plots and scripts to keep the four-weekly schedule fed, and always be looking even further beyond that. There's a rhythm to it all. Problem was, I was struggling to come up with a story to fill the next three-part story slot.

Thank God for good editors! As I was leaving the office one day, Scott said, "Don't think of your plot first, think of a villain and then work out what they want. And cast somebody from television as the villain."

This was a genius note. On the train back up to London from Tunbridge Wells, I started to think about who I would cast as a villain in *Doctor Who* if I were making the show in 1972. Wanda Ventham has always been one of my favourite actresses from that era, so that was an easy decision. I'd also just been watching 1960s/70s ITV drama *Hadleigh*, starring Gerald Harper as a smooth millionaire lord of the manor on a Yorkshire estate. Again, I thought he'd be perfect as a *Doctor Who* villain. From there the idea of a fox hunting parallel came in (it may have been the horsey element in *Hadleigh*), with Ventham and Harper playing privileged and posh alien hunters with a sadistic streak. The rest of the story slotted together very quickly from here.

Staz Johnson was an artist whose work on many American comics I'd greatly admired, so I was thrilled when Scott told me he was coming on board for *Bloodsport*. His fluid and dynamic art perfectly captured the style I wanted for this story. It has a grittiness that captured that early 70s feel, but there's an elegance there too. In discussions we both found a shared love of 70s cops shows, and Staz immediately picked up on how DCI Jack Hayes was my tribute to *The Sweeney* and John Thaw. Maybe one day we'll get our *Doctor Who/The Professionals* crossover comic off the ground. I didn't know it at the time, but Hayes added to our roster of recurring characters, although when the script for Part Two was signed off, I didn't know he'd be coming back.

I went on a location recce to the National Gallery to take lots of photo reference for Staz to work from. One historical detail that came to light was the difference in road layout in front of the gallery building – in 1972, a busy road ran between the gallery and the square, with the pedestrianised walkway and steps only coming in 2003.

*Bloodsport* was a lot of fun to write, and it gave me a chance to put Max Collins front and centre in the action, proving himself to be just as capable a companion to the Doctor as Jess. I also loved what Staz did with the Kolothos hounds – the sleeping hound at the beginning of Part Two still makes me laugh.

I'd love to bring the Kolothos Hunt back at some point. I like Skadi and Broteas, and it reminded me that having the Doctor face off to a proper reactive villain who can banter back is a joy to play around with...

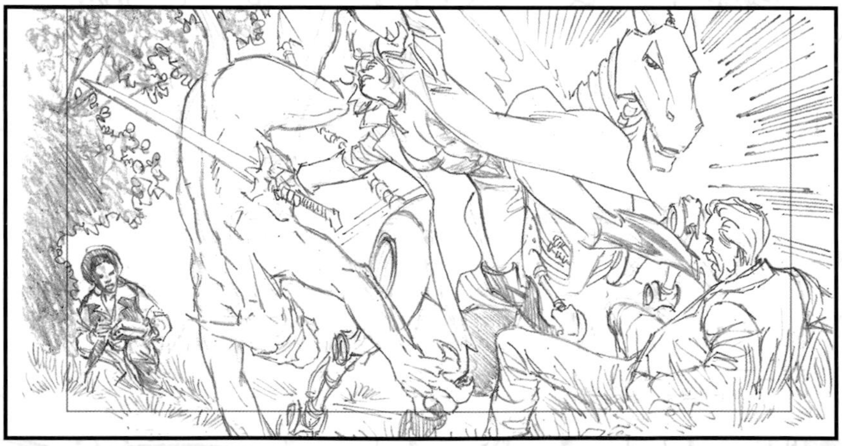

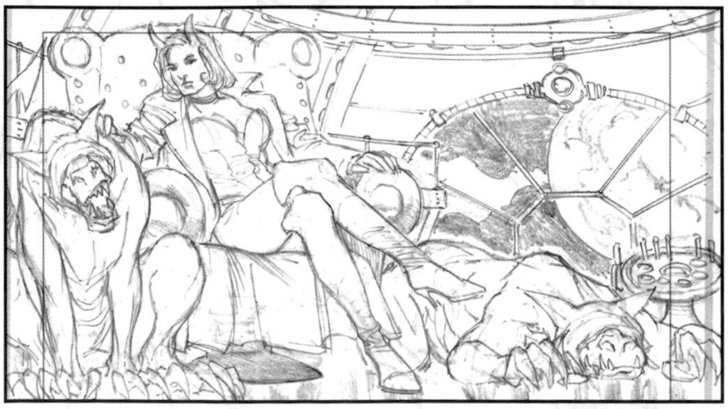

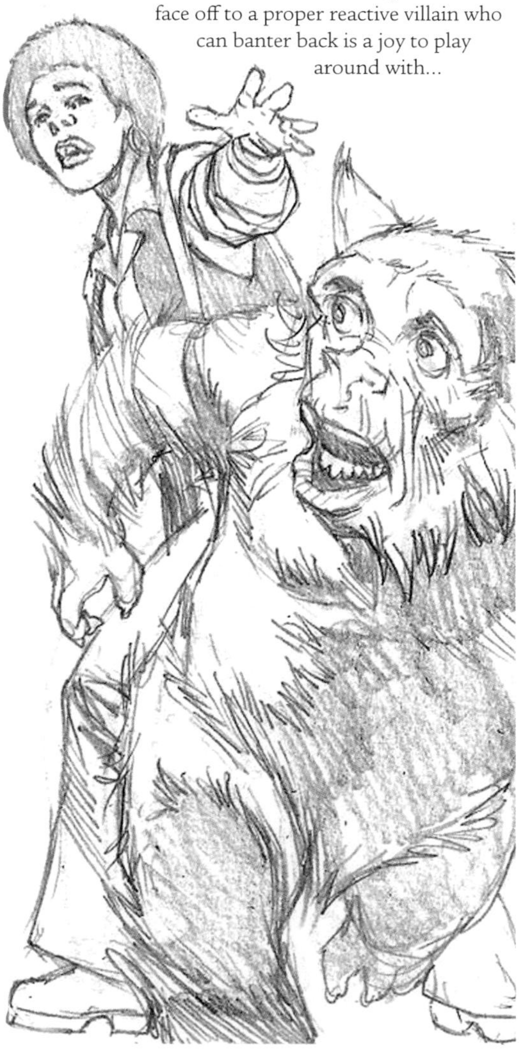

**Far right:** Jess meets the hunted alien in Part One. Pencil art by Staz Johnson.

**Right:** Skadi relaxes with her hounds. Pencil art by Staz Johnson.

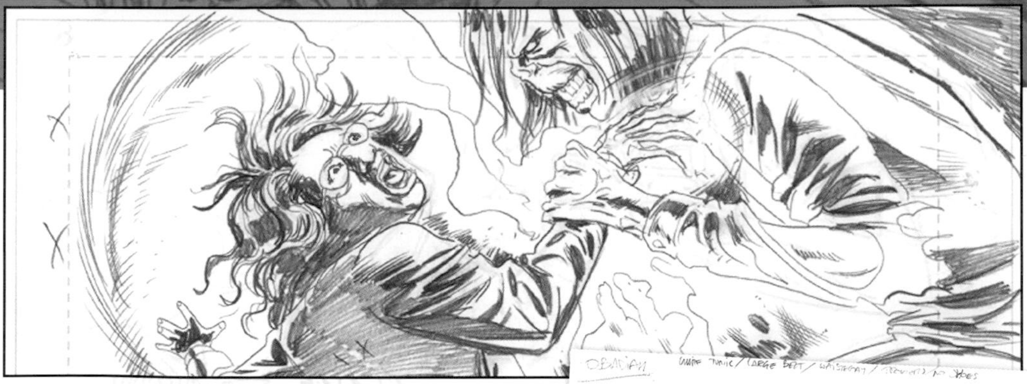

# Be Forgot

## Mark Wright Writer

*Be Forgot* took me by surprise. It wasn't until I had the edited script back from Scott and I found myself in tears on reading it (not because of the edit, I hasten to add!), that I realised just what a personal story this was.

It was a lovely element of having a run on the comic that I got to write the Christmas story. After the action-heavy romp of *Bloodsport*, I wanted to bring things back into the Brixton community that we'd established, and do something a little more contemplative. There was no real intent to do something 'issues' based here, but this story looked at how loneliness can be amplified at times like Christmas; even when we're surrounded by people, we can feel so alone as everyone gets on with their own lives. I also wanted to have the Doctor tackle something that was intangible – he's always looking for the monsters to fight, but in this case the monster was out of reach and needed a different perspective to defeat. This became Devina's moment to shine. It's really her story – and Walter's.

Over the years I've had my own (thankfully brief) brushes with anxiety and depression; moments of darkness, of being trapped and alone however much you're surrounded by loving family and friends. It's a monster that we can't see, we can't touch, but it doesn't mean it isn't real, as the Doctor notes towards the end of this story. Poor Walter, trapped by grief for his mother, his tortured mind creating Obadiah, a mental manifestation to direct his anger towards on the anniversary of her death.

And this is where things took me by surprise. My own mum passed away at the end of 2014, and at the back of my mind I'd had thoughts about writing something to examine my own grief and reactions to the gap that had been left in our lives. My original pitch for *The Highgate Horror* was an attempt to do this, but I realised I was forcing it and so when that version of the plot went away, I let that thought fade away for the time being.

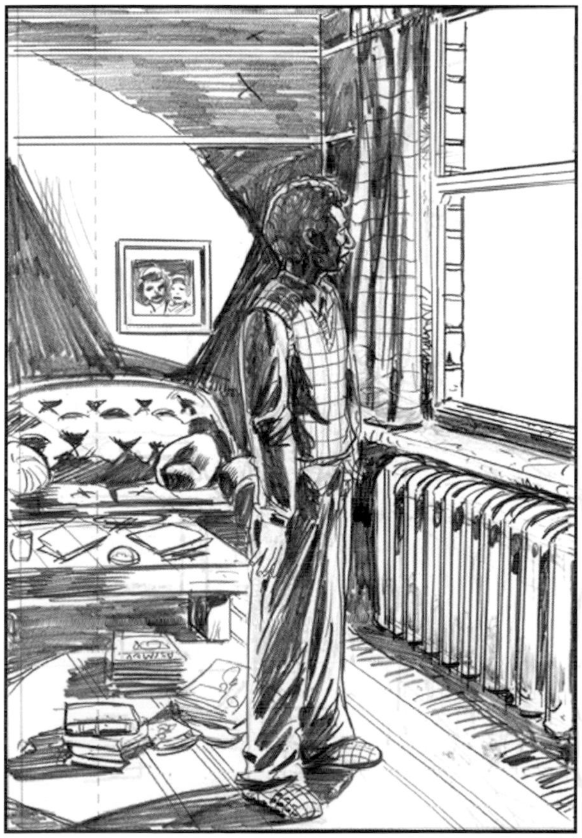

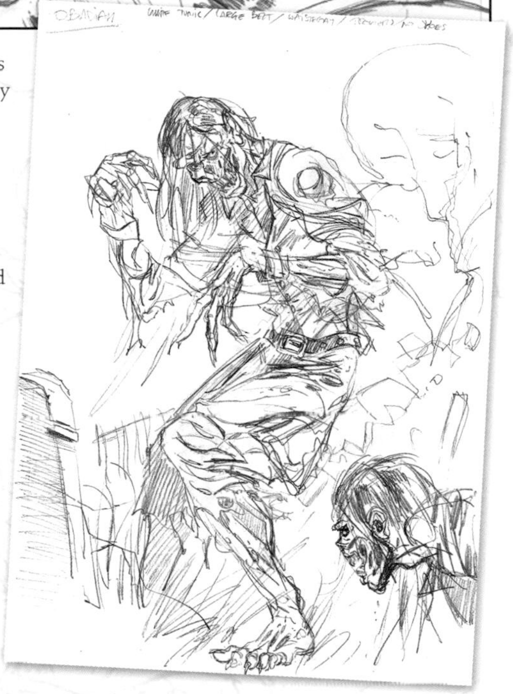
OBADIAH

When I came to write *Be Forgot*, there was no conscious thought about doing a story that looked at grief.

Perhaps that's the point; it came naturally. When I read the final version of the script, having not picked it up for a couple of weeks, it suddenly hit me. I'd finally written about my own grief, how much I missed my mum, and not realised it. Yes, I had a big old cry that day.

Lifting the mood now, it was great to collaborate again with David A Roach – who had performed such wonders on *The Highgate Horror* – and Mike Collins. Apologies to David, who keeps asking to draw a mad alien world story. I ended up giving him living rooms and kitchens in 1972.

As a final note on *Be Forgot*, my mum Val never saw any of my comic work in **DWM**, but I know she was proud of what I was doing and loved that I was involved with the mag, earning a living writing about a TV series she'd seen me grow up adoring. I'm sure I'll write about my mum in other stories in the future, but for now, *Be Forgot* is for her, for all the encouragement she gave me to pursue my dreams.

Thanks, Mum.

## Mike Collins Artist

I was on a break from storyboarding *Doctor Who* for television. The director on that production block didn't need boards, so this dovetailed perfectly with David and Scott calling to see if I could step in to produce the finished pencils for David to ink over. David had done pretty thorough layouts, and it was a great exercise for me to concentrate on the finishes for once instead of the layouts. The monster was a fabulous design by David and the pay-off, that it's the cover of a Warren style 70s b&w magazine, works brilliantly.

This strip is the first where I've pencilled digitally. It's only for two frames that had slipped by in an edit so needed redrawing. I'm fairly certain they blend in seamlessly with David's inks over them but I'd be intrigued if people could spot them.

Unfortunately, as I began the pages, I got a call back on a TV show I'd worked on over the summer that needed more storyboards urgently – I was flown out to Prague to hit the ground running on elaborate sequences involving knights on horses. I went from working on set to back to my hotel to finish off the pages for *Be Forgot* in the evenings – I couldn't let anyone down, so I just did double shifts for a couple of weeks working in two very different periods of history!

It's a cracker of a story, dark but in the end heartwarming, a classic Christmas tale.

## David Roach Artist

As a youngster discovering *Doctor Who* in the Jon Pertwee era, I don't think it crossed my mind that he was perpetually stuck on Earth. As long as there was a steady stream of monsters (Sea Devils, Ogrons, maggots, dinosaurs, you name it), I was

**Top:** Devina is attacked by Obadiah. Pencil art by Mike Collins.

**Above:** David A Roach's character sketch for Obadiah.

**Left:** Walter alone in his flat. Pencil art by Mike Collins.

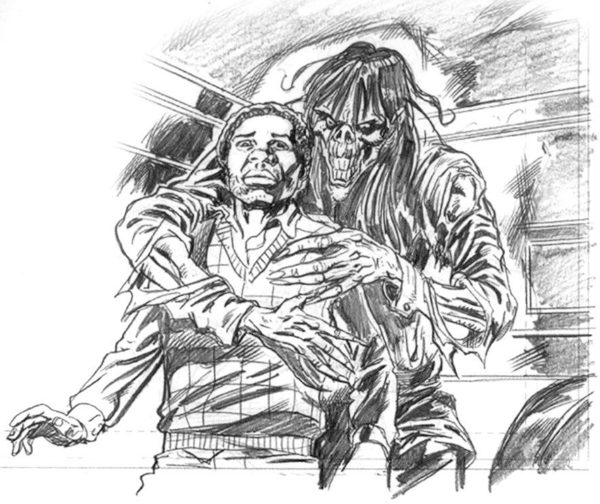

**Above:**
Walter and Obadiah. Pencil art by Mike Collins.

happy. Fittingly, in our comic strip tribute to 1972 the Peter Capaldi incarnation is similarly marooned on Earth, but in the case of *Be Forgot* he is confronted with a monster of an altogether more insidious psychological type; a monster of the mind. We are able to enter the mind of a profoundly disturbed young man in a way that really only works in the comics medium, where words and pictures can so effortlessly evoke multiple realities.

Actually drawing the strip proved to be rather more problematic than usual, though it started off with the enjoyable task of creating a new set of characters. In this case I thought it would be fun to dress Walter, our troubled protagonist, in the classic tank-top outfit of Frank Spencer from *Some Mothers do 'Ave 'Em*, though I don't think any of the readers made that connection. Obadiah by contrast was a chance to reach back to another staple of 70s pop-culture: the classic horror comic. I've long been a devoted fan of American horror comics like *Creepy*, *Eerie* and *The House of Mystery*, and Obadiah's leering, cadaverous form was a welcome chance to imagine myself drawing for these esteemed titles. The story also gave me another chance to draw the Doctor's latest assistant Jess, whom I had originally based on my friend Mélissa Azombo, and had now, thrillingly, become part of *Who* folklore. However, when the script arrived I was still burning the midnight oil editing my latest book (my 15th about art, comics and illustration – check all good booksellers for details!), which in this case was devoted to Spanish comic book artists, primarily of the 70s. Much as I wanted to draw the strip, it seemed as if the pressure of deadlines was going to be too much to take it on. Annoyingly, I was writing about some of the very artists who had inspired the appearance of Obadiah, but in a frustratingly ironic twist that book was preventing me from actually drawing him.

In times of need I always turn to the Speedy Gonzalez of comics, my esteemed colleague Mike Collins. I roughly drew out the strip at A4, scanned the pages in and sent them to our eagle-eyed editor Mr Gray, who then tweaked the odd panel here and there. Mike then tightened the roughs up at our usual size of A3, scanned them in and sent the digital files back to me, which I then printed out in blue and inked in with brush, pen and ink. The end result looked sort of like my art, and sort of like Mike's, and with James Offredi's colours ended up, as if by magic, looking like a rather presentable Christmas story. Phew! But because these various incarnations of each page were whizzed back and forth between our computers I never actually met up with Mike in person and had no idea he wasn't actually in Cardiff. It turns out he was in Prague storyboarding a mediaeval TV show for the History Channel! I rather suspect this is the first time the *Doctor Who* comic strip has been drawn in the Czech Republic... But will it be the last?

## Doorway to Hell

### Mark Wright Writer

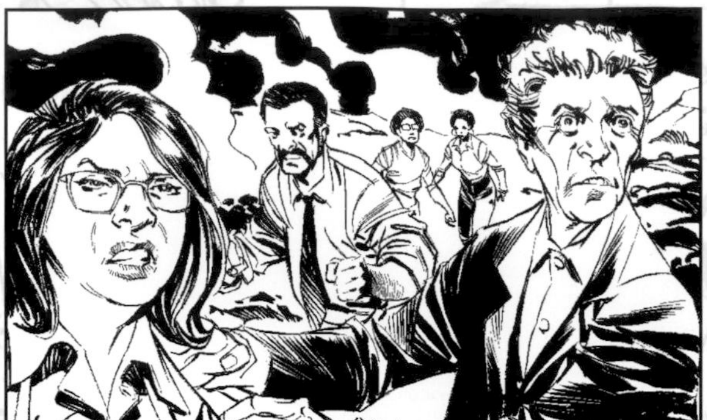

**Top right:**
The Doctor and the Collins family. Art by Staz Johnson.

"Wouldn't it be great if we did the Roger Delgado Master in the comic?" I said enthusiastically to Scott Gray one morning at the office. Scott looked at me over the desk, thought about it for a second, and said, "No, that's a silly idea."

Oh well, I thought, back to the drawing board for the final story of the Brixton arc. The boss has spoken!

Fast-forward 24 hours, and we were on another of those walks into Tunbridge Wells for our daily Americano at the local coffee hostelry. "Yeah," Scott said nonchalantly, "I was thinking on the drive in this morning that maybe it *would* be fun to do the Delgado Master in the comic."

It just seemed so right. With a Doctor on TV who was so steeped in early 70s *Doctor Who*, the prospect of a face-off between him and the original Master was too good to ignore. The great Roger Delgado's portrayal of the Master is one of my favourite things in all of *Doctor Who*. There's an almost avuncular likeability about the character, that suave charm lulling you into a false sense of security before he kills without a second thought. Just what would these two characters make of each other? I got shivers thinking about what Part One's cliffhanger panel would be like: that genial smile, the satanic beard, those hypnotic eyes glittering out of the page.

Of course, having the idea to bring the original Master back is one thing. Plotting an adventure that does him justice and works as a story that's more than just an exercise in nostalgia is something else. This was also going to be the swansong for the Collins family, and from the outset, Scott wanted them put through the wringer.

I dutifully got going with an outline under the title 'Doctor Who and the Master'. It was a very weak, technobabble-heavy story about the Master having been blasted across time tracks and trying to return to his correct timeline before it was too late. Rubbish, of course – how many times have we seen the Master trying to repair a damaged body?

Crucially, though, this version of the outline gave me the opening sequence of Katya and the mercenaries entering the Collins house, although the Doctor was originally present for

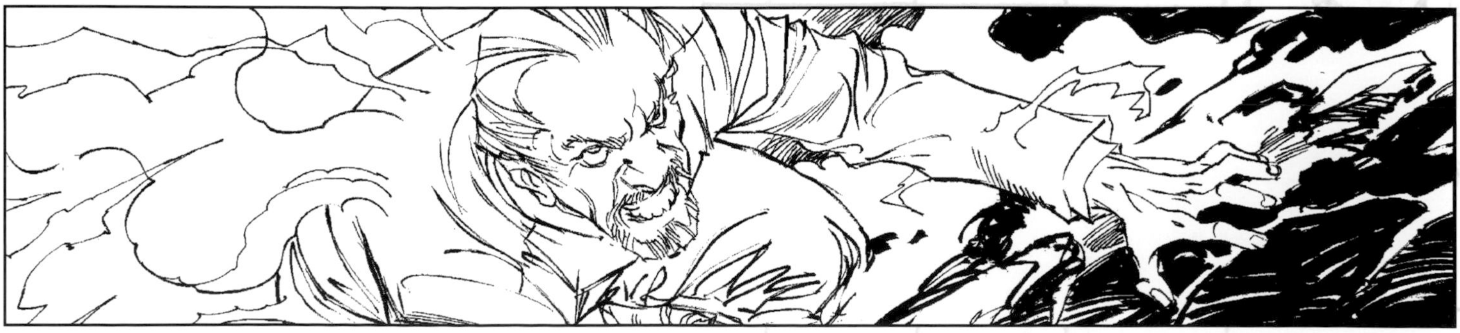

**Below:**
The Master in Part Four. Art by Staz Johnson.

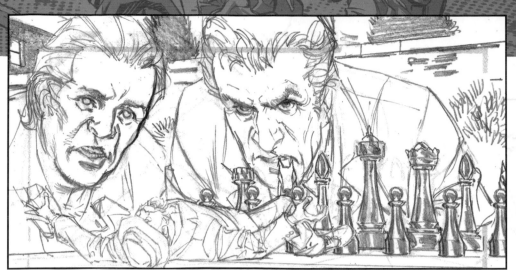

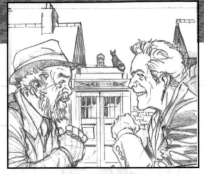

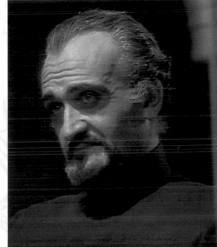

this and tried to fight them off. I also had Jess betray the Doctor at a key moment, and by the cliffhanger, we discovered she was a hypnotised pawn of the Master. Lloyd, who had been at work when the attack happened, teamed up with the Doctor to find Jess. This version also introduced the Master's penthouse apartment on the Thames (I was thinking of the movie *The Long Good Friday*), and the fact that the regenerating TARDIS had done something to the Collins family so the Master could use them to send himself back to his own timestream. At this point, the Master's regeneration was there in the last few pages, as was the final page of Jess at the National Gallery 30 years later.

Structurally a lot was there, but the Master's motivation wasn't. That needed to drive the story. He needed a big super villain plan. For the second pass at the story, Scott sent me an image of the family from the film *Poltergeist II: The Other Side*, looking out over a hellish landscape. He wanted the whole family sent somewhere by the Master, and this was a great note in piecing it all together. I needed to get the Doctor out of the way so the Collinses could be kidnapped; that led me to bringing DCI Hayes back so I could team them up.

My second pass had the title 'The Veil of Questions', and had all the important story beats in place, it just needed finessing a bit. The alien encountered by the Collins family was the embodiment of a super-weapon that constantly questioned everything. It was a curious child, a weaponisation of doubt that destroyed the civilisation that created it, and had been placed in a time lock by the Time Lords. Only the Master would try to unleash something that even the Daleks were too scared to go near. This was okay but needed more time to develop than we had here, so the third and final pass at the plot changed the weaponisation of doubt to the splitting of the chronon. With the addition of a final scrap between the Master and the Doctor, the story was in place.

I must mention poor old Mr Gayle. Scott's note to introduce supporting characters that we could kill came to fruition here. Originally Tibbsy the cat was to end up shrunk on the chessboard, but I think the chess scene between Gayle and the Master and its cliffhanger ending are amongst my favourite moments from this run. And besides, I just couldn't bear to kill Tibbsy. One day I'll write 'Tibbsy's Story', the missing one-shot from this run of stories. Scott suggested an idea for the final part that fell by the wayside, but is just too joyous not to mention here. We considered having a bigger role for Tibbsy, with the Doctor pulling him out at the last second to tip the balance against the Master – all those days and nights of sleeping on top of the TARDIS had made him a missile of orange fur and pure artron energy. A bit silly, perhaps, but fun!

I adored writing the Delgado Master. The dialogue just flowed – I played Dudley Simpson's chilling Master theme from *Terror of the Autons* over and over to get me in the right frame of mind. Holding off the first meeting between the Doctor and the Master until mid-way through Part Three kept that tension going and drove me on through the first two scripts. When the meeting finally happens, I hope the results were as electric as we intended them to be. And if he's read it, I hope Peter Capaldi liked it too!

Everybody pulled out the stops on the art, as they always do. A joy to have Staz as artist again. I do hope we'll collaborate again in the future. And the colours from James Offedi – I can feel the heat coming off the 'hell' scenes in those deep, vivid reds.

There we have it; the end of the Brixton arc. I will miss the Collins family – they've been in my head for the best part of a year. What a thrill to write for Roger Delgado's Master, I hope we did the character and the legacy of a great actor justice. I had my doubts about the regeneration scene – it could have been one step too far – but I'm glad Scott pushed for doing it. And then there's the Twelfth Doctor, off on his adventures in the TARDIS again. I love the contradictions in this incarnation – the sweet and the sour if you will – it made writing him challenging but fun.

Writing a comic strip in **DWM** is something I never thought I'd do, and then they went and gave me a whole run, which blows my mind when I think about it for too long. What a privilege. It's been the most challenging, difficult, frustrating, joyous, fun, brilliant job of my life. I have learnt so much about writing comics, about being able to generate plots and scripts to a tight schedule. It's given me a lot of confidence. Big thanks to Mike Collins, John Ross, David A Roach, James Offredi, Roger Langridge and Staz Johnson for their amazing work on making these stories look superb. Most of all, thanks to Scott Gray for being the best of editors, for having faith in the first place, and for all the encouragement, patience and brilliant notes throughout. Next Americano's on me, mate. ●

YOU WERE ONLY SUPPOSED TO BLOW THE BLOODY DOORS OFF!!

**Top left:** Staz Johnson was dissatisfied with the Doctor's likeness in Part Three's title panel and redrew it.

**Top:** Mr Gayle and the Doctor. Pencil art by Staz Johnson.

**Above:** The original Master, Roger Delgado.

**Below:** Two layout pages, with some additional dialogue from Staz!

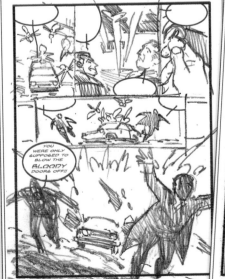

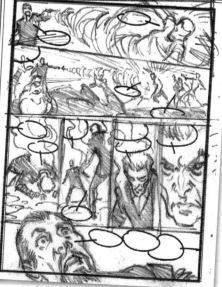

# DOCTOR WHO COMIC COLLECTIONS

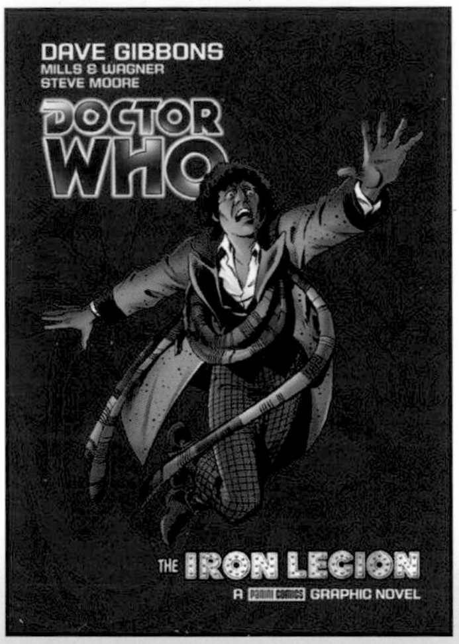
DAVE GIBBONS
MILLS & WAGNER
STEVE MOORE
DOCTOR WHO
THE IRON LEGION
A PANINI COMICS GRAPHIC NOVEL

**THE IRON LEGION** (The Fourth Doctor: Volume 1)
Dave Gibbons, Pat Mills, John Wagner, Steve Moore
164 pages (b&w) £14.99/$24.95 ISBN 978-1-904159-37-7

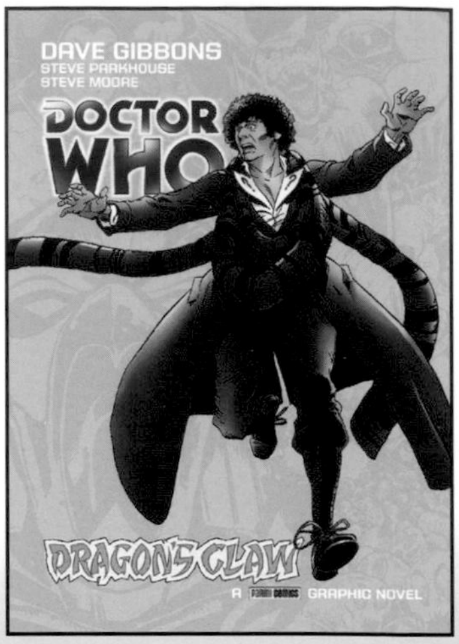
DAVE GIBBONS
STEVE PARKHOUSE
STEVE MOORE
DOCTOR WHO
DRAGON'S CLAW
A PANINI COMICS GRAPHIC NOVEL

**DRAGON'S CLAW** (The Fourth Doctor: Volume 2)
Dave Gibbons, Steve Parkhouse, Steve Moore
164 pages (b&w) £14.99/$24.95 ISBN 1-904159-81-8

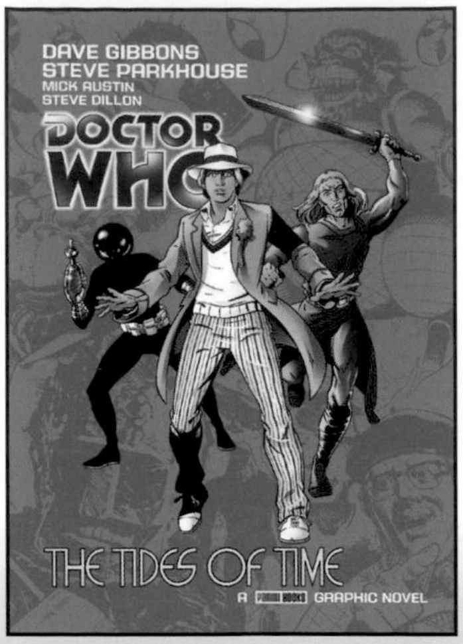
DAVE GIBBONS
STEVE PARKHOUSE
MICK AUSTIN
STEVE DILLON
DOCTOR WHO
THE TIDES OF TIME
A PANINI BOOKS GRAPHIC NOVEL

**THE TIDES OF TIME** (The Fifth Doctor)
Dave Gibbons, Steve Parkhouse, Mick Auston, Steve Dillon
228 pages (b&w) £14.99/$24.95 ISBN 978-1-904159-92-6

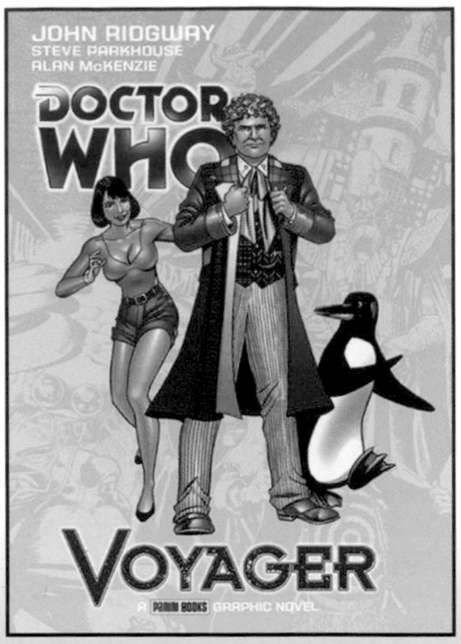
JOHN RIDGWAY
STEVE PARKHOUSE
ALAN McKENZIE
DOCTOR WHO
VOYAGER
A PANINI BOOKS GRAPHIC NOVEL

**VOYAGER** (The Sixth Doctor: Volume 1)
John Ridgway, Steve Parkhouse, Alan McKenzie
172 pages (b&w) £15.99/$31.95 ISBN 978-1-905239-71-9

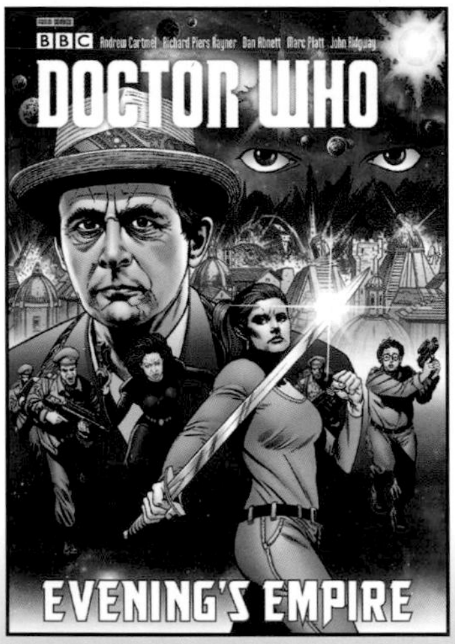
BBC
DOCTOR WHO
EVENING'S EMPIRE

**EVENING'S EMPIRE** (The Seventh Doctor: Volume 4)
Andrew Cartmel, Richard Piers Rayner, Dan Abnett, Marc Platt
132 pages (b&w) £13.99/$19.99 ISBN 978-1-84653-728-8

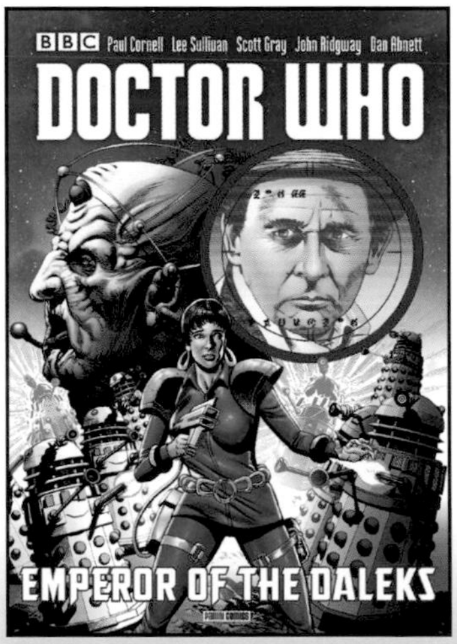
BBC Paul Cornell Lee Sullivan Scott Gray John Ridgway Dan Abnett
DOCTOR WHO
EMPEROR OF THE DALEKS

**EMPEROR OF THE DALEKS** (The Seventh Doctor: Volume 5)
Paul Cornell, Lee Sullivan, Scott Gray, John Ridgway
180 pages (b&w) £14.99/$19.99 ISBN 978-1-84653-807-0

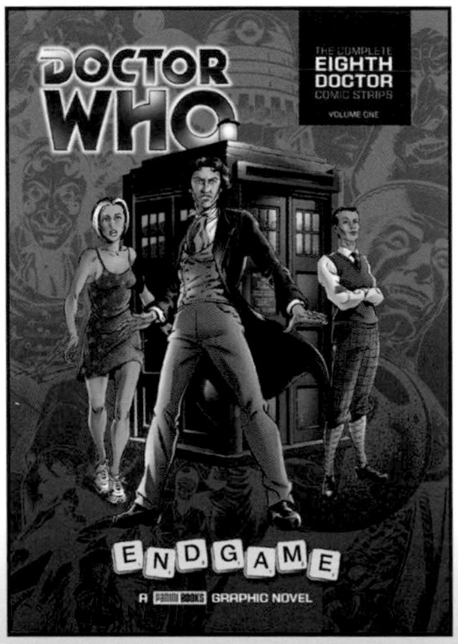
DOCTOR WHO
THE COMPLETE
EIGHTH DOCTOR
COMIC STRIPS
ENDGAME
A PANINI BOOKS GRAPHIC NOVEL

**ENDGAME** (The Eighth Doctor: Volume 1)
Alan Barnes, Martin Geraghty, Scott Gray, Adrian Salmon
228 pages (b&w) £14.99/$24.95 ISBN 978-1-905239-09-2

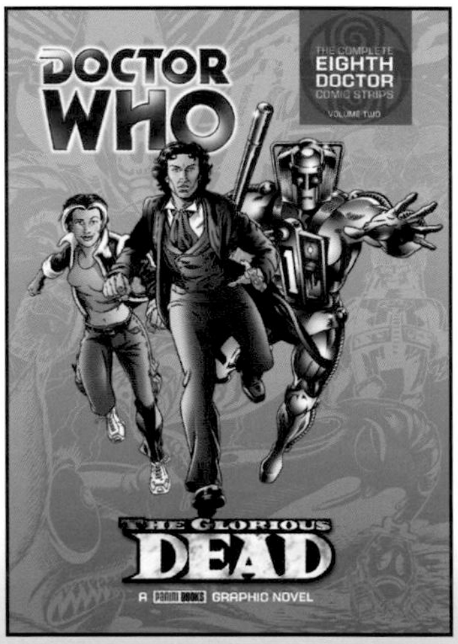
DOCTOR WHO
THE COMPLETE
EIGHTH DOCTOR
COMIC STRIPS
THE GLORIOUS DEAD
A PANINI BOOKS GRAPHIC NOVEL

**THE GLORIOUS DEAD** (The Eighth Doctor: Volume 2)
Scott Gray, Martin Geraghty, Roger Langridge, Alan Barnes
244 pages (b&w) £15.99/$24.99 ISBN 978-1-905239-44-3

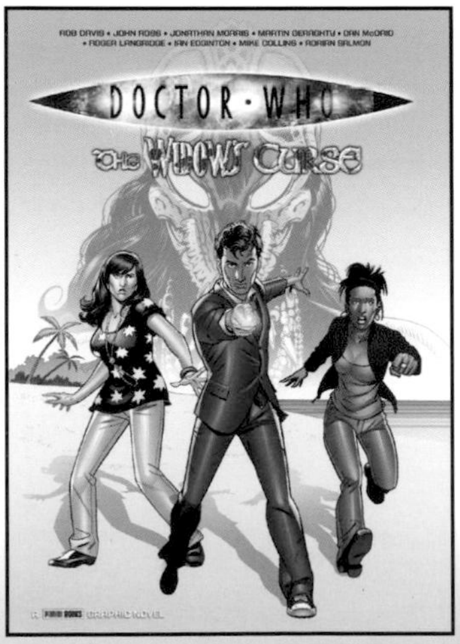
DOCTOR WHO
THE WIDOW'S CURSE

**THE WIDOW'S CURSE** (The Tenth Doctor: Volume 2)
Rob Davis, John Ross, Jonathan Morris, Martin Geraghty
220 pages (colour) £15.99/$24.99 ISBN 978-1-84653-429-4

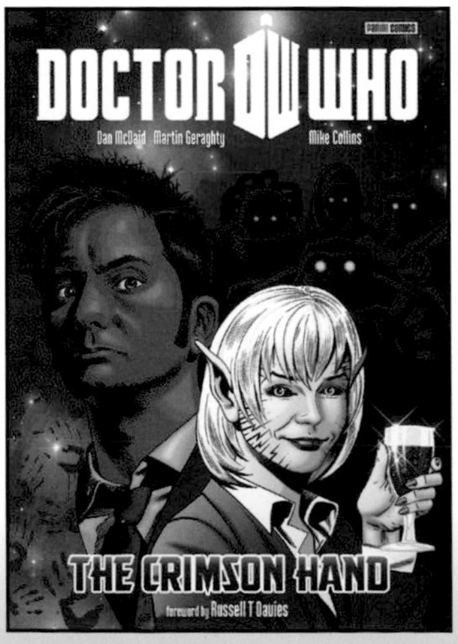
DOCTOR WHO
Dan McDaid Martin Geraghty Mike Collins
THE CRIMSON HAND
foreword by Russell T Davies

**THE CRIMSON HAND** (The Tenth Doctor: Volume 3)
Dan McDaid, Martin Geraghty, Mike Collins
260 pages (colour) £15.99/$31.95 ISBN 978-1-84653-451-5

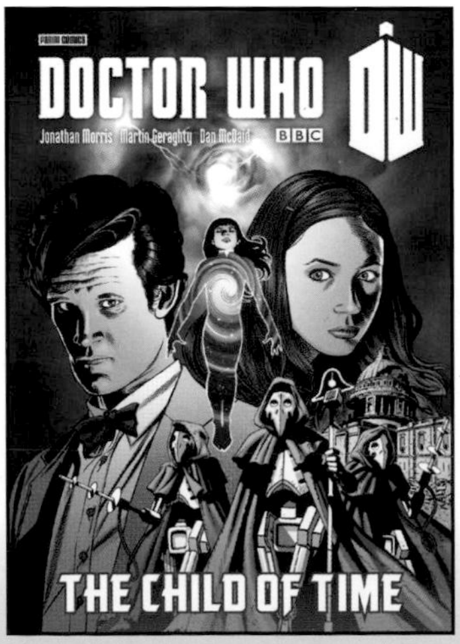
DOCTOR WHO
BBC
THE CHILD OF TIME

**THE CHILD OF TIME** (The Eleventh Doctor: Volume 1)
Jonathan Morris, Martin Geraghty, Dan McDaid
244 pages (colour) £16.99/$24.99 ISBN 978-1-84653-460-7

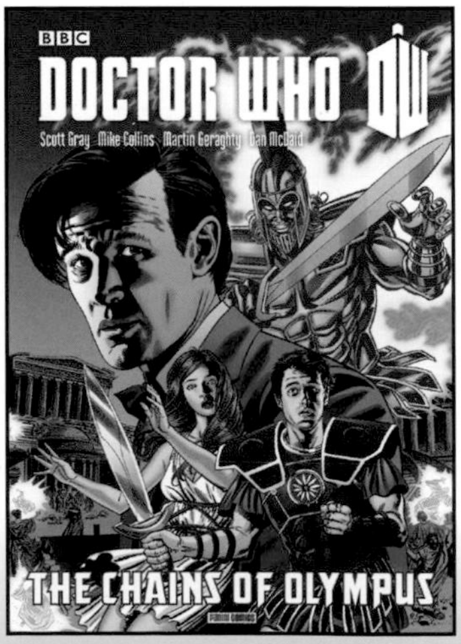
BBC
DOCTOR WHO
THE CHAINS OF OLYMPUS

**THE CHAINS OF OLYMPUS** (The Eleventh Doctor: Volume 2)
Scott Gray, Mike Collins, Martin Geraghty, Dan McDaid
132 pages (colour) £12.99/$18.99 ISBN 978-1-84653-558-1